# Careers

for
dummies®
A Wiley Brand

# Careers

by Marty Nemko, PhD

WITHDRAWN

for dummies®
A Wiley Brand

# Careers For Dummies®

Published by: **John Wiley & Sons, Inc.**, 111 River Street, Hoboken, NJ 07030-5774, www.wiley.com

Copyright © 2018 by John Wiley & Sons, Inc., Hoboken, New Jersey

Published simultaneously in Canada

For general information on our other products and services, please contact our Customer Care Department within the U.S. at 877-762-2974, outside the U.S. at 317-572-3993, or fax 317-572-4002. For technical support, please visit https://hub.wiley.com/community/support/dummies.

Wiley publishes in a variety of print and electronic formats and by print-on-demand. Some material included with standard print versions of this book may not be included in e-books or in print-on-demand. If this book refers to media such as a CD or DVD that is not included in the version you purchased, you may download this material at http://booksupport.wiley.com. For more information about Wiley products, visit www.wiley.com.

Library of Congress Control Number: 2018940765

ISBN: 978-1-119-48233-8; 978-1-119-48234-5 (ebk); 978-1-119-48238-3 (ebk)

Manufactured in the United States of America

V086399_052118

# Contents at a Glance

# Table of Contents

# Foreword

A new career book. Hmm . . . Do we really need another career book? A quick Amazon search of books related to careers brings up 100,000 titles. Job hunting books? 40,000 titles.

The category of career books is crowded with superficial, repetitive, and uninspiring "advice" often from individuals whose only expertise seems to be that they themselves were once hired by someone. Or those who think they have the latest out-of-the-box wild idea like "don't write a resume."

And then I was given the opportunity to read Marty Nemko's latest book, *Careers For Dummies*. I read it cover-to-cover because, despite managing Career Centers at Dickinson College, The University of Texas at Austin, Wake Forest University, and Vanderbilt University, I know there's always something new to learn, particularly when Marty Nemko is involved.

I first encountered Marty's work in 1998 when he published *Cool Careers For Dummies*. I had been working in the field of career services for over ten years at that point, specializing in helping liberal arts students articulate the value of their education to potential employers. Most career books at that time were written with the assumption that the job seeker had a traditional degree (business or engineering) and sought a job in those fields. Not *Cool Careers*. It opened up a world of ideas for my liberal arts students: they didn't have to become bankers, lawyers, or professors. There were plenty of other "cool" careers: interesting careers that would benefit from their knowledge and skills. Over the years, I have purchased copies for all my career coaching staffs so they could use it in their work with students.

I personally "met" Marty in 2009 when the first edition of my book, *You Majored in What?*, was published. Marty asked me to appear as a call-in guest on his radio show, a San Francisco-based National Public Radio program, "Work with Marty Nemko." We had an engaging conversation around chaos theory as it relates to careers of liberal arts students, and it was a pleasure to meet the author behind one of my favorite career books.

So what does Marty's latest career book have to offer? Aside from being well-organized and packed with new ideas and information, this is a book which clears through the clutter. It harnesses the best of the ever-expanding information about career exploration and development. It will help you organize every aspect of your career: from uncovering your strengths to succeeding on the job. It is truly a soup-to-nuts guide to the career search and the career development process.

Career seekers have to consider three main questions: Who am I?; Where can I work?; and How do I get there? Many career books focus on the first and third questions, and Careers For Dummies is no exception. Those topics are covered thoroughly.

But when it comes to the second question, there is a dearth of good information about "what's out there." It's a tough topic to handle because it's at once vast and yet highly specific. Career counselors are often stuck using the less than scintillating *Dictionary of Occupational Titles* or the *Occupational Outlook Handbook*. This is where *Careers For Dummies* shines. In *Part 2: The Careers Catalog* you will be introduced to over 300 interesting and intriguing careers.

Two chapters in particular caught my attention: Chapter 6, "STEM Careers (Science, Technology, Engineering, Math)," and Chapter 7, "STEM + People or Word Careers." Few career books tackle these important areas of employment, and myths abound about these fields, including the myth that STEM jobs are readily available. After all, aren't we always hearing about the lack of people to fill STEM positions? Doesn't Yahoo regularly let us know that the highest paid jobs are in STEM fields?

The truth is, these jobs are highly specialized, often require advanced degrees, and do not fit neatly into one package despite the appealing acronym of STEM. Jobs for a bachelor's level biology major are quite different from jobs for a PhD in physics or a master's degree in math. These two chapters illuminate the variety of careers for individuals with differing STEM backgrounds, describing the typical careers in each field, and then adding what Marty calls "neat niches": interesting lesser-known specialties that might be worth investigating. Careers like cancer registrar, packaging engineer, or virtual reality programmer might not be on Yahoo's top career list — but probably should be. And this section doesn't just list job opportunities; it delves into the mindsets STEM majors will need to develop to succeed, including an interdisciplinary mindset and high emotional intelligence.

Finally, *Careers For Dummies* goes beyond most career books in that it also provides information for succeeding in the workplace once you have the position. This book could quite possibly be the only career book you will need to complete your job search. (Except for mine, of course. Buy them both.)

A new career book. Hmm . . . Do we really need another one? If it's *Careers For Dummies* by Marty Nemko, we do.

Dr. Katharine S. Brooks
Evans Family Executive Director
Vanderbilt University Career Center
Nashville, Tennessee

# Introduction

n our demanding, fast-changing world, it's challenging to pick a career, land a good job, and succeed in it. This book can help.

## About This Book

I hope you'll consider this book your virtual career coach — your little black career book. It shares much of what I've learned from having worked with over 5,000 clients. Here's a walk-through:

I start by helping you look at The Big Trends in Part 1, "Finding Your Place in the Work World." That can help you sail with — instead of against — the wind. It might even help you get in on the ground floor of The Next Big Thing.

In choosing a career, it helps to find out what makes you special. So one chapter helps you do that. Another way to find your specially-suited career is to look under the radar. The book's DIY Under-the-Radar Career Finder can help you find niches that fit you.

After you've gotten to know more about yourself, you can browse Part 2, "The Careers Catalog." It offers a brief scoop on 340 careers: the popular ones plus plenty of under-the-radar options. Each scoop ends with a link to more information. The careers are arranged in categories to make it easier to home in on well-suited choices. In another chapter, I offer my favorite low-risk self-employment ideas, plus a tool to help you decide whether you're likely to be successfully self-employed.

Then I turn to describing how to try on a career. Like a suit of clothes, a career may look good on the rack, but when you try it on, you may love it or cringe. And like a suit, for a career to really work, it may need to be tailored and accessorized. I'll show you how.

It's all well and good to pick a well-matched career, but you need to be well-trained to avoid the imposter syndrome—when you feel less competent than your diploma suggests you are. Sometimes, that means choosing the right major and college- or graduate-school program, but at other times, it's wise to do some (or even all) your career preparation outside the halls of academe. Either way, this book has you covered, even down to how to convince an employer that you're worth hiring *because* you attended "You U" instead of State U.

Of course, career training is important, but we all know people who are well-trained yet don't live up to their potential. They may have issues that keep them from being, as the Army commercial said, "the best you can be." Perhaps they're wrapped up in self-doubt and fear, or they're inveterate procrastinators. So read the chapter: "Getting Emotionally Solid."

Next, it's time to land a job — a good one. The next few chapters show how to do more than just answer ads — how to get referred in, for example. And to summarize those chapters, I list, day by day, what I would actually do to get the essence of my job search done in a week — yes, a week.

Okay, so after you have a job offer, do you just take it or do you negotiate? And if you negotiate, how can you do it without the offer getting pulled or your getting stressed out — well, not too stressed out? That's the topic of the chapter "Negotiating Wisely."

Now you're on the job. How can you get good at it, and maybe even become beloved? I'll talk about the unspoken rules of the workplace: managing your boss, time, stress, and supervisees; cultivating charisma; and even public speaking without fear.

But what if, despite all efforts, you've picked the wrong career or simply decided that you've been there, done that, and it's time for something new? The next chapter shows four approaches to changing careers.

Then I get philosophical: What really matters to you? This chapter can help you decide on your work life's foundational principles. Then I step back and offer a pessimistic view of the future, an optimistic one, and my prediction.

To end on a lighter note, the book concludes with The Part of Tens: ten ultrafast ways to land a job, ten career myths, and, as an opportunity for me to sound like your father, ten (+5) preachy pleas.

# Icons Used in This Book

For Dummies books highlight particularly important text with these icons:

This book is filled with tips, but I mark particularly important or fresh ones with this icon.

You may have heard these ideas before, but they're important enough to deserve a shout-out.

Avoid these common pitfalls and you probably won't bomb out.

# Beyond the Book

In addition to the material in the print or ebook you're now reading, you get a free, access-anywhere Cheat Sheet with even more tips for landing that dream job. To get this Cheat Sheet, visit www.dummies.com and type **Careers For Dummies Cheat Sheet** in the Search box.

After reading this book, if you still have questions, email me at mnemko@comcast.net. I promise to answer you.

*marty nemko*

# Where To Go from Here

You may choose to read this book from cover to cover, or you may prefer to read just what you need when you need it — that's *just-in-time* learning. If you prefer the latter method, just review the table of contents and turn to the page you're motivated to read. In either case, I hope you find this book worthwhile and enjoyable.

# 1

# Finding Your Place in the Work World

# Chapter **1**

# Understanding Today's and Tomorrow's World of Work

This chapter can help you find your place in the world of work, both today and tomorrow.

More specifically, it looks at what's likely to remain the same —and what's likely to change — over the decades of your work life. Although I'm not in possession of a crystal ball, I do have some insights into what you can expect to come down the pike over the course of the next 10, 20, 30, or even 40 years. This chapter spells out some of those insights.

## Timeless Truths

It's been said that the only person who likes change is a wet baby. So let me start by describing what's likely to remain relatively constant over your workspan.

# What employers seek in an employee

Employees with the attributes described in the following list will continue to have good job prospects:

>> **Tech-plus:** Ever more jobs will require both soft and technical skills. Some jobs will continue to require mainly what are referred to as *soft skills* — effective communication, organization, and attention to detail, for example. But ever more jobs will also require skills that are far more technically oriented. It could be simply knowing how to use the field's major software, or it could be having in-depth knowledge of supply chain management or machine learning design.

>> **Reasoning skills:** Most well-paying jobs require employees to make many decisions each day that require good thinking skills, including the not-so-common "common sense."

>> **Emotional solidity:** A person can be smart and knowledgeable yet be unsuccessful. Success requires resilience to life's slings and arrows. You may be able to develop and strengthen that capability to an unexpected degree, as you can see in Chapter 13.

# Large organizations are desirable employers

Start-ups make for lots of sexy-sounding headlines because of a ping-pong and Red Bull culture, and when a start-up goes public, it makes its founders zillionaires. Beyond the headlines, start-ups have other pluses: They often allow you to wear many hats in the service of a cutting-edge product and offer the prospect of a big-buck exit. Just remember that most start-ups quickly go bust, leaving employees jobless and with stock options worth zippo.

Sure, working for a large company has some disadvantages: Your role may be narrow, and you may be forced to follow procedure and the chain of command. But a solid structure can help a company be greater than the sum of its parts. Combine that concept with the deep pockets, refined processes, and good products associated with larger companies and it's easy to understand why many graduates of prestigious colleges continue to want to work for category killers like Apple, Google, Citibank, Johnson & Johnson, Goldman Sachs, 3M, General Electric, and Procter & Gamble. Similarly, people who prefer nonprofits are attracted to major players like UNICEF, Planned Parenthood, and the Bill & Melinda Gates Foundation. And, people who prize job security and a prosocial mission gravitate to the largest employer: the government.

# The importance of choosing a career wisely

Finding a career that matches your abilities, interests, and values will remain important, and not just because your success and happiness matter. If you've picked correctly and thus stayed in your career for at least a few years, you'll have had the time to acquire the in-depth knowledge that many careers require.

# Rigorous hiring practices

Today's job seekers are likely aware that candidates applying for good jobs are often *invited* to apply: They're "referred in" by colleagues, or recruiters find them by trolling professional forums and speakers' lists from professional conferences. (For a database of professional associations, check out www.directoryofassociations.com.)

So, participate in your profession's community. That makes you more employable and competent and, in turn, feeling better about the work you do.

In recent years, job seekers have come to expect multiple rounds of interviews and tests of their technical skills, from typing to coding. That will continue. It means that job seekers will continue to need to show, not just tell. For example, today's winning résumé should usually include a professional development section that lists key learning outcomes from career-specific trainings: from an in-person workshop to an online certificate.

REMEMBER

The good news is that hiring practices involving multiple interviews help ensure that merit, and not other factors, drive hiring decisions. That benefits not only good candidates but also coworkers and customers.

# Home work

More and more people are working from home. Because of the ever-growing traffic in many cities, more employees are asking to *telecommute*, or work from home, at least for part of the work week. Many employers support telecommuting because it saves the expense of providing office space. In addition, cheap, reliable videoconferencing makes video meetings more acceptable than in the past.

# Gigification

Many employees will continue to be needed full-time — 52 weeks a year. But employers will continue to replace other employees with "gig" employees, or *just-in-time* employees, who are contracted to complete specific projects.

Employers are sometimes tempted to replace full-time employees with these "giggers" because it's ever more expensive to hire U.S. workers. That expense includes not just salaries but also government-mandated benefits and protections: increased Social Security and workers' compensation limits, employee lawsuits, and employer-paid healthcare, for example.

**REMEMBER**

Some people lament America's gigification. They prefer stability over having to look for new work every few months. They prefer working with the same people for a long time — it can feel good to experience life's key times together. On the other hand, some people like the gig economy's flexibility: They benefit from the novelty of the experience, the option of taking breaks to complete that dream project or travel destination, or perhaps even a chance at a fresh start after a financial meltdown, for example.

# What Will Likely Change

During your workspan, the world is sure to change dramatically. The following sections take a look at what changes will most likely affect your world of work.

## Yes, the robots are coming — but not so fast

Sure, more jobs are becoming automated, but the worry that robots will entirely take over the workforce may be overblown. Yes, though repetitive work will likely be automated, for at least the next decade, most jobs requiring judgment will be augmented by — but not replaced by — technology. For example, physicians will have sort of a Dr. Watson to aid in diagnosing patients and choosing a treatment — though we're a long way from having to hear the online receptionist say, "The robot will see you now."

The truth of the matter is that every time a new technology has been developed — from the steam engine to the search engine — it was predicted that the technology would kill jobs. More jobs were created, however, including many that couldn't even have been imagined. Plus, in selecting the 340 careers to include in Part 2 of this book, I've considered the risk of a career being automated. There should be ample options, both technological and not, that would capitalize on technological advances. Here are a few examples:

>> **The fashionable future:** It shouldn't be long before you can visit a clothing website, pick a fabric and style, and enter your body measurements — and

then print the perfectly customized item at home on your 3D printer. Yes, this system will eliminate repetitive clothing manufacturing jobs, but those are low-paying and not fun, anyway. The replacement jobs will inevitably be more interesting. For example, people will likely buy more clothes, given how easy and (eventually) inexpensive it will be to purchase what they're in the mood for. That will create jobs for everything from fabric designer to image consultant and from fabric-ink manufacturer to repairer of those printers eternally cranking away in 3D.

>> **Future (Data) Farmers of America:** In this increasingly ever more data-centric world, people will be hired to collect and interpret the information that companies, nonprofits, and government are acquiring. Consider merely how much data Google and Facebook alone already have on each of its users. Artificial intelligence will enable ever more personalized ads to be presented; it will even infer your moods and send you just-in-time ads. That will increase the number of jobs that are available, for example, as data scientist, market researcher, marketing manager, social media marketing specialist, nonprofit fundraiser, and donor database manager.

>> **The future of love:** Even advances in dating will create jobs. Dating already has evolved from the old-fashioned matchmaker to Match.com and a bevy of similar dating sites, from Tinder to J-Date. New jobs will likely be created because of next-generation dating sites: An algorithm will infer your essence from your social media posts and then suggest good fits. Swipe right and you'll see a 3D holographic video of the person introducing himself. (Or herself. I rotate the terms in this book.) Swipe left and you'll teach the algorithm to improve its predictions. Jobs will be created not just for designers of dating sites but also for coaches, for example, to guide your journey to your prince or princess.

>> **Acme Robotics:** And, of course, the more robots that are coming, the more people will be hired to design, build, install, maintain, and repair them.

I wouldn't worry too much about the robots. Hey, they've been trying to sell us robotic vacuum cleaners for almost 20 years now, and most of us are still pushing around our Hoovers.

# Education, reinvented

Campus-based higher education is under increasing scrutiny. In addition to the daunting cost, many people complain that courses are too theoretical or too biased or too saddled with content of little interest to too many students. Those critics cite the Academically Adrift study, which found that more than one-third of college students grew little to not at all between their freshman and senior years in education's core outcomes: analytic reasoning, critical thinking, and writing.

Other criticisms include a residence hall culture that too often is, let's just say, not conducive to studying. And of course, with ever more students graduating, the bachelor's degree no longer confers a large advantage in the job market. A Northeastern University analysis of federal data found that more than half of college graduates under age 25 are unemployed or doing jobs that require no more than a high school education. And that result assumes that they've graduated. Only 59 percent do, even if given six years to complete their studies.

There has been a move to online education. Thousands of undergraduate and graduate courses are available via just two sites: www.coursera.org and www.edx.org. Alas, because many of those courses are similar to the in-person version but without the in-person interaction, the average completion rate is low.

But moving forward, colleges are attempting to compete with short and full-length courses offered by generally more practical providers such as Lynda (www.lynda.com), Udemy (www.udemy.com), and Udacity (www.udacity.com). That competition should result in larger numbers of shorter courses based on interactive videos and led by transformational instructors, including luminary practitioners. For example, MasterClass (www.masterclass.com) offers online courses in filmmaking by Martin Scorsese, writing by Judy Blume and James Patterson, comedy by Steve Martin, fashion by Diane von Furstenberg, architecture by Frank Gehry, singing by Christina Aguilera, jazz by Herbie Hancock, drama by David Mamet, tennis by Serena Williams, and environmental science by Jane Goodall. And each costs just $90. Harvard, let alone No-Name College, needs to respond, lest traditional higher education venues become dinosaurs.

Kindergarten through 12th grade, or K-12, education will progress more slowly toward online education because of its custodial function; the perceived need for a primarily high-touch (rather than high-tech) education; and the heavy unionization and need to protect teachers' jobs. But the United States has largely abandoned ability-grouped classes, especially in grades K-8. Instead, a class today may include special-needs students, gifted students, native speakers of English, and newcomers from many countries. Those diverse needs can be addressed only by technology, using individualized, self-paced instruction taught in multiple languages. Of course, because such classes could be taught primarily on video, the most effective teachers could teach them, enabling rich and poor, from Beverly Hills to Harlem, to obtain a world-class education. The live teacher, or at least a paraprofessional, would still be needed, for example, for classroom discipline, getting kids unstuck, providing emotional support, and presiding over socialization activities.

Of course, this situation has career implications: Would-be teachers or course developers might want to learn the art and science of creating and delivering transformational online courses. Regardless, it will likely be a decade or three until most high school courses (let alone lower grade levels) are delivered online by these "superteachers," so jobs for teachers — especially in science, math, bilingual education, and special education — will likely remain viable.

**TIP**

Whatever your career, in your own education, career preparation, and personal learning, consider the full range of options — on campus and online. (For more on the topic of degree training, see Chapters 11 and 12.)

# Changing health care

Baby Boomers' aging as well as other factors will result in downscaling medical care. Increasingly, the doctor won't see you now; the physician's assistant will. The physical therapist won't help you return to your athletic self, the physical therapy assistant will. These intermediate-healthcare providers, sometimes called *allied health professionals*, should find the job market felicitous.

Cost pressures will also incentivize pharmaceutical and imaging companies to develop more cost-effective diagnostic tests and treatments for patients with acute physical conditions, mental disorders, and chronic disease, driving the need for these companies to bring in more medical researchers.

Cost-control pressures will also boost the need for self-monitoring wearable devices. It won't be long until the concept of today's insulin pump, which continually dispenses the proper amount to the diabetic patient, will be used more widely. Imagine, for example, that instead of your taking a daily fixed amount of birth control medication, your wearable would dispense more of it only when you need it. I can envision a day in which healthcare will center around the mobile phone. One end of a wire will plug into the phone, and the other to a sensor you tape to your skin, perhaps under your shirt or blouse. The sensor would read your health status, automatically dispense any drugs you need, and, as appropriate, contact your healthcare provider.

Becoming a parent also may well change. Prospective parents have long been able to use in vitro fertilization (IVF) to get pregnant and to choose the baby's sex. In the future, embryo selection and repair may enable prospective parents to help ensure that the child is born without serious disease and, if society deems it acceptable, to have genes predisposing to altruism and high intelligence. That would boost the demand for reproductive-choice services.

Of course, all this bodes well for medical researchers, especially those with expertise in the math and physics that undergird people's understanding of medical diagnosis and treatment. But such initiatives also require a wide range of employees, from test tube washers to technicians and from clinical trials coordinators to grant writers.

## Going nuclear

There will likely also be a nuclear energy boon. (I said *boon*, not *boom*.) Pressure will probably continue to grow for people to reduce their carbon footprints and for society to replace oil and natural gas with renewables such as solar and wind. But renewables' physics delimitations should lead to major growth in the use of nuclear energy — it offers an unlimited source of energy with no carbon emissions. The nuclear industry's growth will accelerate as memories of Fukushima, Chernobyl, and Three Mile Island fade and safer technology becomes available — Bill Gates's company TerraPower is focusing on that goal.

## More East–West

Some Asian countries — notably, China and India — have a long tradition of valuing science, technology, engineering, and math (STEM.) Combine that with their large populations, low salaries, and increasing focus on innovation (rather than on simple replication) and Asia will provide ever more formidable competition to U.S. companies and workers. So, subject to political constraints, U.S. businesses and governmental entities will likely increase mutually beneficial collaborations with the East. It will widely be decided that it's wiser to join 'em than to simply try to beat 'em.

**TIP**

To leverage the trend of mutual collaboration with the East, learn how to facilitate such partnerships and joint ventures, whether you're an accountant who understands international rules, a scientist who's bilingual in Mandarin, or an entrepreneur who understands the variations in countries' sales techniques and ethical norms.

## Terrorism 2.0

Small-scale terrorism, such as slamming cars into pedestrians and machine-gunning shoppers, will likely lose impact, causing too much bad PR for any perceived increase in power. So terrorists may turn to weapons of mass destruction. Both groups will find it easier to do so as the cost of developing communicable bioviruses and "suitcase nukes" declines.

## More spiritualism, less religion

The Pew Center for the Study of Religion reports that the fastest-growing religion is no religion. But many people will undoubtedly continue to seek inspiration and comfort beyond day-to-day life. Hence, many people have replaced religiosity with non-deistic spirituality: for example, Buddhism and offshoots such as yoga and meditation. This should result in continued growth in spiritual teachers and leaders of spiritual communities and yes, yoga instructors.

# Taylor's Tale

This story synthesizes common travails in choosing a career. Can you relate?

Taylor was both excited and scared to go to college. Though she was looking forward to the freedom and adventure, she worried whether college would be difficult and whether she would make friends or miss living at home.

She wasn't sure what to major in, so she applied to colleges undeclared.

Taylor got admitted to more colleges than she had anticipated, but, fearing that her family might take on too much student-loan debt, she opted for an in-state public college.

In Taylor's first semester, her favorite course was Introduction to Political Science, taught by a charismatic professor, and she earned an A. Amid the nation's political roiling, her interest in "poli sci" grew, so she declared it as her major.

But some of her subsequent poli sci courses felt "dry," so she switched to psychology. Taylor had personal "issues" and hoped that the major in psychology would help her understand herself, maybe even improve her state of mind, and be more career-relevant. She did enjoy that major.

Taylor mused about possible careers: psychotherapist, social worker, teacher, management trainee. She even wondered whether she should change majors again and go into healthcare, but decided that she didn't want to spend more years as an undergraduate. So she went to the campus career center to explore her options. The counselor there gave her the Strong Interest Inventory and Myers-Briggs Type Indicator, and suggested that Taylor explore the career library using *people careers* as a filter. Taylor scanned its books, videos, and databases, but left feeling that "nothing popped out" at her as a clear winning choice.

So Taylor decided to defer selecting a career, hoping that something would soon emerge.

Taylor graduated in five years, which is about normal for most students these days, and she and her family were proud. After the graduation ceremony, her family took her out for dinner, but when she was asked the time-honored question, "What are you going to do for a career?" Taylor could say only, "I'm exploring."

She decided that travel might help her clarify, so she spent a month touring Europe. When she returned, however, she hadn't gained much clarity. Her parents worried that she'd become the stereotype: lots of student debt but no job, and living with parents again to try to figure it out.

Concerned, Taylor's dad asked whether she might like a job at the nonprofit where he served as human resources manager. Because she was afraid of falling behind her peers, and because she wanted money so that she could move out of her parents' house, she took the job — even though it was only part-time as a volunteer coordinator.

Even though Taylor had an "in" and did well on the job, she wasn't offered a full-time benefited position. She wondered whether she should return to school for a master's degree in psychology or look for a job in the for-profit sector. She decided on the latter because she didn't feel prepared to complete more schooling.

She took a job as a receptionist at a high-tech firm in Silicon Valley. One of her friends said, "You spent all that time and money on college and you're going to be a *receptionist?*" Though that comment gave Taylor pause, another friend told her that being a receptionist for a good company can be a launchpad to a better job, so she took it. And that turned out to be true. She got to know personally many of the company's employees, and one helped her gain a position as a marketing management trainee. But soon she said to herself, "I'm not sure I want to spend my life marketing computer chips," and although she was aware of the standard advice to not leave a job until you have a better one, she quit.

Taylor wondered what she should do next, so she journaled, and she asked friends and family. As time went by and she started missing college, she decided to look for job openings at her alma mater and got one in marketing for its alumni association.

And she liked it, sort of. First, it was just another part-time temporary gig. Then, floating in her brain was a question that she couldn't push out of her mind: "Is that all there is?"

This book can help ensure that your story is better.

# Chapter 2

# Finding What Makes You Special

Sometimes, you just want to feel like you fit in. But especially in choosing a career, you may want to find the answers to such questions as, "Is there anything special about me?" "What work would people pay me well for?" "Do I have a calling?" In short, you're simply asking, "Who am I, Anyway?" This chapter should help you figure it out.

## "Who Am I, Anyway?"

The following sections can help you identify your core abilities, skills, interests, values, and preferences.

### Your abilities

One way to unearth your core abilities is by completing the following steps to mine your accomplishments. Follow these steps:

1. List your accomplishments, big and small, starting with the earliest. Yes, this step can even include reattaching the wheel to your little red wagon or teaching yourself to read or consoling a fellow kindergartener who was crying.

Continue forward to the present — that A grade you earned on a term paper, for example, or that Instagram story you posted that attracted lots of views, your election as club president, that app you developed, the road trip you organized, or the gadget you designed.

2. Next to each accomplishment, write the key embedded ability or two that made the accomplishment possible — quick learning, fixing broken items hands-on, or catching errors in a sheaf of data, for example.

3. Put a star next to those abilities you'd enjoy using in your career.

And, voilà — you've identified the key building blocks in choosing your career.

## Your skills

From infancy, people are continually acquiring skills. More recently, you may have learned how to run a meeting, perform CPR, or query databases with Hadoop. In this section, I'll help you identify one or more skills you want to use in your career.

It's okay if you haven't yet acquired a particular skill. If you have the propensity and the desire, you may be able to sufficiently develop the skill. For example, many people who were afraid of speaking in public have become good at it. I offer a step-by-step plan for developing public-speaking skills in Chapter 20.

**REMEMBER**

Just because you're skilled at a task doesn't necessarily mean that you want to use the skill in your career. For example, you may be good at selling but not want a sales career. No problem — leave that one off your list. You should include only skills that you might well like to use in your career.

Skills tend to fall into one of five categories:

>> **Interpersonal:** You might, for example, be good at motivating people, or at healing, persuading, calming, or teaching them, or at being on a team with them.

Even if you consider yourself a "people person," you're unlikely to be strong in all those areas. So, which interpersonal skills are your strengths? List your last, say, half-dozen successful interactions with people. Do you see common threads?

>> **Word:** Some people are good at writing, reading complicated material, speaking one-on-one, or speaking to groups, and a fortunate few are good at all of the above.

Remember that you don't already need to be highly skilled at any of these. If you feel you have the potential and are motivated, put that skill on your list.

So, is there a word-related skill or two that you'd like to use in your career?

>> **Science, technology, engineering, and math (STEM):** The most valuable skills in these careers are advanced math, software coding, and in-depth knowledge of a scientific field — plant genomics, food chemistry, or the physics of lasers, for example. Do you have (or sense that you could, with reasonable effort, acquire) good skills in one or more of those areas?

>> **Hands-on:** These skills include the artistic — adapting a template website to make it uniquely attractive, for example. They also include the more functional — for example, installing or repairing an industrial robot.

Some people are more skilled in small-scale work — jewelry, die-making, or iPhone repair, for example. Others do better on a grander scale — heating systems, truck repair, or furniture-making, for example.

How about you? Could you see a particular hands-on skill being central to your career? If so, which one? Or, are you like me: When something breaks, my first instinct is to call the repair person?

>> **Entrepreneurial:** Do you think you can identify unmet needs that you could meet while making a profit? You also need to know how to buy low and sell high, plus the art of persuasion: to get vendors to sell cheap and buyers to pay well, all while retaining your ethics. So, should you identify entrepreneurialism as a skill that you want to use in your career?

REMEMBER

You don't need to be self-employed to be entrepreneurial. Indeed, for-profits and nonprofits often welcome *intrapreneurs*, people who can identify a new profit center and drive it through to profitability.

## Your interests

As far as your interests go, *you* identify what turns you on. Combine a core interest with a core ability or skill and you may find yourself with the holy grail: a career that makes you want to jump out of bed in the morning. (Well, most mornings, anyway.)

TIP

A problem with choosing a career based on your interests is that many people's interests cluster in just a few areas: entertainment, the environment, politics, animals, media, sports, fashion, high-tech, food, psychology, or the arts. That usually makes competition for well-paying jobs in those fields quite fierce.

So you have a better shot at finding good work if you can be interested in an area that flies *under the radar* — known by relatively few people, in other words. For example, few people salivate over a career in soybeans, plastics, or high-tech clean rooms. But if you become expert at one of them, you might find yourself *becoming* interested in that.

For example, at Thanksgiving, a young man was asked, "So, you graduated a few months ago. What are you doing for a career?" He replied, "I'm still not sure." The man's cousin said, "Well, I work at the Navistar plant. I probably could get you a job there." The man wanted to be able to afford to move out of his parents' house, so he agreed. His new job was to assemble tractor dashboards. He had no particular interest in dashboards (let alone tractor dashboards), but because he was bright and well-educated, he learned quickly. Soon, other workers on the factory floor came to him with questions, and he got promoted to foreman. When his cousin asked whether he liked his job, the man said, "I actually do." The point is that, sometimes, interest can grow with expertise, and if the field is not well-known, promotion and increased income can show up sooner than if you were to pursue a more popular field.

Of course, I'm not suggesting that everyone should become interested in tractor dashboards and the like. It's just wise to consider a range of options. What would you say are one or two interests that you could see as your career focus?

## Your values

People normally associate values with ethics. For example, most people say that they want to work ethically. But there are many other values you might want to prioritize in choosing your career.

For example, some people value working with particular kinds of people. Perhaps you'd like you work with children with mental or physical disabilities, or with highly accomplished adults. Or with people who share your political world view, or who are businesslike rather than artsy, or vice versa.

Many people value status. For example, even though physician assistants get to carry out most of the tasks that physicians perform, but with far less training and still earning a 6-figure income, status seekers would rather choose the route of becoming an M.D.

Some people are money-driven. They aspire to such careers as executive, investment banker, or big-ticket salesperson because they value financial freedom and a "nice lifestyle." They figure, "If I've got to work, I might as well choose something that pays well." Other people feel that it's unwise to prioritize income, and that it's wiser to focus on work that they're particularly good at and care about.

Some people recognize that they want to work for a nonprofit or as a government employee. Others prefer to work for for-profit companies or to be self-employed. Still others are open to more than one sector.

Many people prioritize work-life balance. Others find working extra hours more rewarding than what they'd otherwise be doing.

Some people place a high priority on job security and predictable salary increases, so they might aim for a career in government. Other people prefer a career in which the risks and rewards may be greater, such as enterprise software sales.

So now it's your turn. Is there a value or two that you want to prioritize?

## Your preferences

Beyond values, you may have work-life preferences to consider as you choose a career.

For example, some people prefer sedentary, predictable work, whereas others prefer not to be stuck behind a desk. Someone may want their job to require far-flung travel, for example, as an international business developer. Or, that person may want only regional travel, for example, as an inspector for a luxury hotel chain.

Adrenaline — some folks thrive on it. They want careers in which risk plays a major role — either physical risk, as in the type that a search-and-rescue pilot experiences, or financial risk, such as the type a bond trader faces.

Some people prefer to work in a particular location — for example, by the water, in an office, at home, outdoors, or in a particular small town, city, or suburb.

Of course, these are but a sampling of preferences. Do you have one or more that should be central to your choice of career, or to how you tailor and accessorize it to fit you?

## Taking a more structured approach

The preceding sections offer an open-ended approach to identifying your abilities, skills, interests, values, and preferences. That process allows you to consider a wide range of options.

It could be, however, that you'd appreciate a more structured approach. To that end, I've created a checklist of abilities, skills, interests, values, and preferences you can use. You can access them for free: Just go to www.dummies.com and type **Careers For Dummies extras** in the Search box.

# The DIY Under-the-Radar Career Finder

Some people are wise to identify a well-suited, under-the-radar niche: a career that excites them but that few others know about or care much about. The following sections describe several ways that you might find a lesser known niche for you.

## Combining two interests or skills

Many people have two disparate interests or skills that can be combined into a custom career. Here are a few examples to trigger your thinking:

>> A bookkeeper who loves art specializes in doing the books for artists.

>> An early-childhood-education major loves being on the water and opens a small childcare center in a lakefront cottage.

>> A sports fan who loves making deals and was considering attending law school takes instead a job as a receptionist for a sports agent. His goal is to become the next Jerry McGuire: "Show me the money!"

## "Niching in" a favorite product's supply chain

Pick a product you like. It can be anything: iPhone, beer, lingerie, basketball, solar panel, skin cream, apple pie.

Now imagine the steps that must be taken to deliver that product, such as beer, to the user:

1. Grow or source the hops, grain (mostly barley), and spices.

   (Did you know that most beers are made with one or more spices: orange peel, lime zest, cinnamon, cloves, and "grains of paradise" — a peppery, citrusy mix?)

2. Ship the ingredients to the brewery.

3. Brew the beer (which involves heating, mashing, fermenting, and, often, cooling under refrigeration), and then carbonate, age, and bottle it (including label and bottle top).

4. Ship the beer to wholesalers or directly to large retailers' warehouses or to ships for export, and then locally to retailers, restaurants, and night clubs.

5. Market the product everywhere, from highway billboards to Instagram to neon signs in a bar's window.

6. Make and distribute beer glasses and steins.

REMEMBER

At each of these steps, many people make a good living. But because most of those steps are not widely known, competition for jobs can be modest. For example, while competition for brewmaster jobs is undoubtedly stiff, it's probably less so for beer spice distributor. Yet you get to live in the beer world. Even if your role isn't sexy, you probably get invited to tastings, parties, and other events, and once in that world, you may find it easier to get into a cooler part of the business.

Now consider the iPhone: What under-the-radar steps occur from the moment the iPhone 10 is merely a twinkle in Apple's eye to the moment you pull it out of the box? Here's the list:

1. Someone manufactures the iPhone's components. It's true that unless you have big-time connections in that world, it probably isn't the source of your under-the-radar career, but we gotta start somewhere.

2. Companies ship the phones from overseas to Apple's warehouses. There are long-distance shippers and local ones, called *drayage*, that remove product from the dock and transport it to local distributors or retailers.

3. Export agents specializing in facilitating international commerce — dealing with tariffs, credit, bills of lading, and currency exchange, for example — ensure that the phones reach their proper destinations with as little hassle as possible.

4. Ad agencies create the ads, film production companies shoot commercials and web videos, and graphic artists create billboards and web pages.

5. Friendly retail salespeople, support personnel, and tech specialists work in the stores and remotely. (No, not all those jobs are offshored. Many have been brought back to the United States.)

6. "Tech tutors" show you how to get the most benefit from your phone.

7. Technicians repair the phone you dropped into the toilet. (That's what you get for texting while on the pot.)

Many people would love to have a career related to basketball, but their thinking often stops at player-and-coach. There's much more. People are needed to

>> Build the arena.

>> Maintain the arena.

>> Run concessions, from food to T-shirts.

>> Recruit players.

>> Condition the athletes.

>> Supply the uniforms, basketballs, and other items.

>> Sell media rights.

>> Sell advertising in the arena, in programs, and on the website.

>> Keep the statistics.

>> Regularly apprise the media.

>> Handle fan and community relations, including in social media.

Finally, here are some buried niches in the lingerie field:

>> Someone has to design it. Is it you?

>> Do you want to source fabric? Companies hire people to do just that.

>> Do you want to be involved in the dyeing process?

>> Do you want to be involved in manufacturing, shipping, selling, installing, or servicing the machines that make the lingerie?

>> Do you want to oversee the factory? (No sweat shops allowed.)

>> Regarding marketing, do you want to stage runway fashion shows? Or perhaps model in them?

>> Do you want to raise money so that the company can expand?

>> Would you enjoy exporting last year's hot designs to a developing nation, where they'd be *au courant*?

These lists only hint at the thousands of under-the-radar niches.

# Going grungy

Rather than focusing on products you like, you can focus on low-popularity areas — I mean, no one grows up saying, "I want to be a mover and shaker in the industrial acid business."

TIP

Yet many people have rewarding careers in industries with grungy products — janitorial, toxic waste, or post-disaster clean-up, for example. But competition there is lighter, so it's easier to rise to prominence and wealth than in a cool, commonly considered field. Most people would like to have important jobs at Google or Apple. Far fewer would want to be even an executive at a bathroom valve company. Yet, perhaps surprisingly, some people find greater satisfaction in less-than-sexy fields because, like the tractor dashboard hero mentioned earlier in this chapter, they can more easily become expert and increase their responsibilities, income level, and job satisfaction.

# 2
# The Careers Catalog

# Chapter **3**

# People Careers

Before we get to this chapter's specific careers, I want to say a word (more accurately, 300 words) about the chapters in this Part: The Careers Catalog.

It offers *scoops* on 340 popular and under-the-radar careers and self-employment options.

How were the careers selected for inclusion in the catalog? Some, like lawyer, couldn't be excluded even though training is long and expensive — and to top it all off the job market is tight and the dissatisfaction rate is high. Such careers are just too popular. Outside of the popular careers, the included ones score well overall on these factors:

» Many people find them enjoyable

» Job prospects are good and the pay ranges from reasonable to excellent

» They are offshore- and automation-resistant

» They make the world better or at least are ethically defensible — you won't see tobacco salesperson listed.

Here's how I selected the link(s) for further information about a career.

>> I preferred authoritative sources but when their reporting seemed governed by undue caution, I chose a less authoritative (but I believe more helpful) source —a forum in which many people in the profession weighed in on their experience, for example.

>> I downgraded sites to the extent they were focused more on recruiting students or members in a professional association than on providing even-handed insight into the career.

>> I included one, two, or three resources depending on a career's popularity and on whether I found a second or a third good resource that added new perspective. And if the first resource focuses on a career's positives, as is usually the case when the resource is a professional association's website, I looked for another resource that, for example, listed pros and cons. If I found a book highly rated on Amazon that offered a more thorough look at a career, I listed that last, because reading a book takes time and it can't, like a website, be accessed instantly and for free.

To ease browsing, the careers are divided into seven chapters:

Chapter 3: People Careers (careers that heavily involve people contact)

Chapter 4: Word Careers (speaking or writing-centric careers)

Chapter 5: People + Word Careers (careers requiring both people and writing or speaking skills)

Chapter 6: STEM (Science, Technology, Engineering, and Math) Careers

Chapter 7: STEM + People or Word Careers

Chapter 8: Hands-On Careers (These include artistic, mechanical, animal, transportation, and some medical careers.)

Chapter 9: Self-Employment Careers (Many of the careers in the previous chapters are sometimes done on a self-employed basis but those listed in this chapter are predominantly so.)

Many careers don't fit neatly into one of the Careers Catalog's seven categories but even if there were 20 categories, much overlap would remain while making the Catalog more difficult to browse. So don't say "Gotcha" when you find a career you think could have gone in another category. It probably could have.

**WARNING**

I reviewed well over 1,000 websites to find those worthy of inclusion. The vast majority prominently featured role models who are female, and only a tiny percent gave even moderate attention to white males. That was true in both male- and female–dominated fields such as nursing and education. Throughout this book, you'll see that I've taken great care to be inclusive. In that spirit, I ask readers reviewing those websites to realize that while, yes, special efforts are being made to attract women and minority employees, all people can still can be viable in all fields. Don't let the pictures fool you.

A final disclaimer. I was tempted to include the typical education requirement for each career and indeed did so in my previous *for Dummies* book, *Cool Careers for Dummies*. But as a number of readers of that book pointed out, there are many exceptions to the usual path. So, in this book, I decided that including an education requirement would unduly restrict your search. Most of the "for more information" resources do include information on the standard education required.

And now, disclaimers made, onward.

# When Helping Is the Main Job

Helping professions include the bloody and the not. (The bloody ones are primarily medical and are profiled in Chapter 7.) In this chapter, I focus on describing the blood-free options. Such professions — counseling and social work are the prime examples —as much art as science. Because these social science fields are still relatively young, practitioners must rely heavily on emotional intelligence (some would say *intuition*, or a "sixth sense") to decide what to do, what to say, and what not to say. If your past experiences suggest that you have that knack, that's a plus for your consideration of a career in the helping professions.

**TIP**

Another helpful attribute is warmth — you could know the science cold yet your clients might blow off your recommendations or not be honest with you. Patience is also key: Few of us change quickly, so patient people do well with, well, patients.

## Caretaking and coaching

Helping people through rough patches or giving them the tools they need to be the best they can be can be very rewarding. The jobs in this section do that.

>> **Mediator:** Traditionally, divorcing couples avoid trying to kill each other by letting their attorneys slug it out. That's expensive, adversarial, and often, just plain yucky. An ever more popular alternative is for the couple to hire a mediator.

In addition to divorce mediation, non-lawyers make a living in community mediation. Example: You're angry at your neighbor for playing loud music every night. Your neighbor is equally angry about your complaints: "Loud music is my way to relax after the workday, and you are not going to deny me my rights."

A good mediator needs the wisdom of Solomon, the patience of Job, and the listening skills of a suicide counselor. Not to worry: Mediation can be a rewarding career, even for mere mortals. Alas, it's a crowded profession, liberally laced with lawyers who'd rather conciliate than litigate.

Check out www.youtube.com/watch?v=BhWsvRUK-nI ("Arbitrator and Mediator Jobs") and mediationchannel.com/2009/07/15/mediation-career-myth-busting-5-urban-legends-its-time-to-debunk ("Mediation Career Myth-busting: 5 Urban Legends It's Time to Debunk").

*Neat Niche:* **Ombudsperson:** Some organizations hire *ombuds* — people who confidentially attempt to mediate conflicts among employees or between the organization and customers. Check out www.ombudsassociation.org/Resources/Frequently-Asked-Questions.aspx.

>> **Psychotherapist:** (For information on personal coaching careers, see Chapter 9.) Demand for psychotherapists is likely to remain strong because the Mental Health Parity Act requires that insurers cover mental illness to the same extent as physical illnesses. In addition, it's tough to cope with life's ever-greater demands. Most psychotherapists deal with depression, anxiety, stress, and — because of the aging population — health psychology. Artificial intelligence (AI) makes this career's future a bit murky. In your workspan, could self-learning AI apps such as WoeBot (www.woebot.io) become smart enough to replace therapists?

Check out www.youtube.com/watch?v=FSy8KGr6ZGI ("A Day In the Life of a Counsellor"), www.apa.org/action/science/clinical/education-training.aspx ("A Career in Clinical or Counseling Psychology"), and www.amazon.com/What-Never-Learned-Graduate-School/dp/0393702421 (*What You Never Learned in Graduate School: A Survival Guide for Therapists,* by Jeffrey A. Kottler and Richard J. Hazler.

*Neat Niche:* **Sports Psychologist:** A golfer has trouble concentrating. A pitcher can't throw strikes under pressure. An entire team can't stand the sight of their teammates. Enter the sports psychologist, whose common tools are guided visualization, rehearsing stressful situations, and breathing exercises. They also help athletes with substance abuse problems and anger issues. That's why some sports psychologists refer to themselves as *performance psychologists* and sometimes are brought into traditional workplaces to help employees excel. Check out www.youtube.com/watch?v=yG7v4y_xwzQ ("Sport Psychology"), www.apa.org/gradpsych/2012/11/sport-psychology.aspx ("Hot Careers: Sport Psychology"), and www.dummies.com/store/product/Sports-Psychology-For-Dummies.productCd-0470676590.html? (*Sports Psychology For Dummies,* written by Leif H. Smith and Todd M. Kays; Wiley Publishing).

*Neat Niche:* **School Psychologist:** In a school psychologist's typical project, Johnny is doing poorly in school. What should the school administrators and parents do to help? The school psychologist observes and tests the child, helps teacher(s) and parent develop an individualized education plan, and then writes up the plan. School psychologists may also present workshops for students or parents on topics from bullying to sexuality, and screen students for programs for gifted students. Check out www.youtube.com/watch?v=CK1006uG-0w ("What Does a School Psychologist Do?") and www.nasponline.org (National Association of School Psychologists).

*Neat Niche:* **Forensic Psychologist:** Is the person sane enough to deserve the death penalty? Rehabilitated enough to be released into society? Competent enough to manage financial affairs without a conservator? More worthy of being the custodial parent? Was the death a disguised suicide to let the beneficiaries cash in on an insurance policy? Forensic psychologists try to get to the truth of the matter. Check out www.psychologytoday.com/blog/witness/201409/forensic-psychology-is-it-the-career-me ("Forensic Psychology: Is it the Career for Me?").

*Neat Niche:* **Men's Therapist:** The past two decades have seen an increase in the number of therapists focused on the issues of women and people of color. Men are now starting to seek counselors specializing in men's issues. Check out www.counseling.org/Publications/FrontMatter/78086-FM.PDF ("A Counselor's Guide to Working with Men").

» **Occupational Therapist:** You help an accident victim relearn how to drive. You find an alternative for an arthritis patient who can no longer button a shirt. Using a combination of psychology, computers, braces, and common sense, the occupational therapist is the practical, patient soul who tries to help clients do what they used to do, and want to do again. Check out www.youtube.com/watch?v=r0aCJtkDdSE ("What Does an Occupational Therapist Do?"), www.aota.org/Education-Careers/Considering-OT-Career.aspx ("Considering an OT Career?"), and www.topoccupationaltherapyschool.com/pros-cons-occupational-therapist ("Pros and Cons of Being an Occupational Therapist").

» **Social Worker:** Many people and families need help: A child is abused; an adult has Alzheimer's disease; a struggling single parent with three kids is devastated to get a diagnosis of AIDS. Few jobs are more intimate and human than the social worker's. This job is also often emotionally draining: The relentless "conveyer belt" of struggling people you counsel can take a personal toll. But despite the frustrations and low pay, most social workers who make it past the first two years like their job. Job security tends to be good, the job can't be offshored, and, alas, it's hard to foresee the need for social workers declining.

**REMEMBER**

Although many social workers have government jobs, some social workers are employed by private agencies such as the Red Cross or are in private practice — for example, as advocates for elders who are ill and trying to obtain needed care and resources.

Check out www.socialworker.com, www.socialworkers.org/Careers/Career-Center/Explore-Social-Work, www.amazon.com/Days-Lives-Social-Workers-Professionals/dp/192910930X (*Days in the Lives of Social Workers,* edited by Linda May Grobman), www.youtube.com/watch?v=_xqSY3nODbg ("A Day in the Life of a Social Worker"), and www.indeed.com/forum/job/social-worker/Is-social-work-bad-idea/t467862 ("Is Social Work a Bad Idea?").

*Neat Niche:* **Adoption and Foster Parenting Specialist:** Public agencies, as well as private licensed ones, hire social workers and counselors to match prospective parents with children and to counsel them and the birth parents. In addition, private agencies may specialize in international adoptions; see www.wikihow.com/Become-an-Adoption-Consultant.

» **Nanny:** Nannies play a key role in raising children during their formative years. Plus, the training is short, the task is manageable (and often pleasurable), and you may get to work in a lovely home. That's an attractive combination, even if the pay is low. If you're good with kids and are reliable, it shouldn't be too tough to find a job. With the increase in single parents and with two-parent families working full time, even many less-than-wealthy people hire nannies. The key to enjoying nannyhood is to get hooked up with a kindhearted family. Check out www.youtube.com/watch?v=n5ZLQqhHbLA ("Day in the Life of a Bel Air Nanny:"), www.nanny.org (International Nanny Association), and www.amazon.com/Supernanny-How-Best-Your-Children/dp/1401308104 (*Supernanny: How to Get the Best from Your Children,* by Jo Frost).

» **Child Life Specialist:** Imagine that you are told that your child has a serious illness and must suddenly face a significant medical procedure. The child life specialist's job is to help children prepare psychologically. For kids who must remain hospitalized for a while, child life specialists also help ensure that they receive an education and experience a bit of fun in their lives. Though it tends to be difficult to find a job and the pay tends to be low, the personal rewards may compensate. Check out www.youtube.com/watch?v=T5JPQdik4J8 ("Day in the Life of a Child Life Specialist"), www.childlife.org (Association of Child-Life Professionals), and answers.yahoo.com/question/index?qid=20110618053123AAtyuwN ("What Are the Pros and Cons in Becoming a Child-Life Specialist?").

» **School Guidance Counselor:** The modern version of this job is more complicated than dealing with kids kicked out of class for chewing gum. School counselors may coordinate sex education, substance abuse programs, career counseling, antibullying initiatives, programs to curb gang violence, and onsite social work services. And yes, counselors still spend a lot of time telling kids that they had better shape up — or else. Check out www.youtube.com/watch?v=ZrKBHSRm07o ("School Counselor: Andrea Rose:"), www.schoolcounselor.org (American School Counselor Association), and www.amazon.com/Elementary-Middle-School-Counselors-Survival/dp/0470560851 (*The Elementary / Middle School Counselor's Survival Guide*, by John J. Schmidt).

>> **College Student Advisor:** In the past, professors advised students, especially undergraduates, but many colleges have realized that the skill set necessary to be an advisor is different from the one held by many professors. So, many colleges now hire counselors to advise undergraduates. Sometimes it's just a matter of reviewing a transcript and suggesting courses, but many students have issues that, while not requiring therapy, go well beyond simply coming up with a semester schedule. Check out www.youtube.com/watch?v=4kHTEUDqUSQ&t=85s ("Academic Advising"), www.nacada.ksu.edu (National Academic Advising Association), and www.amazon.com/Academic-Advising-Comprehensive-Virginia-Gordon/dp/0470371706 (*Academic Advising: A Comprehensive Handbook*, by Virginia N. Gordon, Wesley R. Habley, and Thomas J. Grites)

>> **Organizational Developer:** An organizational developer figures out how to make the organization and its workgroups more effective, sometimes by conducting trainings and sometimes by restructuring. This person may also lead team building, communication, and diversity workshops. Some "ODers" approach those workshops with apprehension, because many participants are often resistant, feel it isn't helpful, or that they can't speak honestly. There's often latent or overt hostility. Check out www.youtube.com/watch?v=RdDg3udzK2E ("Organization Development Animation") and www.odnetwork.org (Organizational Development Network).

>> **Employee Assistance Professional:** Workers show up with problems. Some are prone to violence, some are engaged in substance abuse, some have their finances in disarray, and some have eldercare needs. Employee assistance professionals (EAPs) coordinate programs to help. On the prevention side, EAPs may establish wellness programs, sponsor workshops on time management or career planning, and even arrange carpools. Check out www.eapassn.org (International Employee Assistance Professionals Association) and www.amazon.com/Employee-Assistance-Programs-Enhancement-Programming/dp/0398078394 (*Employee Assistance Programs: Wellness/Enhancement Programming*, by Michael A. Richard, William G. Emener, and William S. Hutchison Jr.).

# Bringing people together

Many people enjoy connecting other people. These bridge-builders may find their ideal career in this section:

» **Personnel Recruiter:** Recruiters find well-suited employees for employers. They don't find candidates simply by posting job ads. In fact, they sometimes don't even post any ads. Increasingly, recruiters solicit referrals from current employees and pluck smart commenters from professional forums and among LinkedIn profiles of people not looking for work. And, recruiters attempt to lure top performers at competing organizations — hence the term *headhunter*.

Recruiters may interview primarily by phone or Skype and use work samples and other assessments to rate applicants more objectively than by questions such as the ol' standard "What's your greatest weakness?" (Recruiters grew tired of hearing, "I work too hard.") But a good recruiter still needs a feel for assessing a person's competence and fit with the job.

A recruiter can work for an individual company or a nonprofit or a recruiting agency. In a recruiting agency, you're part salesperson: You're trying to convince an organization to let you recruit employees for them. That can be challenging in an era in which it's tempting to save on the recruiter's fee and just place an ad on LinkedIn, Craigslist, or Indeed.

REMEMBER

The rate of job growth is fastest in temp agencies. Alas, that may be cost-saving to employers but not good news for many employees, who'd prefer stability and benefits.

Though most external recruiters are motivated by money, they need to also be driven by the desire to be a wise matchmaker and to see good marriages.

Check out www.youtube.com/watch?v=h01GcsTeHpc ("The 10 Skills a Great Recruiter Must Have"), www.ere.net/the-top-20-reasons-why-recruiting-is-an-exciting-and-high-impact-job ("The Top 20 Reasons Why Recruiting Is an Exciting and High-Impact Job"), and www.volt.eu.com/pros-cons-recruitment.aspx ("What Are the Pros and Cons of Working in the Recruitment Industry?").

» **Athlete's Agent or Artist's Agent:** Many artists and athletes aren't entrepreneurial. Left to their own devices, they'd participate in their sport or art form, and the checks would somehow arrive in the mail. The agent's job is to make that happen — for 10 to 15 percent of the take. Agenting can be an enjoyable career because you get to pick out and then champion the talented people you want to represent, work closely with them to ensure that they're well packaged, and help them reach as large an audience as possible — and get as well paid as possible. Plus, being an agent requires no formal credentials.

Most artists' agents learn as an agent's assistant or as a talent buyer — in a book publishing company's Acquisitions department, for example.

When it comes to sports agents, the typical preparation includes a major in sports management or even a law degree, meanwhile working as an assistant in an agency. But perhaps more important for your future success are your innate abilities and a commitment to helping your client, the human being, not just negotiating deals.

Check out superagent Leigh Steinberg's "How to be a Great Sports Agent: "https://www.forbes.com/sites/leighsteinberg/2012/08/15/how-to-be-a-great-sports-agent/#2a26e70a6bf3, www.napama.org (North American Performing Arts Managers and Agents), aaronline.org (Association of Authors' Representatives), and www.amazon.com/Agent-Tells-All-Tony-Martinez/dp/0976143305 (*An Agent Tells All*, by Tony Martinez).

>> **Casting Director:** Would you find it fun to cast a sitcom? An epic motion picture? A toilet paper commercial? Here's what you do as a casting director: You write a breakdown (a list of the needed characters), email it to agents, and wait for submissions (photos and résumés.) Then you pick people to audition. Casting director Lisa Pirriolli says, "Casting is perfect for people who were unpopular in high school. This is their way of getting back at all the people who didn't ask them out." You may have to start as a volunteer. Check out www.castingsociety.com/join/getting-into-casting ("Getting into Casting") and www.amazon.com/Confessions-Casting-Director-Secrets-Audition/dp/0062292099 (*Confessions of a Casting Director,* by Jen Rudin).

# Pressing the Flesh for Fun and Profit

Sales and its nonprofit analogue, fundraising, are among the few potentially lucrative careers that may not require a college degree. What is required is the ability to speak, listen, and be resilient and ethical in the face of many no's, no-responses, and changed minds. Here's a list:

>> **Sales Representative:** When you hear the word *salesperson,* what's the first word that comes to mind? Pushy? Although those types are around, many successful salespeople don't fit the stereotype. They and their nonprofit analogue fundraisers are good listeners at least as much as good talkers. They query or intuit the prospect's practical and psychological motivators. Based on that, they ask questions likely to lead the prospect to say yes.

Though salespeople and fundraisers need product knowledge (of course!), they must also be eager to help prospects solve their problem, even if it doesn't result in a sale. Such generosity often pays off in the long run — and the good salesperson feels okay about such giving even when it doesn't pay off.

On the other hand, salespeople are self-starters who are motivated by money. They're not reluctant to ask for the sale and are resilient when customers decide, despite the salesperson's considerable effort, not to buy or to buy elsewhere.

Many salespeople are surprised to find that they actually spend less than half their time selling. They answer technical questions, write proposals, handle problems with product or delivery, and write reports to management.

However, a sales career offers flexible hours and, if you're an outside sales rep, a chance to travel. Plus, it's nice to know that your income is directly related to your performance: The more you sell, the more you make. Alas, it may be tough to know how much you're likely to sell. Even good salespeople will fail if the product, territory, or commission schedule is poor. Before accepting a job, ask one of the company's other salespeople about those matters.

If you're good, a career as a sales rep is more stable than many other for-profit careers. Employers are loath to lay off the sales team, because they're the link to short-term profits. A sales rep job can also be a good launch pad to promotion. Because the lifeblood of businesses and nonprofits is money, and because salespeople bring in the money, organizations often promote top salespeople to management and leadership positions.

Check out www.bls.gov/careeroutlook/2011/summer/art03.pdf ("Paid to Persuade") and salescareer.net/why-a-career-in-sales-pros-and-cons/6 ("Why a Career in Sales, Pros and Cons").

*Neat Niche:* **Big-Ticket Item Sales:** Some examples are golf courses, airplanes, venues, skyscrapers, and customizable enterprise software, such as Oracle or Salesforce.com.

*Neat Niche:* **Industrial Sales:** I like this niche because it's under-the-radar: Few people grow up thinking, "When I grow up, I want to sell conveyer belts." That means the competition is lighter and the pay is better. And, for the right person, the job can be fun — getting to visit all sorts of manufacturing plants and helping their administrators solve problems. Check out www.peaksalesrecruiting.com/b2b-sales-career ("The Career You Never Thought Of") and www.manaonline.org (Manufacturers' Agents National Association).

» **Fundraiser/Development Specialist:** You may wonder, "Why the term *development?*" Because a nonprofit organization *develops* prospective donors into actual donors — ideally, big donors. For example, your alma mater might start developing you by emailing you invitations to free or low-cost events designed to make you feel closer to the college, such as half-price tickets to the football game, an alumni magazine, or an invitation to speeches by the most compelling speakers on campus. After you're warmed up, they'll start sending you solicitations, usually with email campaigns and telemarketing banks. Plus, if you're a potential big donor (according to the alumni questionnaire you recently completed), the college assigns an alum — with similar interests and who already donates — to personally solicit you. A prospect researcher creates a dossier on you so that the pitcher knows what approach is likely to get you to donate maximally. A development office records how much you donate; the more you donate, the more they ask for the next time. A development officer's crowning achievement is convincing you to put the organization in your will.

**REMEMBER**

Development jobs tend to divide into *cultivators* and *harvesters*. The former stage fundraising events, gather research on prospects, maintain donor databases, and write pitch pieces and grant proposals; the latter make "the ask." Harvesters must have the ability to gain the trust of wealthy people and organization heads, to ask for large sums of money without blinking, and to endure rejection. Knowledge of wills and trusts is helpful. Harvesters are generally older because most people with big dollars are older — it usually takes decades to have accumulated wealth. Former sales managers make especially good fundraising executives.

Check out alumni.virginia.edu/hoosnetwork/2015/04/considering-a-career-in-nonprofit-fundraising-part-i ("Considering a Career in Nonprofit Fundraising (Part I)"), www.youtube.com/watch?v=Qsnap50h8S8 ("Seth Godin on Successful Fundraising"), and www.afpnet.org (Association of Fundraising Professionals).

» **College Admissions Recruiter:** The United States has 4,000 colleges and vocational-technical schools, the vast majority of which must recruit to fill their classrooms. Your title may be college admissions counselor, but you're kind of a salesperson. It's a good job for people who like to travel locally and talk with teens and their parents. Check out www.nacacnet.org (National Association for College Admission Counseling).

**WARNING**

Don't confuse a college admissions *recruiter* with a college admissions *counselor.* The recruiter is hired by a college to recruit students to that college, whereas the counselor is usually employed by a high school or is in private practice to help students find well-suited colleges, gain admission, and maximize financial aid.

# Checking Out Other People-Oriented Careers

Here's a potpourri of other careers for people who prefer to spend much of their workday interacting with people:

>> **Flight Attendant:** Your main role is not to serve food and beverages, but rather to ensure safety. The airlines' remarkably good safety record means that your safety role will almost always be simply to prepare the cabin for take-off and landing, deal calmly but firmly with the occasional difficult passenger, and perhaps make the infamously boring safety announcement — though that task has increasingly been taken over by a video. This career is well-suited to single people because, especially in the earlier years, you're on call and can have irregular schedules. But for many, that's a worthwhile trade-off for getting free trips to exotic place after exotic place. Check out www.thebalance.com/flight-attendant-526020 ("Flight Attendant"), theflightattendantlife.com/prosconsflightattendantlife ("Pros and Cons of Being a Commercial Flight Attendant"), and www.youtube.com/watch?v=sIVqJgkQSoI ("The 'Real Life' of a Flight Attendant").

>> **Event Planner:** This career is the detail-oriented person's dream, with so much to get right, all by an immovable deadline and perhaps with a nervous client adding to the stress level. To boot, you frequently must work nights and weekends. But many of my clients aspire to this career. They say they like working on projects with a definite beginning and end, that it's aesthetic and people-oriented, and that it requires little technical knowledge. Plus, event planning is a large field. The meeting industry alone — predominantly conventions and expos — has a national market of more than $80 billion! Other niches are corporate parties and product rollouts. Check out www.mpiweb.org (Meeting Professionals International), www.managerskills.org/hospitality/pros-v-con ("Pros and Cons of Event Planning"), and www.amazon.com/Event-Planning-Management-Successful-successful/dp/1519178204 (*Event Planning: Management & Marketing For Successful Events*, Alex Genadinik).

*Neat Niche:* **Convention, Trade Show, or Expo Planner:** No matter how much information is available online, and no matter that videoconferencing is cheap or free, people like to meet — to stay current, to network, to check out vendors' new products and, yes, to meet a romantic partner. Check out www.pcma.org (Professional Convention Management Association).

*Neat Niche:* **Wedding Planner:** You handle all the details so That Special Day lives up to the fantasy, without burning all the money that could have been used to buy a house. Check out careers.alot.com/career-paths/pros-and-cons-of-being-a-wedding-planner--8755 ("Pros and Cons of Being a

Wedding Planner") and www.nawp.com (National Association of Wedding Professionals).

*Neat Niche:* **Reunion Planner:** "I can't believe it. Back when we were in school, he was skinny and had a full head of hair!" High school reunions are intriguing events, but who has the time to send invitations, take reservations, hire the DJ, find food, arrange hotels, line up child care, plan activities, and dig up all those missing class members? The reunion planner, that's who. Tracking down long-lost folks, mainly using online databases, adds a detective component to an already pleasant job. Check out www.reunions.com (National Association of Reunion Managers).

» **Police Officer:** Most police officers are valued, trusted protectors of a community's people and property, but in recent years the bad actions of a few have meant that cops in general have come under closer scrutiny by society at large. The main takeaway here is that *the* crucial skill that everyone involved in law enforcement must have is the ability to remain calm under extremely stressful circumstances while simultaneously being able to calm the people you're interacting with. Check out www.youtube.com/watch?v=6Jh7FIm5w34 ("What's It Really Like Being a Police Officer"), www.criminaljusticedegreeschools.com/criminal-justice-careers/police-officer ("Police Officer: Career Guide"), and www.policeone.com/opinion/articles/231426006-The-pros-and-cons-of-being-a-police-officer ("The Pros and Cons of Being a Police Officer").

» **Military Officer:** This job title is a catchall for hundreds of occupations, from manager to doctor, from accountant to engineer. A military career offers many pluses: fine free training, extensive benefits, and esprit de corps unmatched in most civilian jobs. Of course, you must accept a life of uniforms, bureaucracy, and transfers to places you might not choose, and there's some chance you'll get hurt — or worse. Among the many routes you can take are ROTC, enlistment, officers' candidate schools, and the prestigious service academies, such as West Point (Army), the Naval Academy, the Air Force Academy, and the Coast Guard Academy. These schools offer small classes taught by unusually dedicated instructors and — in exchange for a 4- to 5-year post-graduation commitment to serve — free tuition and room and board. When I visited the Air Force Academy, the cadets were more enthusiastic about their college experience than students at any of the 100-plus colleges I've visited, including Harvard and Stanford. If you think you may like to "be all you can be," start by checking out the clearinghouse for military-related careers at www.todaysmilitary.com; for balance, take a look at www.thebalance.com/what-the-recruiter-never-told-you-3332706 ("What the Military Recruiter Never Told You").

» **FBI Special Agent:** Are you an aspiring James or Jane Bond? The reality is usually less exotic, investigating such mundane dalliances as your basic fraudulent bankruptcy, but some FBI special agents do search out terrorists, corrupt officials, kidnappers, hackers, drug traffickers, identity thieves, mobsters, and bank robbers. The downsides are that you travel a lot and are alone most of the time. The FBI employs more than 10,000 special agents and prefers a graduate degree in law or accounting or fluency in a foreign language — Middle Eastern languages are in particular demand. Are you 37 or older? Forget it; the FBI wants to hire young. So do most employers, but age discrimination laws prevent it. The FBI is above all that. Entry-level job title: clandestine service trainee. Check out www.youtube.com/watch?v=d4NSfrOtMfU ("FBI Special Agent Careers"), www.indeed.com/cmp/FBI/reviews?fjobtitle=Special+Agent&fcountry=ALL ("FBI Employee Reviews for Special Agent"), and www.amazon.com/FBI-Career-Guide-Information-Prestigious/dp/0814473172 (*The FBI Career Guide*, Joseph W. Koletar).

*Neat Niche:* **Secret Service Agent:** The United States Secret Service employs over 6,000 people to, yes, protect the U.S. president (and former presidents), vice president, and their family members, but also, working alongside the FBI, to unearth other threats, from counterfeiting to cyberterrorism. Check out www.youtube.com/watch?v=ZvXgHiS9-zQ ("10 Hidden Details the Secret Service Doesn't Want You to Know").

» **Bail Bond Investigator (Bounty Hunter):** Few tasks are riskier than pursuing criminals on the run. Believe it or not, the police are often too busy to find them. That's where bail bond investigators come in. First, you must track down leads. Computers can help, but the ability to find snitches is the key. (One woman bailed her grandson out of jail by posting her house as a bond, but he skipped town, and guess who turned him in? Dear grandma.) An adrenaline rush comes during the actual chase and takedown — many people who skip bail won't go back to jail without a fight. So it's not surprising that successful bail bond investigators can earn a 6-figure income. (I wouldn't do it for seven figures.) Check out www.youtube.com/watch?v=PGJBb9nnuMo ("Breaking Bond") and www.bountyhunteredu.org/careers ("Bounty Hunter Careers and Job Description").

» **Producer:** Whether it's a hip-hop concert, a local production of a play, or a virtual-reality trip to Tahiti, few activities are more fun than coming up with an idea and putting the pieces together so that it becomes a reality. That's what a producer does. I'm not talking just about raising money and hiring the actors and crew. I'm talking about solving countless problems like this one: In the book *Gig: Americans Talk about Their Jobs* (written by Marisa Bowe, John Bowe, and Sabin Streeter), producer Jerry Bruckheimer tells of having spent a million dollars designing space suits in which the actors in the movie *Armageddon* could breathe. In the middle of the shoot, Ben Affleck fell to the floor, suffocating in his space suit. The oxygen system had stopped working, and someone had to cut open the suit. No harm was done, except that it stopped production and, for every lost minute, hundreds of people must be paid — an expensive meter always is running. Bruckheimer said, "So there's a little set story for you. And there are a million of those."

How to become a producer? David Wolper — the producer of *Roots,* the Los Angeles Summer Olympics, and the Jacques Cousteau *National Geographic* special — believes that if you're a go-getter, producing isn't rocket science. Just find a cool idea you'd like to make happen, gather a team of experts to agree to participate if funding is available, tap all the talented, unemployed film production people you know (they're around), and then pitch well-off people to fund it.

Be sure to check out www.youtube.com/watch?v=IzynSBPtS4U ("Things to Know If You Want to Be a Film Producer"), www.prospects.ac.uk/job-profiles/television-film-video-producer ("Television/Film/Video Producer"), and www.amazon.com/Complete-Production-Handbook-American-Presents/dp/024081150X (*The Complete Film Production Handbook,* by Eve Light Honthaner).

*Neat Niche:* **Expo/Show Producer:** As an expo producer, you may put on a bridal show, an art fair, a plastic manufacturer's convention, or a conference on nanotechnology. Identify a need and gather plenty of exhibitors and enough attendees to keep them happy, and you may be able to make a year's income in a few months. Check out www.iaee.com (International Association of Exhibitions and Events), and www.ifea.com (International Festivals and Events Association).

» **Relocation Specialist:** You're moving to a new city. What's the best neighborhood to live in? Which are the best schools? Where should your spouse look for a job? A relocation specialist living in that city can help you. Based on answers to a questionnaire about your wants and needs, the relocation specialist points you in the right direction. It's like having a wise, local relative. How do you get a job as a relocation consultant? You might approach the local offices of national real estate chains or the HR departments of locally based corporations. More complex versions of this job are global: helping employers move employees to new locations worldwide, which can include immigration and tax issues. Check out www.erc.org (Employee Relocation Council).

» **Trial Consultant:** This field has evolved from its start, when a few activist social scientists tried to help Vietnam war protesters win their cases. Then, hiring a trial consultant became *de rigueur* for celebrity defendants: If O.J. Simpson hadn't retained a trial consultant, who knows whether he would have been found innocent in his first criminal trial? Dr. Phil met Oprah Winfrey when she hired his trial consulting firm to aid in her defense at her 1996 "mad cow disease" trial in Amarillo, Texas. Now trial consultants are frequently used by a wider range of clients.

Most people think of trial consultants as helping to pick a jury, but they also coach witnesses and conduct mock trials and focus groups to try out different strategies. (Beware if you're the defendant and the other attorney has retained a trial consultant.) This is an appealing career for lawyers who don't want to argue, psychologists who don't want to listen to patients' problems all day, and market researchers who'd rather deal with people than with data. Check out www.astcweb.org (American Society of Trial Consultants) and www.amazon.com/Principles-Practice-Consultation-Stanley-Brodsky/dp/1606231731 (*Principles and Practice of Trial Consulting*, by Stanley L. Brodsky).

» **Funeral Director:** Some people cringe at the thought of working in this profession, but funeral directors are proud of their work. When a death occurs, a funeral director who helps family members make arrangements that feel right can be of benefit in a time of need. Alas, some funeral directors take that opportunity to push a $5,000 casket when a $500 one would do: "You wouldn't want to be cheap with your mother, now would you?"

Training is moderate in length, pay is substantial, and demand is growing because of the aging U.S. population and because many funeral directors are about to retire — not a bad combination. Of course, before choosing this career, spend some time at a funeral home. And despite projected fast growth in this field, landing a job isn't easy. Many people keep this business in the family. It may take a while to convince an employer that you're (pardon the expression) dying for the job. Check out www.youtube.com/watch?v=3MNkx49Nma8 ("Funeral Director. It's a Calling"), https://funeralbusinessadvisor.com/a-good-funeral-director-is-hard-to-find/funeral-business-advisor ("A Good Funeral Director is Hard to Find"), and www.nfda.org (National Funeral Directors Association).

# Chapter **4**

# Word Careers

Everyone can speak and write, at least to some extent. So (especially if you're not inordinately social or STEM-oriented) it can be tempting to consider a word-centric career. These true-false questions may help validate if a language-focused career would be a wise choice for you:

» Your speaking and/or writing are more precise, clear, and concise than that of most of your peers.

» You relish rather than are intimidated by the thought of speaking to a group.

» You've been told that you're an effective communicator.

## Writing for a Living

The careers described in this section focus on full-time employed positions rather than on freelance gigs. Alas, many writing jobs are now freelance or no-pay — for info on making it as a freelance writer, check out www.thebalance.com/freelance-consulting-4074015 ("How Does Freelance Writing Work, Exactly?").

» **Organizational Communicator:** Companies, nonprofits, and governments employ writers to create a wide range of documents. Some examples are the email from a nonprofit urging you to donate, the instructions on the hair dye bottle, the FEMA advisory following a natural disaster, and, yes, the annual report you received because you own a single share of Disney stock.

Someone working under the umbrella term *organizational communicator* — which includes public relations, media relations, community affairs, marketing communication, donor relations, and investor relations — is tasked with producing such documents.

A *business communicator* may also focus on *internal* communication, such as your organization's employee manual, the newsletter for employees' eyes only, and even the boss's speech to the troops.

Then there's the *marketing communicator.* This person writes the pun-filled copy for the Trader Joe's *Frequent Flyer* catalog, the up-sell brochure that the installer left when hooking up your cable, and, yes, your junk mail.

For more info on the profession as a whole, check out www.youtube.com/watch?v=e5oXygLGMuY&t=510 ("What Is Organizational Communication?") and www.iabc.com (International Association of Business Communicators).

*Neat Niche:* **Medical Writer:** Many medical writers translate prevention practices and treatments into plain English — for example, "Preparing for Your Knee Surgery." But the job can go well beyond that. Employers of medical writers include WebMD, Mayo Clinic, university medical schools and nutrition departments, professional associations, medical book companies, pharmaceutical companies, health insurers, hospitals, and even small medical practices. Biotech and pharmaceutical companies may hire you to produce regulatory documents. Check out www.amwa.org/page/toolkit_Details#Understand_Role (American Medical Writers Association).

*Neat Niche:* **Public Relations:** I held the stereotypically dubious view of public relations until I wrote my first book. In my heart, I believed that the book deserved to be read, but how was I to get it noticed among the 60,000 other books that were published *that year?* That situation made me realize that publicists can serve an honorable purpose.

**REMEMBER**

*Publicist* is actually only one specialization within the public relations field. Public relations types also develop corporate images that are consistent with community values; promote anyone from rock star to seminar leader; and, yes, do damage control, for example, when a politician is found to not walk the talk.

For a "reverse psychology" view of the public relations profession, check out www.prdaily.com/Main/Articles/5_signs_PR_is_the_wrong_career_for_you_15091.aspx ("Five Signs PR Is the Wrong Career for You"). For a more traditional view of the profession, see www.prsa.org (Public Relations Society of America).

*Neat Niche:* **Technical Writer:** You create user manuals, articles describing new products, instruction booklets, press releases, and online training or Help files. You must be able to work on deadline because you usually have to write documents when products are otherwise ready to go to market. Check out www.monster.com/career-advice/article/technical-writing-careers ("A Guide to Careers in Technical Writing") and www.stc.org (Society for Technical Communication).

>> **Book, Magazine, or Website Editor:** Book editors come in flavors. For example, the publisher of this book uses an acquisitions editor to develop ideas for books that fill a need, to find appropriate authors and work with them to create the table of contents, and to negotiate the contract. The project editor supervises the book's writing to ensure coherence of content and address problems as they arise. A copy editor reviews the manuscript, sentence by sentence, to ensure clarity, proper grammar, and so on.

Magazine and website editors are different. Even publications that use mostly freelancers and no-pay writers employ editors to oversee the business side of the magazine and to direct production of the publication's content. An editor on the editorial side of the house gets paid even if most of the writers are volunteers, because that person's job is mission-critical. S/he might, say, develop a vision for the publication that will attract visitors and advertisers and generate content ideas — a four-part series on body acceptance, including links to social media, for example. The role may include finding writers and graphical artists who will produce quality material despite modest or no pay. And, to ensure that the articles are read, she may optimize them for search engines. Check out www.prospects.ac.uk/job-profiles/magazine-features-editor ("Magazine Features Editor").

*Neat Niche:* **Copy Editor:** Many people write, but getting their writing into publishable form, with crystal-clear wording, often takes some doing. That's why writers and publishers (including the publisher of this book) hire copy editors. Check out www.copydesk.org (American Copy Editors Society).

>> **Proposal Writer:** Every year, federal and state governments issue thousands of requests for proposals (RFPs) for every imaginable product and service. They may request, for example, proposals for a state-of-the-art data management system, 300 desks for IRS offices, or 50,000 Navy uniforms. Thousands of private and corporate foundations issue even more RFPs. To maximize the chance of receiving grants, organizations hire proposal writers to search RFP databases to find ones that the organization might qualify for. The proposal writer then talks to in-house staff, reviews the relevant literature, perhaps consults with outside experts, and then crafts the proposal. It's a career that's endlessly innovative and creative. Not surprisingly, writers can be hired to

write both RFPs and grant proposals. Check out www.tgci.com (The Grantsmanship Center) and www.amazon.com/Proposal-Writing-Effective-Grantsmanship-Sourcebooks/dp/1483376435 (*Proposal Writing: Effective Grantsmanship for Funding,* by Soraya M. Coley and Cynthia A. Scheinber).

>> **Political Writer:** Most politicians, from the town councilperson to the president, need writers. Political writers craft copy for the pol's site, fundraising letters, speeches, and see-how-much-I'm-doing-for-you newsletters. One approach to landing a job is to write a fundraising letter for your favorite local politician and then send it as a sample. This work's pinnacle is as speechwriter. (See the Speechwriter entry later in this list.) You may have to start as a volunteer to do some basic writing for your favorite local elected official. For Al Gore's speechwriter's take on the speechwriter's life, check out opinionator.blogs.nytimes.com/2012/11/03/the-political-speechwriters-life.

>> **Ghostwriter:** Many notable people, world famous or little-known, didn't achieve their success because of their writing skill. So they often turn to ghostwriters to pen everything from a blog to a book about their breakthrough product or a would-be-president's memoir.

**REMEMBER**

Less august people also may use a ghostwriter. A psychologist might have someone write his Facebook posts; a high school basketball coach her column for the school website; a local eminent a newsletter trying to attract more customers or become a national thought leader. Check out www.thebalance.com/hiring-a-ghostwriter-2799856 ("Learn About Ghostwriting").

*Neat Niche:* **Speechwriter:** This one requires melding the speaker's content, values, and style — and, sometimes, market research data. A good speech uses tactics to enhance memorability — for example, emotional anecdotes or a repeated catchphrase, as in Martin Luther King's "I Have a Dream" speech.

*Neat Niche:* **Celebrity Ghostwriter:** This career is for people with a track record of published work. Here's how I'd try to land a celebrity ghostwriting book gig: I'd contact luminaries I respect who have been outside the headlines for a year — last year's hero may fear that he has already had his 15 minutes of fame. I'd say something like this: "I like and respect you because X, and I wonder whether you might like me to be the scribe of your autobiography. I'll ask you about your life and then massage it into a book. Because the content is all yours and I'm merely the writer, the cover would read, 'By you, with (in smaller letters) me.'"

Here's a real-world example: "Kareem Abdul-Jabbar with Mignon McCarthy." In a counterexample, John F. Kennedy notoriously did not credit his speechwriter, Ted Sorenson, for the (substantial) work Sorenson did on JFK's Pulitzer-Prize-winning book, *Profiles in Courage.*

For more on the ghostwriting profession, check out www.amazon.com/Ghostwriting-Murphey-Method-Cecil/dp/1621840824 (*Ghostwriting: The Murphey Method*, by Cecil Murphey).

» **Journalist:** If you can land a decent-paying job, journalism is a great career. You have opportunities for creativity, you're often learning something new, and you feel that you make a difference. Many factors, however, make it ever more difficult to find a journalism job that pays at least a middle-class salary. Print and broadcast organizations are merging or folding, and many remaining ones are using more nationally syndicated content. And thousands of "citizen journalists" are participating in journalism for free. Media outlets such as the Associated Press (AP) and *Los Angeles Times* are even using automated article-generation for basic business and sports articles.

**REMEMBER**

Like a career in acting or film directing, journalism is, alas, one of those job aspirations that too often results in poverty. I was on a top floor of the Time-Life Building talking with four editors from one of Time-Warner's major magazines, and everyone agreed that it was obscene that colleges continue to welcome more and more journalism majors even though only a small fraction will ever make a middle-class living in even a related field.

To increase your chances of landing a good job, specialize: Science, technology, and experts in racial or ethnic issues may have an edge. Check out www.spj.org/genj.asp (Society for Professional Journalists).

**WARNING**

Many articles and TV news segments — especially those on the fringes — are slanted more than the Leaning Tower of Pisa. Such biased coverage is the main reason the media is often distrusted. A recent Gallup poll found journalists among the least trusted professionals, about equal with lawyers and politicians. You may never completely control your biases, but the public trust demands that you make your best effort.

# Talking for a Living

Many people dread public speaking, but if you think it could be your dream career, this section is for you:

» **Professional Speaker:** Despite the plethora of electronic alternatives, people still want to hear live speakers. Competition is fierce, but some people make a living speaking at conventions, on college campuses, at corporate headquarters, and in public forums. Even cruise ships have speakers on their menus of entertainment. Find an in-demand topic on which you are an expert. Then read, for example, this book's section about compelling public speaking without fear in Chapter 20 and books such as the National Speakers Association's *Paid to Speak*, www.amazon.com/Paid-Speak-Practices-Building-Successful/dp/1608321312; study YouTube videos of speakers you like; craft a solid outline of your speech; and practice, practice, practice. Try to get some honest feedback from friends, and then tweak your delivery until you're truly able to convey something of substance while connecting with your audience. Consider joining a local chapter of Toastmasters, where you learn public speaking and get to give talks to fellow members (a sympathetic audience). When you have a strong sample video, post it on YouTube and send it to conference program chairs and speakers' bureaus. Check out www.nsaspeaker.org (National Speakers Association) and the aforementioned *Paid to Speak*, (www.amazon.com/Paid-Speak-Practices-Building-Successful/dp/1608321312).

>> **Talk Show Host:** It's tough to make a living as a talk show host, but it's rewarding because you can express your opinions and you get to interview interesting people and callers — I speak from firsthand experience. To get started, first think about what would make you both distinctive yet of broad-enough interest. If you're unusually intuitive about people's emotions, you might create a show in which people call in about their personal problems. If you're knowledgeable and passionate about politics, you might start by focusing on local issues. If you're into health and wellness, or even pets, those could be viable niches too. Then practice with your friends until you feel ready to post shows as podcasts. Do some marketing, perhaps on social media, to drive traffic to your show. If you're getting a positive response and traffic, send the link to your podcast and the audience analytics to local radio and perhaps to TV stations' program directors. That's a variant of what I did, and now I'm the host of "Work with Marty Nemko" on a National Public Radio affiliate in San Francisco. Check out www.talkers.com (*Talker's magazine*), blog.bufferapp.com/podcasting-for-beginners ("Podcasting for Beginners"), and http://www.dummies.com/social-media/podcasting-dummies-3rd-edition/ (*Podcasting For Dummies,* by Tee Morris, Chuck Tomasi).

>> **Radio/TV News Reporter:** This is one of those long-shot glamour professions that may be worth the risk. You get to investigate fast-breaking stories (sometimes in dangerous environments) and report your findings live. Even in non-emergency situations, you usually have just an hour or two to gather pertinent information before making your report. Considering the thousands of local news broadcasts, you may be able to land a job, at least if you're willing to start out in a small market and work nights and weekends.

Requirements are the ability to write concisely and quickly, a good memory, and an authoritative on-air presence. News reporting is a launch pad for a news anchor position, which, in addition to offering prominence, pays well for a job that consists heavily of reading aloud.

For more on the profession, check out www.spj.org (Society of Professional Journalists), www.ire.org ("The Rules of Undercover Reporting"), and www.amazon.com/Writing-Reporting-News-Communication-Journalism/dp/1305077334 (*Writing and Reporting News,* by Carole Rich).

» **Sports Announcer:** Sports continues to be a passion for millions of people. Demand exists for sports announcers on radio, TV, and podcasts before, during, and after the game. How do you boost your chances of making a living at it? Be able to analyze what's going on beneath the surface, and be filled with interesting trivia to fill the game's (considerable) dead time. Pluses are an appealing voice and a quick wit, having been a well-known athlete, and a degree from a top broadcast journalism program, such as Northwestern, Syracuse, or Missouri. Even then, your first job is likely to sound like this: "We're in the top of the fifth. Jasper High School is up 1-0." Check out www.thebalance.com/job-profile-sports-announcer-3113313 ("Sports Announcer") and www.youtube.com/watch?v=Lfk4wWCL0KQ ("A Week in the Life of ESPN Sports Broadcaster Bob Wischusen").

» **Sports Information Director:** The public craves information about its teams, and you're happy to give it to them. After all, it helps fill the seats and boosts TV, radio, and website revenue. Your job is to create and distribute information to media representatives and to field their questions. Writing has always been key to this job, but social media expertise is ever more important. Your athletes and fans, young and old alike, are on Twitter, Facebook, and Instagram. Social media keeps them engaged. Your working environment is pleasant, and you're closer to the team than anyone except the coaches. Oh, and you get great seats to the big game for free. Check out www.thebalance.com/job-profile-sports-information-director-3113309 ("Sports Information Director").

# Using the Word in Other Ways

Here are a few other word-centric careers for your consideration.

» **Librarian:** If you're picturing a mousy bookworm, update your stereotype. Today's librarian is often a sociable computer whiz whose job increasingly focuses on helping patrons retrieve obscure information from masses of electronic and print resources. This is an underrated career. Most librarians enjoy helping patrons dig up information — they learn in the process and keep up-to-date on the latest books and online resources. Librarians who specialize in medicine and other sciences, law, or engineering may find it easier to land a job. Indeed, that may be the field's biggest liability: It's tough to land a job.

Check out www.reddit.com/r/Libraries/comments/1d2zro/what_are_the_pros_and_cons_of_being_a_librarian ("What Are the Pros and Cons of Being a Librarian?"), www.ala.org/educationcareers/careers/librarycareerssite/home ("Start Your Journey"), and www.amazon.com/Rethinking-Information-Work-Librarians-Professionals/dp/1610699599 (*Rethinking Information Work: A Career Guide for Librarians and Other Information Professionals,* by G. Kim Dority).

*Neat Niche:* **Private Librarian:** Hospitals, government agencies, prisons, magazines, TV and radio station news departments, and research departments of corporations and nonprofit organizations have libraries. Would you ever have thought that Revlon had a library? The Brookings Institute? The United States Air Force? *U.S. News?* Most large law firms? All hire librarians. I gave a talk to 100 special librarians — most of them love their careers. Check out www.sla.org (Special Libraries Association).

» **Archivist:** What part of the National Park Service's enormous collection of information should be permanently maintained? Which items should be exhibited in national parks? How can the rest of the information be stored for easy access? Which rare paper documents are worth storing in original form, and which electronically? Archivists answer such questions. Another typical archivist job: Create online access to rare papers, photos, and films for a university, corporation, or museum. Archivists are often viewed as simply filing dusty old papers, but job seekers may be particularly successful if they specialize in digital record and document storage. Best background: a major in history or political science and a master's degree in library science from a school that offers a specialty in archival management. Check out www.careeronestop.org/toolkit/careers/occupations/occupation-profile.aspx?keyword=Archivists&onetcode=25401100&location=California&lang=en ("Archivists") and www2.archivists.org/careers/beanarchivist ("So You Want to Be an Archivist?").

» **Ethicist:** Here is a dilemma an ethicist might address: Scientists are discovering ever more genes that contribute to memory and reasoning ability — what is commonly referred to as *intelligence.* Should an "intelligence pill" be allowed and/or taxpayer-funded? Embedded ethical questions include these: What is the likelihood that people will be coerced to use it? Will subsidizing it for the poor (as is done with other medical services) be adequate? If not, will the benefits to society outweigh an exacerbation of difference between society's haves and have-nots? Of course, ethical issues are also inherent at the individual level — for example, "When should doctors stop treating a dying patient?" (This is a career I'd seriously consider if I were choosing a new one for myself.) See the American Society of Law, Medicine, and Ethics: www.aslme.org.

» **Educating others**

» **Defending or prosecuting others**

» **Exploring a potpourri of other people+word careers**

# Chapter 5

# People+Word Careers

This is the first of three chapters that profile careers requiring more than one of the big four skills: people, word, STEM, and hands-on. The careers in this chapter require both people skills and word skills.

## Managing and Leading

A career in management appeals to many people. Compared with individual contributors, managers may have more control, influence, and pay. Besides, it can feel more prestigious to say that you're a manager. Plus, management is a path to leadership positions where significant gains in income are possible.

In addition, management jobs come in many flavors — for-profit, nonprofit, government, people, product, project, sales, marketing, finance and accounting, operations, and fundraising — and in all fields, from high-tech to high touch, aesthetic or all business, from watch batteries to electric car batteries, and from nuts to bolts. This section provides profiles of many popular and under-the-radar management specialties.

Of course, like all occupations, management careers have downsides. First, you probably won't start out as a manager. You must usually begin as an individual contributor, as a management trainee, or, perhaps, as a manager of a not-so-hot place of employment. Another minus: Most organizations need many more

Indians than chiefs, so even after you've paid your dues, your ascension to management is far from guaranteed.

Be aware that some managers feel caught in the middle between higher-ups asking for more stuff done faster and supervisees who may not be as enthusiastic about that task. And today's flattened hierarchies make for decreased power: Today's supervisees may expect more influence and deference.

Finally, though your gross pay may be higher than that of worker bees', managers aren't eligible for overtime. You may well work more than 40 hours a week but not get paid any more while your supervisees get paid time-and-a-half when the clock ticks past eight hours.

## For-profit environments

The for-profit sector offers a wide range of management careers. This section offers samples that jibe with careers likely to be of particular interest to a broad readership.

>> **Project Manager:** Your project could be a conversion of an app from Apple to Android, getting a prototype made in China, or building a self-teaching vacuum cleaner. In any case, the project manager's job is to lead a project's design, budget, and timeline, often using project management software. This career is good for someone who is second best in many areas. For example, a medical device project manager needs to be good, if not tops, in bioengineering, sourcing, people managing, and marketing. Many project managers like their job because it has defined milestones and a concrete "big win" at the end. Check out www.beinggeeks.com/2017/02/pros-cons-career-project-management.html ("The Pros and Cons of a Career in Project Management") and www.amazon.com/Project-Management-Absolute-Beginners-Guide/dp/0789756757 (*Project Management Absolute Beginner's Guide,* by Greg Horine).

>> **Product Manager:** Being in charge of a product, even if it's toilet paper, can be fun. Using both technical and business skills, you play a key role in many decisions: Does the market really need *another* toilet paper? If so, at what balance of strength, softness, and cost? Should it be embossed with dots or doves? Where should it be manufactured? How should it be shipped? What picture should go on the packaging? How should the sales force pitch the product? Should ad dollars be weighted more heavily toward print, TV, web, or point-of-purchase? Should the ads show the product being used? (Well, maybe not in this case.) Check out www.clarizen.com/pros-cons-becoming-product-manager ("What Are the Pros and Cons of Becoming a Product Manager?") and www.dummies.com/careers/project-management/product-management-dummies/ (*Product Management For Dummies,* by Brian Lawley and Pamela Schure).

>> **Human Resources Manager:** HR managers usually wear one of three hats. You can be a hiring specialist, trying to recruit, say, those tough-to-find AI software developers. Or you can be a benefits expert, helping employers find and make the most of their options. Or you can be an organizational developer. In that role, you develop programs to prevent or address communication problems, workplace violence, substance abuse, and race and gender issues. You may also serve as mediator when problems arise.

The good news is that organizational developers generally get to be the good egg. Whereas other managers' main job may be to get workers to do more better and faster, your job, at least ostensibly, is to keep things human. Yes, you're also trying to build the bottom line, but your efforts generally have a more compassionate quality.

For more on human resources, check out www.thebalance.com/human-resources-4074009 ("Everything You Need to Know About Human Resources:"), www.shrm.org (Society for Human Resource Management), and www.amazon.com/Essential-HR-Handbook-Sharon-Armstrong/dp/9386215012 (*The Essential HR Handbook*, by Sharon Armstrong).

*Neat Niche:* **Violence Prevention/Resolution:** Workplace violence is a serious problem. According to the U.S. Department of Labor, nearly two million incidents of workplace violence occur *every year*. Perhaps surprisingly, among the most common victims are executives and nurses. Courts have found that the lack of a thorough violence prevention and intervention plan is evidence of liability if a worker assaults another worker. So HR people might want to gain expertise in this niche, especially in high-risk places such as courts, financial institutions, hospitals, and the U.S. Postal Service. Check out "Workplace Violence Prevention and Intervention" at www.shrm.org/ResourcesAndTools/tools-and-samples/toolkits/Documents/WVPI%20STD.pdf.

>> **Performing Arts Manager:** Many aspiring actors, singers, and dancers found out why the word *starving* often adjoins the word *artist*. That motivates some people to move to the office as a way of staying around the field they love.

**REMEMBER**

Today's performing arts managers do more than supervise ticket sales. Indeed, their main job is often to find additional ways to make money: offer classes, recruit and manage wealthy board members, coordinate fundraising events and email solicitations, and solicit potential donors.

Performing arts manager salaries generally are low, but many people are willing to live modestly for a life related to their creative passion.

Check out philanthropynewsdigest.org/off-the-shelf/the-cycle-a-practical-approach-to-managing-arts-organizations ("The Cycle: A Practical Approach to Managing Arts Organizations").

*Neat Niche:* **Director:** In this career, you literally run the show. You envision a production's look and feel. For example, I recently saw a version of Neil Simon's *Lost in Yonkers,* a play about 1930s traditional Jews, but in this version, two of the main characters were cross-dressers. (I didn't think that worked.) You then work with set, costume, lighting, and sound specialists to help implement your vision. You recruit and audition performers. You direct rehearsals, balancing between encouraging actors' choice-making and providing needed feedback — tact is especially important in coaching actors. You may also assist in planning and even implementing the production's marketing — as they say, "putting butts in seats." *Artistic directors* have a more macro role: With producers, they determine what plays, concerts, and so on go onstage, and they also select the director, crew, and perhaps performers for each production.

>> **Facilities Manager:** You run an organization's facilities — deciding where to lease, furnishing the place, hiring the maintenance crew, reducing the carbon footprint, and planning for emergencies. Some subniches are sports or performance venues, airports, and conference centers. Check out www.ifma.org (International Facility Management Association) and www.amazon.com/Facility-Management-Handbook-Kathy-Roper/dp/0814432158 (*The Facility Management Handbook,* by Kathy O. Roper and Richard P. Payant).

>> **Construction Manager:** Imagine being able to look at an office building, an arena, a freeway cloverleaf, a school, or a biotech lab and say, "I directed the building of that." Construction managers do one or more of these tasks: help owners and architects clarify their desires, bid the job, hire subcontractors, plan the project's timeline and budget, direct the project's execution, and help solve problems — when workers, supplies, and government inspectors aren't in sync, for example. Downside: You may be on-call 24/7 to deal with delays, weather, and jobsite emergencies. But you do get to see the fruits of your labors for the rest of your life. Check out www.youtube.com/watch?v=ZMaN8yc2PAA ("Construction Manager").

# Government and nonprofit

*Note: Management and Leadership careers in education are profiled in the next section.*

Some people like the idea of working in management but prefer not-for-profits. No problem: The government and non-profit sectors employ many managers. Here are examples.

>> **Political Campaign Manager:** Everyone who runs for office, from park board member to president of the United States, needs a campaign manager. People in this career use data analytics to understand voter opinion and to

identify the supporters, opponents, and undecideds. Increasingly, that's done down to the single neighborhood block! Campaign managers also use the data to develop the candidate's themes, direct fundraising, allocate resources, and coordinate the website, social media, email, and snail mail strategy. Campaign managers also hire staff; train phone bank workers; coordinate the door-to-door campaign; entice the media; lead damage control; and even design the campaign button, bumper sticker, and lawn sign. Of course, larger campaigns use multiple people to do all that.

Managing a campaign is exciting — you're in charge of a winner-take-all contest that may make a difference in society. Start out by volunteering to assist in running the campaign for a local politician.

For more on campaign managing, check out www.localvictory.com/organization/political-campaign-manager.html ("How to Be a Great Political Campaign Manager") and www.amazon.com/Campaign-Manager-Running-Winning-Elections/dp/0813350794 (*The Campaign Manager: Running and Winning Local Elections,* by Catherine Shaw).

I can't resist offering an opinion here. Our political leaders get elected largely on who presses the most flesh, buys the best database of undecided voters, makes the speech with the most focus-group-approved sound bites, has the best "ground game" and digital operation, and perhaps most important, extracts the most dollars from special interests. If I had my way, election campaigns would be just three weeks long and funded completely with a modest amount of tax dollars. Each registered voter would receive an email or booklet with each candidate's voting record and personal statement. During those three weeks, the candidate could use the tax dollars to campaign as s/he saw fit and would be required to participate in at least one televised debate moderated by a person acceptable to both candidates in which candidates could not dictate the terms. That's it. More substance, less fluff, and less chance of politicians in the hip pockets of special interest groups. Perhaps more important, because of the brief, honorable campaign, outstanding candidates, daunted or disgusted by what it currently takes to get elected, would more likely come forward.

>> **Lobbyist:** We all know about lobbying's dark side: former legislators become lobbyists for special interests that don't serve the common good. Lobbying firms can even serve as go-betweens to get around campaign finance limits. But let's focus on lobbyists' more justifiable purposes. Let's say you're a lobbyist for the National Abortion Rights League. A law you want to pass would solidify a teen's right to have an abortion without parental permission. You may draft the legislation, and you certainly have unearthed research that supports its benefits. You meet with legislators, staffers, and the media to make your case. That's the life of a lobbyist, a professional persuader of politicians. A law degree

is a plus but isn't always required. Check out www.princetonreview.com/careers/88/lobbyist ("Lobbyist") and www.amazon.com/Lobbying-Advocacy-Strategies-Recommendations-Compliance/dp/1587331004 (*Lobbying and Advocacy*, by Deanna Gelak).

>> **Government Manager:** Aspiring managers shouldn't overlook government positions. Eighty percent of government jobs are managerial and professional, compared with just 25 percent in the private sector. In addition to quantity, government jobs often offer better benefits, stability, offshore resistance, and colleagues who are dedicated to the public interest. Surprisingly, per a recent study, federal jobs may even offer better pay for equivalent work in the private sector. Among the more interesting government manager jobs is program administrator. Government funds various programs, each using one or more administrators to run them. Check out www.usajobs.gov/Help/working-in-government/unique-hiring-paths/students ("Federal Programs for Students and Recent Grads") and icma.org/careersinlg ("Careers in Local Government Management").

*Neat Niche:* **City Manager:** You're involved in all aspects of running a city, from distributing the budget to overseeing park renovation to hiring key personnel. City managers are among the more powerful government officials who don't have to run for election. But in the U.S. democracy, implementing initiatives even as small as a ban on leaf blowers may require community meetings, lobbying efforts, legal challenges, and real-world implementation more diluted than what would have served the common good. The city manager is merely the lead dancer in an allemande. Check out www.icma.org (International City/County Management Association) and www.amazon.com/City-Management-Orville-W-Powell/dp/1403323038 (*City Management: Keys to Success,* by Orville W. Powell).

*Neat Niche:* **Court Administrator:** For many employees, a job's setting can be as important as its tasks. Courts tend to be attractive, peaceful workplaces — unless, of course, two lawyers are screaming at each other or a perpetrator decides to go ballistic. (Oh, that was a TV show. Sorry.) Courts need administrators to coordinate judges' schedules, plan budgets, provide information resources to judges, figure out how to install enough jurors, and develop more efficient systems for processing traffic tickets. (I have a bachelor's degree in traffic school.) Check out www.nacmnet.org/sites/default/files/publications/Guides/The_Court_Manual_Colorization_2016.pdf ("The Court Administrator").

>> **Nonprofit Manager:** Nonprofit management can be difficult because the staff is often largely volunteer, funds are limited, the root causes are tough to address, and the salaries (except for major fundraisers and executive directors) are low. Nevertheless, many people believe deeply in the causes they

work for and therefore think the price is worth it. Check out casefoundation. org/blog/pros-and-cons-working-nonprofit-sector ("The Pros and Cons of Working in the Nonprofit Sector").

*Neat Niche:* **Foundation Program Manager:** How'd you like to supervise the giving of money to non-profit causes? Corporations, school districts, and wealthy individuals set up foundations to distribute money to nonprofits. Foundations hire program managers, often called *grantmakers,* to supervise the funded programs to help ensure that the money is well spent. Check out www.philanthropynewyork.org/so-you-want-job-philanthropy (*So You Want a Job in Philanthropy*) and www.amazon.com/Insiders-Guide-Grantmaking-Joel-Orosz/dp/0787952389 (*The Insider's Guide to Grantmaking,* by Joel J. Orosz).

*Neat Niche:* **Association Manager:** Thousands of professional organizations exist, from the American Psychological Association to the Amador County Association of Realtors. Each uses managers. What do they do? Typically, they plan new-member recruitment, training, meeting, and conference planning and promotion. One way to get a job created for you is to approach organizations that have been volunteer-run and are ready for a step up. Check out www.associationcareerhq.org/job_search_strategies/why_work_associations ("Why Work for an Association?").

# Educating Children and Adults

We all need hope, and education is a major source. We may hope that education or training will help us not only prepare for a career but also become wiser human beings. If our past hasn't been ideal, we may hope that education or training will help us be more successful in the future. This section describes careers in education and training, both within and outside academic settings:

>> **Teacher:** If you have "the gift," teaching can be a most rewarding career. The gift is the ability to get the kids to want to behave and work hard for you. That requires you to convey that you're firm, but only because you care deeply about kids and learning. "The gift" also entails your being able to clearly explain difficult (and sometimes real-world-irrelevant) material — and on multiple levels. A classroom today may include special-needs and gifted students, native speakers of English, and newcomers.

*Good news:* Teachers may not be as underpaid as some people believe. Whereas, as in most professions, starting salaries for teachers are modest, with experience, the pay — even for kindergarten teachers in many metropolitan areas — can rise to six figures. And the teachers' unions have gotten their teachers lifetime tenure after just two or three years. Plus, teacher benefits are excellent. For example, teaching is among the few remaining professions in which you get a pension. And although many teachers work far longer than the less-than-180-day, 6-hour-per-day school year, not all do.

And, if you burn out, there's a career ladder, for example, to assistant principal, dean, principal, or district, county, regional, state, or federal administrator. The federal education department alone has 4,400 employees who administer a $70 billion dollar budget *every year*. Or you can work in curriculum development or as an employee trainer in corporations, nonprofits, and government.

For more on the teaching profession, check out www.thoughtco.com/becoming-a-teacher-4132510 ("Becoming a Teacher") and www.amazon.com/First-Year-Teacher-Twenty-Five-Experiences/dp/0451188918 (*My First Year as a Teacher: Twenty-Five Teachers Talk About Their Amazing First-Year Classroom Experiences*, edited by Pearl Rock Kane).

*Neat Niche:* **Career-Technical Teacher:** Increasingly in high schools and, of course, community colleges, teachers are hired in fields such as technology repair, business education, agriculture, protective services, and entry-level healthcare careers. If that sounds like something you'd like to do, check out The Association for Career and Technical Education at https://acteonline.org.

» **Professor:** A professorship has many upsides: the joy of creating knowledge and helping others acquire it through classes, advising, writings, and conference presentations. You have intelligent, civilized (usually) colleagues, and, after a few years, tenure for life. Plus, you get to work on a college campus, which is one of the more appealing work environments.

The professoriate also has downsides. First, there are many more people, including those holding a PhD plus a post doctorate, who want to be professors than there are professorships. And so, institutions of higher education can get away with hiring many part-time or temporary faculty members to avoid paying benefits and awarding tenure.

Another downside of the professorial career is that because of the societal push to send a higher proportion of high school graduates to college, many of that new cohort aren't prepared for college-level work. Yet professors, except at 2-year colleges, usually need a doctorate, which, depending on the field, takes an average of six to ten post-bachelor's years. The disparity between the intellect and drive demonstrated by professors and that shown by students can be frustrating.

Also, there's usually pressure to publish journal articles, even if they're obscure, when you'd rather be teaching. Ernest Boyer, the late head of the Carnegie Foundation for the Advancement of Teaching, wrote, "Winning the campus teaching award is often the kiss of death for promotion and tenure."

One last thing to consider: At many (but not all) universities, a conservative may well have a difficult time getting hired as a professor, and if hired, find him or herself with limited ideological support on campus."

For more on jobs in academia, check out www.phdstudies.com/article/Pros-and-Cons-of-Continuing-into-an-Academic-Career ("Pros and Cons of Continuing into an Academic Career") and www.amazon.com/Professor-Essential-Guide-Turning-Ph-D/dp/0553419420 (*The Professor Is In: The Essential Guide to Turning Your Ph.D. into an Academic Job,* by Karen Kelsky).

*Neat Niche:* **Online Course Developer and Instructor:** Many people are opting to take individual classes or earn entire degrees online. Websites such as www.coursera.org and www.edx.org aggregate large numbers of online courses from many colleges. In addition, sites such as www.udemy.com www.lynda.com, and www.udacity.com offer more practical courses. It takes special skills to teach an online course, so if you can make that your specialty, you'll likely be in demand. Check out ctl.mesacc.edu/teaching/designing-an-online-course ("Designing an Online Course") and www.amazon.com/Online-Teaching-Survival-Guide-Pedagogical/dp/1119147689 (*The Online Teaching Survival Guide,* by Judith V. Boettcher and Rita-Marie Conrad).

**Education Administrator:** You wouldn't think that turnover is high among school principals — it's a prestigious job with an important mission. Yet turnover *is* high. Some leave the career because they believe their training didn't adequately prepare them. Others are frustrated by low student achievement and limited influence on teacher performance. Still others leave a principalship for a higher salary or a less demanding school.

Another source of principals' stress is that they often must take on more tasks than in the past. For example, they may be charged with leading school-based antiviolence and substance abuse programs.

The principal's supervisees — teachers — have ever-tougher jobs because special education and gifted native-speakers of English and newcomers are now often placed in the same class. And those varied students must not only be served but also achieve the new mantra, "All students can learn to high standards," as defined by the rigorous Common Core. Could you meet even the eighth grade math standards, as outlined at www.corestandards.org/Math/Content/8/introduction? Principals must manage to keep teacher morale high under these circumstances.

A silver lining is that the job market for aspiring principals is good. Plus, a principalship is a launch pad for jobs as district, county, regional, state, and federal education administrators.

For more on this topic, check out www.amazon.com/Principals-Survival-Guide-Where-Succeed/dp/1575424916 (*The Principal's Survival Guide: Where*

*Do I Start? How Do I Succeed? When Do I Sleep?,* by Susan Stone Kessler, April M. Snodgrass, and Andrew T. Davis).

*Neat Niche:* **College Administrator:** A college campus is a great place to be a manager. Who could resist a beautiful environment, intelligent people, learning opportunities all around, a prosocial mission, and work hours that tend to be more moderate than in the private sector? Plus, the environment lightens up between terms and all summer. And few organizations hire as many managers — often, multiple layers of management — for everything from governmental affairs to the physical plant. A downside is that, on many campuses, office politics are often challenging. It's been said that nowhere else is there so much fighting over so little. Check out www.princetonreview.com/careers/40/college-administrator ("College Administrator") and www.amazon.com/Career-Aspirations-Expeditions-Advancing-Administration/dp/1588742679 (*Career Aspirations & Expeditions:* Advancing Your Career in Higher Education Administration, by Nancy Archer Martin and Jennifer L. Bloom).

*Neat Subniche:* **Student Affairs Administrator:** This career has nothing to do with steamy dorm room flings. College student affairs administrators coordinate the nonacademic part of student life, from student orientation to graduation. For example, they supervise the fraternities and sororities, coordinate residence hall activities and intramural sports, and sponsor antidrug programs. Check out www.naspa.org (National Association of Student Personnel Administrators).

>> **College Admission Counselor:** "Which college should I go to?" "How do I get in?" "How do I find the money?" In high schools, counselors typically help students answer these questions, mainly with group presentations and handouts. In private practice, it's one-on-one. As usual, specializing is wise. You can focus, for example, on students with learning problems or those aiming for designer-label colleges. Check out www.nacacnet.org (National Association for College Admission Counseling) and www.iecaonline.com (Independent Educational Consultants Association).

*Neat Niche:* **College-Bound Athlete Consultant:** Many high school students aren't eager to complete their college applications. Not so with college athletes: They may not care more than their peers about the joys of learning, but they do care about playing their sport. Those motivated clients make your job fun. You help Bruiser figure out which colleges will let him play a lot and satisfy him academically and socially. You're a bit like a junior Jerry Maguire: "Show me the scholarship!" Check out professionals.collegeboard.org/guidance/prepare/athletes (Working with Student Athletes) and www.ncaapublications.com/DownloadPublication.aspx?download=CBSA18.pdf ("NCAA Guide for the College-Bound Student-Athlete").

# Teaching the Practical

Might you prefer to teach away from the halls of academe? If so, this section is for you.

>> **Employee Trainer:** (not including Athletic Trainer, which is profiled in Chapter 7 in the health care section.) Employee trainers teach job-specific skills such as software or sales. They also conduct trainings to comply with government mandates for training designed to address harassment, diversity issues, and workplace violence. Health insurers and government agencies hire trainers to do workshops in communities with a high rate of obesity, tobacco use, and substance abuse.

The need for training is great. Many students graduate from high school and even college without basic skills at the same time that today's workplace demands are ever greater. In addition, many older workers must stay current lest they be permanently put out to pasture. Trainers are needed in many areas: from basic reading to advanced regulatory compliance, from peak performance to retirement planning, or from database management to diversity management. Check out www.td.org/Publications/Blogs/Career-Development-Blog/2015/01/Is-Training-Development-the-Right-Career-for-You ("Is Training and Development the Right Career for You?") and www.amazon.com/Telling-Aint-Training-Expanded-Enhanced/dp/1562867016 (*Telling Ain't Training,* by Harold D. Stolovitch and Erica J. Keeps).

*Neat Niche:* **Online Training Developer:** In person, a top trainer or teacher can serve only a relatively few students. Reliable videoconferencing and sophisticated but easy-to-use software will allow online trainer developers to create a more effective next-generation of online instruction: simulation-rich, individualized online modules taught by a dream team of instructors. That would make world-class instruction available to employees at their workplace or at home in their comfies rather than needing to fly to a far-flung place. Of course, that has implications for K-20 education: Students from Beverly Hills to Harlem, and from Tokyo to Togoland, could have world-class teachers.

>> **Athletic Coach:** I coached a Boys Club basketball team. I went in with visions of using hoops to help kids triumph over life circumstances, but that strategy proved overly ambitious. Nevertheless, it was fun, and the games provided a rush from constantly figuring out what to do to give my team an edge while trying to be a good role model. Plus, I hope that my one-on-one life-skills mentoring did some good.

The usual starting coaching position is in a children's league or at a high school, but you only start to earn a decent income at the college level. There, you have additional responsibilities, such as meeting with members of the media and donors. And you must make recruiting trips to convince high school athletes that even though they have a C average at a low-rigor high school, they can succeed in college classes.

For more on the coaching life, check out www.thebalance.com/athletic-coach-524874 ("Athletic Coach Career Information") and www.amazon.com/Power-Double-Goal-Coaching-Developing-Winners/dp/0982131747 (*The Power of Double-Goal Coaching: Developing Winners in Sports and Life,* Jim Thompson).

>> **Speech-Language Therapist:** Think of how you feel when you listen to someone who stutters. Now imagine how that person feels. The speech-language therapist treats stuttering and other voice and speaking problems, from cleft palate to limited vocabulary to stroke victims trying to recover speech. For many patients, progress is slow; patience is mandatory. Speech therapists who work in schools have relatively short workdays and ample time off. They may also work in hospitals and clinics and in private practice. Many speech therapists choose a combination. Check out www.asha.org (American Speech-Language-Hearing Association).

# Legally Speaking

Our system of jurisprudence is widely admired, designed to ensure just treatment for all. As with all human pursuits, implementation isn't always so perfect, though we shouldn't be too cynical about the law or lawyers. It has yielded much good. Regardless, I'd be remiss in proceeding to describe legal careers without at least providing one lawyer joke: What do you call a lawyer gone bad? Senator.

>> **Attorney:** It's an understandable career choice: prestige, money, the hopes of using the law to make a better world. Besides, you're better with words than with science.

And, of course, some lawyers are happy with their choice, my daughter included. They may land a public-interest job that they find meaningful. Or they find meaning in corporate work — for example, defending a company against an unfair lawsuit or ensuring that it is treated fairly in a contract negotiation.

There also are reasons that many lawyers would not choose the profession if they were starting over:

- There are few public-interest law jobs, and the competition for them is fierce. I know a Yale Law School graduate who clerked for a U.S. Circuit Court of Appeals judge, yet could not land even a low-paying job at a nonprofit.

- The pressure to win is ever greater. There's an oversupply of lawyers, ever greater competition among law firms, and escalating legal technology. That increases the job's pressure as well as its ethical temptations.

- Lawyers who succeed tend to be workhorses or rainmakers. They must work long billable hours or be out selling successfully, able to join and impress on volunteer boards, make compelling presentations at conferences, and so on. The hours tend to be long. It's telling that some lawyers have futons in their offices.

- Cost-control pressures and improved software enable law firms and in-house legal departments to shift work from lawyers to paralegals. That creates an oversupply of lawyers, which lowers salaries. Also, shunting lower-level work to paralegals means that an ever larger percentage of lawyers' work is difficult.

- The image of lawyers spending most of their time in courtrooms is incorrect. Even litigators must spend much of their time poring over often-dry material in preparing for trial. And a large percentage of lawyers rarely see a courtroom. They're transactional attorneys, whose job is to prepare, review, and negotiate documents.

To get a better sense of the pros and cons of lawyering, check out www.lawyeredu.org/law-careers.html (Lawyeredu.org) and www.businessnewsdaily.com/8417-lawyers-career-pros-cons.html ("Seven Lawyers on What They Love and Hate About Their Jobs").

On the other hand, certain legal niches promise greater job satisfaction. Here are some:

*Neat Niche:* **Mediator/Arbitrator:** See the Mediator profile in Chapter 3, in the section about caretaking and coaching.

*Neat Niche:* **Adoption Attorney:** How different adoption law is from traditional adversarial lawyering — helping to match children with parents wanting to adopt. Check out www.adoptionattorneys.org (Academy of Adoption and Assisted Reproduction Attorneys) and www.amazon.com/Somebodys-Child-Stories-Adoption-Attorney/dp/0399528164 (*Somebody's Child: Stories from the Private Files of an Adoption Attorney,* by Randi Barrow).

*Neat Niche:* **Assisted Reproduction Attorney:** This field is growing as assisted-reproductive technologies come into wider use, including *in vitro* fertilization, surrogate parenting, and, soon, gene editing. Assisted-reproduction attorneys may be involved in helping draft government laws and insurance company policies, or could litigate on behalf of a birth parent, adoptive parent, company, or government. Check out apps.americanbar.org/dch/committee.cfm?com=FL142000 ("Section of Family Law: Assisted Reproductive Technologies").

*Neat Niche:* **Education Lawyer:** Johnny has gone through 12 years of school-ing and his reading comprehension is at the 5th grade level. Who's respon-sible? Many parents are claiming that the schools should be and they're hiring lawyers to file lawsuits against school districts. Education lawyers also defend school districts against these and other claims.

For example: a dismissed teacher claims that due process was violated, an activist group sues a school district because a disproportionate number of student suspensions are of a particular race, a parent demands more special-education services or claims inadequate supervision after her child fell off a schoolyard play structure.

Some education lawyers are lobbyists. The following example focuses on the other end of the achievement continuum. A lobbyist could represent the National Association for Gifted Children and urge that gifted kids should be, as special kids are, legally entitled to appropriate-level education. Or they could represent the other side: a lobbying group that advocates for more funds reallocated to special-education students.

For more on education and the law, check out `hls.harvard.edu/content/uploads/2008/07/2015_educationlawguide_final.pdf` ("Education Law: A Career Guide").

*Neat Niche:* **Small-Town or Exurb Attorney:** There's money to be made in them thar hills. Most lawyers choose to live in or near a big city, but lawyers are also employed in more halcyon environs. Not only is the competition there milder, but the pressures may be, too. Plus, the opportunity for ongoing one-on-one relationships with clients may be greater — as the traditional family lawyer who handles issues from prenup to estate planning, for example.

*Neat Niche:* **Patent Lawyer:** When you think of patents, contraptions may come to mind, but patents are now often awarded for such concepts as genes, computer chips, medical devices, drugs, and genetically engineered mice. Most commonly, patent lawyers are hired to challenge or defend an existing patent, though some do work to get intellectual property patented. So it's no surprise that most intellectual property lawyers have a science or engineering back-ground in addition to a law degree. Robert Benson, a patent attorney for Human Genome Sciences, loves his job: "In the lab, you can only do so much research work, but as a patent attorney, you get to experience literally hun-dreds of lifetimes of research work." Check out `careers.findlaw.com/legal-career-options/is-a-career-in-intellectual-property-law-for-you.html` ("Is a Career in Intellectual Property Law for You?").

*Neat Niche:* **Space Lawyer:** More than a half-million satellites and other objects now orbit the earth. Space lawyers figure out how to deal with collisions. If the moon or a planet were to be mined or colonized, what rules should apply? By midcentury, people will be able to circle the planet in a spacecraft. What laws should govern licensure and liability? U.S. companies would like to sell their satellite and other space technologies to other countries. What rules and principles should be adopted? Space law is a new frontier. Check out www.americanbar.org/groups/young_lawyers/publications/the_101_201_practice_series/space_law_101_an_introduction_to_space_law.html ("Space Law 101: Introduction to Space Law").

*Neat Niche:* **Tax Attorney:** This is among law's highest-paid specialties and it's easy to understand why. A company is structuring a deal — do it right and it can save a fortune in taxes. Considering the U.S. tax code's complexity, there also are gray areas. Tax lawyers try to help their clients win the gray. Even plain ol' people may be willing to pay a tax attorney —when being audited for deducting the family's trip to Tahiti, for example. Check out www.lawcrossing.com/article/900044271/What-it-is-Like-to-Be-a-Tax-Law-Attorney--Tax-Attorney-Careers ("What's It Like to Be a Tax Law Attorney?").

*Neat Niche:* **Estate Attorney:** Over a lifetime of work, a person has accumulated serious savings. Although she's already been taxed on that income, the government wants to tax it again when she dies — not the nicest way for the government to offer its condolences. The estate attorney's job is to write wills and trusts to minimize this double taxation. Estate attorneys also help ensure that as much of the client's assets as possible go to whom — and to any nonprofits — they intend. That may include litigation. For example, occasionally, even ostensibly nice people unreasonably contest a will. Estate litigation specialists file those claims as well as argue that the will should be honored. As the baby boomers age, this specialty continues to grow. Check out www.lawcrossing.com/article/4746/Trusts-and-Estates-Attorney-Jobs ("Choosing a Career As a Trusts and Estate Attorney").

>> **Paralegal:** To cut costs, paralegals are doing much of the work that lawyers used to do: researching cases, locating and interviewing witnesses and clients, drafting legal documents, summarizing depositions and testimony, attending trials — just about everything but representing a client in court. Paralegals get to do that without needing a bachelor's degree plus three expensive years of law school. Many firms hire non-degree-holding graduates of 2-year paralegal training programs. Job-market dampener: An excess of lawyers is resulting in their being hired as paralegals. Check out www.nala.org (National Association of Legal Assistants).

>> **Administrative Law Judge/Hearing Officials:** Government employs administrative law judges to resolve disputes with constituents. Typical examples include denied claims for welfare benefits, workers' compensation, discrimination, and special-education services. They may also adjudicate

traffic tickets, public-housing disputes, or a student's appealing being expelled. Telephonic hearings are increasing because claimants are more geographically dispersed and because they can serve to accommodate special-needs claimants. This is a somewhat easier way to become a judge, though you still usually must be an attorney with successful litigation experience and a measured temperament. Plus, as in all competitive fields, it helps to have friends in high places. Check out www.naho.org (National Association of Hearing Officials) and www.amazon.com/Administrative-Law-Process-Nutshell-Nutshells/dp/1628103558 (*Administrative Law and Process in a Nutshell,* by Ronald Levin and Jeffrey Lubbers).

# Other Word+People Careers

Of course, many additional careers require both word and people skills. Here are popular ones that many people find rewarding:

» **Politician:** Yes, pols always have to have their hands out, and their reputation isn't sparkling, but most politicians I know do try to be fine leaders. And although the wheels of government turn slowly, its goal is benevolent: the commonweal. Another plus: Though many politicians were political science majors and/or lawyers, no specific training is required, although you must be instantly likeable, a compelling speaker and savvy negotiator, and have a thick skin (In the weeks before an election, dirt so "conveniently" seems to emerge.) And you do have to value being in the public eye more than preserving your privacy.

Politicians exist at all levels, from part-time school board member to full-time congressperson and, yes (the dream of millions of children), president of the United States. Another upside of the politician's career is that government isn't going away any time soon, nor can this job be offshored, so the job market should remain at least stable. Plus, if you decide to switch careers (or voters decide for you), the connections you've made may well help you land a job.

For more on the political life, check out www.princetonreview.com/careers/123/politician ("Politician"), www.amazon.com/Political-Ladder-Insider-Getting-Politics/dp/0615604811 (*The Political Ladder: Insider Tips On Getting a Job in Politics,* by Alexandra Acker-Lyons), and www.amazon.com/Politicians-Are-People-Richard-Benedetto/dp/0761834222 (Richard Benedetto's book *Politicians Are People, Too*).

» **City Planner:** Should WalMart be allowed to open a store in your city? What's the wisest plan for revitalizing downtown? How can you make the county reduce its carbon footprint without killing jobs or impacting people's quality of life to an unsupportable degree? To address such questions, the planner reviews data, conducts studies and public hearings, and, before making a recommendation, probably wears many hats, including that of an engineer, economist, architect, sociologist, and politician. A silver tongue is essential if you expect your plan to survive the input of community groups and special interests. Many planners specialize in urban or rural land use, transportation, housing, air quality, water quality, health and human services, historic preservation, or hazardous materials. Check out www.planning.org (American Planning Association) and www.amazon.com/Contemporary-Urban-Planning-John-Levy/dp/1138666386 (*Contemporary Urban Planning,* by John M. Levy).

>> **Foreign Service Officer:** You work in the United States embassy or consulate anywhere from Afghanistan to Zimbabwe. Though your first job may include helping people who lost their visas, the situation can get more interesting. Your job may include keeping abreast of political and economic conditions so that you can brief American policymakers. You may be the point person for American citizens after a disaster. You may arrange cocktail parties for your host country's business and political leaders. Landing this job isn't easy. For example, you need to be a good reader and writer and be able to fulfill the requirement of learning a foreign language in six months — and another language two years later. Is Urdu for you? Check out en.wikipedia.org/wiki/Foreign_Service_Officer.

>> **Park Ranger:** People think that this career is for shy souls who spend their lives alone, searching for forest fires through binoculars. Granted, some of those jobs exist, but most park rangers spend much of their time with people — expounding on the glories of nature or pestering park patrons: "Do you have a fishing license?" "No dogs allowed," and "I'm going to have to ask you (you drunken fool) to leave the campground." A park ranger's first job usually includes physically demanding tasks such as shoring up eroding paths.

TIP

Jobs are available in national parks, and especially in state and regional parks. Insider's secret: Job seekers tend to overlook jobs available on federal lands other than parks. Check out national forests, wilderness areas, wildlife refuges, and scenic rivers.

Starting pay may be low, but for those cut out for this career, that's a small price to pay for a life in the wilderness.

Check out www.environmentalscience.org/career/park-ranger ("What Is a Park Ranger?").

>> **Sports Referee/Umpire:** I loved being an umpire. It was fun making a decision every few seconds that was respected — usually. Somehow, even getting booed wasn't so bad when I was able to remind myself that in the larger scheme of things, it matters little whether it was a ball or a strike. And umpiring is a way to be a part of the game even if you're not a great ballplayer.

Don't count on making full-time money as an ump. Sure, pro officials make six figures, but for most high school and college refs, officiating is a sideline, as much for the fun as for the money. There are perks, though. You get to travel and, in sports such as basketball or soccer, it's a fun way to stay in shape. And demand is high. You, however, need skills: competent decision making under pressure and the ability to stay cool when coaches and fans yell, "Ump, you're blind!"

Check out www.bls.gov/ooh/entertainment-and-sports/umpires-referees-and-other-sports-officials.htm ("Umpires, Referees and Other Sports Officials") and www.amazon.com/Successful-Officiating-2nd-American-Education-Program/dp/0736098291 (The American Sport Education Program's *Successful Sports Officiating*).

» **Private Investigator (PI):** You're worried that your nanny might be neglecting your child, that your spouse is cheating on you, or that one of your employees is collecting disability but is, in fact, on the golf course. Who you gonna call? A private investigator. She'll hang out in the neighborhood, talk with folks, dig through online public information, and use that time-honored PI technique: dumpster diving. PIs must be able to read people and persuade them to give up information. But today, many more cases are solved by a computer search than by stakeout. Check out www.thebalance.com/private-investigator-career-information-974475 ("Private Investigator Career Information") and www.amazon.com/Private-Eyes-What-Investigators-Really/dp/1466275189 (*Private Eyes: What Private Investigators Really Do*, by Sam Brown and Gini Graham Scott).

» **Administrative Assistant:** Many of my clients like being the righthand person, and this career affords that opportunity. Trusted administrative assistants can have a varied workday: Draft a letter, conduct research on the Net, plan a luncheon, create a PowerPoint presentation, organize the boss's file system, prepare a spreadsheet, arrange travel, appease a client, screen mail and calls, and enjoy a close relationship with the boss. And unlike the boss, admins are usually out the door at 5:00, with little or no work to take home. Increasingly, bosses allow admins to work from home at least one day a week. Check out www.bls.gov/ooh/office-and-administrative-support/secretaries-and-administrative-assistants.htm ("Secretaries and Administrative Assistants") and www.amazon.com/Organized-Admin-Organizing-Overwhelm-Productivity/dp/0982943067 (*The Organized Admin: Leverage Your Unique Organizing Style to Create Systems, Reduce Overwhelm, and Increase Productivity*, by Julie Perrine).

*Neat Niche:* **Personal Assistant:** A typical day in the life of Olympia Dukakis's personal assistant consists of rendering a second opinion on a movie contract, dropping off her dry cleaning, picking up her dog's gourmet dog food, and suggesting ideas for marketing Dukakis's salad dressing.

Of course, not only celebrities need assistants. These days, most busy people could use one. Sometimes, the job may be more like an office assistant — writing letters, coordinating a project, and handling the bookkeeping — but Beth Berg made a good living with none of that. She started Dial-a-Wife: She plans the meal, waits for the plumber, takes kiddo and friends to soccer, perhaps plants the herb garden, and even does (or at least has done) the initial house hunting. Sounds like a traditional wife, but she gets paid well. Berg's first ad simply said, "Buy time." For more on working as a personal assistant, check out www.amazon.com/Ultimate-Assistant-celebrity-assistants-high-powered/dp/0976326817 (*Be the Ultimate Assistant: A Celebrity Assistant's Secrets to Working with Any High-Powered Employer*, by Bonnie Low-Kramen).

>> **Spiritual Leader/Clergy:** A career in the clergy offers the opportunity for unmitigated do-gooding. Of course, clerics must have the desire to serve others, speak well and listen better, and welcome the opportunity to not only preside over life's happiest moments but also provide comfort during its saddest. This is no 9-to-5 job. Though we all have times when we wish we could just clock out, that's difficult in the clergy. Also, most clergypersons must spend a lot of time on fundraising and, perhaps surprisingly, on paperwork. Another perhaps surprising truth is that unshakeable faith in God is not a requirement — even most clergy have doubts now and then.

One thing on which there is little doubt is that clergy pay is generally modest, and the job market is equally so. After all, according to Pew and *National Geographic* studies, the fastest-growing religion is no religion. Many more people are abandoning religion in favor of spirituality, which often doesn't require a spiritual leader. Check out study.com/articles/Clergy_Professions_Job_Description_and_Information_for_Students_Considering_a_Career_in_the_Clergy_Professions.html ("Clergy Professions").

>> **Actor:** Like many creative pursuits, acting may be a better hobby than a career. Expressing creativity is a primal need — so primal, in fact, that the competition even for volunteer work in the creative arts is intense. I drove a friend who's a professional actress to an audition for a midsize role in a Walnut Creek, California (an awful long way from Broadway) production of *Les Misérables*. One hundred people auditioned for that modest role, even though the pay would be just $50 a performance and $0 for rehearsals.

The good news is that the job market for actors may be improving. With the proliferation of Internet video for commercials, training, and entertainment, increased cable viewership, and more foreign demand for American productions, the need for actors is growing. But most actors don't make enough from their acting, so they typically have a day job and still live a modest lifestyle, perhaps living with roommates.

The term *actor* is misleading. It implies that you're acting, doing something. For the most part, actors wait. They wait to be hired. After they're hired, on the set, they wait for their turn; for the weather to clear; for the tech people to set things up; for the producer and directors to make up their minds. Casting director Lisa Pirriolli, in the book *Gig,* adds, "It's a horrible life . . . it's all about getting the job and about rejection. If you do get the job, it's all about doing it correctly and getting the next one, and the next one, just trying to become famous. And if you do become famous, it's all about being famous. And then it's about when your star is going to fall."

If you're going to be an actor who needs a day job, you might consider one that could improve your acting: mock trial participant, mock patient (used in medical school training), role-player in employee training seminars or police crisis simulations, traffic school instructor, and Santa Claus. (Don't let your small child read that.) Check out www.amazon.com/Acting-Professionally-Facts-about-Careers/dp/1137605863 (*Acting Professionally: Raw Facts about Careers in Acting,* by James Calleri and Robert Cohen).

# Chapter **6**

# STEM Careers (Science, Technology, Engineering, and Math)

When I think of all the ways that people in STEM careers have improved my life, I am grateful: the people who designed and built the computer on which I'm writing this book, the people who designed and built the house I'm sitting in, the people who manufactured the coffee mug I'm sipping from. You get the point.

Today, most STEM careers are interdisciplinary, but to facilitate browsing, this chapter lists the careers in their best-fit category: biology, chemistry, physics, computer, engineering, or math.

In part because of that interdisciplinarity, even researcher and analyst types will find people skills valuable. So, even though Chapter 7 focuses on careers that require STEM-plus-people-skills, such as in healthcare, recognize that your prospects even in this chapter's careers will improve if you have, or can boost, your emotional intelligence. (For some advice on that, see Chapter 13.)

# Working in Biology

Terms like *amazing* and *awesome* get cheaply tossed around — to describe shoes or a rock band, for example. More worthy are items that biologists study, like birth and growth:

>> **Biologist:** No field has done more to improve life. In the past decade alone, people working in biology and biotechnology have developed

- Food crops that can grow in a previously infertile section of Latin America that covers 800,000 square miles — an area larger than the size of Mexico. Thousands of formerly starving people can now eat.

- A method to identify a criminal (DNA analysis) that is thousands of times more accurate than conventional methods.

- New categories of drug, like proteins that lessen the effect of heart attacks, and drugs that have turned AIDS from a death sentence to a manageable condition. Hundreds of biotech drug products and vaccines are available or in clinical trials targeting most major diseases. For example, CAR-T cell immunotherapy uses the patient's own antibodies genetically engineered to attack only the person's cancer cells.

I attended a presentation by five Nobel Prize winners. One of the few things they agreed on was that the field that will make the greatest contribution to humankind in the coming decades is molecular biology.

Today, the name *biologist* is misleading. Now, most biologists are part biologist, part chemist, part mathematician, and/or part programmer. They spend much of their time on the computer. Those with only a whole-animal biology background will usually be limited to positions such as field data collector, zoologist, lab assistant, high school teacher, and environmental educator in zoos, parks, and museums.

**TIP**

For a good number of years now, students have become aware of this field's potency, so there's an oversupply even of molecular biology PhDs with post-docs. So, to have a good chance at landing a job directing research studies at universities, or even in industry, typically requires particularly good math or computer science chops and a fundable research focus, for example, autism, cancer, and Alzheimer's rather than a rarer disease.

The good news is that bachelor- and master-level jobs are available at biotech and pharmaceutical firms. In such jobs, you may be running experiments, perhaps assisting in designing them and writing them up, and even co-presenting at conferences. Check out www.aibs.org/careers ("Careers in the Biological Sciences").

*Neat Niche:* **Gene Editing:** It's increasingly clear that even attributes assumed to be environmentally determined, such as political affiliation, are partly under genetic control. At the same time, techniques such as CRISPR-cas13 are enabling researchers to develop gene therapy approaches to preventing and curing disease and, subject to regulation, enhancement of everything from appearance to intelligence and maybe even altruism.

TIP

In the 1967 movie *The Graduate,* Dustin Hoffman received a career tip: plastics. Today, if I were to give such a tip, it would be gene editing. Check out www.yourgenome.org/facts/what-is-genome-editing ("What Is Genome Editing?").

*Neat Niche:* **Plant Geneticist/Botanist:** Plant geneticists have created high-protein grain that has saved many lives in developing nations. Less dramatically, orchids used to be affordable only by the wealthy. Now, thanks to plant cloning and tissue culture, you can buy a world-class orchid in bloom at Trader Joe's for $9.99. Plant geneticists and botanists also cross-breed varieties to obtain (among other products) roses that needn't be sprayed with fungicides and tomatoes that taste and ship better.

Plant geneticists even play a role in figuring out how humans develop from one cell into highly differentiated adults. This understanding is crucial to preventing and curing disease. Although some of this research can be done only on animals, much can be done ethically and inexpensively with plants. As a plant lover who likes intellectual challenges and wants to make a difference, if I were starting over, this is a career I would consider. Check out botany.org/Resources/Botany.php ("What Is Botany?").

*Neat Niche:* **Entomologist:** Locally or in remote jungles, you may gather and study data on the thousands of new insect species discovered each year. Which are threats? Allies? How to deal with them? Or you may visit a farm infested with some little terror and figure out how to nuke it without nuking the rest of us. Check out www.youtube.com/watch?v=VqDBQOSTCk0 ("Leggy! Entomology Careers") and www.entsoc.org (Entomological Society of America).

*Neat Niche:* **Marine Biologist:** Beyond liking dolphins, boats, and water, marine biologists have to be, well, scientists. And today, that means as much math and computer science as biological science. You may be observing, collecting, and analyzing data on anything from plankton to whales to, yes, dolphins. The purpose usually is to figure out how to strike a balance between man's and marine animals' use of bodies of water. Check out www.youtube.com/watch?v=WgPVa8EDnkg ("What's It Like Actually to be a Marine Biologist?")

and www.environmentalscience.org/career/marine-biologist ("What Is a Marine Biologist?").

>> **Silviculturist:** Silviculturists are forest builders. You create, restore, or maintain a forest or tree nursery. Your job is to pick the right tree varieties and supervise planting, pruning, and harvesting. Also, you may conduct research on topics such as the best way to ensure rapid tree growth or the effects of animal grazing on the forest. Although most silviculturists live in isolated locations, urban forestry is a possibility as cities look to provide islands of respite amid the maelstrom. Check out www.youtube.com/watch?v=UCIPZjWC6g4 ("What Is Silviculture?") and www.amazon.com/Silviculture-Concepts-Applications-Ralph-Nyland/dp/147862714X (*Silviculture: Concepts and Applications*, by Ralph D. Nyland, Laura S. Kenefic, Kimberly K. Bohn, and Susan L. Stout).

>> **Viticulturist:** In plain English, this is a grape grower and often a vineyard manager. Typically, you work for a winery and direct its field operations. With an *enologist* (wine expert), you decide which grape varieties and rootstocks to plant, how to grow them for best flavor and ease of care and harvest. You make decisions about irrigation and how to control insects and fungus. Because you're a manager, it helps if you know accounting. Although you aren't the farmer, you may do a lot of bending. Don't worry: There's free wine to dull any aches. Check out www.agcareers.com/career-profiles/viticulturist.cfm ("Viticulturist") and www.youtube.com/watch?v=awp1lCXUsug ("A Career in Viticulture").

>> **Exercise Physiologist:** Athletes are learning to perform better, not just with a coach's help but with an exercise physiologist's. The latter may, for example, show an athlete how to improve by using slow-motion, computer-analyzed video of exactly what the muscles are doing. In addition to consulting with teams, exercise physiologists get jobs in sports medicine, cardiac rehab, and corporate fitness. Check out explorehealthcareers.org/career/sports-medicine/exercise-physiologist/ ("Exercise Physiologist") and www.amazon.com/Essentials-Exercise-Physiology-William-McArdle/dp/1496302095/ref=sr_1_1?s=books&ie=UTF8&qid=1512414220&sr=1-1&keywords=Essentials+of+Exercise+Physiology (*Essentials of Exercise Physiology*, by William D. McArdle, Frank I. Katch, and Victor L. Katch).

>> **Cancer Registrar:** Because most cancers don't have a single foolproof cure, many treatment protocols are tried for each type of cancer. One way to figure out which methods work best for whom (for example, African-Americans in their 60s with leiomyosarcoma Stage 1b and diabetes) is to accumulate treatment records of every cancer case. Most insurance companies and government healthcare providers do that, and the person in charge is the cancer registrar. This person doesn't just enter submitted information into the database, she often speaks with the physician, and even the patient,

for clarification. May you never get a call from a cancer registrar. Check out www.ncra-usa.org (National Cancer Registrars Association).

» **Epidemiologist:** With the world becoming ever smaller, diseases can spread fast. And with bioterrorism an increasing risk, those diseases can be either manmade or natural. Epidemiologists may track and predict an outbreak's spread and develop plans for its mitigation. (Think ebola.) Or, using a combination of hard science and social science methods, they may help governments develop plans and policies to help prevent conditions such as obesity and AIDS. Check out www.publichealthonline.org/epidemiology ("A Guide to Careers in Epidemiology").

» **Coroner:** Did Professor Plum do it with the candlestick in the conservatory? Or did the victim die of natural causes? Coroners are medical detectives who answer such questions. It isn't the sort of medical career that makes a great first impression: You cure no one, and you spend your life mucking around with dead people. Fortunately, after a period of desensitization, working with corpses begins to feel normal.

And it is rewarding work. It's the only career in which you enable dead people to save lives. Here's a perhaps surprising fact: Coroners don't need to be MDs. A related field, medical examiner, does require an MD, and has broader responsibilities; they may, for example, work more closely with law enforcement. Check out www.mynextmove.org/profile/summary/13-1041.06 ("Coroners") and www.amazon.com/Education-Coroner-Lessons-Investigating-Death/dp/1501168223 (*The Education of a Coroner: Lessons in Investigating Death,* by John Bateson).

» **Criminalist:** He's lying dead. Near the corpse lies a tiny white hair. The criminalist picks it up. Under the microscope, he sees that it's a pet hair. A visit to three suspects' homes finds that one of them has a pet whose hair matches this strand of hair exactly. No, it's not just a "CSI" episode. Real-life criminalists search crime scenes to unearth physical evidence — a weapon, fingerprints, a clothing fiber, blood, drugs, even vapors — and then perform tests to see whether they link the suspect and the victim. It's safer than a detective job because you usually show up after the danger is over. More advanced criminalists may analyze DNA, ballistics, fingerprints, arson, forgeries, and crime patterns to help the cops plan their strategy. Check out www.thebalance.com/criminal-justice-and-criminology-careers-974797 ("Criminal Justice and Criminology Careers").

» **Accident Reconstructor:** "It was his fault. He ran right into me!" It's the job of the accident reconstructor to find out whether that person is telling the truth. Using photographs of the crime scene, statements from drivers and witnesses, knowledge of the physics of what is and isn't possible, and computer simulations, accident reconstructors try to discover what really happened. Check out www.accidentreconstruction.com (Accident Reconstruction Communications Network).

# Going the Engineering, Physics, or Chemistry Route

Careers in the fields of engineering, physics, or chemistry may not deal directly with the study of human life, but they do greatly affect it. Engineers create most products we use: from the food we eat to the microwave that reheats it, from our air conditioner to our hair conditioner.

*Note:* Engineering traditionally has divided into electrical, civil, chemical, mechanical, and software categories. But because of growing interdisciplinarity and because many engineers are motivated by the type of project they're working on, each profiled Neat Niche is for a type of product:

» **Engineer:** This is a career for math and science junkies who like to solve practical problems, usually by designing an object. Perhaps it's a snowboard that turns better, a remote sensor that monitors the air for bioweapons, a hydrogen-powered car, a machine to pull plastic from the ocean floor, a heat shield for commercial satellites, a microscope that enables us to see individual molecules or a telescope that lets us see stars 10 billion light-years away. Check out www.discovere.org/discover-engineering/engineering-careers ("Engineering Careers").

*Neat Niche:* **Hardware Engineer:** Your job is to design and produce electronic devices. You may, for example, design the wireless module for the next-generation iPhone, a computer chip for a robotic hand that enables a world-class surgeon to do brain surgery on a patient halfway around the globe, or the machine for mass-producing that chip. Check out www.computerscience.org/careers/computer-hardware-engineer ("Hardware Engineer").

*Subniche:* **Robotic Engineer:** Robots are now used not just for welding cars but also for everything from crop-picking to nuclear plant maintenance to battle-field surveillance. For example, you're leading a troop in war. Can you safely move over the hill? A robot will tell you. Thousands of Cambodians lost limbs to land mines. Some of those mines still remain. How can they be removed without more loss of life and limb? Check out www.bostondynamics.com/atlas ("Atlas, the World's Most Dynamic Humanoid"), www.a3automate.org/resources/videos ("Why I Automate"), careers.stateuniversity.com/pages/416/Robotics-Engineer.html ("Robotics Engineer Job Description"), and blog.robotiq.com/what-to-study-for-a-career-in-robotics ("What to Study for a Career in Robotics?").

*Neat Niche:* **Biomedical Engineer:** You may design a better artificial heart, a device that will cure disease at the subcellular level, a noninvasive alternative to biopsies, an implantable device to address depression, or a vital-signs monitor for patients, astronauts, or deep-sea divers. Check out navigate.aimbe.org ("Discover Biomedical Engineering").

*Neat Niche:* **Energy Engineer:** Petroleum and nuclear engineering are, in some circles, not particularly welcome, but they remain a significant part of our energy mix. If you're comfortable being a contrarian, it may be easier to land a good energy engineering job in those specialties than in, for example, solar or wind.

Nuclear, an unlimited source of clean energy, may experience a resurgence of interest if government decides that the new generations of nuclear plants will be sufficiently safe. No less than Bill Gates thinks so. He's the founder and Chairman of TerraPower, whose mission is safer, more compact nuclear energy.

The job market should be viable in both energy creation and energy management — think of the U.S. electrical grid and, on a smaller scale, improving buildings' and vehicles' energy efficiency. Check out www.troopstoenergyjobs.com/energycareers/engineers.php ("Engineer").

*Neat Niche:* **Industrial Design Engineer:** Your alarm clock buzzes and you flail to find the Snooze button, to no avail. Industrial designers try to design better ones. Your smartphone can do all sorts of things, but you know how to use only some of its capabilities. An industrial designer tries to increase the percentage. Sometimes, this career is divided: The *designer* is more of an artisan, creating something that looks good and has the right features and user interface. The *engineer* makes sure it can actually be manufactured at the right price. Check out www.idsa.org/education/interviews ("Industrial Designers Society of America: Interviews") and www10.mcadcafe.com/nbc/articles/view_article.php?articleid=318078 ("The Difference Between Industrial Design and Design Engineering").

*Neat Niche:* **Packaging Engineer:** How should a small toy be packaged so that it's theft- and tamper-resistant yet allows the shopper to play with it so that he can plead, "Mommy, can I have it?" How should a drug be packaged so that it's childproof yet accessible to an arthritic adult? What's the most cost-effective way to add a sensor to a dog food bag so that it cues Amazon to deliver more when it's empty? Check out career.iresearchnet.com/career-information/packaging-engineer-career ("Packaging Engineer Career").

*Neat Niche:* **Sales Engineer:** Salespeople who sell technical products often bring a sales engineer on sales calls or consults with one in response to a customer's question. This tends to be a well-paying career because it's directly linked to growing revenue. Check out www.bls.gov/ooh/sales/sales-engineers.htm#tab-1 ("Sales Engineer").

*Neat Niche:* **Ship Engineer:** Some people love a life at sea. If you don't mind monitoring a ship's engine, pumps, and air-conditioning systems for hours at a time, you may find this career to be smooth sailing. Check out bigfuture. collegeboard.org/careers/transportation-ship-engineers ("Ship Engineer").

*Neat Niche:* **Spacecraft Engineer:** More passenger spacecrafts are in the offing, but, for the next decade, more growth will be in designing and building un-crewed vehicles. Such satellites may broadcast TV shows worldwide, monitor rogue nations' and nonstate nuclear activities, predict the weather, and document climate and pollution change. Many people think that spacecraft engineering mainly involves designing the vehicle itself. Actually, the main work is designing the thousands of computer programs needed to drive its many systems. Don't worry: You can still say that you're a rocket scientist. Check out www.amazon.com/Spacecraft-Systems-Engineering-Peter-Fortescue/dp/047075012X (*Spacecraft Systems Engineering,* edited by Peter Fortescue, Graham Swinerd, and John Stark).

» **Broadcast Technician/Broadcast Engineer:** Broadcast technologists operate and maintain the recording equipment in radio stations and TV studios and on remotes. An utterly nonrandom example is going to Hawaii to cover the Aloha Bowl. The bad news is that you must often work nights and weekends, and the pay can be modest. Training is less than a year at a private technical school or a bit longer at a community college. But there's an alternative: The broadcast engineer at the radio station where I host a program told me that in decades past, techie teens would, like groupies, hang out at radio stations to learn broadcast engineering. Now few do, perhaps because most teens view radio as passé. That leaves an opportunity for you. Check out www.amazon.com/Broadcast-Engineering-Tutorial-Non-Engineers/dp/0415733391 (*A Broadcast Engineering Tutorial for Non-Engineers,* by Skip Pizzi and Graham Jones).

» **Engineering Technician:** Your job is to assist an engineer in designing and developing products. For example, you may test and troubleshoot electrical and computer systems or work on a survey party, calculating land areas, estimating costs, and inspecting construction projects. A 2-year degree in engineering technology is the norm. In choosing to be an engineering technologist rather than a full-fledged engineer, you trade some prestige for shorter training, yet still often end up with an interesting job. Check out study.com/articles/Engineering_Technician_Job_Description_Duties_and_Requirements.html ("Engineering Technician").

» **Physicist:** Want to figure out how the universe began? Create nano-size machines to cure disease? Develop the science behind the next generation of fuel cells or medical imaging machines? How about studying issues with no practical application, like string theory? I listened to an NPR show on that topic, and all I remember is that string theory has something to do with groups of quarks (items much smaller than electrons) acting like guitar strings.

I think I'll leave string theory to the physicists. Increasingly, even a PhD in physics may need to be viewed as a gateway to other careers. For example, see www.physics.org/careers.asp?contentid=381 ("Careers from Physics") and www.aps.org/careers/physicists/index.cfm ("Becoming a Physicist").

*Neat Niche:* **Photonics Specialist:** Your job is to figure out how to move photons (elemental particles of light) so that they do good. And, indeed, they can. They're used in developing autonomous vehicles (LIDAR), missile defense, correction of poor sight, better lighting, higher-resolution TV screens (OLED, for example), and fun stuff like laser light shows, holograms, and tattoo removal. Well, that may not be so much fun. Check out www.aip.org/jobs/profiles/photonics-careers ("Photonics Careers").

*Neat Niche:* **Acoustician:** You probably know that acousticians ensure good sound in a concert hall, but they also keep offices quiet enough to concentrate (sort of) and homes quiet so that you can sleep. In addition, acousticians help design loudspeakers and microphones, and recording and film studios. Acousticians also are the folks who created sonograms — safer alternatives to X-rays and invasive diagnostic tests. Check out acousticalsociety.org/education_outreach/careers_in_acoustics ("Acoustics and You").

» **Geologist:** This is a career for people with and without rocks in their heads. (It's okay — you can groan.) Many geologists — petroleum geologists, for example — don't even see the rocks they're studying, because they're far below the earth's surface. Those geologists use computer data to answer a key question: Where should we drill for oil? Guess wrong and the company loses millions. Guess right and you're a genius.

You do have cool tools like gamma ray detectors to help you guess correctly. Much of the work is outdoors and can be in remote locations for long periods, so it's a poor choice if you value family life and a stable work environment. Most of the unexplored oil locations are abroad, so if you can speak a foreign language and are willing to relocate, job opportunities should be ample. The growth area in U.S. geology jobs is in cleaning up ground-based pollution. What luck: Most of the oil is far away, but the pollution is right here. New employers of geologists are seismic data-brokering companies, but the largest employers are oil companies and the U.S. departments of agriculture, interior, and defense. Check out www.geology.pitt.edu/geology-bs/careers-geology ("Careers in Geology").

*Neat Niche:* **Geophysicist:** Usually, the earth doesn't move. That is, unless you're in love or there's a volcano or earthquake. Geophysicists focus on the latter two in these neat niches. Check out earthquake.usgs.gov/learn/kids/become.php ("Become a Geophysicist").

*Subniche:* **Volcanologist:** When will a volcano erupt? Volcanologists had better not guess wrong. If they predict an imminent gusher and nothing happens, many people have been needlessly terrified and evacuated. If the volcanologist says, "No problem" and the volcano blows, you have a fried community. According to *Time,* "Volcanology may be *the* most dangerous science since those vast laboratories can explode at any moment with a force equal to thousands of atom bombs." Alas, though this may literally be a hot career, the job market is not hot. Check out www.environmentalscience.org/career/volcanologist ("What Is a Volcanologist?").

*Subniche:* **Seismologist:** So you think that seismologists predict earthquakes? Actually, most seismologists earn their living *creating* earth vibrations. Why would they do that? One reason is that it's a good way to determine where to drill for oil. Other seismologists figure out how to prevent mining disasters — and what to do when they guess wrong. Of course, some seismologists get involved with earthquakes. They may help design a plan to make a building earthquake-resistant and try to predict when and where the next Big One will strike. Check out www.environmentalscience.org/career/seismologist ("What Is a Seismologist?").

>> **Hydrologist:** Without water, we have nothing. Hydrologists ensure that water is as safe as possible. They gather data and then make water-saving proposals to corporations or government agencies. They may predict whether sufficient quantities are available and remediate polluted water sources. Although some hydrologists work in labs doing testing and computer modeling, others have offices in the great outdoors, including at the water's source: cold mountains and glaciers. Check out www.environmentalscience.org/career/hydrologist ("What Is a Hydrologist?").

>> **Meteorologist and Atmospheric Scientist:** They're getting better at predicting the weather — not only tomorrow's but also next year's. This has important implications. For example, imagine you're a farmer and you know how wet and warm the next season will be. You can pick the perfect crop for that weather.

**REMEMBER**

You can be a meteorologist even if you're too shy to give the weather report on TV. Meteorologists may work for cruise lines, ski resorts, the Department of Defense, and airlines. Slightly broader in scope are atmospheric scientists who may work for environmental agencies and nonprofits. Both are options for the math and computer person who doesn't want to be a coder. Half the meteorologists are hired by the National Weather Service. Check out www.ametsoc.org/ams/index.cfm/education-careers/career-guides-tools/all-about-careers-in-meteorology ("All About Careers in Meteorology").

» **Chemist:** Yes, you get paid to play with a grown-up's version of a chemistry set, but it's more complicated than mixing two potions and seeing whether the mixture turns green. You need advanced math, and many chemist jobs also require some knowledge of physics, biology, or engineering. Chemists are hired not just by companies but also by government and environmental groups. (The latter may want someone to work on how to mitigate the effects of industrial effluents.) Whatever you do, try not to blow up the lab, huh? Check out www.acs.org/content/acs/en/careers/college-to-career/chemistry-careers.html ("Chemistry Careers").

*Neat Niche:* **Battery Developer:** Batteries store energy, and storage is the key to improving electric and hybrid vehicles. It's also central to boosting solar energy's usefulness: How can the energy from solar farms most efficiently be stored at night and during not-sunny weather? Of course, better batteries are also the key to our smartphones, iPads, and laptops. Today, we're always aware: "Do I have enough juice?" Well, imagine a battery that would run for months without a charge. Battery developers could make that a reality. Check out study.com/articles/Battery_Technology_Training_and_Education_Program_Overviews.html ("Battery Technology Training and Education Program Overview").

*Neat Niche:* **Food Scientist:** How can we make a veggie burger that looks and tastes as good as the beef version? Bill Gates-funded Impossible Foods has done just that. More mundane but still important, how can chicken processors reduce bacteria, which sickens thousands of people every year? Food scientists work for food processing companies to make tastier, healthier foods, and for government agencies to help ensure food safety. Check out www.ift.org/knowledge-center/learn-about-food-science/day-in-the-life.aspx ("Day in the Life of a Food Scientist").

*Neat Niche:* **Toxicologist:** Toxicologists assess the safety of products from shampoo to shellfish. They also may work after the fact — determining whether someone who died unexpectedly was poisoned, for example. Or they may search for the source of an outbreak of a food-borne disease. After a recent *e. coli* outbreak, toxicologists matched the DNA in a disease-causing head of lettuce with the DNA found on one farm.

The Texas A&M toxicology home page warned that such incidents are far from rare: "Hardly a week goes by without hearing about a chemical that may threaten our health: pesticides in the food we eat, pollutants in the air we breathe, chemicals in the water we drink. Are these chemicals really dangerous? How much does it take to cause harm? Toxicologists answer these questions." The terrorism threat further increases the demand for toxicologists. Check out www.toxicology.org/careers/toxicologist/becomeTox.asp ("Becoming a Toxicologist").

*Neat Niche:* **Perfumer:** Come up with a fragrance that smells great and different — that's what perfumers do in the creation of new soaps, laundry products, shampoos, lotions, candles, and, yes, perfumes. Most perfumers learn their art in an extensive apprenticeship. Procter & Gamble offers a prestigious one. Check out `volatilefiction.wordpress.com/2014/04/27/ what-is-a-perfumer-how-to-become-a-perfumer` ("What Is a Perfumer and How to Become One").

# Finding a Career in Computers

You don't need this book to tell you that there are, and will likely continue to be, lots of computer-centric careers. Here are common ones, plus some neat niches:

>> **Software Developer:** Nowadays, *software developer* (along with *coder*) has become the more common term for *computer programmer.* Whatever the job title, today's software is typically developed by a team of them. That can make it easy to lose sight of the importance of each developer, but collectively they do make a big difference in our lives, That's true even in seemingly mundane projects, such as a website for a nonprofit, a business, a government entity, or a political campaign that's more useful or appealing than template DIY websites.

Of course, there are sexier projects. For example, software developers gave us Google and our smartphones. Moving forward, you may help develop software to enable medical wearables to dispense the correct amount of medication through an implanted pump and, as needed, wirelessly message their healthcare provider. Or you might help develop the software behind an automatic "dimmer switch" that would be attached to every street lamp. Each night, depending on how strong the moonlight is and how much light is generated from surrounding buildings, each street lamp's "dimmer switch" would adjust its brightness. That would save lots of energy while inconveniencing no one.

Likely to remain in-demand niches include artificial intelligence (AI) and its related specialties: machine learning (self-teaching computers), cryptocurrency (for example, Bitcoin), wearables such as medical monitoring devices, and virtual and augmented reality systems.

**REMEMBER**

Perhaps surprisingly, a degree is not necessarily required for a successful computer career. Good programming skills, a strong work ethic, and detail-orientedness are. Many programmers are learning their craft online with training at CodeAcademy, Treehouse, Udacity, Lynda, and Coursera.

*Neat Niche:* **Artificial Intelligence Specialist:** Many AI specialists work on specific applications — for example, an expert system that will assist healthcare providers in diagnosis and treatment. An example is WoeBot (www.woepot.io). It's an AI/self-teaching mental health app that has been found to reduce depression and anxiety in two weeks — and if, in the middle of the night, you're freaking out, it's more available than a therapist.

An example of a fundamental problem that AI specialists are working on is to teach computers to be curious about what they don't know but potentially could control. So, a self-teaching FedEx logistics computer might focus on unexpected results. For example, its computer predicted that a truck would be full, yet it wasn't. The computer would be "curious" about that and use its previous experience and "brain power" to improve its future predictions. The curiosity-enhanced computer wouldn't, however, focus on unpredicted rain, because the computer couldn't solve that problem.

Software developers proficient in using such AI-dedicated frameworks as SPARK, such languages as TensorFlow and Gluon, and such broader-use languages as Python, R, and Java should find ample employment opportunities, especially if they specialize in neural networks, robotics, evolutionary computation, expert systems, speech processing, or machine learning. Check out blog.hackerearth.com/2015/12/artificial-intelligence-101-how-to-get-started.html ("Artificial Intelligence 101: How to Get Started").

*Neat Niche:* **Computer Security Programmer:** The threat of cyberterrorism and previous breaches of major websites from IRS to Equifax to Target reinforce the need for computer security professionals to try to stay a step ahead of the black-hatters. Government and companies cite a great shortage. Check out en.wikipedia.org/wiki/Computer_security ("Computer Security").

*Neat Niche:* **Augmented Reality/Virtual Reality Programmer:** Already, Amazon and Ikea use augmented reality software that allows you to see what thousands of items look like in your space. AR will soon allow your phone to identify objects, from that cute blouse you see someone wearing to that mole on your shoulder. It may then be able to Google-search it and post top hits on your phone. Truck mechanics will be able to see what's hard to see when repairing an engine's innards, and remote surgeons will be able to "feel" what the tissue is like as they're making an incision.

**REMEMBER**

Virtual reality programmers also write software that's the ultimate training method, by putting students in a virtual duplicate of the real-world situation: military officers in war zones, doctors and medical students in surgery, schoolchildren learning what to do in case of fire, and astronauts in spaceships. And, of course, virtual reality is the goal of many video games. Check out en.wikipedia.org/wiki/Virtual_reality.

*Neat Niche:* **Game Developer:** Of course, this is cool. The question is, how do you get hired? Many developers learn on their own, but some take online courses such as those offered by Microsoft, Udemy, or Udacity. When you create a cool sample program, send it to game companies. Check out www.gamasutra.com/blogs/BobEdwards/20130808/197934/Breaking_into_the_Video_Game_Industry_A_AAA_Perspective.php ("Breaking into the Video Game Industry: A Triple AAA Perspective").

*Neat Niche:* **Project Lead or Manager:** Much basic programming is now done in low-cost countries, but project management jobs are less likely to be offshored, because they generally require cultural competence in the home country. So people with good people- and project-management skills atop programming chops should find themselves in demand. Check out "What The Hell Is Project Management, Anyway?" at www.fastcompany.com/1822525/what-hell-project-management-anyway.

» **Software Architect:** This is a common promotion for an experienced programmer with good strategic and communication skills. Software architects talk with stakeholders to tease out what the software should do. They synthesize that information into a blueprint for the software, usually containing multiple modules. A software *designer* then designs the specific modules, and the programmers and software developers code the actual software. Check out lifehacker.com/career-spotlight-what-i-do-as-a-software-architect-1699203274 ("What I Do as a Software Architect").

» **Database Administrator:** Among an organization's most valuable possessions are its databases. The database administrator's (DBA's) job is to protect them. With datasets ever larger and often in varied formats — often residing in the cloud, perhaps outside the security firewall — the DBA's job has become more complex. Check out www.roberthalf.com/blog/salaries-and-skills/the-evolving-role-of-database-administrators ("The Evolving Role of the Database Administrator").

» **Network Administrator:** "The network is down. What the heck happened?" "I don't believe it — I lost my data!" Network administrators, sometimes called *system* administrators, install and repair computer networks. You're a combination mega-Tinker Toy assembler, electrician, programmer, and fix-it person, and you're crucial to everyone who uses the network — which means that you receive heartfelt thank-yous when you get people back up and running. Network administrators also are consulted by management in deciding whether and how to expand the network and on preventive maintenance. Check out www.bls.gov/ooh/computer-and-information-technology/network-and-computer-systems-administrators.htm ("Network and Computer Systems Administrator").

» **Employee Background Checker:** When one of former San Francisco mayor Willie Brown's key employees was caught lying on his résumé, hizzoner shrugged, "Everyone lies on their résumé." Alas, he's not wrong. Depending on which study you believe, 20 to 45 percent of job applications contain "creative writing" — inflated work history, a degree never completed, a claim of no criminal record, and so on. Employers and landlords use computer sleuths to unearth the truth. Check out www.napbs.com/resources/about-screening ("About Screening").

# Pursuing a Career in Math

Many science, computer, and engineering fields depend on math whizzes. Here are some options for them.

*Note:* You may be expecting to find *accountant* in this section, but because accountants have, in practice, more people contact than one might expect, it's profiled in Chapter 7.

>> **Data Scientist or Analyst:** Data scientists and analysts use mathematical models to tease out information from databases. For example, they may infer our buying preferences from our Google and Facebook interactions. Or they may query data sets from genomic assays to identify gene clusters that may cure disease, predict what techniques will motivate a particular donor to give more, or monitor Internet activity to foil terrorist plots. Check out www.infoworld.com/article/3190008/big-data/3-reasons-why-data-scientist-remains-the-top-job-in-america.html ("Three Reasons Why Data Scientist Remains the Top Job in America").

*Neat Niche:* **Environmental Analyst:** Yes, environmental analysts may do research on climate change, but they also may do lower-profile work. Here's one example: In an area with higher-than-normal cancer rates, environmental analysts look for aberrations in the composition of the air, soil, and water and then play detective and try to figure out whether any of those are causing the problem. If analysts find unexpected chemicals, they check to see whether local companies are culprits and — consistent with local, state, and federal laws — what levers can be pushed. Environmental analysts are hired by federal, state, and local environmental protection agencies or by consulting firms. Check out www.naep.org (National Association of Environmental Professionals).

*Neat Niche:* **Operations Research Analyst:** One way the U.S. stays competitive in the global economy is its ability to create efficient production systems. The operations research analyst, a practically oriented math whiz, is one of the brains behind it all. They may, for example, help Bird's Eye figure out how much broccoli to plant and when to plant it. They may shorten the time it takes to cash a paycheck. They may even develop a system to ensure an adequate AIDS-free blood supply in the nation's hospitals. A recent example: Operations research analysts figured out a way for Norfolk Southern Railways to coordinate its automated dispatching across its 20,000 miles on track in 22 states, resulting in faster shipments and major savings. Check out www.bls.gov/ooh/math/operations-research-analysts.htm ("Operations Research Analysts").

*Neat Niche:* **Market Research Analyst:** What products and styles will teens crave next? What do you, as an individual, prefer — Coke or Jamba Juice? Toyota or Schwinn? DIY or full-serve? Market research analysts develop surveys and review data sets to present — using words, charts, and infographics — predictions of what will sell and what you, as an individual will want. With that information, manufacturers can tweak a product so that it contains the features you want, can produce advertising that reflects that fact, and can then place the ads where you'll see them. We all dislike ads — especially blinking, noisy banner ads — but market research analysts help ensure at least that the ads are for products we might actually care about. For example, millennials are more likely to see an ad for Google than for Depends adult diapers. Check out www.bls.gov/ooh/business-and-financial/market-research-analysts.htm#tab-1 ("Market Research Analysts").

*Neat Niche:* **Analyst for Government:** Government jobs offer solid benefits, job security, and, perhaps surprisingly, good pay. A Congressional Budget Office study found that, for equivalent work, federal pay is higher than in the private sector. Government employs many people in analyst roles. Analyst jobs tend to divide into program or budget. Program analysts may review the literature in an area the government wants to fund. Or they may develop a request for proposals or guidelines for existing programs, or specify how the program is to be evaluated and review the results. A budget analyst usually develops or reviews budgets for agencies, subagencies, or specific government initiatives. Check out www.aabpa.org (American Association for Budget and Program Analysis).

*Neat Niche:* **Securities Analyst:** Might you find it fun to figure out whether a company's stock or bond is a bargain? That's what securities analysts do. They're mathematical detectives who interview company employees and crunch a lot of numbers. They're hired by pension funds, mutual funds, corporations, insurance companies, and universities.

*Subniche:* **Portfolio Manager:** After you've been an analyst for a while, this job is a big step up. You develop models for analysts to use in evaluating stocks, bonds, or other financial instruments. You review the results, add your own thoughts, and then decide which instruments to keep in the organization's portfolio. Check out www.cfainstitute.org (Chartered Financial Analyst Institute).

TIP

Want to play with other people's money but don't see yourself getting the MBA or CFA certification that's usually required to be a portfolio manager? See the financial advisor profile in Chapter 9.

>> **Statistician:** It's difficult to ascertain truth. Often, the best you can hope for is high probability. That's true in everything from deciding where a politician should campaign hardest to how much a professional baseball player is worth. Statisticians boost confidence in decision-making. After determining what information is needed, they design surveys and questionnaires, analyze results, and present them in an accessible format. Florence Nightingale said that statistics is the most important science in the whole world, for upon it depends the practical application of every other science. Check out www.bls.gov/ooh/math/statisticians.htm#tab-1 ("Mathematicians and Statisticians").

*Neat Niche:* **Biostatistician:** You answer questions such as "How effective is a new drug? How sure are we that this gene expresses this protein across an entire population? What are the chances of a side effect in pregnant women?" Check out thisisstatistics.org/what-does-a-career-in-biostatistics-actually-look-like ("What Does a Career in Biostatistics Actually Look Like?"), www.dummies.com/education/math/statistics/biostatistics-for-dummies/ (*Biostatistics For Dummies,* by John Pezzullo).

*Neat Niche:* **Sports Statistician:** Were you the kid who calculated the likelihood of this or that happening during the game? Sports statistician may be your dream career. They are numeric journalists, creating elucidating stats that enrich a journalist's article, broadcaster's reporting, or coach's decision-making: in a given situation, whom to play and bench, where to position the players, what play to call?

TIP

To maximize your chances of making a living as a sports statistician, hone your craft as a high school or college team's statistician. Don't record just the basics; be creative. For example, in the game's final minutes when the outcome is in doubt, Biff completes 40 percent fewer passes than during the rest of the game (Mr. Choke) while Rick completes 20 percent *more* passes (Mr. Clutch).

If you prove yourself at the high school or college level, send work samples — especially that creative stuff — to producers of pro sports TV shows. Their names are mentioned or listed at the end of the game. You might even send your material to the Elias Sports Bureau, which produces stats for Major League Baseball, the NFL, and the NBA. Check out stattrak.amstat.org/2012/08/01/sports-statistician ("Preparing for a Career as a Sports Statistician").

>> **Actuary:** How much should an insurance company charge each employee of Western Widget Waxing Company for health insurance? That's a typical question asked of an actuary. Actuary is a good career for someone who wants a career that applies math to practical decisions and that offers 6-figure pay. More good news: You can achieve the highest level of actuary (Fellow) without a graduate degree. You do have to pass a series of arduous exams for which you can study at home or take classes at local actuary clubs or at universities.

Check out www.soa.org/future-actuaries/what-is-an-actuary ("What Is an Actuary?").

>> **Economist:** This is another career for the math-centric person who wants to do something that's potentially practical. Economists answer such questions as, "How will our company be affected if the minimum wage rises?" "What are the costs and benefits of legalizing gambling in this county?" "What will likely happen to solar installations after the federal subsidy expires?" In other words, economists predict and analyze production and consumption trends to help governments and companies make policy. Check out www.princetonreview.com/careers/56/economist ("A Day in the Life of an Economist").

*Neat Niche:* **Environmental Economist:** You figure out the economic costs and benefits of activities such as a carbon tax, the building of a transnational oil pipeline, or a policy that prohibits new freeway building, which actually has been enacted in the San Francisco Bay Area. Check out www.environmentalscience.org/career/environmental-economist ("What Is an Environmental Economist?").

*Neat Niche:* **Forensic Economist:** You claim that your business partner ruined your business. How large were the damages, if any? A forensic economist can tell you. Your spouse got run over by a car. How much money should you get? An estimate will come from a forensic economist. Your spouse needn't die for you to need a forensic economist. Let's say you're divorcing. How much spousal support do you need to pay? A forensic economist can tell you. Check out www.monster.com/career-advice/article/forensic-economists ("Forensic Economists").

>> **Cryptographer:** The government has just intercepted a secret message from a terrorist organization — cryptographers decode it. A website contains thousands of customers' credit card numbers — cryptographers encode it to deter hackers. In short, cryptographers make and break secret codes. Most cryptographers have a PhD in math — a secret decoder ring won't quite cut it. However, despite having only a bachelor's degree, my cryptographer friend (forgive the name-dropping) Whitfield Diffie won the Turing Prize (the equivalent of a Nobel in computer science.) Check out careersthatdontsuck.com/2007/02/24/career-profile-cryptologis ("Career Profile: Cryptographer").

>> **Appraiser:** Yes, there's the mundane sort of appraising businesses, machinery, and real estate. But some appraisers are more like professional treasure hunters, sifting through collections of coins, stamps, jewelry, antiques, or art and figuring out whether there's booty among the ordinary. You can find oddball niches, too — for example, appraising race horses or Lionel train collections. As businesses turn over more quickly and the population ages, the need for appraisers is increasing: in estate planning or in divvying up the pie after the fact. Check out www.appraisers.org (American Society of Appraisers).

# Chapter 7

# STEM + People or Word Careers

I f you're STEM-oriented but are also good with people or with words, you may well find a well-suited career in this chapter.

## Healing Others

For a variety of reasons, healthcare is being downscaled, provided by what are called intermediate-level healthcare providers. This trend is likely to continue. So, much physician work will be done by physician assistants; physical therapy work by physical therapy assistants; anesthesiology by nurse anesthetists; psychiatrist and psychologist work by counselors; and so on.

A career as an intermediate-level care provider is well suited to detail-oriented, caring people who can handle the still significant preparatory science courses. Such careers pay well and require far less schooling than their more prestigious analogues. In this chapter, I profile many of these intermediate healthcare careers, which sometimes are called allied health careers, as well as their more impressive counterparts.

**WARNING**

At least 300,000 patients die *every year* because of medical errors at hospitals alone. You should consider one of the following healthcare careers *only* if you are, even when stressed, caring and detail-oriented:

>> **Physician Assistant or Nurse Practitioner:** In both of these professions, you derive most of the benefits of being a physician with few of the liabilities. You get to do the pleasant parts of doctoring: exams, health education, medication prescriptions and treatment, lab test interpretations, procedures, and even surgery assistance. And if the situation gets too difficult, you can ask your MD supervisor to take over.

In addition, you don't need to complete four expensive, difficult years of medical school plus three to seven years of residency — get a master's degree and you're in, and with solid pay to boot. Differences are subtle between the career of physician assistant and nurse practitioner. Nurse practitioners must first be nurses, but may have more autonomy and authority, whereas physician assistants may, in some cases, require closer MD supervision. Check out www.aapa.org (American Academy of Physician Assistants) and www.aanp.org/all-about-nps/what-is-an-np#why-nps-are-important ("What's an NP?").

>> **Registered Nurse:** Of course, you have to get used to being around bodily fluids, but most nurses do eventually desensitize and find the career a calling. They recognize that a patient's outcome may depend as much on the nurse as on the doctor. Plus, as cost-cutting pressures increase, registered nurses are performing ever more substantive medical care, not just as nurse practitioners, as just described, but (as you can see in the following three *Neat Niche* bullets) having an RN degree opens doors to a variety of patient care, administrative, and research careers. Some nurses are rankled by being subject to an MD's orders. In any case, most doctors are now more respectful of nurses than they may have been in the past. Check out www.discovernursing.com/future-nurses-start-here# ("Future Nurses Start Here") and www.amazon.com/Life-Support-Nurses-Culture-Politics/dp/0801474280/ref=sr_1_1?ie=UTF8&qid=1512437572 &sr=8-1&keywords=three+nurses+on+the+front+line (*Life Support: Three Nurses on the Front Lines,* by Suzanne Gordon).

*Neat Niche:* **Nurse Anesthetist:** Anesthesiologists are among the highest-paid physicians, and much of their work doesn't need so highly trained a person. So, under cost control pressures, nurse anesthetists and anesthesiology assistants increasingly do much of an anesthesiologist's work — calling for advice and help as needed, of course. But especially in nonmetropolitan areas, nurse anesthetists work quite autonomously. Nurse anesthetists make less than anesthesiologists but still are well paid. Check out www.aana.com (American Association of Nurse Anesthetists).

*Neat Niche:* **Obstetrics Nurse:** Experience the miracle of childbirth every day. Even normal births can be stressful, so OB-GYN nurses particularly need a calm demeanor. Check out www.discovernursing.com/specialty/obstetrics-nurse-gynecology-nurse#.Wdp1fWeAamA ("Obstetrics Nurse/Gynecology Nurse").

*Neat Niche:* **Nurse Informatician:** Nurses need to access lots of data: patient records, drug contraindications, disease ins-and-outs, and insurance gobble-dygook. A current priority is improving the ability to access and enter patient data in an electronic medical record system. The nurse informatician is part of a team that attempts to improve and implement such systems. It's a nursing career with no blood and gore. Check out www.ania.org (American Nursing Informatics Association).

*Neat Niche:* **Legal Nurse Consultant:** Some people consider suing a doctor or hospital. To evaluate those claims' legitimacy, lawyers hire nurses to review the medical records, participate in interviewing potential clients, and, if the case seems meritorious and involves nursing malpractice, research the nursing literature to develop the case's foundation. Legal nurse consultants also testify in trials as expert witnesses. Check out www.aalnc.org/page/what-is-an-lnc#Q2 ("What Is an LNC?").

» **Physician:** This career may be overrated. Of course it's prestigious and potentially lucrative, and you help prevent and cure disease —unquestionably a noble pursuit.

But here it's worth focusing on the profession's downsides because they're little known and significant, especially moving forward.

First I describe a downside that would surprise few readers. The training is long, difficult, and expensive. As an undergraduate, though you needn't major in premed, you must take a half-dozen challenging science and math courses and earn A's and B's. To have a good chance of getting into medical school, you need not only to earn a high overall GPA and MCAT score but also significant relevant experience working in a hospital or research lab. (One of my clients is hoping that her experience working in an optometrist's office will work. I'm not so sure.)

If you're accepted into medical school, you face four years of intense and costly education. Even at a public medical school, you're talking over $200,000. At the University of California, San Francisco School of Medicine, where I teach, the all-in 4-year sticker price is $300,000; The average student debt is $170,000. At the private Harvard Medical School, the total tab is $400,000.

You must pass a 3-step set of medical board exams before being allowed to graduate. After medical school is the required 3- to 7-year low-pay residency, after which you must pass a rigorous examination to be allowed to practice.

Once certified, physicians may receive lower compensation than in the past. Cost-control pressures are reducing Medicare, MediCal, and private-insurance reimbursements.

The job of MD may also become more difficult. The easier-to-succeed-with patients will mainly be seen by physician assistants and nurse practitioners. Many patients have high needs but demonstrate a not-so-high likelihood of compliance with physician recommendations. Then there are those sophisticated patients who are convinced, after a few Google search sessions, that they know more about their condition than does the physician, or at least enough to make them argue with their clinical judgment.

Then there's the imposter syndrome. Because medicine is changing rapidly, it's nearly impossible to keep up. So some physicians feel guilty that, because of their own lack of knowledge and insurer constraints, they may not be providing the level of care that they wish they could.

There's also the physician's longstanding burden of dealing with death and often difficult dying. The medical profession, despite progress, still has a hard time beating the common Big Diseases: cancer, cardiovascular disease, and diabetes, let alone rarer diseases that attract fewer research dollars.

Then there's the paperwork. Some of my physician clients complain that they must spend a lot of time on paperwork to comply with government, insurer, and employer requirements. One said, "I became a doctor to heal, not to fill out forms."

So it's not surprising that many doctors are unhappy. They have high rates of substance abuse, and many leave clinical practice. Indeed, in my career counseling practice, my most frequent clients are doctors and lawyers.

That's why I encourage many would-be physicians to consider a career as a physician assistant, as mentioned earlier in this section. But some people simply feel that they're meant to be doctors. They're driven to serve, or they want the status and they hope for big dollars; and, ideally, they have the gift for the art as much as the science of medicine. For them, being a physician indeed can be the perfect career.

For more on being a doctor, check out www.bls.gov/ooh/healthcare/physicians-and-surgeons.htm#tab-1 ("Physicians and Surgeons") and www.amazon.com/Med-School-Confidential-Complete-Experience/dp/0312330081 (*Med School Confidential: A Complete Guide to the Medical School Experience: By Students, for Students*, by Robert H. Miller and Dan Bissell M.D.).

*Neat Niche:* **Infectious Disease Specialist:** As you're reading this section, terrorist groups and governments are likely developing biological weapons of mass destruction — smallpox mutated so that there's no vaccine, for example. The chance of that situation affecting you remains small, but that's not true of the following: Natural selection is creating superbacteria that are resistant even to the most powerful antibiotics. In addition, the odds of contracting infectious diseases is growing because of easier worldwide travel and continued migration to crowded, urban areas. And then there's AIDS — the virus itself and the myriad opportunistic infections that its victims contract. Infectious disease researchers and practitioners do some of humankind's most important and challenging work. Check out www.idsociety.org/ ID_Careers ("Career Paths in Infectious Diseases").

*Neat Niche:* **Radiologist:** Few medical fields have advanced more in recent decades. *Diagnostic* radiologists used to rely mainly on X-rays, which produce crude images while exposing patients to significant radiation. Today, ultrasound, and especially CT and MRI scans, enable far more useful images with lower risk to the patient. Next-generation, higher-resolution imaging promises to be even more valuable. *Interventional* radiologists use ever more targeted radiation therapy for cancer and in opening blood vessels and inserting stents in diseased arteries. Check out meded.ucsf.edu/ume/career-information- diagnostic-radiology ("Diagnostic Radiology") and www.sirweb.org/ patient-center/what-is-ir ("What Is Interventional Radiology?").

*Neat Niche:* **Dermatologist:** After med school, you choose a specialty, and dermatology is among the most competitive because it's so desirable: You help most of your patients, whether medically or cosmetically and, unlike certain specialties, the hours are regular. Check out en.wikipedia.org/ wiki/Dermatology.

*Subniche:* **Mohs Surgeon:** Skin cancers are common and, usually, curable. Sometimes, excision is a wise choice. Especially on the face, the incision needs to be as small and shallow as possible to avoid a large scar. Mohs microsurgery minimizes that. Also, because skin cancer surgery needn't be done immediately, Mohs surgeons, unlike most surgeons, work regular hours, and each of the one to three excisions takes just minutes. Contrast that with standard surgeons, who must sometimes work for hours to complete a surgery. Plus, for now at least, dermatologists can perform Mohs surgery without extensive training. For an eye-opening article not just about Mohs surgeons but also about the motives of physicians and regulators, check out www.mdedge.com/edermatologynews/article/113747/should-we- pursue-board-certification-mohs-micrographic-surgery ("Should We Pursue Board Certification in Mohs?").

*Neat Niche:* **Sports Medicine:** How'd you like to be the team physician for a football team and/or treat weekend warriors' sprains and concussions? Here's another physician specialty in which you succeed with a large percentage of your patients. Check out www.amssm.org (American Medical Society for Sports Medicine).

*Neat Niche:* **Infertility Specialist:** Ever-more women are deferring parenthood until the age when getting pregnant isn't so easy. Enter the infertility doctor, with an ever-growing array of solutions. Today, fertility docs even allow you to pick your baby's sex. What's next — ensuring that your child isn't ugly? Or has a high IQ? Check out www.asrm.org (American Society for Reproductive Medicine).

*Neat Niche:* **College-Based Physician:** College student health problems are usually curable, you have no overhead, and you work in an attractive, stimulating setting: a college campus.

*Neat Niche:* **Medical Informatician:** As mentioned in the earlier registered nurse profile, medical informatics is the future, whether in improving artificial intelligence tools for healthcare providers or abetting the transition between paper and electronic medical records. And physicians will obviously play a key role. Check out explorehealthcareers.org/field/informatics ("Informatics Overview").

>> **Optometrist:** "Better with lens A or lens B?" After a while, I can never tell and I feel like a dunce. But I digress. Optometrists examine, diagnose, and treat eye conditions, usually by prescribing glasses or contact lenses. In some states, they're allowed to perform some minor surgery. Optometry is among the more rewarding health careers because it identifies problems that usually have a ready cure. And because the population is aging and optometrists are a lower-cost alternative to ophthalmologists (medical eye doctors), the job market for optometrists is good. In any case, online vision exams are becoming more popular and could make your vision of a career in optometry fuzzier. Check out optometriceducation.org/wp-content/uploads/2016/03/ASCO-CareerGuide-2016-v3.pdf ("Optometry: A Career Guide").

>> **Orthoptist:** This is another option for people who want to be a doctor but lack the grades or desire to spend a great deal of time in school. Under the general supervision of an ophthalmologist (MD), you assess visual acuity, depth perception, and eye muscle problems, do patient education, and help manage patients, especially children whose eyes don't work in tandem: amblyopia ("lazy or wandering eye") and strabismus ("cross-eye.") Check out www.orthoptics.org (American Association of Certified Orthoptists).

>> **Audiologist:** As baby boomers age, they may develop hearing loss, so demand for audiologists should be loud and clear. Plus, you're ever more likely to satisfy customers because hearing aids are improving. For the self-conscious, some hearing aids are so tiny that everything fits into the ear canal. (Perhaps the nation's most famous user is Bill Clinton.) Many audiologists get out of the office and spend part of each week in hospitals, rehab centers, or special schools. Check out www.bls.gov/ooh/healthcare/audiologists.htm ("Audiologists") and www.amazon.com/Introduction-Audiology-Communication-Sciences-Disorders/dp/0133491463 (*Introduction to Audiology,* by Frederick N. Martin and John Greer Clark).

» **Dentist:** It's a myth that you must be excellent with your hands to be a good dentist. Studies find that an average person can develop the hands-on skills. You must, however, be able to engage pleasantly with patients, communicate clearly, and exude calm confidence. You also need good back muscles. Many dentists develop back problems from continually leaning over patients. And dentistry is stressful. It's no fun to see patients flinch (hopefully, not writhe) in response to your gentle touch. This is another of the medical professions in which you cure most patients' problems. Plus, it's one of the few remaining medical professions in which self-employment remains a viable option. Check out www.ada.org/en/education-careers/careers-in-dentistry ("Careers in Dentistry"), www.bls.gov/ooh/healthcare/dentists.htm ("Dentists"), and www.amazon.com/Art-Science-Being-Dentist-Professional/dp/1587621622 (*The Art and Science of Being a Dentist: Leading Dentists Reveal the Secrets to Professional and Personal Success*).

*Neat Niche:* **Orthodontist:** You probably know that orthodontists fix misaligned teeth, those that occur naturally or the result of an accident. What you may not know is that this career requires extensive training: four years of dental school followed by a 2- to 3-year orthodontics program. But its rewards can be great, both financially and in its high success rate with patients, both medically and cosmetically, which is fun to see. Plus, because you see most patients frequently over an extended period, you have the time to develop a relationship. And you rarely get a night or weekend call: "Doctor, my rubber band broke!" Check out www.asdanet.org/utility-navigation/career-compass-home/grad-career-options/Life-of-a-Dentist/Orthodontics ("Orthodontics").

» **Dental Hygienist:** More than simply cleaning your teeth, a dental hygienist takes and develops X-rays and administers anesthesia. In some states, hygienists even examine patients who are unable to come to the dentist's office. And, of course, part of the job is to show you ugly pictures of diseased gums to guilt-trip you into flossing more often. Like dentists, dental hygienists must take precautions to avoid repetitive strain injuries and back pain. Most dental hygienists will continue to work in private practice, but more are working in public health clinics, even in shopping malls. See www.adha.org/professional-roles ("Dental Hygiene Career Paths").

» **Physical Therapist:** An executive who suffers from a bad case of "smartphone thumb" from texting too often, an older person recovering from a stroke, and an infant with a birth defect — each of these can be a physical therapy (PT) patient. The physical therapist's job is to develop programs to relieve pain and restore function. Many people think of a physical therapist as the person who coaches the patient through exercises but in many cases that's done mainly by less expensive physical therapy assistants (as described in the following paragraph). Increasingly, the physical therapist is primarily the patient's plan-maker and perhaps initial instructor, and consults with the patient's physician. The aging population is boosting the demand for physical therapists. Admission to PT school has become difficult — only a notch easier than medical school. This is another of those fields in which a doctoral degree has become the standard. Check out www.apta.org (American Physical Therapy Association).

*Neat Niche:* **Physical Therapy Assistant:** The physical therapy assistant implements the patient care designed by the physical therapist, including instructing patients on exercises, helping them use equipment, and fitting and instructing them on how to use braces, prostheses, and crutches. Check out "About Physical Therapist Assistant (PTA) Careers" at www.apta.org/PTACareers/Overview/.

*Neat Niche:* **Sports Physical Therapist:** Helping people who hurt themselves while playing a sport or trying to keep themselves in shape tends to be a less burnout-prone niche than general physical therapy, which more often treats slow-progress patients. You need to acquire the technical competence to assess a patient's risk-reward of resuming various levels of sports activity, plus the emotional intelligence to convince the athlete to not rush the process (a natural tendency). Many sports physical therapists work in specialty sports medicine clinics but, of course, the glamorous work is in helping high-performing athletes get back in the game. Check out www.exercise-science-guide.com/careers/sports-physical-therapist ("Sports Physical Therapist: Career Overview").

>> **Veterinarian:** A vet is like a doctor except that you need to know a half-dozen species, none of which can describe their symptoms to you. Veterinary medicine offers advantages over being a physician: You get to perform a wider range of procedures because, in many specialties, board certification isn't required. Plus, most veterinary medicine is fee-for-service, so you aren't saddled with labyrinthine regulations and paperwork. One downside is that veterinary offices tend to be loud: lots of barking. More serious, vets have a high depression and suicide rate — it's tough having to put down a family pet, especially if a long, expensive treatment might or might not help. Check out www.amazon.com/Ask-Animals-Vets-Eye-View-People-ebook/dp/B002LA09M6 (*Ask the Animals: A Vet's-Eye View of Pets and the People They Love*, by Bruce R. Coston).

*Neat Niche:* **Veterinary Cardiologist:** Demand is growing, treatments are improving, and earnings are excellent for these heart specialists. Check out blog.sfgate.com/pets/2011/09/07/qa-with-veterinary-cardiologist-dr-justin-williams ("Q&A with Veterinary Cardiologist Dr. Justin Williams").

>> **Veterinary Technologist:** This career requires a much shorter training time than for veterinarians, yet "vet techs" get to do much of what vets do. Say that poor Fifi isn't feeling well. The vet tech (who speaks Dog) may take her medical

history, complete the exam, and take her blood sample (poor Fifi.) The vet diagnoses the problem as a bladder infection and prescribes an injection that you administer.

Next, even poorer Bowser comes in: He was run over by a car. The vet decides to operate. You administer the anesthetic and assist in surgery. You're even allowed to stitch up Bowser. He also has a broken leg. You take the X-rays, the vet sets the leg, and you apply the cast. Finally, you educate Bowser's human parent about how to take care of Bowser during his recovery.

You needn't be dogged to land a job because there are four job openings for every vet tech graduate in the United States. But because many people would love a career working with animals that doesn't require massive amounts of schooling, salaries are <ahem> poopy. Check out www.indeed.com/forum/job/veterinary-technician/CONS-being-vet-tech/t84798 ("What Are the Cons of Being a Vet Tech?").

>> **Pharmacist:** You're not just filling prescriptions. You're often a frontline healthcare provider, teaching diabetics how to inject themselves with insulin, assisting with blood pressure monitoring, and ensuring that people know how to take their medications. The latter isn't as easy as it sounds. Many older people must take numerous medications, each of which must be taken at a different time — some of which must be taken on an empty stomach and others when not drowsy.

Perhaps the most important task a pharmacist performs is to ensure that drugs that *should* not be taken together are in fact *not* taken together. The TV show *Dateline* showed an obviously pregnant woman walking into ten pharmacies and asking whether two drugs could be taken together. Six of the ten pharmacists said yes. In fact, when a pregnant woman takes those two drugs together, it's lethal. Each year, thousands of people are hospitalized because they take prescription medications improperly. When they do their job correctly, pharmacists can be lifesavers.

Some of the more interesting pharmacy jobs are in pharmaceutical companies' research departments and in hospital pharmacies. In the latter, in addition to filling prescriptions, you may attend grand rounds, instruct interns, and assist surgeons in preparing infusions. Standard drugstore pharmacy jobs are less desirable because of lots of repetitive work and night and weekend hours. As in many other fields, the training requirements have been ratcheted up: Now a Doctor of Pharmacy degree is standard. Check out the Occupational Outlook Handbook's profile on Pharmacists at https://www.bls.gov/ooh/healthcare/pharmacists.htm as well as "Pros and Cons of Being a Pharmacist" (https://www.vfu.cz/informace-o-univerzite/organizacni-schema/jazyky/vyucovane-predmety/vyukove-materialy-faf-zs-2011-2012/week-ii_pros-and-cons-of-being-a-pharmacist.pdf).

>> **Genetic Counselor:** People are ever more aware that they're much affected by their genes. What do genetic counselors do? Here's an example: A husband and wife both suffer from severe depression. They're thinking about having a child. A genetic counselor helps them understand the odds that their child will suffer from depression, facilitates their decision whether to get pregnant, helps them make peace with their decision, and, possibly, persuades insurers to cover treatments. Check out www.nsgc.org/page/becomeageneticcounselor ("Interested in Becoming a Genetic Counselor?").

>> **Health Educator:** An ounce of prevention may not only be better than a pound of cure but also cost less. So insurers, employers, nonprofits, and government hire health educators to teach people such lessons as how to lose weight, stop substance abuse, manage diabetes, and improve their diets — as though people don't know that broccoli is good and supersize bacon-cheeseburgers are bad. Check out www.bls.gov/ooh/community-and-social-service/health-educators.htm#tab-1 ("Health Educators and Community Health Workers").

>> **Dietitian/Nutritionist:** People in this career are no longer located only in the hospital basement. Companies now hire dietitians to plan healthy meals to be served in their employee cafeterias, and to promote sensible eating habits. Government uses dietitians to plan such things as school menus. Food manufacturers and supermarket chains use dietitians to evaluate prepared foods and identify "interesting" low-calorie recipes, such as endive salad with radicchio and sun-dried tomatoes. (I think I'll pass.)

Health spas, weight-loss clinics, and prisons use dietitians to ensure that visitors eat a balanced diet. My daughter says that our fridge contains a different four basic food groups: snack foods, jams, condiments, and science experiments.

**REMEMBER**

The previously mentioned dietitian careers are growing, but most dietitians still remain busy with hypertension, diabetes, and obesity in hospitals, clinics, and their own private practices. Check out www.eatrightpro.org (Academy of Nutrition and Dietetics).

>> **Paramedic:** A person is having a heart attack. Or three teens are down after a gang war. Or bleeding passengers from a bad car accident are tangled in the wreckage. The paramedic is first on the scene to try to save the day. If you thrive on adrenaline but can stay calm and be gratified by your saves — and not burned out by your losses — this career can be rewarding.

Initial certification as an emergency medical technician (EMT) requires just 120 to 150 hours. Full paramedic status requires 1,200 to 1,800 hours and certifies you to do the stuff they do on *ER* or *Grey's Anatomy.* Many paramedics burn out, so after a few years they train to become a nurse or a physician assistant. Check out www.thebalance.com/emt-and-paramedic-526010 ("EMT and Paramedic") and www.naemt.org (National Association of Emergency Medical Technicians).

>> **Healthcare Administrator:** What's a healthcare system to do? Technology is advancing, healthcare laws are changing, HMOs are squeezing, the population is aging, hospitals are closing, stand-alone clinics are opening, home health-care is burgeoning, regulations are increasing, and the healthcare system is morphing. The answer: Hire more administrators to make sense of it all. A typical challenge: An emergency room administrator tries to balance the budget in the face of more parsimonious insurers and nonpaying patients. Check out explorehealthcareers.org/career/health-administration-management/health-administrator ("Health Administrator") and www.achca.org (American College of Health Care Administrators).

*Neat Niche:* **Public Health Administrator:** Working for a government agency, you may, for example, coordinate healthcare programs for the poor, direct a safe-sex campaign, or administer vaccination programs. Check out www.princetonreview.com/careers/131/public-health-administrator ("Public Health Administrator") and www.aspph.org (Association of Schools and Programs of Public Health).

>> **Surgical Technologist:** Simply earn a bachelor's degree, or sometimes quite a bit less, and you can play a role in the life-and-death drama of the operating room. The surgical technologist preps the patient (I remember having my chest shaved before my appendectomy — embarrassing!), provides emotional support (I needed that), and prepares the surgical tools and machines in the operating room. During the operation, when the surgeon on the medical TV shows calls, "Sutures! Clamp! Retractor!" the surgical technologist is the one who's being called. Check out explorehealthcareers.org/caree/allied-health-professions/surgical-technologist ("Surgical Technologist") and www.ast.org (Association of Surgical Technologists).

>> **Cardiovascular Technologist:** Heart disease is the number-one cause of death in the United States and the leading reason that men die five years earlier than women. The cardiology technologist plays a key role in diagnosing the problem before it's too late. The range of diagnostic tools has advanced well beyond the traditional electrocardiogram. Cardiovascular techs have a stressful job, especially if they're assisting in heart catheterization — an invasive but accurate test for heart blockages. It helps to have a knack for calming people down. Check out explorehealthcareers.org/career/allied-health-professions/cardiovascular-technologist-technician ("Cardiovascular Technologist/Technician").

>> **Athletic Team Trainer:** Suddenly a player goes down. You race onto the field and must make an instant evaluation: How bad? Do we need the stretcher? A doctor? You don't want to overreact — the player, the team, and the fans want to see the person play again, or at least walk off the field, but, of course, better safe than sorry. The athletic trainer's key skill is decision-making.

The athletic team trainer also has important decisions to make before and after the game. For example, an injured athlete is dying to play again. The doctor has given the okay, but as you tape up the player, you notice a wince. What should you do? Other interesting parts of the job: developing conditioning programs for the team and rehab regimens for injured athletes, and motivating them to implement those programs. And there's more. Michael O'Shea, a trainer at the University of Louisville, explains, "The trainer is a 24-hour father confessor."

Training jobs for sports teams are tough to land, but trainers are also employed at corporate fitness centers, sports medicine clinics, and hospitals.

For more on athletic training as a profession, check out www.nata.org (National Athletic Trainers' Association).

» **Massage Therapist:** This is among the few careers in which nearly every customer is extremely satisfied. The best massage therapists not only are great with their hands but also exude caring. After the short training time — a few hundred hours — you may work at a spa or massage studio; do corporate work; ply your trade for an athletic team, a hospital, or an assisted-care facility; or do home visits. The downsides? The money can be meager, you're on your feet all day doing physical work, and you run the risk of repetitive strain injury. Plus, some friends and relatives may look askance at this career. But providing pleasure and stress relief is not to be denigrated. Check out www.amtamassage.org/professional_development/starting.html ("Starting a Career in Massage Therapy: What You Need to Know") and www.amazon.com/Massage-Career-at-Your-Fingertips/dp/0964466252/ref=sr_1_sc_1?ie=UTF8&qid=1512495868&sr=8-1-spell&keywords=massafe+a+career+at+your+fingerttips (*Massage, A Career at Your Fingertips*, by Martin Ashley).

*Neat Niche:* **Employee Massage:** A massage therapist for employees is a stress-buster who gives in-chair (or on a massage table in the conference room) massages to employees. Massage — it's the new coffee break. How do you convince employers to hire you? You might say, "No perk costs less and increases morale more. And your company is seen as benevolent, which can boost sales and make it easier to attract quality employees." Some employers are "going halfsies:" They pay half, the employee pays half. It sounds like a deal to me, but at least one employer isn't at ease with onsite massage: The IRS office in San Jose offered onsite massage to its employees but had one problem: the sound. The IRS's Morgan Banks explains, "You can't have taxpayers coming into an audit hearing 'oohs' and 'ahhs.' Now we're looking for a room with thicker walls." Check out www.infinitemassage.com ("Infinite Massage").

# Making Business Your Business

There's a perhaps irresolvable debate about whether a person can do more good working in the private or public sector.

These days, it seems that business has acquired a bad reputation. Of course, the world of business includes some bad actors, and some firms are downright sleazy. But business includes many good ones. Indeed, business is responsible for making products available that previously were unimaginable: from the telephone and phonograph in the 19th century to the car, airplane, and computer in the 20th and onward to the smartphone- and solar-powered house of the 21st. And beyond cool items, think about the basics — your refrigerator, home, shoes, and even that apple you're munching on as you're reading this chapter. All were probably produced and made affordable by business.

If you come down on the private sector side of that debate, this section's for you.

>> **Accountant:** The stereotype is that the accountant finds security in the black-and-white truth of numbers and that accountants don't need people skills. Neither belief is quite right. At low levels of employment, such as your basic bookkeeper, those beliefs may be valid. But to rise, both nuance and people skills are important. Indeed, one of the field's more significant downsides is that you must impart, in a helpful way, bad news: "No, you can't deduct that. No, you calculated that fee incorrectly. No, that's inadequate documentation." "No, you haven't saved enough for retirement."

But for certified public accountants (CPAs) who have people skills, there's light at the end of the green-eyeshade tunnel. Employers promote good accountants to positions such as comptroller and chief financial officer, where they function more like financial physicians than bean-counting bookkeepers. They're involved in decisions about developing and marketing new products, how to best use existing capital and raise more, and even how to structure the organization. Accountants and their closely related finance specialists are an organization's antidote to decision-making based on gut feeling. And some accountants are hired by big-name consulting firms that have their roots in accounting — PwC, for example, as well as Deloitte, KPMG, and EY. Other accountants hang their own shingles, specializing in individual and small-business tax planning and return preparation, for example. Check out www.accounting.com/careers ("Careers in Accounting") and www.amazon.com/Need-Know-about-Accounting-Accountants/dp/1492283673 (*All You Need to Know about Accounting and Accountants: A Student's Guide to Careers in Accounting*, by Robert Louis Grottke).

*Neat Niche:* **Forensic Accountant:** Routine accounting will increasingly be done by computer. After all, millions of people already use TurboTax. But forensic accountants will be needed to sniff out malfeasance, from employee embezzlement to phony insurance claims to insider securities trading. Forensic accountants attempt to follow the money to the criminal. They may not only write reports but also testify in court. Many accountants enjoy this career's detective work.

Forensic accountants are hired by law firms, government agencies, and corporations. The Big Four firms alone hire many forensic accountants every year, and so does the FBI. Who knows? You may be asked to follow the money as it moves from religious charities to terrorist organizations, or to investigate the finances of Tommy the Blade's cement business. Check out www.acfe.com/forensic-accountant.aspx ("Forensic Accountant") and www.accounting.com/careers/forensic-accounting ("An Overview of Forensic Accounting").

*Neat Niche:* **International Accountant:** With business ever more global, companies need international accountants. Though internationally accepted accounting principles (GAAP) exist, myriad issues remain — for example, different countries' tax laws, auditing principles, and currency exchanges. Because of the nuance involved, it certainly helps if you're bilingual and bicultural. Check out www.monster.com/career-advice/article/global-accounting-careers ("Accounting Careers Go Global") and www.topaccountingdegrees.org/faq/what-careers-are-in-international-accounting ("What Careers Are in International Accounting?").

*Neat Niche:* **Environmental Accountant:** Government agencies and nonprofits are using more environmental accountants to argue that the environmental damages caused by a company outweigh the benefits. And many companies — especially utilities, manufacturers, and chemical companies — hire other environmental accountants to prove the opposite, or simply to help comply with the regulations. CPAs who also are engineers are in particular demand. Check out www.environmentalscience.org/career/environmental-accountant ("What Is an Environmental Accountant?") and www.accountingweb.com/aa/auditing/what-is-environmental-accounting ("What Is Environmental Accounting?").

*Neat Niche:* **Business Valuator:** Every day, companies merge or are acquired. Who knows? Maybe eventually a grand total of only one company will exist. Every merger and acquisition requires someone to figure out the value of the company being merged or acquired, and those high stakes mean serious dollars for the valuator. Valuators are also used whenever wealthy people divorce or die, to determine the value of a spouse's business. Check out the National Association of Certified Valuators and Analysts at www.nacva.com

>> **Commercial Banker:** These are traditional bankers, who may approve loans and safeguard the bank's assets. But banks no longer are limited to offering only loans, checking accounts, and savings accounts. They can sell stocks, bonds, insurance, estate and trust products, and video games. (Well, not video games.) Even if cryptocurrencies like Bitcoin gain wider use, banks are now investing resources in preparing to be players in that space.

Entry-level jobs such as personal banker may require only a bachelor's degree, but having an MBA helps. The good news is that the term "banker's hours," referring to relatively short ones, still may apply. That's in contrast with the investment banker, who may well invest in 70-hour workweeks but also make more money. In any case, commercial bankers don't starve. Check out `www.investopedia.com/articles/professionals/091615/career-advice-investment-banking-vscommercial-banking.asp` ("Investment Banking vs. Commercial Banking").

>> **Investment Banker:** Business's growth hormone is money. A common investment banker's assignment is to get money on the best terms. Here's how investment bankers work: A growing private company needs more money. Should it go public? Acquire private equity funding? Spin off a division? Get bought out? You do complex calculations to help the company come up with answers. Say that the company decides to go public and issue stock. You attempt to price it right. Then you hand off the project to a different kind of investment banker — a salesperson — who attempts to convince banks, mutual fund managers, and pension fund managers to buy your stock or bond offering. To sell requires more than a slick tongue, though that certainly helps.

Most investment bankers are first hired with only a bachelor's degree (in any field, as long as it's from a designer-label college at which you earned good grades). Your first job is usually as an analyst, a numbers-cruncher who typically determines assets' value. Before making the big bucks, you usually need an MBA and sophisticated sales skills. A couple of years as an investment banking analyst can be the ticket, perhaps company-paid, to top-name MBA programs. But I'm talking full years. In her book *The Fast Track*, Mariam Naficy writes, "The amount you'll work in investment banking cannot be overstated. One analyst reported that he bought 50 pairs of underwear because he had no time to do laundry."

Many people, thanks in part to movies like *The Wolf of Wall Street* and books like *Liar's Poker*, believe that investment bankers do nothing that's good for the world. In fact, these bankers' job is to help companies raise money so that they can bring a better product to market. Even the media-reviled investment banker Michael Milken, by raising money for MCI as an investment banker, was central to making the telecommunications industry more competitive, and in turn lowering everyone's phone bills. Another example: You wouldn't be able to buy a Tesla if it weren't for investment bankers. They raised $738 million to jump-start that innovative car manufacturer.

The most sought-after investment banking jobs are at "bulge bracket" firms: Goldman Sachs, Bank of America/Merrill Lynch, Citigroup, JP Morgan Chase, and Morgan Stanley, though boutique firms exist that specialize in an industry or a product. Players include Evercore, Moelis, and Lazard. Also, some traditional banks do investment banking. Check out www.careers-in-finance.com/ib.htm ("Careers in Investment Banking") and www.idealsvdr.com/blog/is-investment-banking-really-that-bad ("The Good, Bad, and Ugly of Investment Banking").

>> **Venture Capitalist:** On behalf of a pension fund, a foundation, a bank, an insurance company, or individuals, a VC looks for businesses to invest in — most often, small, fast-growing software or biotech firms, but occasionally low-tech ideas such as retail or restaurants. Many proposals show up unsolicited by fund-seekers eager for a one-on-one meeting or just an invitation to an event at which they can pitch an audience of VCs and other would-be investors.

Though VCs outsource technical evaluation, they must be able to assess businesses' viability and technical quality. VCs also need a nose for judging people — any business succeeds or fails as much on its people as on its product. After VCs are convinced that a business is worth investing in, they make much more money if they can sell shares to sophisticated investors. After funding is obtained, VCs may take a role in guiding the business's development.

Most VCs either work for a VC firm or join one of the banks or companies, such as Google and Microsoft, that have in-house VC arms. As you might guess, this is not a career for an inexperienced person. The most viable VC is often an engineer or VC-track graduate from a designer-label college, like Harvard or Stanford, who rose to become the CEO of one or more tech-centric companies. Check out www.cbinsights.com/research/venture-capital-jobs ("How to Get a Job in Venture Capital: 45 VCs Offer Advice on Getting into the Game").

>> **Business Developer:** Though *biz dev* is often used to describe the job of anyone from product developer to salesperson, I'm referring here to the kind of business developer who's a dealmaker. Working for a company, this person searches out and negotiates joint ventures, licensing agreements, mergers, and acquisitions. For example, Company A makes an energy drink, and Company B has a greener, cheaper can. The business developer arranges to have Company A license the can technology or perhaps acquire or merge with Company B. Business development requires an unusual combination of skills: valuation, quick learning, reasoning, and, yes, sales. Check out www.wetfeet.com/articles/career-overview-business-development ("Business Development").

*Neat Niche:* **Business Broker:** As small-business-owning baby boomers retire, they look to sell their companies. Meanwhile, many people want to buy — people who couldn't find a well-paying job and so are looking to own their own businesses, for example. The business broker brings them together. It's an option for sales-oriented people with accounting and general business analysis skills. But buying and selling a business usually isn't just about cash flow; it's about hopes and dreams, sometimes unfulfilled. So an underdiscussed key to being a successful business broker is empathy. Check out businessbrokeragepress. com/become-a-business-broker ("Become a Business Broker").

» **Management Consultant:** Your job is to solve problems that are too tough for an organization to solve by itself. Examples: A firm wants to start selling in Asia, a nonprofit needs a better system for managing the information flow, or a start-up has a great idea — but now what?

Yes, to address such problems, you need top analytical skills, but you also must be persuasive and tactful — even though you're a 20-something with little real-life work experience, you're telling a veteran what to do. You also must be willing to work long hours. The typical management consultant for a major firm works 50 to 80 hours a week and travels half the time.

Management consulting is a good career for learning about the business world, to have an impact on a company while you're still in your 20s, and to hang around with smart (and well-paid) people. However, for a decent shot at being hired by a top consulting firm, such as McKinsey, Boston Consulting Group, Bain, PwC, EY, Deloitte, or KPMG, you must have good grades from a designer-label college and make a great impression in tough interviews. Alternatives include small management consulting firms and self-employment.

In fairness, many insiders feel that management consulting provides poor value for the substantial prices charged. The joke is, "A management consultant steals your watch to tell you what time it is."

For more on management consulting, check out 80000hours.org/career-guide/reports/management-consulting ("Management Consulting").

*Neat Niche:* **Corporate Intelligence Officer:** An article in *Working Woman* magazine reassures people who are considering this career: "No need for a cloak or dagger." Corporate intelligence staffers comb through perfectly legitimate sources of information — websites, competitors' sales materials, speeches, credit reports, databases, and interviews — for the goods on competitors. In addition, you may have to be good at finding unpublished information, which means getting people to trust you. Check out www.scip. org (Strategic and Competitive Intelligence Professionals) and www.amazon. com/Business-Competitive-Analysis-Effective-Application/ dp/0133086402 (*Business and Competitive Analysis: Effective Application of New and Classic Methods*, by Craig S. Fleisher and Babette E. Bensoussan).

» **Marketer:** Your company wants to introduce a product — a virtually augmented (VA) teen-girl-oriented game, for example. You review the competition to identify a gap in the market (perhaps no good such game exists with lower-middle-class protagonists and settings). Then, with that general product in mind, you consult the analytics from sites that are frequented by the game's target market — Instagram, for example — to develop marketing messages that will most appeal. Based on your inferences, you conduct surveys and focus groups to confirm or refute your ideas as well as to identify game features that would attract your target market. In light of all that, you help select packaging, a marketing message, and wise marketing channels — perhaps those social media sites, targeted Facebook ads, print magazines, point-of-purchase displays in shopping malls' game stores, or even high schools' websites.

Demand is great for marketers with technical backgrounds capable of developing, for example, a marketing plan for an Internet of Things (IoT) product such as a remote biosensor. That's easier if you're an engineer.

For more on being a marketer, check out www.thebalance.com/exploring-careers-in-marketing-2294887 ("5 Marketing Careers You Should Explore"), www.amazon.com/dp/B00NH0XZR0?psc=1 (*SEO 2018: Learn Search Engine Optimization with Smart Internet Marketing Strategies,* by Adam Clarke), www.amazon.com/All-Marketers-are-Liars-Works/dp/1591845335/ref=sr_1_sc_1?ie=UTF8&qid=1512525275&sr=8-1-spell&keywords=all+marketeres+are+liars (*All Marketers Are Liars*, by Seth Godin), and www.psychologytoday.com/blog/how-do-life/201701/marketing-is-evil ("Marketing Is Evil").

*Neat Niche:* **Marketing Researcher:** You design surveys and focus groups. Then you analyze results regarding, for example, products, political issues, or societal problems. In addition to in-house corporate or nonprofit marketing departments, you can work for politicians or for independent polling organizations such as Gallup or Harris. Pollsters have great power — a subtle change of wording can dramatically change a poll's results. The question "Would you eat corn that came from seeds specially bred to produce sweeter corn?" will yield quite a different result than "Are you concerned about eating genetically modified corn?" Check out www.insightsassociation.org/career-guide ("Career Guide to the Survey, Opinion, & Marketing Research Industry").

*Neat Niche:* **Social Marketer:** The same techniques that Madison Avenue uses to convince you to buy a brand of cigarettes, alcohol, or marijuana, social marketers use to get you to stop using them. For example, the U.S. government spends a fortune every year on commercials, mainly to spread anti-substance-abuse messages. It's the flip side of product marketing: You're trying to build market share of *non*-use. Of course, social marketing can also be used to encourage use. For example, in high-risk communities, a social

marketing initiative might encourage safer-sex practices. Check out
en.wikipedia.org/wiki/Social_marketing ("Social Marketing") and
www.amazon.com/Social-Marketing-Philip-Kotler/dp/0029184614
(*Social Marketing: Strategies for Changing Public Behavior*, by Philip Kotler).

» **Supply Chain Manager, Purchasing Specialist:** How'd you like to get paid for
shopping? Well, it's not quite like at the mall. Purchasing specialists do the
shopping for companies and government agencies. Of course, it doesn't hurt to
have a good instinct for when it is and isn't worth pursuing a bargain, but this job
has rapidly gone technological. Supply chain software helps ensure that your
employer gets what's needed when it's needed instead of, as in the old way,
leaving lots of costly inventory sitting in a warehouse. Demand is strong for
people graduating from supply chain management programs, such as the ones
at Arizona State and Michigan State University, but any bachelor's degree plus an
enthusiastic interest in purchasing may be enough to get your foot in the door.
Check out www.investopedia.com/terms/s/scm.asp ("Supply Chain
Management") and www.ism.ws (Institute for Supply Management).

*Neat Niche*: **Business Equipment Broker/Lessor:** Many people start businesses,
and many people end them. Business equipment brokers profit from both. They
lease to new businesses and buy used equipment from companies going bust.
And they handle upgrades. As technology advances ever faster, rather than buy,
many businesses prefer to lease the latest model and then, in a few years, lease
the next-generation one. Check out businessbrokeragepress.com/become-
a-business-broker ("Become a Business Broker").

» **Risk Manager:** Companies face many risks: For example, is the company's
manufacturing operation in China safe for workers and are the products of
consistently good-enough quality? If not, how much money should be spent to
cut the risk to an acceptable limit? And, should that amount be spent on
making modest improvements in the existing factory, building a new one, or
outsourcing manufacturing to a higher-quality manufacturer? Another
example: The company's new cardiac stent has passed FDA scrutiny, but,
given the human and fiscal cost of its failing, should the company conduct
additional tests, restrict its use to low-risk patients, or perhaps buy a bigger
insurance policy on it? Of course, each such decision must consider the
opportunity cost: No company has unlimited resources, so the amount spent
to reduce Risk A makes money unavailable to control Risk B or, for example,
to fund the development of an even better cardiac stent. Check out en.
wikipedia.org/wiki/Risk_management ("Risk Management").

*Neat Niche:* **Credit Risk Manager:** This isn't a sexy career, but it's high-paying
and in demand. Credit risk managers work for organizations that extend
credit: credit card companies and other corporations, universities, even
government agencies. Your job is to figure out who should get credit and how
much. Check out www.nacm.org (National Association of Credit Management).

>> **College Financial Aid Officer:** At most colleges, more than half the students apply for financial aid. With only so much money available, your job is to distribute it equitably and to mollify or negotiate with students who get less than they had hoped. It's a nice job because it can feel good to support students in need, there are sizable breathing periods between crunch times, you need only a bachelor's degree, and you get to work on a college campus — a pleasant work environment. Check out www.nasfaa.org (National Association of Student Financial Aid Administrators).

# Other STEM + People or Word Careers

Of course, many careers other than the ones I've described in this chapter require STEM plus people skills or word skills. Here are a few that I want to bring to your attention:

>> **Terrorism Expert:** Alas, terrorism is likely to continue providing plenty of job and consulting openings. Of course, the term *terrorism expert* includes many specialties. For example, one might focus on state, nonstate, or lone wolf actors. Or a person could be an expert on conventional, biological, chemical, cyber, nuclear, or radiological ("dirty nuke") attacks. Others could specialize in protecting the food or water supply, public venues (arenas or trains, for example), port security, or corporate or community preparedness.

The federal government hires the most terrorism experts, but states, cities, and midsize to large companies also hire them. Also, some jobs may be available at disaster-related nonprofit organizations such as the Red Cross. Check out www.thebalance.com/careers-in-counter-terrorism-4020787 ("Careers in Counter-Terrorism").

*Neat Niche:* **Behavior Change Expert:** It's impossible to foil all attacks. Remember that it doesn't require even a safe house to spawn terrorism. One terrorism "marketer" can, on a phone, simply post messages on social media to inspire lone wolves. So rather than take a purely information-gathering and technical approach to quell terrorism, future efforts will likely focus on attempting to understand and work with terrorist groups and individuals so that they're less likely to want to be violent. If you're interested in such a career, search on such terms as *consultant ISIS, terrorist psychology,* and *expert lone wolves.*

*Neat Niche:* **Biological Weapons Deterrence Specialist:** Biological weapons may be more dangerous even than nuclear weapons. An airborne-communicable biovirus or *Bacillus* released on just a single subway car could kill thousands, or maybe even millions of people.

And bioweapons are far more portable than nuclear weapons — enough airborne-communicable bioviruses to commit mass murder could fit in a vial. The National Academy of Sciences worries even more about custom-created bioweapons — there isn't time to develop an antidote every time a new one is created. The need to hire deterrence experts is obvious, and the federal budget for it has grown. For the unusually intelligent, scientifically trained but humanly attuned person, this career could enable you to save many lives. Check out en.wikipedia.org/wiki/Biological_warfare.

» **Program Evaluator:** In the spirit of full disclosure, let me admit that I'm biased toward this career. My PhD is in this field, and I think it's an underdiscussed career.

"You're judgmental!" That's usually a criticism, but in this profession, you're paid to be judgmental. Here's a typical scenario: You're hired to evaluate a school district's new reading program, so you interview students and teachers, compare test scores with a control group, and write and orally present a report of your findings. Being an evaluator is fun because you get to check out lots of innovative programs, see what works and what doesn't, and make recommendations for improvement.

The bad part is that many program sponsors don't really want your input; they hire you mainly to meet a government requirement. After all, few people like to be evaluated, especially negatively. Though a master's or doctorate degree filled with statistics courses is usually the profession's admission ticket, program evaluators often use just the statistics they learn in an introductory statistics course. If needed, advanced methods are outsourced to a statistician. What's most required is the ability to quickly size up what's happening in a program based on data, observation, and human interaction. Also required is the ability to engender the program's staff and clients' confidence — crucial to obtaining valid information. Check out www.eval.org (American Evaluation Association) and www.amazon.com/Program-Evaluation-Practice-Concepts-Discussion/dp/1118345827/ref=sr_1_sc_1?ie=UTF8&qid=1512526725&sr=8-1-spell&keywords=program+evaluatiom+in+practce (*Program Evaluation in Practice: Core Concepts and Examples for Discussion and Analysis,* by Dean T. Spaulding).

*Neat Niche:* **Foundation Program Officer:** In this sought-after career, you help a corporate or personal foundation develop requests for proposals to solve a social ill, review the proposals, decide which to fund, and supervise their implementation — that means providing support and ideas, and perhaps evaluating their effectiveness. You may write reports, present to the foundation's leaders, and even raise more money for the foundation. Check out www.cof.org (Council on Foundations).

» **School Technology Coach:** Though most schools are filled with computers and many kids have smartphones or laptops, these items are insufficiently integrated into the curriculum. A main reason is that many teachers lack the knowledge or motivation to use them well. Enter the school technology coach: a combination of teacher trainer and troubleshooter, with a knack for figuring out how to motivate teachers to use those ever more powerful learning tools. Check out www.edweek.org/ew/articles/2016/06/09/ed-tech-coaches-becoming-steadier-fixture-in-classrooms.html ("Ed-Tech Coaches Becoming Steadier Fixture in Classrooms") and www.iste.org (International Society for Technology in Education).

# Chapter **8**

# Hands-On Careers

T rue, many formerly hands-on careers are becoming automated, but this chapter is proof that many remain and are likely to remain.

**TIP**

Though the careers described in this chapter have you working primarily with your hands, as with many careers in this book, you'll usually do better if you have also developed some people skills and some emotional intelligence (see Chapter 19) so that you can communicate effectively with the people you're building or fixing things for.

## Mainly Mechanical

Here are some possible careers in case you're the install-it-or-fix-it type:

>> **Computer Technician:** As products become ever more computerized — from PET scanners to Amazon's Echo — ever more people are needed to repair them. You may be hired by a company's IT department, a computer support firm, or a government agency to do such tasks as answer user questions and troubleshoot — perhaps by responding to frustrated computer users who fear that they've lost their data, to take one common example. You'll also install and customize software, and you may also be responsible for managing the network. Or you might work in-house for a computer-centric

product's manufacturer. This job is in demand — plus, when you fix their mission-critical problem, they'll love you. For more info, check out "Computer Technician" at www.techopedia.com/definition/13420/computer-technician.

*Neat Niche:* **Robotics Technologist:** Your job is to build, install, maintain, and repair robots. And they're ever more widely used. Not long ago, robots mainly welded cars and elevated highway beams. Today, they assist with hip replacement surgery, build cars, climb and paint rusty utility towers, and install space stations. One perhaps surprising job requirement: the ability to lift 50 pounds. (Robots haven't yet been to Weight Watchers.) Check out "Robotics Technicians" (www.cacareerzone.org/profile/17-3024.01) and "Robotics Online Beginner's Guide: Helpful Resources for People Just Starting Out in Robotics" (www.robotics.org/Beginners-Guide.)

*Neat Niche:* **Biomedical Equipment Technician:** This high-tech repair niche pays well because when the machine is broken, it must be fixed perfectly and fast — a patient on a heart-lung machine can't wait long. A calm personality helps. Your job may also include training medical professionals on using the equipment. Check out "Biomedical Equipment Technician" at portals.clevelandclinic.org/healthscienceseducation/ExploreaCareer/CareerOptions/BiomedicalEquipmentTechnicianBMET/tabid/7703/Default.aspx and "An Introduction to the Biomedical Technician Training Program at The Wistar Institute" (www.youtube.com/watch?v=CoepT3XC1G4).

>> **Computer Chip Layout Designer:** This job essentially requires you to fit New York City onto a postage stamp. It sounds harder than it is. But like a chip — a potato chip — it's addictive. You can find yourself working 24 hours straight because, "I'm getting it. I'm getting it. It's almost done." You take engineer's specs for the 10,000-device chip and feed that information into a computer program that lays it out for you. The computer layout usually has errors that you have to fix by hand. That's where the art comes in. Your job is to cram those devices in as tightly as possible and still get the chip to work. Check out "Integrated Circuit Layout Designer" at dot-job-descriptions.careerplanner.com/INTEGRATED-CIRCUIT-LAYOUT-DESIGNER.cfm and *IC Layout Basics: A Practical Guide,* by Christopher Saint and Judy Saint (www.amazon.com/IC-Layout-Basics-Practical-Guide/dp/0071386254).

>> **Vehicle Mechanic:** Get that image of a grease-covered dude out of your head. Today's automotive technician may spend almost as much time with a computer as with a wrench. Newer cars are heavily computer controlled, as is the equipment used to diagnose problems. If you have the ability to understand a complicated repair manual and a nose for diagnosing what's wrong, this is a better career than it used to be. More good news: Many car mechanics snag their first professional job with no training other than having played around with their own cars. New opportunities are available for women because the work has become more automated, and physical strength is

less important. Check out "Automotive Service Technicians and Mechanics" at www.bls.gov/ooh/installation-maintenance-and-repair/automotive-service-technicians-and-mechanics.htm.

*Neat Niche:* **Diesel Mechanic:** These mechanics work on not only truck engines but also trains, farm equipment, and generators. Tightened pollution regulations have helped create many more jobs for diesel mechanics. Check out "5 Top Jobs to Pursue After Diesel Mechanic Training" at www.auto.edu/blog/5-top-jobs-to-pursue-after-diesel-mechanic-training.

» **Electrician:** Our ever more electrified lives demand electricians. They may install new lines for voice or data in our homes or businesses; add smart home systems that automate lighting, air conditioning, and security; expand a home from 110 volt to 220; troubleshoot the cause of those blown circuit breakers; install lighting systems for businesses and cities; or build electrical systems from scratch in new residences, businesses, and hospitals.

Surprisingly, electricians are seriously injured by electricity at only half the rate of the general population. Just don't be color-blind: Many electrical wires are color-coded.

Training is usually a 4- or 5-year apprenticeship, but that investment can pay off. Everyone's lives seem to get more and more technology driven, so this offshore-proof career will likely remain <ahem> current. Check out "Electrician" at www.princetonreview.com/careers/59/electrician and "What Can You Expect from a Job as an Electrician?" at www.careerbuilder.com/advice/what-can-you-expect-from-a-job-as-an-electrician.

*Neat Niche:* **Avionics Technician:** In a $20 million airplane, $16 million is avionics (electronic equipment.) Today's airplanes are flying computers. That means plenty of avionics to fix, and plenty to upgrade. Because electronics are always getting better, many people are retrofitting — much cheaper than buying a new plane. Avionics technology is a career for tinkerers who read publications such as *Popular Mechanics* and who, of course, like airplanes. Check out "Aircraft and Avionics Equipment Mechanics and Technicians" at www.bls.gov/ooh/installation-maintenance-and-repair/aircraft-and-avionics-equipment-mechanics-and-technicians.htm-tab-1.

» **Alternative Energy Technician:** The dominant work in this field is as a solar energy technician. The good news about this career is that solar continues to be, well, hot, and some government job retraining programs are paying for people to acquire the necessary training.

I should mention, though, that the last few of my clients who tried to land jobs as solar installers insist that the job market is saturated. Yes, inferring the job market from that small sample could be invalid, but sometimes government-provided data isn't as current as is the word on the street. As usual, it helps to bring an extra something to the table: the ability to handle challenging installations, to close sales, or to manage other workers and budgets.

Another downside of this job is its working conditions. Roof work can be dangerous, and you may be working in attics, which may be cramped and/or hot. For hands-on types for whom environmentalism is central, however, there may be no sunnier option. Check out "These Two Industries Are Major Job Generators" at www.monster.com/career-advice/article/tech-alternative-energy-wind-solar-jobs-0117.

*Neat Niche:* **Wind Turbine Technician:** This career will get you in shape. You climb wind turbine towers a few times a day and then perhaps wrestle with blades and such. Of course, there's demand in windy Midwestern states and in environment-focused California, but, in addition, offshore wind farms are slated to be operational within a few years.

**REMEMBER**

You can train with a short course provided by a wind turbine company such as Airstreams Renewables, Inc., or a 9-month to 2-year program at a community college. The early salary isn't great, but when you've gained expertise in industrial hydraulics and in electronic and systems troubleshooting, your pay will blow upward. Check out "A Day in the Life of a Wind Turbine Technician" at www.windpowerengineering.com/featured/day-life-wind-tech. (Read the comments as well as the article.)

*Neat Niche:* **Nuclear Reactor Operator:** This is a contrarian career choice because it's politically out of favor relative to solar and wind and because some career-seekers fear radiation exposure, especially in a disaster. But the probabilities are high that you'll stay safe and that nuclear energy will burgeon. Nuclear is the only renewable source that's capable of creating unlimited energy with no carbon footprint. And you're operating and moderating dials in a comfortable setting rather than struggling with heavy equipment on top of roofs or wind towers. Plus, it's a career that pays well yet doesn't require a college degree. Check out "Reactor Operators: What It Takes To Do This Important Job" at public-blog.nrc-gateway.gov/2012/11/14/reactor-operators-what-it-takes-to-do-this-important-job.

» **Elevator Installer and Repairer:** This is among the better-paying trades. Alas, part of the reason is that you spend much time in cramped, high elevator shafts, although you may also work on escalators and moving walkways. But this career is recession resistant; that is, it has few <ahem> ups and downs. Check out "Elevator Installers and Repairers" at www.bls.gov/ooh/construction-and-extraction/elevator-installers-and-repairers.htm.

» **Industrial Mechanic:** Few people without a college degree picture themselves as crucial to the operation of a megacorporation, yet industrial mechanics are. They install and repair heavy, so-called *stationary* equipment — conveying systems, production machinery, and packaging equipment, for example. And it can be rewarding work — it can feel good to be called on to figure out what's wrong and, under time pressure, solve a problem that affects an entire plant's operation.

You're also called in whenever a new piece of million-dollar heavy machinery is delivered. You're there to unload, inspect, and move it into position. That can mean deciding which ropes, cables, and hoists to use. It often means constructing special wood or metal foundations and using lasers to narrow the accuracy to the millimeter. Most industrial mechanics learn as apprentices or in community college programs. It's a largely unionized field, so the pay is good. Check out "Industrial Machinery Mechanic" at www.bls.gov/ooh/installation-maintenance-and-repair/industrial-machinery-mechanics-and-maintenance-workers-and-millwrights.htm-tab-1.

>> **Machinist:** Machinists make precision metal parts for everything from Harleys to Hoovers and from garbage disposals to artificial limbs. If your high school math was solid and you're detail oriented, you may be hirable with just a high school diploma and short training period. Though, yes, much manufacturing has gone overseas, the United States still has a shortage of precision machinists. For you, it could be a career to "die" for. Check out the Precision Machined Products Association site at www.pmpa.org/careers/overview.

>> **Locksmith:** This is the only career in which you don't get arrested for picking locks. It's one of the better hands-on, physically undemanding occupations — a short training period and many grateful customers. Just think of all those people locked out of their homes or cars, and companies and homeowners who need to keep the bad guys out. As security threats increase, the demand for high-tech entry systems grows. So locksmiths may install and troubleshoot closed-circuit TV and other computer-controlled computer systems. Locksmiths serving commercial customers have a better chance of earning a good living. Check out the Associated Locksmiths of America site at www.aloa.org and *The Complete Book of Locks and Locksmithing,* by Bill Phillips (www.amazon.com/Complete-Book-Locks-Locksmithing-Seventh/dp/1259834689.

>> **Irrigation Technician:** Nearly every homeowner, farmer, park, or golf course owner needs an irrigation system. And if they already have one, it may need to be fixed or upgraded. Irrigation technician is a good career for someone who likes a combination of indoors and outdoors, and business and environmentalism. Environmentalism? Yup, because irrigation systems save water, and fertilizing through the irrigation system allows less chemical fertilizer to be used. Check out "What Does an Irrigation Technician do?" at www.sokanu.com/careers/irrigation-technician.

>> **Golf Course Superintendent:** Where do we put that new bunker? How do we schedule the groundskeepers? What's the best way to keep those greens perfect without using too much water or too many chemicals? To answer these questions, every golf course has a superintendent. This is another career that doesn't require a bachelor's degree. Though the training period is short, you probably need to pay your dues by working on a golf course maintenance crew. Check out "Preparing for a Career as a Golf Course Superintendent" at www.gcsaa.org/career/students/pursuing-a-career.

# Air, Land, and Sea

The careers described in this section span the earth's layers: from pilot to geographer to diver:

**TIP**

>> **Pilot:** I've often wondered whether this career is boring. After all, it seems that you're basically just a bus driver whose bus has wings. Yet many people aspire to be pilots. I guess it's the takeoff, landing, aerial view, prestige, good pay — and exotic travel.

Most pilots like their careers, but how to land a job? Those plum commercial airline jobs mainly go to former military pilots and to others with thousands of air hours and certifications from an FAA-certified training school. The good news is that many under-the-radar pilot jobs exist. And they may be more interesting than long-distance commercial flights on which you spend hours staring at instruments that are actually flying the plane, and as a reward for all that staring, you get jet lag.

Some under-the-radar piloting jobs include small planes fractionally owned by individuals and companies, corporate and individual charter flights, rescues of injured people, aerial advertising, fish spotting, flight instructing, criminal tracking, burials at sea, drops of aerodynamically packaged seedlings for reforestation, helicopter-based radio/TV traffic reports, emergency-parts delivery, and wilderness patrol. Oil and electric companies also have pilots fly over pipelines and electrical lines to check for leaks. Check out "The Truth About the Profession" at http://thetruthabouttheprofession.weebly.com/typical-career-paths.html as well as the Flight Info message board at https://forums.flightinfo.com/.

>> **Harbor Pilot:** This is a sailor's job that doesn't require long stints away from home. Your job is to dock ships or take them — the world's largest moveable manmade objects — out to sea. You start as a decently paid deck hand or engineer and move up to captain. If you're talented and a good networker, you may get to be a harbor pilot and earn a salary that can exceed $300,000 a year.

Why does this job pay so much? Because even most experienced sea captains lack the skills to navigate all sorts of vessels through the shallow, tricky port waters. And sometimes, after steering the ship to sea, the harbor pilot must climb down from the ship and into a small boat to get back to shore — which can be dangerous.

The job market for the top-paying jobs is tight as a jib, but jobs that pay a middle-class salary are more available: Fear of oil spills has evoked regulations that require most large ships to be towed into dock, often by a tug, but sometimes simply by advising the ship captain. Some tug operators and aspiring harbor pilots get their experience by working on party or fishing boats or by attending a 2-year maritime program, such as the one at the National Maritime Academy or one of the five state maritime academies — California, Maine, Massachusetts, New York, and Texas. Check out "Harbor Pilots Reap High Rewards for Dangerous Job" at www.npr.org/2012/03/21/149091141/harbor-pilots-reap-high-rewards-for-dangerous-job.

>> **Railroad Engineer:** Were you the kid who always liked to play with model trains? After a short training period and probably a stint in the railyard, you can be driving a locomotive and transporting people and the nation's goods. During your railyard work, you're paying your dues: You must work in all sorts of weather and all hours of the day, and after you're an engineer, you're away from home a lot. But for that Lionel kid, there may not be much better than living on and around trains. Check out "What Does a Railroad Engineer Do?" at learn.org/articles/What_Does_a_Railroad_Engineer_Do.html and "Railroad Jobs" at www.aar.org/Pages/Careers.aspx.

>> **Geographer:** Michael Jordan was a geography major. Can you just imagine him debating: "Hmm, should I be a geographer or a pro basketball player?" Well, assuming that you have no pro basketball potential, geography offers some good careers. First, to correct a common misconception, most geographers aren't mapmakers, who are officially called *cartographers*.

Rather, most geographers divide into two categories: Physical geographers study the earth, from Afghani terrain to climate change. Human geographers might study a natural or terrorist-caused disaster's impact on a locale's culture or economy. Or their project might be to recommend where Trader Joe's should open more stores or to help the government decide where to allow economic development.

Many geographers have a title other than geographer, but whatever the title, you'll be in good company: Mother Teresa started out as a geography teacher.

Check out "Careers and Professional Development Resources" at www.aag.org/galleries/jobs-careers-files/Careers_resources_overview_02192013.pdf.

*Neat Niche:* **Geospatial Analyst:** A landfill needs to be located wherever it imposes the least risk. A farmer or commodities trader is trying to assess whether a crop is likely to be bumper. Firefighters are developing a plan for putting out a rash of forest fires. The military is attempting to map out a strategy for attacking a country that's threatening to use nuclear weapons against another country. Geospatial analysts make recommendations based on analyzing data from remote sensors, GIS and GPS systems, as well as satellite and even old-school aerial photographs. Check out "What Does a Geospatial Information Scientist Do?" at www.sokanu.com/careers/geospatial-information-scientist.

>> **Surveyor:** Exactly where should each square foot of that new light-rail system go? Where should the fence between homeowners be located? Where is that oil spill moving? How does a cartographer obtain the information needed to create an underwater map? (Only 5 percent of oceans have been mapped, so there's demand.) Surveyors figure these things out. They may still use the old-fashioned theodolites on tripods, but they now often use satellite-based geographic information systems, remote sensors, and other technology. Surveying is a career for someone without a college degree but who is comfortable around algebra and geometry, likes to learn as an apprentice, and wants an outdoor career with some status. The director of California's state apprenticeship programs told me that, of the hundreds of apprentice-able careers, he considers surveying the best. Check out "All About Surveying" at www.beasurveyor.com.

>> **Firefighter:** Most firefighters like their jobs. Disadvantages such as irregular hours, frequently breathing noxious fire fumes, and living in a firehouse are usually outweighed by the exciting, rewarding work of responding to emergencies and helping people. Most firefighters spend more time dealing with medical rescues than saving people from a burning building. Check out "Four Reasons You Shouldn't Become a Firefighter" at www.firerescue1.com/fire-career/articles/2165186-4-reasons-you-shouldnt-become-a-firefighter/ and *The Fire Inside: Firefighters Talk About Their Lives*, edited by Steve Delsohn (www.amazon.com/Fire-Inside-Firefighters-About-Their/dp/0060176652).

>> **Commercial Diver:** I wish I could tell you that the reality matches the stereotype: gliding through glistening tropical waters, harvesting pearls. Fact is, 90 percent of divers are construction workers for whom diving is just a mode of transportation to the job site — except that there's the added challenge of working under the sea, so you can't run down to Home Depot to get a part. Before you take the plunge (I couldn't resist), do remember that a typical job is working in the Gulf of Mexico welding leaky pipes in an oil rig. That said, commercial diving has pluses: It's among the few outdoor careers that doesn't require a college education, and, after just a few years on the job, you can earn six figures for a 9-month work year. Engineers can make more. You get to travel all over the world — often on a moment's notice. And there are prized neat niches: research divers who assist marine biologists, journalist divers who write articles and take pictures for websites and books, and police divers who look for guys who have been fitted with cement shoes. Check out "Getting In Deep: Considering a Career as a Commercial Diver" at dtmag.com/thelibrary/getting-in-deep-considering-a-career-in-commercial-diving.

# Medical mechanics.

Health care depends not only on medical providers and administrators, but also on people to install, run, service, and repair the machines that contribute to quality health care.

>> **Medical Imaging Technician:** You may do basic X-rays, fluoroscopes, sonograms, or CAT scans as well as higher-resolution MRI, PET, and CT scans, which no doubt will yield to next-generation imaging, in which resolutions of just a few nanometers will be possible. That will make imaging an ever more attractive diagnostic option — imaging is a lot cheaper than invasive testing. So the need for imaging technicians should grow. What does it take to do it well? Yes, pass the science courses, but you must also be meticulous (and sometimes physically strong) in positioning patients and in using the imaging equipment. Plus, you need the ability to keep patients calm and still while you say "Cheese." Check out "What Are a Medical Imaging Tech's Duties and Responsibilities?" at careertrend.com/medical-imaging-techs-duties-responsibilities-32292.html.

*Neat Niche:* **Sonographer:** Is it a boy or a girl? Commonly known as *ultrasound technologists,* sonographers perform sonograms to not only answer that question but also assess knee damage and cardiovascular blockage — all non-invasively and without radiation. Typical training is a 1- or 2-year community college program. Check out the Society of Diagnostic Medical Sonography's Careers page at www.sdms.org/resources/careers.

>> **Electro-Neurodiagnostic Technician (formerly EEG Technician):** The END tech monitors brain waves. Why would you want to do that? In surgery, brain waves indicate how well the anesthesia is working. In a sleep clinic, brain waves help figure out what's causing a person's insomnia. Doctors use EEGs to determine how well a medication is helping an epileptic patient. Despite its important healthcare role, training is short, perhaps at a community college or even on the job. And employment prospects are good. Check out "Neurodiagnostic Technologist" at explorehealthcareers.org/career/allied-health-professions/neurodiagnostic-technologist.

>> **Medical Technologist and Technician:** Often called a *lab technician,* this is another medical career that should burgeon because of improvements in the diagnostic use of blood, urine, and tissue samples as well as the need to control medical costs. Because the field is ever changing and lab techs usually get to rotate across test types, this can be a surprisingly interesting career. Lab techs also work in research labs. For example, molecular biology technologists perform complex DNA and protein tests on cell samples. A medical technician, who typically has an associate's degree, does routine tests and monitors automated ones, whereas a medical *technologist,* who has a bachelor's degree, performs more complex ones. Check out "Medical and Clinical Laboratory Technologists and Technicians" at www.bls.gov/ooh/healthcare/medical-and-clinical-laboratory-technologists-and-technicians.htm#tab-.

>> **Heart-Lung Perfusionist:** In open heart surgery, the surgeon can't work on the heart if blood is squirting all over the place. So a machine is hooked up to an artery to receive the blood. The machine then, like a heart and lungs, pumps blood and air back into an artery on the other side of the heart and lungs, and circulation continues. Meanwhile, the heart is relatively bloodless so that the surgeon can work. The surgeon hooks up the blood vessels, and the perfusionist runs the machine. It all sounds straightforward, but talk to any perfusionist and she'll say that the job is stressful. One mistake can be one too many for a patient. Only calm people with a high tolerance for stress do well. Perfusion is the smallest healthcare profession, with only 4,000 practitioners in the United States, and, because of the aging population, there's a shortage. Check out Perfusionist at explorehealthcareers.org/career/allied-health-professions/perfusionist.

>> **Prosthetist/Orthotist:** An amputee walks in. You're going to make his artificial limb or brace. You must be able to work face-to-face with amputees and create limbs and braces with precision. After all, you're preparing a device on which that person's ability to use hands or feet depends. Extensive training is required, but many of the schools are public, so it doesn't cost an arm and a leg. Check out "OP Careers" at www.opcareers.org.

*Neat Niche:* **Pedorthist:** A person needs special shoes — not to match an outfit but because the feet are deformed from disease or injury. A *podiatrist* (foot doctor) sends the patient with a shoe prescription to a pedorthist, who examines and measures the feet and then designs or modifies shoes to fit. The demand for pedorthists exceeds supply, and training tends to be short. Check out "Pedorthists" at www.opcareers.org/professionals/pedorthists.

>> **Polygraph Examiner:** Are you a calm, analytical, detail-oriented person who'd enjoy figuring out whether people are telling the truth? That's what polygraph (lie detector) examiners attempt to do — hook up subjects to a machine that monitors various physiological functions. If things start spiking when you ask, "Did you murder your spouse?" your subject may be a step closer to Ol' Sparky. Most polygraphers work for law enforcement agencies, but polygraph tests are also used in pre-employment testing in sensitive fields such as day care and by attorneys trying to prove that their clients are upstanding citizens. Check out Polygraph Examiner Career Profile at www.thebalance.com/polygraph-examiner-career-profile-974652.

# Animal Care

Many of my clients love animals. (Me too!) Here are some careers that enable you to make a living around your four-legged friends.

>> **Farrier:** Horses' hooves grow like humans' nails do, and when they're overgrown, a farrier must trim them and reshoe the horse. The saying goes: "No hoof, no horse." The pay is good, perhaps because few farriers can do the job after age 45. It's said that every farrier has only so many shoeings in him. Other downsides: You must be careful to ensure that you don't cripple the horse and that it doesn't give you a career-ending kick. But if you love the idea of doing physically demanding work with horses, are good with your hands, and don't mind having to face a career change in your 40s, a career in horseshoeing can be lucky. Check out "A Job of a Farrier" at https://www.youtube.com/watch?v=1eGpKzJZbOw.

>> **Dog Trainer:** Do you have the patience to teach Rover not to chew the furniture or pee on the floor when Rover's owner has run out of patience? Do you like the challenge of convincing Rover to let you walk him rather than have him walk you? Consider a career in dog training. One way for *you* to train is to visit a few local training centers, watch a few pros work, and ask your favorite for an apprenticeship. Most states have no licensure requirements. Anyone can claim to be a dog trainer, so choose your mentor carefully to avoid getting bitten. Check out "Ever Wanted to Be a Dog Trainer?" at www.precision-dog-training.com/become-a-dog-trainer.html and "So You Want to be a Dog Trainer!" at apdt.com/resource-center/career.

*Neat Niche:* **Service Dog Trainer:** We all know about guide dogs for the blind, but demand is increasing for dogs for the deaf. Your job is to train the dog to alert her master to specific sounds like a smoke alarm, a ringing phone, and a knock at the door. Service dogs for diabetics alert their owners to low blood sugar before it becomes dangerous. Because service dogs are generally large, and much of the training requires moving the dog, assistance dog trainers must be physically strong. Check out "Service Dog Training 101: Everything You Need to Know" at www.akc.org/content/entertainment/articles/service-dog-training-101 and "Working with Assistance Dogs" at www.assistancedogsinternational.org/faq-category/working-with-assistance-dogs/#how-do-i-decide-if-i-should-train-service-dogs.

*Neat Niche:* **Working Dog Trainer:** Typical jobs are sheepherding, sniffing out drugs, and finding injured people in wrecks or collapsed buildings. Check out "Working Dogs" at www.workingdogs.com.

# Artistic and Aesthetic

You may have noticed the generally optimistic tone regarding the careers profiled heretofore. Unfortunately, I can't be as sanguine about the careers in this section.

Many people would like careers that use artistic talent or aesthetic sensibilities. Though some can make a living at it, the abundance of wannabes enables employers to pay poorly, if at all. Therein lies the dilemma: Do you relegate your artistic essence to avocational status or risk being another example of why the words *starving* and *artist* so often adjoin?

**WARNING**

Many visual and performing arts schools' websites, brochures, and salespeople (admissions "counselors") paint an overly optimistic picture of graduates' career prospects. For example, a site may highlight a few successful graduates. They're less likely to address *the* question:

> What percent of students who start attending your school end up earning enough money from their art to have paid for their education and stably earn even a modestly middle-class living?

If you're interested in such schools, ask that question of the admissions representative. I hope you get a straight answer, but if the percentage was high, the admissions rep would likely know it and answer your question directly. Indeed, that statistic would likely be trumpeted in the institution's marketing material. Regardless, if you're at least tempted by artistic and aesthetic careers, read on. Obviously, some people do make a living in the artistic and aesthetic world:

>> **Artist/Graphic Artist:** A *Princeton Review* profile of artist careers reported that, in this purely self-expressing career, "90 percent of artists make under $1,000 per year on their art." If you expect to defy the odds, know that 75 percent of the art in the United States is produced by the advertising industry.

Good graphic artist jobs that are offshore-resistant tend to require a trio of skills:

- *Hand-drawing prowess:* Despite the ubiquity of computer-assisted image creation, many if not most good-paying graphic artist positions require the ability to create images the old-fashioned way: with pen-and-ink, maybe even watercolor.

- *Mastery of the Adobe software suite:* You need skills in Illustrator and Photoshop for sure, and then perhaps InDesign, After Effects, Animate, or Dreamweaver.

- *A solid business sense:* You should have the ability to translate market research data into compelling ads, product labels, logos, and other elements. This one is often the key.

To make a living as a *fine* artist, you probably need to spend considerable effort in marketing — attend networking events with potential buyers of your work, for example, or be an expert at using social media if your target buyer does. I have a client who is a successful rocker. He spends at least an hour a day replying to fans on Facebook, Twitter, and Instagram. Check out "The AIGA Guide to Careers in Graphic & Communication Design" (www.aiga.org/guide-careerguide) and "The Art Career Project" (www.theartcareerproject.com/).

>> **Fashion Designer:** "Next year, I think our line of children's swimsuits should add more cotton to the Lycra-poly, and let's try earth tones; they give off an 'enviro' feel. And parents are tired of cutesy — for a change, we might try a design that comes down lower on the leg. Here's a sketch of a few designs. If you like any of them, I'll cut a few samples. Maybe we could get reactions at the sales meeting or at a fashion show." That's what a fashion designer might do.

**REMEMBER**

People often think of designers focusing on haute couture, but a great deal of design is more ordinary — a polo shirt that might be sold on Amazon, for example.

**TIP**

Would-be designers improve their chances of landing a job if they're diligent networkers and distributors of their portfolios, and especially if they pick an under-the-radar niche such as uniforms, skiwear, or hospital garb. How about trying to bring style to the patient gown?

Check out "Becoming a Fashion Designer: Advice from the Experts" at www.theguardian.com/careers/fashion-design-careers.

*Neat Niche:* **Accessory Designer:** Designs for shoes and handbags change almost as often as for clothing, yet many aspiring clothing designers don't consider designing accessories, so it isn't quite as crowded. Even less crowded might be accessories for men. Less crowded still is creating a mass-customized accessory. Read this: "The Build-Your-Own-Handbag Startup That's Perfected Mass Customization" (www.fastcompany.com/3067830/the-build-your-own-handbag-startup-thats-perfected-mass-customization).

>> **Architect:** Few careers have received as much positive media as has architecture. It seems that half the heroes in nonviolent movies are architects. After all, architecture is creative yet practical, and the career is prestigious. It's even green. And think of how cool it would be to design a building that everyone recognizes.

Unfortunately, in the real world, especially in the first years, most architects are less likely to design even a tract home than to draft construction documents for designs created by others, verify that a ventilation system meets city code requirements, or design a staircase that the contractor then alters to save $100. And that's after training that, for full licensure, requires five years for a bachelor of architecture or three years for a masters, plus three-plus years of experience and often a year or more to pass the seven licensure exams. A decade!

What does it take to be a good architect? You must be an excellent communicator — able, for example, to convince the city leaders that the ventilation system deserves a variance to Section 13.02.05. When customer-facing, you must have the ability and willingness to tease out what the client really wants rather than half-listen and subtly impose your own vision.

**REMEMBER**

Some architects have "cool" ideas that customers consider too expensive — it's the customer's usually hard-earned money.

Increasing amounts of architectural work are being automated or offshored. So, moving forward, successful architects need offshore-resistant skills: client relations, sales, and macro project planning.

Check out "Architects" at www.bls.gov/ooh/architecture-and-engineering/architects.htm and "What Are the Pros and Cons of the Architecture Profession?" at www.quora.com/What-are-pros-and-cons-of-the-architecture-profession.

>> **Landscape Architect:** A landscape architect's projects can be mundane, like designing the spaces between buildings in an industrial park or building an artificial pond in a homeowner's backyard. Or they can be exotic, like designing the landscapes of resorts, golf courses, zoos, urban plazas, colleges, cemeteries, landmark monuments, wetlands, or scenic highways. For example, landscape architects designed the U.S. Capitol grounds, preserved Yosemite Park, and created Boston's "Emerald Necklace" of green spaces tying the city to the suburbs.

**REMEMBER**

Because most landscape architecture projects have fewer components than in designing a building, young landscape architects, unlike building architects, may more quickly get to design entire projects. Also, the training period is shorter: You typically can get a job with a master's or even a bachelor's degree and an internship of a year or less. A downside: Landscape architects are subject to a thicket of environmental regulations — you're more likely to stay calm if you're an ardent environmentalist. Check out the American Society of Landscape Architects at www.asla.org.

>> **Arborist:** This is a career in which you start at the top — of the tree, that is: prune it, top it, brace it, and spray it. When you climb down, you also advise on which tree to put where and how to plant and care for it so that (unlike the struggling specimen in front of my house) it thrives. Do a good job and you'll have bolstered Joyce Kilmer's case: "I think that I shall never see a poem lovely as a tree." Check out "What Is an Arborist?" at www.environmentalscience.org/career/arborist.

>> **Interior Designer:** Many people find it fun to help people figure out how to make their homes or offices beautiful and functional. And you get to go on shopping sprees. But if you expect to make a living, the job usually requires more than shopping: You read blueprints, create estimates for commercial

and residential projects, develop mock-ups using computer-aided design (CAD) systems, and know whether you can knock down a wall without the building collapsing. In short, you're somewhere between a decorator and an architect.

Interior *decorators* often practice without credentials, but interior *designers* must have a bachelor's degree and, to get the respected American Society of Interior Designers certification, must know building codes and space planning. The ivillage.com site explained the latter: "If a person enters a building's lobby and can't easily figure out how to get to the bathroom or the elevator, then back to the lobby, you've got a problem." Side benefit: You may need to have a cool-looking office. Check out "Ten Things You Should Know About Becoming an Interior Designer: freshome.com/2014/10/13/10-things-you-should-know-about-becoming-an-interior-designer and *The Interior Design Business Handbook: A Complete Guide to Profitability,* by Mary V. Knackstedt (www.amazon.com/Interior-Design-Business-Handbook-Profitability/dp/1118139879).

» **Hairstylist/Barber:** Job satisfaction surveys place haircutter near the top. That's because appearance is important to many people, haircutters succeed with most customers, the workplace atmosphere is pleasant, and you can develop ongoing relationships. As with most people-centric careers, success requires not only competence but also likeability. Downsides? The low barrier to entry can mean low pay. And if you're successful, you're on your feet eight hours a day and often work evenings and weekends. Too, there's a risk of repetitive strain injury and tight shoulder muscles. One thing you needn't worry about is that your job will be offshored. (To cut an American's hair from India, the scissors would have to be awfully long.) Check out "What Is It Like to Be a Hairstylist?" at www.thebalance.com/what-is-it-like-to-be-a-hair-stylist-525730.

» **Cosmetologist/Makeup Artist:** It can be fun to make people look attractive while chatting with them. And the training time is short. Although most cosmetologists don't get rich, some, like my sister, do just fine. Sandy always loved putting makeup on others, so she learned everything she could about it and went to a manufacturer, who put Sandy's brand name on ready-made cosmetics. Then Sandy opened a store called *Let's Make Up.* There, she did free makeovers and showed people how to do it themselves. When the women saw how good they looked, they usually bought fistfuls of the stuff. Within two years, Sandy was making fistfuls of money. Check out Kevin Aucoin's *Face Forward* (www.amazon.com/Face-Forward-Kevyn-Aucoin/dp/0316287059) and the article "Quit Job to Go to Cosmetology School?" at www.indeed.com/forum/job/hairstylist/Quit-Job-go-Cosmetology-School/t92608.

>> **Gemologist:** It's a gem <groan> of a career: looking at beautiful jewelry all day and deciding how much each piece is worth. Even better, the training time is short. Never again will anyone be able to convince you that a cubic zirconium is a diamond. Options range from retail to unearthing raw stones from mines. Other niches include gem cutting, grading, and appraising; jewelry designing; and repair. If you can live with the possibility of rhinestone pay, you may find a gemologist career sparkling. Check out "Guide to Career Options in Gemology" at www.gemsociety.org/article/guide-career-options-gemology.

>> **Filmmaker:** It sounds quite cool: "Hi, I'm a filmmaker." Beyond sounding cool, directing or producing films *is* cool. You get to orchestrate the telling of a story that you put in front of lots of viewers. And the process is the ultimate in creativity and camaraderie, with you leading your film crew, working intensely for a stretch, and then it's done — you can sit back and watch your masterpiece (and perhaps the money) roll in. What a dream!

Unfortunately, for the vast majority of aspiring filmmakers, it is only a dream. Even many graduates of the top film schools (UCLA, USC, and NYU) end up never earning enough even to pay back their student loans, let alone make a subsistence living as a filmmaker. Nevertheless, if my daughter said, "Dad, I want to be a Hollywood filmmaker," I wouldn't discourage her — the prospect is just too exciting. I'd feel that if she couldn't make it as a Hollywood film-maker, she could somehow make a living in another Hollywood career, like studio executive, or by directing educational or training videos. Just as important, she'd have acquired skills that are transferable to other careers. In the worst-case scenario, in a few years she'd have to read the next edition of *Careers For Dummies*. For more on filmmaking as a career, check out "Eight Mistakes Filmmakers Make That Kill Their Careers" at www.raindance. org/8-mistakes-filmmakers-make-that-kill-their-careers.

>> **Cinematographer:** It seems that everyone wants to be a film director. The question then is, how can you derive many of directing's benefits yet find a field with fewer people competing for jobs? The answer may be cinematography. Like directors, cinematographers direct on film sets. The major difference is that rather than direct people, they direct the cameras. And, of course, cinematographers aren't used just for feature films but also for commercials and even videos on the Net. And the ever better technology makes the creation of brilliant visuals easier. Like all competitive careers, drive and talent prevail — sometimes. Check out the Cinematography forum at www. cinematography.com.

>> **Lighting Designer:** This is another back door into a film or theatrical career. Lighting designers are hired not only in film and theater but also for trade shows and for lighting major buildings — hotels, corporate lobbies, museums, concerts, and theme parks. Check out "Lighting Designer: The Real Poop" at www.shmoop.com/careers/lighting-designer.

>> **Exhibit Designer/Builder:** Though many artistic types who like to sling a hammer dream of becoming film or theater set designers, that market is tight. But exhibit designing/building, a similar field, is less known and is thus easier to break into. You build the equivalent of theater sets for trade shows, expos, and museums. Check out "Exhibitor: Best Practices in Trade Shows and Events at exhibitoronline.com and the Experiential Designers and Producers Association at www.edpa.com.

>> **Stuntperson:** Ready to dive from a cruise ship into a frigid ocean? How about getting set on fire — while leaping from a tall building? If so, maybe you'd like to be a stuntperson. Be sure your health insurance is in place. Most of the "gags" that pay well don't just look dangerous; they are. The risk doesn't deter aspirants; competition for stunt jobs is fierce. You usually need to be quite an athlete and well trained. Check out "Movie Stuntman Jobs" at www.jobmonkey.com/uniquejobs/stuntman.

>> **Magician:** Oh, to pull a rabbit out of a hat, link the solid rings, or saw a woman in half. And to do it in Vegas or L.A.'s Magic Castle, America's centers of magic. But that requires years of practice, plus showmanship and a sense of humor.

Though most magicians don't end up in Vegas, you have a chance of conjuring up a living at magic by convincing companies to hire you for their parties and trade shows. You may also have to fill in with street shows in tourist areas, in train or bus stations, at parades, and at private parties for kids and adults, like me, who continue to be fascinated with prestidigitation, welcoming it as a low-tech escape from a too-serious world. Despite the liabilities, few careers are as, well, magical. Check out the International Brotherhood of Magicians at www.magician.org and *Hiding the Elephant: How Magicians Invented the Impossible and Learned to Disappear,* by Jim Steinmeyer (www.amazon.com/Hiding-Elephant-Magicians-Impossible-Disappear/dp/0786714018). Be sure to also check out my favorite magician, Shin Lim, at www.youtube.com/watch?v=thI1xChNYqk.

>> **Photographer:** As with most artistic careers, to be successful you must be both talented and a willing and able marketer. Photographer Dennis Miller says, "Photography is 75 percent sales — *if* you're very talented; 95 percent if you're not." To be competitive, a photographer must be expert at both still and video, in using post-production software, and at using the web for sales and marketing. Check out *Photographer's Market 2018,* by Noel Rivera (https://www.amazon.com/Photographers-Market-2018-Noel-Rivera/dp/1440352534/ref=sr_1_sc_1?ie=UTF8&qid=1515872611&sr=8-1-spell&keywords=photographers+markt), *What They Didn't Teach You in Photo School,* by Demetrius Fordham (https://www.amazon.com/What-Didn%C2%92t-Teach-Photo-School/dp/1781572690/ref=sr_1_1?ie=UTF8&qid=1515872745&sr=8-1&keywords=What+They+Didn%E2%80%99t+Teach+You+in+Photo+School), and Sobering Truths About Making a Career Out of Photography" at aphotoeditor.com/2011/05/26/sobering-truths-about-making-a-career-out-of-photography.

*Neat Niche:* **Government Photographer:** Government work can be an island of security in the photographer's fickle sea. The feds may hire you to take aerial photographs. Law enforcement agencies hire forensic photographers: "Did that piece of headlight come from a suspect's car?" Enhanced photographs of evidence can tell the tale. Even the U.S. Supreme Court recently hired a photographer. Federal job openings are on www.USAjobs.gov, and the website www.governmentjobs.com aggregates state and local job openings.

» **Curator:** A museum exhibition begins with the curator's idea. She then chooses the objects that best convey it and creates an innovative way to install the exhibit. Then she works to publicize it. Between exhibitions, she tries to acquire interesting exhibit material, all in a peaceful environment.

Most curators major in an academic field such as art, history, archeology, or computer science and then join a museum, zoo, or college or government library. To advance to a curator position, you usually need a master's degree in library science or a PhD in a museum's specialty — modern art, for example. Museums are expensive to maintain, so to land a good museum job, you usually must have business expertise, perhaps acquired as part of an MBA or through your own work experience. As you move ahead, you'll write scripts for audio tours, grant proposals, and perhaps meet with funders and the media. Check out "Curator" at www.princetonreview.com/careers/48/curator.

» **Musician:** Perhaps nothing soothes like music. It can lift a depression, tame an angry soul, or move one to gyrate with joy — even if you're alone in your kitchen. How great to have a career in which music is your main activity.

But how do you fight the odds against making a living as a musician? First, you must find out whether you have enough talent. Your teachers may not be candid, because they have an interest in encouraging you and because it's difficult for someone who knows you to tell you you're not good enough.

**TIP**

How do you discover the truth about your talent? Play for (or send a recording to) people who don't know you but are in a position to pay you for your work: nightclub owners, orchestra conductors, studio gig contractors, wedding band leaders — whatever your niche is. If you audition 20 times and receive little encouragement, you might want to cut your losses. Make music your after-work passion. For example, join a community chorus or orchestra.

If you receive consistent encouragement from customers but not a full-time paying gig, you may have to be entrepreneurial to make a middle-class living. With all the music pirating going on, the money is in live events rather than recorded music. If you want club gigs, to get decent pay, you'll probably need to guarantee perhaps 25 attendees.

So you have to build a fan base. To that end, put video of you in action on social media and ask for Likes, in the hope of building enough of a following to get a sufficient number of people to come to your live events. If you're a wedding musician, get some good musicians to form a group and participate in such marketing activities as throwing a party for wedding and corporate event planners with great food and drink while you play your best stuff so that it's clear you're worth the price of multiple musicians rather than of one DJ. Are you a classical buff? Audition, audition, audition. If by age 20-something you're still in a low- or no-pay orchestra, form a chamber group — it's a great hobby. Check out "Musicians and Singers" at www.bls.gov/ooh/entertainment-and-sports/musicians-and-singers.htm.

» **Composer:** Increasingly, soundtracks, especially for computer games, are created as much by computer cutting-and-pasting as by musical wizards. Rather than stand in the orchestra pit, this conductor sits at a computer with a library of sounds, special effects, and music clips and creates the mood of a computer game, commercial, or film trailer. Of course, traditional composers and songwriters are still out there, but the job market is *largo* (slow.) Check out "Composer" at www.careersinmusic.com/composer.

» **Specialty Sewing Professional:** Rhonda Webb fits women who have had mastectomies with prosthetic breasts and special lingerie. She markets through surgeons and oncologists and meets clients in their own homes. She says, "People are very appreciative. It's so much more relaxed than walking into a cold department store with everyone hearing what your problem is." Other under-the-radar niches: paraplegics and quadriplegics, orthodox Muslims, corporate concierge sewing, wheelchair accessories, doll clothing, wedding gowns, and custom sails and parachutes. Check out "Advice for Those Thinking About a Career in Sewing or Design" at www.threadsmagazine.com/item/14212/advice-for-those-thinking-about-a-career-in-sewing-or-design and *Sewing to Sell: The Beginner's Guide to Starting a Craft Business,* by Virginia Lindsay (www.amazon.com/Sewing-Sell-Beginners-Starting-Business/dp/1607059037).

» Looking at five counterintuitive keys to successful self-employment

» Exploring low-risk and high-enough-payoff business ideas

» Deploying the handy DIY Under-the-Radar Business Finder

# Chapter **9**

# Self-Employment Careers

Perhaps you've always wanted to be self-employed. Or maybe you've always preferred to be employed by an organization but haven't been able to land something good. In either case, self-employment can be an attractive option — but only if you succeed. This chapter should help.

## Becoming Self-Employed

Here are the core attributes of the successfully self-employed. The more of these that describe you, the better your chances:

» **You're a self-starter.** It's the key because, unlike when you're an employee, no one will push you to keep working.

» **You're money-motivated yet ethical.** Most successfully self-employed people are motivated by money but manage to stay ethical, even though they have no boss to monitor them. These people have the strength of character to resist cutting ethical corners, even at the risk of losing money. That's a high bar, but it's the right one.

- » **You're smart about spending.** Successful people husband their money so that they maximize their chances of surviving long enough to become profitable. For example, they may often comparison-shop while remaining aware of when the lowest-priced product or supplier isn't the wisest choice. They may remain as a 1-person operation they run from home. Are you reluctant to start your business by yourself? Rather than take a partner, hire a consultant short-term, or a trusted friend ongoing, and part-time if possible.

- » **Getting yeses comes naturally to you.** If you're a business owner, you need lots of yeses: people willing to work for you for stock and little or no cash, vendors willing to sell to you on credit, people willing to let you share their space or equipment for little or no money, and customers willing to buy your product at a price with a good profit margin. The successfully self-employed person has the ability to get people to say yes without exerting undue pressure. Look back at your track record, not just professionally but also personally. Do people tend to agree with you, to say yes to your requests?

- » **You can handle diverse problems on the fly.** Time is money, and you can't afford to hire help for too many tasks.

- » **You are resilient.** Even if they're well-run, most businesses suffer setbacks. Successfully self-employed people see whether there's a lesson to be learned and then, rather than wallow, move forward. Yet they're objective enough to know when a wiser use of further time and money is to replace their business with one of greater potential or to resume looking to be employed by others.

Honestly, to what extent do the qualities in this list describe you?

# Earning the Un-MBA

Most of this book's advice is mainstream, but here, I go radical.

**TIP**

In this chapter, I suggest that you consider starting businesses that MBA programs wouldn't tout. Further, I recommend that you run your business using principles that are often different from core MBA ones: For most one- and few-people businesses, such core precepts are usually wrong because they're designed to prepare people to work for deep-pocket corporations that can afford to have multiple business ideas fail. Most people contemplating self-employment can't afford to join the 50 percent that go broke in the first few years.

So this chapter's focus is on low-risk, low-investment, simple businesses that put the odds in your favor. First, I'll lay out 5 *un*-MBA principles and then offer 24 examples of businesses that incorporate those principles.

## Choose a low-investment business

MBAers may intone, "It takes money to make money," but the self-employed person is wiser to choose a low-investment business — especially the first time out. The fact is, you'll probably make costly errors starting out, and with money being a business's lifeblood, each error bleeds you. You don't want your business to bleed out before you can make it healthy.

## Recognize that status is the enemy of success

MBA programs encourage students to start high-status, cool-sounding businesses — high-tech, biotech, entertainment, or environmental, for example. But high-status businesses attract the best and the brightest. Your odds of success improve if you compete with lesser lights. Status is the enemy of success.

Even if it's a low-status business, you'll find that you'll feel good about it as long as you're successful and ethical at it. And if you're worried about telling your friends what you're doing, one approach is to realize that, if they think less of you because you own, say, a small chain of coffee carts, they're not worth caring about. But if you can't bring yourself to accept that idea, you can frame your business in ways that increase your status — for example, "I'm the president and CEO of the California Cappuccino Company with branches throughout the San Francisco Bay Area."

## Don't innovate; replicate

MBA programs urge students to innovate. Easy for them to say. In the real world, new ideas are too prone to fail: You misread the market, have no comparable businesses to copy ideas from, and have to educate your market on your innovation. And if your idea works too well, a better-funded entity could compete you into the ground. The leading edge is often the bleeding edge. Guinea pigs often die. Don't innovate; replicate.

## Keep it simple

MBA courses are often taught by professors who are attracted to complexity. So their classes tend to focus on complex businesses. Sure, it's more impressive to know and to tell people you own a multiproduct, high-tech, international business, but the more complex it is, the more there is to go wrong. It's far less impressive to tell people you've gone bust.

Are you worried that you might be bored running a simple business? No need. It's a challenge for even a smart, entrepreneurial person to make even a simple business work, and to keep it working in the face of the inevitable challenges. So keep it simple.

## Stay small

MBA programs urge businesses to *scale*, to get big. That takes not only money but also lots of high-quality employees, who aren't easy for a start-up to find. In addition, quality tends to drop with each additional location because there's more to keep track of and supervise. You can make enough money with a small number of locations — perhaps just one, and maybe just a website. Stay small.

These are the reasons that the small-business ideas I offer in this chapter are all low-investment, simple ones that are far from the cutting edge.

# Pursuing Low-Risk, High-Enough-Payoff Business Ideas

In this section, I describe 24 low-risk yet high-enough-payoff self-employment ideas to consider. Of course, this is just a sampling of worthy options. For example, many careers in earlier chapters can be carried out on a self-employed basis, but those listed here are mainly for the self-employed.

(You can generate your own custom-tailored self-employment ideas by using this chapter's finale: The DIY Under-the-Radar Business Idea Finder.)

## Personal services

Many of the self-employed find their work particularly rewarding when providing a needed service to people. It feels, well, human.

>> **Financial Advisor:** Many people worry about how in the world they're going to have enough money to buy a house, have kids, pay for a college education, or for graduate school — let alone the jillion dollars the experts say we need for retirement. Social Security may not be solvent enough to help. Enter the financial planner.

The good financial advisor is as much a financial therapist as a numbers cruncher or mutual fund picker. Some people, for example, overspend to get a transient shopper's high or in a vain attempt to fill an emotional hole in themselves. The wise financial planner listens well and has the gift of engendering change.

To resist ethical temptations, it's normally best for financial planners to work on a fee basis — perhaps, per year, 1/2 to 1 percent of the person's assets she'll be investing with you. In addition, agree to make investments only in low-cost ways, such as Vanguard mutual funds.

**TIP**

How to get clients? Develop relationships with accountants and estate planning attorneys, and make presentations at employee workplaces and alumni association events.

Some people believe that the best training to become a financial planner is the skill set you can acquire if you're hired by a major financial service, such as Schwab, Fidelity, or the aforementioned Vanguard. One option is to work there for a year or two and then decide whether you want to stay put or hang a shingle. Check out "Financial Advisor Training: Real World Advice from a Successful CFP at wealthpilgrim.com/financial-advisor-training-real-world-advice-from-a-successful-cfpr.

>> **Patient Advocate:** It requires a Magellan to navigate the labyrinthine U.S. healthcare system. Most people, especially when diagnosed with a serious disease, aren't the best navigators. Enter the patient advocate. You help ensure, sometimes with assertiveness, that the patient gets to see the needed specialist. You do research so that the patient is more informed at that appointment. You may accompany the patient to provide a second ear and ask questions and check in on the patient in the hospital. You might sort through the bills and, if necessary, negotiate fees with the healthcare provider, insurance company, or government.

The confluence of aging baby boomers with the complex U.S. healthcare system means great demand for a persuasive, persistent person willing to do the vital work of patient advocacy. Some hospitals and HMOs hire nurses and social workers as patient advocates, but significant unmet need remains. Medical advocates may attract clients by contacting oncologists, cardiologists, and endocrinologists (they serve many diabetes patients,) or by speaking to support groups for newly diagnosed people.

Check out "Patient Advocates: The Coach in Your Corner for Taking On the Health Care System" at www.nerdwallet.com/blog/health/managing-medical-bills/patient-advocates-medical-billing-advocates and the Patient Advocate Foundation at www.patientadvocate.org.

*Neat Niche:* **Geriatric Care Manager:** In addition to the patient advocate I just mentioned, and in collaboration with an older person's family, the geriatric care manager helps older people find appropriate services that may enable them to age in place or find appropriate assisted living. Care managers may visit the patient to check in and coordinate with family, and even help resolve disputes. Such disagreements may be especially likely when the elder is experiencing both physical and mental declines. Check out the Aging Life Care Association at www.aginglifecare.org.

>> **Doula:** Labor, childbirth, and postpartum weeks can be exhausting. Throughout, the doula can be there to provide nonmedical pain-decreasing strategies — from breathing techniques to different positions, and from aromatherapy to massage. Doulas also provide support and advice. Some evidence suggests that doula-assisted births result in shorter labor, fewer Caesarean and forceps births, and less need for pain medication. Check out Doulas of North America at www.dona.org.

>> **Independent Researcher:** Fiction and nonfiction writers, business or nonprofit employees, and anyone interested in learning about a topic may hire a researcher. Typically, this person searches the Net and perhaps databases and print materials. She may even interview the right people. Then she distills all that into a digest of the most useful information.

The information mountain is overwhelming, so information professionals often specialize — in genomics, engineering, politics, or digital art, for example, or perhaps mergers and acquisitions. How might you get clients? One way is to pick a specialty and give talks or write articles on the art of research for that field's professional association. You might place an ad on a site read by your target customer. For example, if you're good at digging up ancestry, take an ad on or write an article for a genealogy website. Check out the Association of Independent Information Professionals at www.aiip.org.

>> **Personal Chef:** The United States Personal Chef Association estimates that the number of personal chefs could double to 20,000 in the next five years. This career is better than restaurant cheffing because you cook smaller numbers of meals — you needn't spend long days, nights, and weekends standing over a hot stove. And unlike when starting out in a restaurant, you design all the menus; you're a veritable executive chef. Check out the United States Personal Chef Association at www.uspca.com and the American Personal & Private Chef Association at www.personalchef.com.

>> **Handyperson:** When I tell friends that I have a good handyperson, their eyes light up — good help is hard to find. That's largely because ever more students are eschewing the trades for white collar careers. So, if you have handyperson skills, you'll likely find yourself with plenty of customers grateful to pay you well. Being a handyperson can be enjoyable because you get to work on a range of projects that are fairly simple. (Well, not simple for a klutz like me.) Check out *How to Start a Home-Based Handyman Business*, by Terry Meany (www.amazon.com/Start-Home-Based-Handyman-Business-Mouth/dp/0762752777/ref=sr_1_1?ie=UTF8&qid=1514555366&sr=8-1&keywords=How+to+Start+a+Home-Based+Handyman+Business).

*Neat Niche:* **Noise Control Specialist:** Many owners of residences and workplaces near airports, freeways, schools, and factories willingly pay for some peace and quiet. This is a high-value specialty, yet the skills required are often modest. Often, all you're doing is insulating, installing double-glazed windows, and weather-stripping windows and doors.

*Neat Niche:* **Senior Retrofitter:** Making stairs easier to climb or lowering light switches may ease the aging process, but many seniors won't seek out such retrofits. So handypersons may suggest retrofitting while doing routine jobs in seniors' homes.

>> **Tile-and-Marble Setter:** This is among the more desirable construction trades. Progress on each job is steady and readily apparent, and the results look attractive. Training is brief, usually on-the-job, although apprenticeships are available. Plus, the pay is higher than for most construction trades. Perhaps that's because you have to do a lot of bending, kneeling, and reaching, and unless you're diligent in wearing rubber gloves, the chemicals can take a toll on your hands. The job market is strong, as evidenced by the fact that many tile setters are successfully self-employed. Check out "Tile Setters Career Overview" at www.youtube.com/watch?v=IeU31JU-8vM.

>> **Home Inspector:** Though buying a home can be love at first sight, love can be blind. Enter the home inspector, whose job is to help the blind to see. No surprise: You'll need to know how to assess the soundness of a home's wiring, plumbing, heating, building materials, and other factors. Market your service to local real estate agents, perhaps by giving lectures titled "How to Keep an Inspection from Killing the Deal" at local Board of Realtor meetings. Check out the American Society of Home Inspectors at www.ashi.com and the International Association of Certified Home Inspectors at www.nachi.org.

>> **Home Stager:** This is a well-paying career for artistic types who'd rather work with rooms than watercolors. When a homeowner decides to sell, she's willing to invest some bucks to make the house look its best. Stagers visit the house to recommend moving and removing furniture and decorations. ("That stuffed moose head simply must go!") To create the right effect, they may also suggest leasing other furniture or low-cost improvements, such as painting one wall a dramatic color to enliven a nondescript room.

Because the home seller stands to make big bucks, home stagers can earn good money, and although it's an artistic career, staging doesn't require a Rembrandt. Check out "How to Start a Home Staging Business" at www.wikihow.com/Start-a-Home-Staging-Business and "10 Ugly Truths to Know Before Becoming a Home Stager" at www.staged4more.com/blog/so-you-want-to-be-a-home-stager.

**>> Tutor:** Many tutors enjoy the close one-on-one relationships that can come with tutoring. (The visible progress you can see and the fact that you can earn money with minimal start-up costs and without endless training are also pluses.) How do you make a decent living as a tutor? Perhaps let local public school teachers know that, unlike chains such as Sylvan Learning, you make house calls or facilitate sessions by phone or Skype.

TIP

It helps to specialize — helping students with attention deficit disorder, for example, or math for girls or music lessons on Skype or one of the *neat niches* described in this section. You also might post your profile on Wyzant.com and Tutor.com.

I often give just one word of advice to people with patience and the ability to explain things clearly, motivate others, and self-promote: Tutor.

Check out "How to Set Up a Home Tutoring Business" at www.wikihow.com/ Set-up-a-Home-Tutoring-Business.

*Neat Niche:* **Autism Behavior Specialist:** People on the autism spectrum benefit from one-on-one behavior coaching to increase behaviors such as eye contact and decrease behaviors such as wailing and arm-flapping. Because this work usually requires great patience, it is in demand, especially if you are certificated — for example, BCAT or BCBA or CAS. Check out Autism Tutors at www.AutismTutors.com.

*Neat Niche:* **Computer Tutor:** Get referrals from employers, computer retailers, or local Internet service providers. Or emulate the guerrilla marketer who attracted plenty of clients just by standing in front of a computer store and giving his pitch to everyone walking out with a new computer.

*Neat Niche:* **Speaking or Writing Advisor:** Whether it's part of an attempt to make an actual living at writing or speaking or it stems from a general desire to improve their communication skills, people want to get better at speaking and writing — witness the popularity of Toastmasters clubs and the many novel and screenwriting workshops and degree programs in creative writing. If you're a good writer or public speaker and you know how to strike the balance between support and tactful suggestions, you might teach others what you've learned. Acquire clients by giving talks on how to give a speech at conferences, libraries, and adult education schools. This writing coach's website www.lisatener.com/ book-writing-coach gives a flavor of this niche. And here's a cautionary note from a former speaking coach: www.forbes.com/sites/work-in-progress/ 2012/04/19/public-speaking-trainer-confesses-dont-waste-your- money-on-this/3/#184b480e5230.

*Sub-Niche:* **Thesis Completion Coach:** Many graduate students get close to finishing their degrees but drop out because they have trouble completing their master's theses or doctoral dissertations. Can you help? You may guide the student to develop the questions to be addressed, plan the research's structure and analysis, including or not including statistics, and review a draft. Check out the Association for Support of Graduate Students at www.asgs.org.

*Neat Niche:* **Accent Neutralization Specialist:** When you call tech support, it's nice to hear someone whose accent you can understand. To that end, companies hire accent neutralization specialists (also known as *accent reduction specialists*). In addition, many immigrants to the United States, especially those in professional jobs, are eager to improve their accents. In either case, to find clients, contact human resource departments at high-tech and biotech companies. They often recruit from abroad to fill programmer, engineer, and scientist positions. Check out "An Overview of Accent Neutralization and Accent Reduction" at www.thoughtco.com/accent-neutralization-accent-reduction-overview-1212077.

» **Personal Coach:** Do you like to help others but would rather deal with problems easier to address than reconstructing a personality or curing a serious disease? Personal coaching is some combination of goal-setting advisor, time-management consultant, motivator, sounding board, confidant, dream-builder, image instructor, and cheerleader. Alas, most coaches must market heavily to get clients — there seems to be a coach under every rock. Coaching is increasingly done by phone and Skype. Check out the International Coach Federation at https://coachfederation.org/ and "What Life Coaches Won't Tell You" at www.nextavenue.org/10-things-life-coaches-wont-tell-you.

*Neat Niche:* **Career Advisor:** This is what I do, and as with most professionals, we all do things differently. But here's what I think is the best way to proceed. First, choose a niche. You're more helpful if you specialize. If you're a 20-something female with a liberal arts degree, you'll probably do better specializing in people like you than if you're a generic career coach. Katharine Brooks, the author of this book's foreword, wrote a fine book on this topic: *You Majored in What?* It's at www.amazon.com/You-Majored-What-Designing-College/dp/0452296005/ref=sr_1_sc_1?ie=UTF8&qid=1514560078&sr=8-1-spell&keywords=you+majoered+in+what%3F.

Then learn by watching master coaches. In the career advisor example, perhaps you'd ask a young female career coach who has excellent Yelp reviews whether you might watch her in sessions and if she would watch you in a few sessions with friends that you'd do for free. Of course, you may have to pay the coach, but that's cheap tuition.

Develop a style that matches your strengths. Yes, I listen and ask questions to help the client generate their own solutions, but if I feel that their well has run dry, I tactfully offer suggestions, emphasizing that I'm merely the advisor and that they're the CEO of their life. Other coaches, especially younger ones,

REMEMBER

correctly feel that they have less expertise, experience, and wisdom than do their clients. They would be wise to stick to facilitator mode: asking questions to help lead the client to their own answers and, when clients lack knowledge, letting them or helping them find it on the Internet or through personal connections.

I've tried to follow the advice I've given in this book to tailor and accessorize the career so that it fits me well. I love working at home: I love the peace and quiet and the lack of commute, and my doggie, Einstein, can be my receptionist and stress buster. I specialize now in high-powered people who nonetheless are unhappy or less successful than they could be. My clients include lots of doctors, lawyers, executives, and even college presidents. We may focus on a job change or even a career change, but, as often, we work on their skills — leadership, public speaking, and emotional intelligence — and factors outside of work that affect them, such as their romantic relationships or lack thereof, their relationships with money and materialism, and even figuring out what, for them, are their life's foundational principles.

*Neat Niche:* **Dating Coach:** A dating coach could do some or all of the following:

- Help the client clarify what sort of relationship he wants: adventurous to stable or short-term hook-up to marriage, for example.

- Determine, in light of the preceding task and the person's personality, what combination of activities should be in the plan: dating sites, setups from friends, taking or teaching a class (Dance? Finance?), or traveling with or without a wing person. Put the strategy and specific action plan in writing.

- Help the client create an online dating profile that accurately reflects who he is and the kind of person he's looking for. It may include taking photos for the profile.

**TIP**

After creating an impressive portfolio of such profiles, you might try to get hired as a dating site's in-house profile writer. You would

- Help decide which profiles to reach out to and respond to.

- Role-play flirting and dates. This strategy can not only provide useful feedback and tips, but shy or socially anxious clients could also benefit from the desensitizing effect. You could put it on video. After all, video is used to provide feedback during all sorts of lessons, from golf to interviewing, so why not dating?

- Assist in selecting clothes, hair, and makeup. Perhaps even accompany the client on a shopping trip.

- Double-date with the client and, afterward, provide feedback.

- Meet regularly to discuss the progress and, if needed, make changes.

- Coach the client on turning a good first date into a blossoming relationship.

- You might even offer a group activity, such as a long-term-relationship boot camp. That could be highlighted by video-recorded mock mini dates, on which each person would get and give feedback. Of course, the boot camp's leaders would also provide input.

Check out "How to Become a Dating Coach: The 2 Most Important Steps" at coachestrainingblog.com/becomeacoach/category/relationship-coach/how-to-become-a-dating-coach.

*Neat Niche:* **Organizing Coach:** Work and home lives are increasingly compli-cated and cluttered, so it's no surprise that there's demand for organizing coaches, even for people who would never make it onto the TV show *Hoarders.* It's usually not enough to help the person organize their space. Often, there are internal, irrational drivers that would make the person soon clutter up again. So, although not a psychotherapist, the useful organizing coach must be able to unlock some of that.

TIP

A good marketing tactic is to contact HR or training departments at nearby businesses, nonprofits, or even government agencies. Suggest that they hire you to do "organizing makeovers" for any employees who feel they need it. Check out the National Association of Productivity & Organizing Professional Organizers at www.napo.net as well as *Shed Your Stuff, Change Your Life: A Four-Step Guide to Getting Unstuck,* by Julie Morgenstern (www.amazon.com/SHED-Your-Stuff-Change-Life/dp/0743250907/ref=sr_1_1?ie=UTF8&qid=1514561445&sr=8-1&keywords=shed+your+stuff+change+your+life).

*Neat Niche:* **Parenting Coach:** Whether a parent has a newborn or an adult child who just moved back home, many parents worry that they're not good-enough parents. They don't want a therapist; they just want help in getting their pride and joy to not drive them crazy. Parents with a special-needs child or one with a substance abuse problem may particularly call on you. You can market to individual parents — by offering free seminars at PTA meetings or public libraries, for example. Or see whether you can get referrals from your child's pediatrician. Check out "Becoming a Parenting Coach: The Basics" at www.wahm.com/articles/becoming-a-parenting-coach-the-basics.html.

*Neat Niche:* **Home Schooling Consultant:** Some parents don't feel comfortable sending their child to public school, which tempts them to home-school. And they're reassured when they read media reports that home-schooled kids do well in college admission. So it isn't surprising that 2 million children are now home-schooled. But home schooling is no easy feat. As a consultant, you help parents and kids design learning programs, perhaps do some one-on-one or small-group teaching, and iron out problems. For more info, go to the forums at Mothering.com (http://www.mothering.com/forum/index.php) and enter "Starting a Home-Schooling Consulting Business" in the Search box.

*Neat Niche:* **One-on-One Athletic Coach:** Even as young as in elementary school, many athletes want to improve their game. So their parents may hire a one-on-one coach, say, for their Little League pitcher who mainly sits on the bench and is hankerin' to get in the game.

I haven't heard of adults hiring such coaches, but if I had known of a one-on-one coach who specialized in watching schoolyard basketball players in action and then giving tips, I could see having hired one for myself, although I probably would ask that he simply join the game so that my fellow players wouldn't think I was weird. To get clients, you might ask coaches at local schools. Check out CoachUp at www.coachup.com.

*Neat Niche:* **Retirement Coach:** Baby boomers are now reaching retirement age, many with trepidation. They may need to plan on living another 30 years but have saved only for a fraction of that. Work is central to their identity and, even with a bit of part-time work and volunteering, they worry that they'll feel out-to-pasture. Couples in retirement suddenly find themselves spending more time together and may find the proximity difficult. Enter the retirement coach, who may assist in financial planning, helping the client figure out how to fill days, and/or readjust to seeing the spouse more often. Check out the Retirement Coaches Association at retirementcoachesassociation.org.

## Not-so-personal businesses

Some people prefer to interact more with products than with people. Here are some options.

>> **Selling products online:** If you keep it simple, you have a reasonable chance at earning at least a sideline income while you sleep:

1. *Pick a niche:* It might be genome lab consumables, *netsuke* (antique miniature Japanese sculptures), or whatever else you know a lot about. Don't pick anything that's easily understandable. Customers will probably just buy such items at Amazon or a big-box store. Don't choose anything perishable, either — like African violets. It may take too long to accurately estimate the next days' sales, so you may end up with a roomful of dead plants.

   If you're not sure what to sell, select 10 or 20 best-selling, best-value, and/or highest-quality items sold on Amazon or other sites within a category you like.

2. *Decide where to sell.* You need your own site, but you need to decide whether you'll try to get all sales from that site, rack up sales as an Amazon, eBay, and/or Etsy reseller, or use a combination of approaches.

Think about being an affiliate. Instead of people buying directly from you, they click on an item on your site, which takes them to the product's page on Amazon (for example), and if they buy, for most sales, you get 5 percent. You can attract customers with the quality of your products and reviews, as well as the site being well optimized for search engines.

3. *Come up with a self-explanatory name for your site.* If you want to sell *netsuke*, for example, go to a domain-registration and website-creator site such as squarespace.com and find a domain name close to netsuke.com. (You can't have netsuke.com, because it's already taken. Squarespace.com is kind enough to offer suggestions for domain names. For example, at the time of this writing, bestnetsuke.com was available. Good enough.

4. *Create and host your site.* The options keep improving, but, as of this writing, I do recommend squarespace.com, which has gorgeous designs and easy setup, is well-suited for small businesses, and is affordable.

5. *Make your site definitive in your niche.* For example, if you're selling window boxes, be sure your site has a large or well-curated selection of fairly priced ones. The .jpg image of each should be of high quality but small enough that the pages load quickly. The descriptions should be written from a consumer-advocacy rather than "sales-y" perspective, perhaps integrating your own expertise with the Net's collective wisdom. For example, if an item is sold on Amazon and other sites, synthesize their reviews with your own.

6. *Optimize for search engines.* Frequently use terms that potential customers will likely use. If you're selling supplies for computer-chip clean rooms, search terms might be *clean room apparel, clean room consumables,* or *best clean room consumables,* for example. Most importantly, be sure to use such terms in the titles of web pages, menu items, and page titles. If you want to be more thorough, find keywords by searching Google AdSense, and, if you want to see whether any words capitalize on what's hot, use Google Trends.

7. *Build your customer list.* Use as many of the techniques in the following list as you feel are worth the effort:

Offer a discount to entice visitors to sign up to get emails about your site's special offers and new products.

Start a community forum on the site.

On social media, offer discounts, tips, and contests, for example, for the best photos and stories using your product.

Put a helpful yet entertaining 1- to 2-minute explanatory video on your site and YouTube. Whiteboard videos now can be bought inexpensively. (Try upwork.com.) End with a call to action: "Order using the code 'YouTube' and you'll get 25 percent off your first order."

Write an article for a publication read by your target customer. Include a tagline offering that first-timer discount.

Give live or online classes, of course, collecting the names of attendees.

8. *Promote the site.* One strategy is to email a link to the site to highly ranked Alexa bloggers and other thought leaders related to your product category, along with a flattering, smart note. Also tout it regularly on social media.

9. *Leverage your data.* Use sales numbers to decide which products to delete, replace, or move to a more or less prominent place on your site.

Compared with most businesses, online selling requires little time and no money, and it doesn't force you to quit your job or to stop trying to find a job. If your e-commerce business fails, it's been an interesting experiment. If it succeeds and, as they say, "the money rolls in while you sleep," you have an income stream that could free you up to quit your job or job search and/or to find a second such set of products to sell online.

Check out "What to Sell in 2018: How to Find a Product Niche and Start Selling Online" at www.bigcommerce.com/blog/find-product-niche-start-selling-online, "What to Sell Online: 8 Strategies for Finding Your First Product" at www.shopify.com/blog/12932121-what-to-sell-online-8-strategies-for-finding-your-first-product, and *SEO 2018: Learn Search Engine Optimization with Smart Internet Marketing Strategies,* by Adam Clarke (www.amazon.com/dp/B00NH0XZR0?psc=1).

» **Selling timely items from a cart:** The beauty of this sales strategy is that rent is usually free, inventory can change as needed, and it's mobile. So, subject to local restrictions on where you can park your cart, on weekday mornings you can sell — depending on the weather — sunglasses, hats, scarves, gloves, and/or umbrellas at a busy mass transit station or in front of a leviathan office building. In the middle of the day, you can sell local yummies in a tourist area, and, for the return rush hour, return to your morning location, perhaps adding flowers for people to give to their sweeties. On the weekends, sell the local team's hats, T-shirts, and pennants near the stadium.

TIP

You may not make enough money from one cart, so, after you've mastered the process, hire a trusted friend to run it while you look for another good location. A variation is the pop-up shop. You rent a small space for a week or two for your usually seasonal business: Halloween, Valentine's Day, Mother's Day, and Christmas. Check out "What Is a Pop-Up Shop?" at blog.thestorefront.com/what-exactly-is-a-pop-up-shop.

» **Online Selling Assistant:** Many small businesses — often 1-person operations — want to sell their products on Amazon, eBay, or Etsy but don't have the skills to write copy, take great-looking photos, price appropriately, ship efficiently, and so on. You collect their products, answer shopper questions, and when an item is bought, you ship it. Check out "How to Make Money from Home as an eBay Selling Assistant" at www.mytopbusinessideas.com/ebay-selling-assistant.

» **Importer:** Many people dream of traveling to far-flung places to search for beautiful items, buying as many as desired. Being an importer can allow you to do that. Key here is to not give too much weight to your own preferences: You can't mainly sell what you like. You have to sense what will sell and through which channels. You also need the knack of buying for 70 to 90 percent less than what the product could consistently sell for at retail, yet be ethical enough to ensure that the seller makes a decent profit. You'd be surprised at how many creators of art sell at a loss because they want to get their work "out there."

A client of mine went to China. In the street fairs, many artists sell beautiful watercolors of camellias, azaleas, and nature scenes on elegant deckled rice paper for $1.00 a piece. When my client said that she wanted to buy in quantities of 25 and asked each seller whether she could make a decent profit by selling them to you for 30 cents each, most willingly agreed. She brought back 200 in her suitcase, a value below the limit for tariffs. Back in the States, she bought 200 frames wholesale for $1 apiece, so her total cost per framed watercolor was $1.30. She sold most of them online and at street fairs for $30 each and the 20 remaining ones to an Asian art gallery for $15 each. I can't think of a product with a higher profit margin, at least a legal one. Subsequently, by phone, she found a local in China who would visit the street fairs to replenish her stock, freeing her to travel to a different dream spot.

What made this business work was that my client bought only what was clearly commercial at a profit margin that enabled her to make a middle-class living without undue effort. Plus, her product has unlimited shelf life and was lightweight, so it was cheap to ship.

Do you think you could consistently pull off something like that? It may not always be that simple. The article "How to Start an Import/Export Business" describes import/export operations in more detail (and with more examples): www.entrepreneur.com/article/41846.

» **Small-Business Consultant:** Many of the myriad people who start a business are scared of failing. Even if it's a running concern, the owner could use help with marketing, accounting, finance, or technology. Check out *An Insider's Guide to Building a Successful Consulting Practice,* by Bruce L. Katcher (www.amazon.com/Insiders-Building-Successful-Consulting-Practice/dp/0814414362/ref=sr_1_1?ie=UTF8&qid=1514569857&sr=8-1&keywords=An+Insider%27s+Guide+to+Building+a+Successful+Consulting+Practice).

*Neat Niche:* **Private-Practice Consultant:** Many doctors, dentists, psychotherapists, orthodontists, veterinarians, lawyers, and CPAs are aware that being good practitioners doesn't make them good businesspersons, especially in a rapidly changing, ever more paperwork-centric, compliance-heavy, multipayer environment. So they're turning to consultants to help recruit new customers and develop better systems for billing and collections, payroll, records management, and personnel. Demand is strong, and you work with educated people with the money and motivation to pay you well. Check out National Society of Certified Healthcare Business Consultants at nschbc.org.

*Neat Niche:* **Government Procurement Consultant:** The nation's largest customer is the government — and it may be willing to pay $85 for a hammer. That's the sort of customer that all businesses love, but many companies don't know how to get the government to buy from them. Your job is to teach them. Check out the U.S. Small Business Administration's Government Contracting Division at www.sba.gov/GC as well as *The Small-Business Guide to Government Contracts,* by Steven J. Koprince (www.amazon.com/Small-Business-Guide-Government-Contracts-Regulations/dp/0814431933).

*Neat Niche:* **Business Plan Writer:** Many business owners know that they need a business plan but don't know how to create one. Inexpensive software such as LivePlan can help you make business plans look professional, though the key to being a good business plan writer is understanding what it takes to identify and market a winning product or service, and the wisest way to raise money for and operate the business.

This seems like an enjoyable career: You help come up with the business idea and implementation plan without incurring any financial risk or having to deal with the headaches of running the business. Here's a way to find clients: Teach a class at a public library or college's extension school on how to write a business plan. Check out "14 Exceptionally Useful Tools for Business Plan Writing" at www.thebalance.com/business-plan-writing-tools-2951568.

>> **Debt Collection Specialist:** If you don't mind representing a business or college against a debtor, this can be a good career. It's one-on-one problem solving — the sort of work many people like. And if the debtor can't pay, the world doesn't end. There's always another debtor to call on. That's the key to success in this business: Stay pleasant and solution-oriented. It's a great home business. You can sit at home with your feet up, with no overhead, and earn 25 percent to 50 percent of every dollar you retrieve. And there are plenty of dollars to retrieve. Consumer debt is $13 trillion dollars. Check out *Starting a Collection Agency FAQs: Making Money Collecting Money,* by Michelle Dunn (www.amazon.com/Starting-Collection-Agency-FAQs-collecting/dp/1482023407/ref=sr_1_2?ie=UTF8&qid=1516152423&sr=8-2&keywords=starting+a+collection+agency, and the Association of Credit and Collection Professionals at www.acainternational.org.

» **"Dull-Normal" Business Owner:** Thomas Stanley, author of *The Millionaire Next Door,* found that a disproportionate number of millionaires own what he calls "dull-normal businesses," such as welding contracting, pest control, transmission repair, and mobile home park maintenance. The book goes on to say that these people, despite their career's lack of status, are generally happy with their work lives. Check out *The Millionaire Next Door: The Surprising Secrets of America's Wealthy,* by Thomas J. Stanley and William D. Danko (www. amazon.com/Millionaire-Next-Door-Surprising-Americas/ dp/1589795474.

» **Virtual Assistant:** This is an option for someone who wants to use administrative skills such as word processing, database management, routine email responding, social media posting, travel arranging, event planning, and bookkeeping at home. Virtual assisting is especially appealing if you have a disability or want a portable business because your spouse's career requires frequent moving — or simply because you love the idea of taking breaks whenever you want to play in your garden or with your dog. There's no commute and no office politics. A *Newsweek* article describes this career as an administrative assistant without a boss looking over your shoulder. Check out the International Virtual Assistants Association at ivaa.org and the Virtual Assistant Training program at www.assistu.com.

» **Indexer:** An index can make the difference between a book and a good book. Peter Farrell calls a good index "a minor work of art but also the product of clean thought and meticulous care." That work of art must usually be done quickly — publishers usually give indexers just a week or two to complete the work. Check out the American Society for Indexing at www.asindexing.org.

» **Mobile Auto Repairperson:** Every car needs tune-ups, brake jobs, and so on, and nearly every car owner finds it a hassle to get them: Drop off the car and somehow get to work in the morning, and then somehow get back to the shop after work. Enter the mobile auto repairperson. He does the work where you park your car for work. Perhaps you can even do it "wholesale:" for companies with an employee parking lot. Explain to their human resources manager that by allowing you to offer repairs in the lot, employees won't need to take time off work to get their cars serviced.

*Neat Niche:* **Mobile Car Detailer:** Many people want their cars polished and cleaned inside and out but don't have the time to do it themselves or to take it to a shop where they have to sit around waiting for it to be done. Enter the mobile car detailer. While the customer's car is parked at work or at home, the mobile car detailer does the job. This is another of those low-investment, no-brains, high-markup, easy-to-satisfy-the-customer businesses. One marketing approach is to get local new car dealers, especially luxury brands, to give a coupon for a half-price detailing to each new-car buyer. Luxury car buyers want their baby to keep looking good, and you know they have disposable income. One discounted detailing may yield a customer who'll keep buying your service for years. A variation: Set up shop in an airport, employee, or shopping mall parking lot. Check out *How to Start a Home-Based Car Detailing Business*, by Renny Doyle (www.amazon.com/Start-Home-based-Detailing-Business-Home-Based/dp/0762778768).

» **Musical Instrument Repairperson:** Kids aren't known for their tender treatment of anything, even school musical instruments. That means plenty of repairs are needed. And, of course, even some older folks' instruments need work. Musical instrument repair is a good career for fix-it types who prefer to avoid things electrical, although there are specialists, for example, in synthesizers and amps. It's a low-stress job. Working conditions are usually ideal, and you're nearly always assured of pleasing your customer. You should know how to play the instrument. Otherwise, how do you know whether you fixed it? Check out "Musical Instrument Repair Technician" at www.youtube.com/watch?v=M_cl_z4ZC28.

*Neat Niche:* **Piano Technician:** This is a good niche if you prefer to be out and about rather than in your workshop all day. And, if you get bored with just tuning, you can learn piano repair, or even rebuilding. Despite the presence of electronic aids, piano tuners need a good ear. Unfortunately, the market for piano technicians is poor — synthesizers sound as good as many pianos, are portable and less expensive, can create many more sounds, and needn't be tuned. But some people, including me, love a regular piano. Check out the Piano Technicians Guild at www.ptg.org/document//27.

» **Inventor:** Sixty thousand kids a year are treated in hospitals for trampoline-related injuries. So Mark Publicover invented JumpSport (www.jumpsport.com), which provides 360-degree protection around standard-size trampolines. JumpSport is for sale in hundreds of outlets.

How does an invention get invented? It can start by asking yourself, "What's annoying?" and then "What could I invent that would solve the problem?" Inventors, mostly engineering types, usually develop their prototypes as an after-work spice to their day jobs.

How to invent successfully? You needn't build the prototype yourself. Find a model maker (www.modelmakers.org has a directory). Then test your prototype on potential customers and retailers. If it passes muster, find out what it would cost to manufacture — use ThomasNet's database of 600,000 manufacturers (www.thomasnet.com) to find an appropriate one. Can it be made inexpensively enough to allow ample profit? Have them make a small run that you could then distribute through trade shows, a website, or wholesale to retailers. Or try to get a company to buy or license your invention. See an intellectual property lawyer first. Think three times before using services that promise to take your idea and turn it into a moneymaker. They usually aren't worth it. Check out *Stand Alone, Inventor!* by Robert Merrick (www.amazon.com/Stand-Alone-Inventor-Robert-Merrick/dp/0964383209/

ref=sr_1_1?ie=UTF8&qid=1516152642&sr=8-1&keywords=stand+alone+inventor) and *Secrets from an Inventor's Notebook: Advice on Inventing Success,* by Maurice Kanbar (www.amazon.com/Secrets-Inventors-Notebook-Inventing-Success/dp/1571783288).

>> **Succession Advisor:** A tough time for employed individuals reaching retirement age or for a principal in the family business is when the person realizes, or management says, that it's time for the next generation to take over. The person and colleagues may be too emotionally involved to develop a wise succession plan on their own. Enter the succession consultant, a combination businessperson-and-psychologist. Check out "Succession Planning" at en.wikipedia.org/wiki/Succession_planning and *Family Business Succession: The Final Test of Greatness,* by C. Aronoff, S. McClure, and J. Ward (www.amazon.com/Family-Business-Succession-Greatness-Publication/dp/0230111009).

# The DIY Under-the-Radar Business Idea Finder

Chapter 2 of this book includes a DIY Under-the-Radar *Career* Finder. Here's an analogous approach to finding a business idea that you like but may never have otherwise thought of.

## Combining two or more interests or skills

Some people choose a business primarily on its money-making potential, but others need it to fit their knowledge, skills, interests, or values. A way to find a niche especially well-suited to you is to think of businesses that would combine two or more of your core interests, skills, and values.

Let's say that you care about the environment, you are a computer geek, and you love gadgets. How about creating a website with the coolest energy-saving programmable gadgets — for example, home automation systems. Don't just sell them but also offer to chat by Skype (or in person if they're local) to custom-program them and help customers get them running.

Or, suppose that you have a degree in engineering and you enjoy building things, listening to music, and interviewing people. How about being a home music consultant? You help people pick out the perfect system for listening to music and watching big-screen TV throughout their house, buy the gear at a good price, install it, break open walls if necessary, and train the users how to use the remote.

You love animals and music. So does Lisa Spector. She made recordings of music to calm anxious dogs. And she gives piano concerts in which dogs are often invited. That's her under-the-radar niche and successful small business. Check her out at www.lisaspector.com.

# Niching in your favorite product's supply chain

Let's say you like wine. Here are potential small-business niches in the vino supply chain:

>> Real estate agents facilitate buying, selling, and leasing vineyard property.

>> Viticulture consultants evaluate sites for growing grapes.

>> Equipment is manufactured, marketed, sold, installed, and maintained, cultivating tractors, harvesters, crushers, filters, storage tanks, oak barrels, bottlers, corkers, and labelers. Small businesses may specialize in consulting on the right equipment for the situation, by selling, delivering, or servicing.

>> Farmers grow root- and plant-stock, bud those together, and market, sell, and deliver the plants.

>> Someone needs to build the trellises on which the grapes grow as well as fences to keep out grape-eating animals.

>> The soil is amended and perhaps fumigated. Those tasks — especially fumigation — may be outsourced to a small business.

>> An irrigation specialist designs the timer, valve, and emitter system. A supplier provides the equipment, and another business may be in charge of installation.

>> People plant and later train the grape plants onto the trellis, and then fertilize and protect against insects and mildew — occasionally, by aircraft spraying. The latter service is usually outsourced to a firm that specializes in it.

>> A viticulturist, sometimes an outside consultant, tests the grapes during the growing season to determine whether cultivation changes are required and when it's time for harvest.

>> The grapes are harvested and crushed, and the juice is pumped into tanks and barrels for aging and then pumped into bottles. Then the bottles are sealed — usually, with lead capsules and natural or plastic corks. A small-business person could specialize in capsules and corks, down to embossing or printing them with grapes or the winery's name.

>> The finished bottles may be aged more or shipped to distributors, retailers, or individuals. Small-business people can be involved in any of those tasks. For example, a small business could specialize in establishing, marketing, and fulfilling orders for a winery's wine-of-the-month club. Or the business could become a shipping specialist, knowing all there is to know about laws, restrictions, temperature-controlled shipping, and best pricing for each package.

>> The wine must be marketed to rise above the wine lake. Especially in Napa and Sonoma, much wine is grown (including by celebrities who don't mind losing money as long they can tell their friends they own a winery). There's a whole wine marketing industry, laced with small-business owners. For example, a client of mine is a photographer who does nothing but take marketing photos of wine bottles. Apparently, there's an art to getting white wine to glisten and red wine to look appetizing rather than black.

>> Then there are sellers of wines: from independent distributors who go from restaurant to restaurant to those who export wine to an underserved area from Kalamazoo to Kathmandu. Others open a wine bar. I have a client, a sommelier, whose business is hosting wine-tasting parties for corporations and individuals.

>> Small businesses have made serious money simply by making or selling wine glasses. For example, Kurt Zalto, a glassblower, worked with a local priest with a renowned wine palate to create a glass that now sells (and sells a lot) at $59 a pop. Check out his work at gearpatrol.com/2017/06/29/zalto-glassware-grail.

>> Wine reviewers make their name by giving points to wine. (Studies show, however, that in blind tastings a reviewer will give a different rating to the same wine! And *Consumer Reports* rated both red and white Trader Joe's Charles Shaw "Three-Buck Chuck" wine higher than wine many times as expensive, but I digress.

You get the point. If you're a wine lover, many under-the-radar small-business opportunities exist that will put you in the wine world. Even if you're just selling equipment, you get to talk wine — and taste it.

# Going grungy

Everyone's visceral reaction to garbage (let alone sewage; let alone toxic waste) is "Ugh."

But the fact is, if you run a grungy business, you probably desensitize soon, and you may feel good about being in that business because you're doing worthy work that few people are willing to do. Yet it's easier to succeed at than in a more competitive field. Again, the key is realizing that status is often the enemy of success. Of course, going grungy may be anathema to you. Fine. That's merely one of this book's many paths to success. But if the concept appeals to you, here are a few examples:

>> Federal and local governments issue requests for proposals for hazardous materials to be transported and safely disposed of. Of course, you need a special truck (such as this example at www.svitrucks.com/hazmat) as well as other specialized equipment, but if you make that investment, you may find it a solid approach to transporting serious dollars into your bank account.

>> A client was barely five feet tall. He became self-employed by cleaning the inside of oil refinery tanks. Only someone that small could fit into the crevices, ducts, and pipes. He had little competition, it was a task that had to be done, and oil companies have money, so I imagine he charges a tidy sum for his far-from-tidy job.

>> As mentioned earlier in this chapter, Thomas Stanley, the author of the book *The Millionaire Next Door*, interviewed 750 millionaires to uncover commonalities. Many of them owned "dull-normal" businesses — for example, mobile-home-park maintenance, sandblasting, and used truck parts — grungies all.

» Mastering the art of informational interviewing

» Taking an appropriate shortcut

» Tailoring your career to your needs

» Avoiding indecision

Chapter **10**

# Making Your Choice

I magine that you've been dropped from a helicopter onto a frigid mountaintop. You have to hike down to the happy village — a career. You see a number of possible paths, but because of the fog, you can see only a few yards ahead. If you just stand there, unwilling to pick a path to try, you'll die. The answer, of course, is to start down the path that you sense is best. You could end up at the happy village, find a side path to an even happier village, or, in the worst case, return to the top to try another path.

It's like that with the careers you're considering: If you wait until a career feels perfect upfront, you'll probably freeze. It's better to simply start down a path. If it's feeling good, stroll on toward the happy village, perhaps finding along the way a path to an even happier option. If your path of first choice ends up feeling bad, you can always try another.

Here's a bit of reassurance: Your career path needn't feel perfect — just promising. Most people who are pleased with their careers weren't sure that they would be, until after they had gone down the path: Become good at your work, and then tailor and accessorize the career to fit your needs.

So there's no need to wait to start down a path. Just follow these general steps:

1. Check out one or more careers using this chapter's suggestions. Pick the one that feels best.

2. Do a thorough job search and vet employers carefully so that you've maximized the chance that your first job will be well-suited to you.

3. Tailor and accessorize your job to fit. Or try self-employment, where custom-tailoring is easier.

That's a more likely path to the happy village than to wait at the top of the mountain for perfection to descend on you.

# Using Google to Find the Best Articles and Videos

Because a Google search is free and instantly available, many people take it for granted. But it may be the most valuable tool for learning about a career — actually, for almost any topic. Google Search curates incomprehensibly large amounts of data to present you with on-target websites in text and video, in likely order of utility.

A few of the strategies described in this list can help you get more from a Google search:

>> **Enclose phrases into quotation marks.** In other words, enter *astronomer "day in the life"* rather than *astronomer day in the life*. That tells Google to ignore sites with the word-string *astronomer day*, which likely refers to astronomers' attempts to see stars during the day. That's not quite what you were looking for.

>> **Trust Google Search's algorithm.** Some smart people have figured out how to curate search results, so do initially consider the first few results.

>> **Resist the temptation to instantly click on any result.** The page of results shows the first few lines of each website. First skim those and then ask, "Should I click on one of these sites, or do I see an even better search term within those few lines?" This suggestion makes your search more time-effective.

**TIP**

>> **(Optional) Zero in on videos.** If you like learning from videos, take advantage of Google's Video tab. Though one or two videos may appear near the top of a normal Google Search result by default, you can find more videos by doing a separate search using this tab. (It's at the top of the screen).

>> **Limit the number of results that you click.** When you've clicked on a site, you additionally improve your time-effectiveness by skimming them, being sure to read or watch only the material that you sense has a good chance of being useful.

>> **When you find a nugget, copy it into a Word file that you've created for that career.** A typical nugget is a not-so-obvious aspect of a day-in-the-life that's a turn-on or a turn-off. For example, you may learn that surgeons have far more irregular hours than do pediatricians. Or you may believe that a question deserves to be followed up in another Google search or to be saved for an informational interview (see the later section "Making the Most of Informational Interviewing"). For example, a video might say that *most* social workers have a master's degree, but you might be curious about options for people who have only a bachelor's degree. In that case, you would search for *"Social work" jobs bachelor's.*

# Making the Most of Informational Interviewing

In the past, it was standard practice to recommend that career-seekers complete an informational interview before picking a career path. Now that practice is not so clearly correct. People are busier now. Unless they already know and like you, a common response to a request for an informational interview is no response. And if you're a low priority, you may not be scheduled for several weeks out. Worse, the wait may not be worth your time: You could be receiving idiosyncratic input. After all, some people love their career; others in the same career hate it. Or they could hate it that day. It's a sample of one. Or their specific job could be particularly good or bad. But it still may be worth doing an informational interview or two, especially if you do it right.

## Preparing for the interview

First, do the Google search I mention in the preceding paragraph. That way, in the informational interview, you can ask about topics you couldn't have learned about on your own. And your Google search may generate good questions. Submit your best two or three in your request for an informational interview. That will make the person more likely to grant you one.

Here are some sources of people to ask for informational interviews:

>> The membership or leadership in your field's professional association

>> Members of your college alumni association (usually provided in a database of members and their occupations)

>> Friends and family members

>> LinkedIn connections

Look for people with whom you're likely to bond — you may both be alums of the same small college, for example. (Being fellow alums at a large institution is likely to be less compelling.) An even stronger bond is a negative situation that you have in common, such as not finishing college and looking for someone in that career who also didn't finish. Stronger still may be a political affiliation — people on the same side of the political aisle will likely bond more than those on opposite sides of the aisle.

Seekers of informational interviews (all of us, actually) become frustrated from sending off emails and making phone calls, and even applying for jobs, and not receiving even the courtesy of a rejection message. Though there's no foolproof antidote to the societal devaluation of courtesy, my clients have found the following procedure helpful in boosting their response rates — I call it "call–email–call:"

Call: After hours, leave a voicemail, such as this one:

*Hi, my name is Mary Jones. I just finished my BA in psychology and am contemplating a career as an eating-disorders specialist. I've done a fair amount of reading about the career, which has generated a few questions that I can't seem to get answered in print — for example [include two questions that your Internet research has triggered.] I wonder if you'd be willing to talk with me for a few minutes by phone or Skype, or in person, to answer my questions and perhaps tell me a little about your work as an eating-disorders specialist. I'd be honored. As soon as I hang up the phone, I'll send you an email reiterating my request. My number is 311-555-2368. That's 311-555-2368.*

Email: Promptly send that person a résumé and a brief cover letter reiterating the information in your call.

*Call:* If you haven't heard from the person in three days, call during work hours. If you get voicemail, that's okay. Leave a message such as this one:

*Hi, this is Mary Jones again. I'm contemplating a career as an eating-disorders specialist. Having not heard from you, I'm assuming that you're too busy. I understand, but I know that things can fall between the cracks, so I'm taking the liberty of calling to follow up. I'd be honored if you'd call back to answer a few questions and perhaps tell me a little about your work as an eating-disorders specialist. But if I don't hear from you, don't worry — I won't be a pest and keep calling. But if you do decide to call me, my number again is 311-555-2368. That's 311-555-2368. Thank you for considering it.*

**TIP**

If the person is local, it's usually worth your time to try to get an in-person appointment. The chemistry works better, which boosts your chances of getting more inside-baseball information, of getting help in landing a job, and even being offered one.

## Doing it

The term *informational interview* is a misnomer. Sure, you may want information, but if the interviewee happens to offer you a cool job, you might well take it. So be as prepared as you would be for a job interview. Bring stories or evidence of your accomplishments, even if it's a term paper or another work product you completed for school.

Every situation is different, of course, though the following outline works well in many informational interviews:

1. Thank the person for being willing to talk with you.

2. Using at most a minute, tell the story of how you became interested in the career, perhaps embedding an accomplishment or two. That can motivate the person to give you more time and a job lead. If ad libbing is scary, script the story, reduce it to a few bullet points, and practice delivering it to a mirror or to your mobile phone — use Voice Memos on the iPhone or Smart Voice Recorder on Android to make a recording. Keep practicing until you sound crisp and natural.

3. To additionally engage the interviewer, show that you see her as a person, not just as an information resource who's no different from a book. Start by asking about her life in the career you're inquiring about, such as "Would you mind telling me what made you decide to get into this field?"

   Often, that's enough to start the person off and running in describing training and day-to-day life in the profession. If not, be specific — for example, "What would you suggest for a good way, or place, to get training?" or "Can you walk me through a typical day in your work life?"

4. Trust your intuition. Do you sense that the person wants to end the interview, or might she be willing to answer one or more questions? Here are some that often elicit useful information:

   - What would you say are the not-obvious best and worst things about the profession?

   - What ends up being the crucial attributes for being good at this profession?

   - What might surprise me about your career?

- Why do people decide to leave the profession?

- Do you have any suggestions for what my next step should be?

  The response is usually something to read or watch, or a conference to attend. If you follow through and then tell the person what you learned, you will strengthen your relationship, making her more likely to help you further, as a mentor or a source of job leads.

- It's a judgment call whether to ask, "Might you suggest someone else I should talk with?" or "Is there any chance I might be able to work for you?"

5. End with a catch-all question, such as "Anything else you'd like to tell me or ask me?" It's wise to end most interviews and conversations this way. Often, it can tease out something useful that you wouldn't have thought to ask.

# Shortcutting the Process

Doing an informational interview is worth your time, but some people want a simpler process. You'd still be ahead of the game with most career-seekers if you simply visited www.mynextmove.org. This site enables you to find your career your way. The process works in one of three ways:

>> You describe your dream career in a few words. The site then searches descriptions of hundreds of careers to find matching terms.

>> You complete an interests inventory and it shows you matches.

>> You peruse categorized lists of careers.

The site then provides information, and perhaps videos, about each career, including places to get training. Good stuff.

Or use the Pathsource app, which is free on iOS and Android. It offers a career-finding matching program, more than 2,600 informational interviews on video, links to colleges offering preparation for a particular career, and a large database of job fairs. It even includes a résumé builder.

Want more videos? The U.S. Department of Labor offers a collection of short, captioned introductions to careers at www.careeronestop.org/videos/careervideos/career-videos.aspx.

Then just pick the career that best fits your needs, and use www.mynextmove.org to find the best way to train. It's easy-peasy and still a more likely path to career contentment than the one most people take.

# Tailoring and Accessorizing Your Career

Off the rack, a career probably will feel just okay. It will feel much better, if you tailor and accessorize it to your tastes.

Perhaps the examples in this section will trigger your own ideas for personalizing your career:

Sandy loved to take photos, but knew the long odds against making a living at it. So she decided to use her ability as a computer programmer (knowing that Silicon Valley is looking to hire women) and became a software developer. Instead of displaying the usual sterile photos of executive team members on the company website, she shot and then posted edgy shots of everyone in the building, from CEO to janitor.

Michael had two loves — acting and hiking — but couldn't foresee making a living at either, so he became a high school history teacher. He incorporated his two loves by dressing up in costume whenever the class discussed major historical events, and he frequently took classes on hikes to historic sites.

Here's how I made a good fit of my off-the-rack career as a career counselor. I enjoy playing the piano for people. So, whenever we need a break during a session, I play something for my clients. As a sideline, I perform my 1-man shows (www.youtube.com/watch?v=umnVd_FrhX0) and accompany singers (www.youtube.com/watch?v=4q61rNqU8DA). I also host a radio program (www.martynemko.com/radio-show). I work at home because I don't like commuting, and that way, my doggie doesn't have to deal with his separation issues. And as you may know, because I like to write, I write a lot about careers — including, of course, this book. That process made an otherwise good career fit into one that I love.

With all this as a possible trigger, how might you take your own off-the-shelf career and make it a great fit for you?

# Resolving Indecision

Sometimes a person can narrow her choices to two or three possible careers, but can't decide which to pick. This technique, which I often use with clients, may help:

1. Write the advantages and disadvantages of choosing Career 1.

2. Write the advantages and disadvantages of Career 2 and, if desired, Career 3.

3. Put a plus sign or two next to the most important advantages and a minus sign or two next to the most significant disadvantages.

4. Review those advantages and disadvantages, and pick one of the careers. How are you feeling? If you're disappointed, what advantages and disadvantages do you need to give more consideration to?

5. Remind yourself that, by tailoring and accessorizing a career, it will fit better in the long run.

6. Using only your gut feeling, make your choice. The gut feeling will have incorporated many factors — those you consciously considered, plus others you can't articulate. Using this chapter's strategies for choosing a career puts you ahead of most other career-seekers. Chances are, you've made a wise choice.

# 3

# Getting Trained, Getting Confident

Get competent within the halls of academe

Get competent outside the halls of academe

Get psychologically solid

Chapter **11**

# Getting Trained by Degrees

Y ou've chosen a career direction. A key to your success, of course, is getting well trained for it.

In Chapter 12, I discuss less traditional ways to get trained; in this chapter, however, I offer ideas on how to make the most of the mainstream route for most white collar professions: a college degree, maybe a graduate degree.

## Choosing a Major

If you don't already have a bachelor's degree and your career normally requires at least that degree, you need to choose a major. Career-minded people are tempted to pick a direct route: for example, nursing, business, computer science, accounting, architecture, or engineering. Sometimes that's wise: Not only does that provide more direct preparation for your career, but most employers also prefer or require that major.

For many careers, however, you can choose virtually any major. Some lawyers majored in theatre, and some businesspeople in English, and although physicians took the required handful of science courses, some majored in art. The link at the end of each career scoop in Part 2 should tell you how much flexibility you'd likely have in choosing a major.

In this chapter, I'd just like to offer some perhaps not-so-obvious thoughts about a dozen popular majors.

## English

This one comes in two flavors: literature and writing.

An argument for choosing the literature major is that it increases your aesthetic appreciation and exposes you to thoughtful explorations of life's major issues — for example, love, money, and the life well-led. Alas, the courses' reading lists can be voluminous, affording insufficient time to explore those universal themes. That may partly explain why *Cliff's Notes* and *SparkNotes* are popular.

An argument for the writing major is that it affords much opportunity for self-expression. In addition, if the program includes practical and not just creative writing, you learn a skill that's valuable in most careers. Plus, if you get substantive feedback on your writing, your thinking skills may improve. After all, writing is thought written. Alas, especially in institutions with large classes, you may get less feedback than is desirable. As you decide which instructors' courses to take, consider reviews (on ratemyprofessor.com, for example) to see whether students feel they were given sufficient feedback. Saying simply, "B+, Good job" won't do.

## Theatre

Theatre is an underrated major, in part because the public knows that few theatre majors can make a living in the dramatic arts. What's under-recognized is that the theatre major is a good vehicle for learning the universal themes mentioned in the preceding section. That's because, if you're in a play — whether as an actor or a director or behind the scenes — you're experiencing the play again and again, making its explorations of life issues more likely to suffuse into your fabric rather than something to be forgotten soon after the exam. An acting-centric theatre major is also good for building poise and public speaking, which are useful in many careers. Plus, the theatre major can be unusually pleasurable. Few activities are as fun as being part of a play: a big project with a public culmination.

## Communication or rhetoric

This major, too, is underrated. The ability to communicate, especially to persuade, is helpful in nearly all careers, not to mention in personal life. Communication majors learn the art of oral and written persuasion.

## Computer science

If you have a strong aptitude for computer science, that major should be a career-door opener. CS grads work on likely-to-stay-in-demand, cutting-edge problems such as virtual physicians that learn from experience and bioterrorism sensor-development. But the people who get hired for good, offshoring-resistant jobs have an unusual combination of skills: coding, communication, business, and/or interpersonal moxie. With training, these people can become project architects, managers, and executives. Those careers, unlike coding, are offshore-resistant.

## Nursing

The job market for nurses will almost certainly remain strong, largely because of the sizable aging baby boomer cohort. That will mean that work formerly done by physicians will be done by nurses: nurse practitioners and nurse anesthetists, for example. But nursing must be a calling. Many nurses face an endless conveyer belt of illness, pain, and death. Nurses must not only be unusually caring — they must also, in the face of ongoing stress, remain extremely detail-oriented: A misplaced decimal point can mean that a patient dies of an overdose.

## Molecular biology and genetics

I had the privilege of attending a panel discussion among five Nobel Prize winners. They disagreed on all manner of topics but concurred that molecular biology, which subsumes genetics, would be the coming decades' most impactful field.

## Applied math

This major is the key to the evolving fields of finance, computer programming, and marketing. A variant, statistics, teaches skills that are valuable in, for example, artificial intelligence, evaluation of innovative social programs, biomedical research, politics, and sports. For the practically oriented math nerd, applied math is an underconsidered major compared with, for example, computer science or molecular biology.

# Entomology

Entomology, the study of insects, is an underconsidered route into the overcrowded job market for environmentalists.

# Architecture

Too many architects are underemployed. They're less likely to design buildings than to draft plans for heating, ventilation, and air conditioning systems. Or their job may heavily entail submitting documents for approval by the government.

Worse, ever more architectural work will be automated or offshored. For example, thousands of blueprints are already available inexpensively online. That kills architect jobs. Beyond design, some architectural work can be offshored to low-cost countries.

Plus, hiring a residential architect is a luxury. The economy may not support enough people who can afford an architect and who instead will live in tract homes, purchase an ever better premanufactured home, or merely adapt the aforementioned online blueprints.

Because architecture training is narrowly focused, with much learning that isn't transferrable to other fields, and full licensure requires 7 to 11 years, architecture isn't a major I can embrace unless you're confident that it's your unique calling.

# Journalism

Journalism is an enticing major. Many people are intrigued by doing investigative journalism: shining light on societal wrongs in the hope of contributing to a better tomorrow. Alas, it's enticing to too many people. The result is a great oversupply of journalism graduates who are bearing the usual mountain of student debt but who are usually expected to work for little or nothing — for example, write a free-lance article for under $100, with no benefits. (I wrote 20 articles for TIME.com's Ideas section, and although I'm not shy about negotiation, the total pay was $0. They said, "Take it or leave it.")

# Foreign language

After early childhood, it is difficult to master a foreign language sufficiently to significantly enhance your career. So unless your goal is to immerse yourself in a foreign language's *literature*, it's wise to avoid this major. Sure, some knowledge of Spanish or Chinese, for example, will be a plus. That could justify self-study using commercial software, but doesn't argue for foreign language being the best choice of major.

## Music

Like studio art, this is another major you shouldn't think of as preparation for your career unless it's already clear that you're at least a potential star. Unfortunately, even many Julliard and Chicago Art Institute grads are forced to relegate their art to avocational status. Regardless, pleasure is an underconsidered factor in choosing a major. Remember: Many people pursue careers having nothing to do with their majors. Music and art give many people, including me, inordinate pleasure. So a major that involves listening to and producing music or viewing and creating art has much to recommend it, even if your career has no more to do with music than working while listening to tunes.

# Choosing a Graduate Program

If you're thinking of graduate school, you're probably appropriately focusing on a program that will prepare you explicitly for your career. Popular examples are law school, master's in social work (MSW), occupational therapy, business administration (MBA), medical school (MD), doctor of physical therapy, doctor of audiology, and doctor of optometry. Less common but underconsidered options are practically oriented doctorates — for example, doctor of business administration (DBA,) doctor of psychology (PsyD), and doctor of education (EdD.)

TIP

Turn down Harvard for No-Name U? Believe it or not, that can make sense. Of course, a designer label on the diploma opens career doors, but you pay a price for that: You may receive an education that doesn't prepare you as well for your career. You see, universities accrue prestige not mainly from their teaching but from their research, and the more prestigious the university, the more likely it is to focus on research — often esoteric research that is less important for students to learn than what they otherwise could have. Of course, it's tempting to choose the most prestigious institution to which you can gain admission, but if you'd rather focus on steak than on sizzle, on career competence rather than on perceived competence, do consider less august institutions.

For example, in my PhD's specialty, the evaluation of innovative programs, I chose the most prestigiously named school to which I was admitted: the University of California, Berkeley. Later, I discovered that a better program in that field is at Western Michigan University.

These are the key factors in choosing graduate programs to apply to:

>> **Geography:** Most people end up living near where they attend graduate school because their fieldwork, internships, and networking connections are local. So focus your search on locales you could see living in after graduation.

>> **The curriculum:** Even programs with the same title can vary greatly. For example, a clinical psychology PhD program might specialize in cognitive-behavioral interventions, the biological basis of mental illness, or the increasingly out-of-favor Freudian theory. Variation in emphasis can be true even in a discipline as seemingly prescribed as medical school. For example, I teach in the University of California, San Francisco School of Medicine. It prioritizes training doctors to meet vulnerable populations' needs and to change our healthcare system to better accommodate them. So, on each prospective program's website, look at the required courses and available electives, and check out the faculty's research and service interests.

>> **Your advisor:** Even in master's degree programs but especially in doctoral ones, your advisor is a key to your success and, yes, happiness. She can help you map out a program that will meet your needs, hire you as a teaching or research assistant, open doors to good jobs, and (as has been the case with my advisor, philosopher, and evaluation luminary Michael Scriven) become a lifelong friend.

>> **The tone:** Many programs have a political tinge: liberal, moderate, and, less commonly, conservative. Because political affiliation is among people's strongest bonds, you may want to choose a program consonant with your political beliefs. Or, if you're more interested in broadening your perspective, give brownie points to programs offering a different slant. Also, some programs, even within prestigious institutions, are more rigorous than others. At one, the typical student might study five hours a night; at another, just one. You can often learn about the workload by asking the admissions counselor about it or even if a student or two would phone you to discuss the program.

>> **Selectivity:** Reflexively, most students choose the institution that's hardest to get into, because that usually means a more prestigious name on the diploma and because they may learn more by having classmates who are brighter and more motivated.

But many students would be wiser to choose an institution at which they're just average: That enables them to be around some unusually stimulating students, but they don't have to wipe themselves out to get decent grades and so they have time for extracurricular activities and a personal life.

Still other students thrive as the big fish in the less selective pond. For example, a student who is anxiety-prone or who tends to close down when he's not a top-level student might choose the least selective college to which he has been admitted. As a bonus, doing that often yields a better financial

TIP

aid package because the institution wants to upgrade its student body. A student who is a big fish in a less selective pond benefits also because he tends to get higher GPAs, and get noticed by professors, and is offered plum opportunities and glowing letters of recommendation.

>> **Cost:** It's difficult to ascertain upfront how much you'll pay. Some students pay far less than the sticker price. Some of that is determined by evaluating your ability to pay based on your verified FAFSA and perhaps Profile form. But some institutions have other money to distribute. That's why it's wise to apply to a good number of programs, perhaps as many as ten, compare offers, and even play one against the other. Do distinguish between discounts that are loan versus grant. Obviously, you have to pay back the loan. And the powerful higher-education lobby convinced Congress to make student loans virtually the only loan that cannot be discharged in bankruptcy.

# Online Degrees

The number of online degree programs has grown, at both the undergraduate and graduate levels.

Quality can vary, perhaps even more so than in traditional degree programs. So, in addition to the screening criteria in the previous section, consider these:

>> **Interactivity:** Good online programs offer at least some of these: video simulations, videoconference discussions, online group projects, forums, and the opportunity to email the instructor and fellow students.

>> **Completion rate:** Ask the admissions person, "What's the normal range of time it takes for students to complete this program?" Asking for "the normal range" will give you a better sense than just asking for "the average," let alone "the expected" time to completion. You may get a more accurate answer if you ask by email rather than by phone.

>> **Career services:** Only some online programs offer students full access to the university's career services.

>> **Career enhancement:** Most programs' websites offer anecdotal success stories. Better to ask, "What data do you have that assesses how much a person's career prospects are improved by graduating from this program?" That question is broad enough to accommodate the different ways an institution might collect such data.

# Getting In

Average students can gain admission to all but the small percentage of brand-name institutions, which as I point out earlier in this chapter, may provide less practical training than would a less prestigious institution.

That said, here are several tips for maximizing your chances of admission to a selective institution and even getting better financial aid:

>> No surprise, because universities are in the business of giving grades, they like students with good grades, especially in hard courses. Are we having fun yet?

>> Even though tests such as the SAT, GRE, LSAT, and GMAT are moderately coachable, they carry significant weight in most colleges' admission decisions. If you're self-motivated, I recommend foregoing expensive prep courses and tutors in favor of the dramatically cheaper prep book or software. Many highly rated ones are available on Amazon.

>> Having relevant work experience is a plus. If you're applying to a career-preparatory program, — an MBA, for example — it's often wise to have a couple years of career-relevant work experience under your belt before applying. That can increase your admissibility, because it's evidence that you know what the career is like and it gives you real-world knowledge that can enrich classroom discussions. Having those couple years of real-world experience benefits you because it can solidify whether you want to pursue that degree. In addition, that real-world experience gives you something concrete to apply to what you'll be taught in graduate school.

>> Colleges want a well-rounded class, but when it comes to individuals, they're looking for extracurricular *depth*. So they're more likely to be impressed if you've been immersed in a specific cause for a few years than if you dabbled in a few. If you're applying for a specific major or graduate program, they prefer that depth be related. For example, if you're applying to medical school, they'd likely be more impressed if you worked in a clinic or research lab or as a medical scribe than if you were the star of the bowling team.

>> Most essay questions reduce to one. At the undergraduate level, it's "Tell me an anecdote that reveals one of your essential qualities." At the graduate level, it's usually, "Why choose this career and this institution's program?" Thoughtfully addressing that question not only enhances your admissibility, but it can also be personally clarifying for you.

**TIP**

>> At your top-choice school(s), review the faculty bios in your prospective major or graduate program to identify someone whose interests and persona seem most attractive. Perhaps read an article or two of theirs. Most professors include their *curriculum vitae* (a fancy word for academic résumé), which lists

their publications. Google the name of the article, and if you're lucky, it, or at least an abstract, will come up. Or see whether a local college subscribes to the journal in which the article appeared.

After reading the article, phone the professor during office hours. Explain that you're considering applying to her program, found her bio interesting, read one of her articles, and wonder whether she might chat a bit to discuss whether it's an appropriate program for you — and perhaps even whether she might be an appropriate advisor. That shows unusual initiative, and if you click with the professor, could yield advice to enhance your application and maybe even a letter recommending your admission.

# Making Your Education Career-Ready

Of course, study skills can help you become better educated and, in turn, may boost your career, but other skills are also important. The next few sections highlight some keys to academic success.

## Choosing courses carefully

Even in required courses, you may have a choice of professors, and in elective courses, you usually have more choices. Select courses that would help you become more qualified for your career goal, but, when in doubt, choose the better teacher even if the course title isn't as on-target. For example, even if you think you don't care about the history of your field, the professor of that course who engages, enlightens, and even transforms will likely be of value to you professionally and personally. In finding the best instructors, use scuttlebutt, syllabus review, and online professor review sites. Check out "What to Know about Professor Rating Websites" at www.fastweb.com/student-life/articles/what-to-know-about-professor-rating-websites.

TIP

You may be able to get permission to take courses at other institutions.

## Reading in advance

You can make a good first impression on an instructor while reducing your stress and getting a head start toward a good grade by completing the first assigned reading before the first class session and continuing to stay ahead. That will help you understand what's going on in class and make you more likely to ask thoughtful questions and make interesting comments.

## Taking a moderate amount of notes

Of course, taking too few notes can hurt, but so can taking too many — that's overwhelming. Your notes should consist of material you'll use to study for an upcoming test. So don't write information that you already know or details that you sense the professor doesn't care much about. Of course, keep your antennae out for signs of importance: The professor's voice gets louder or slower. She may even explicitly say, "Remember this for the midterm!" Perhaps most important, write things you personally care to remember, whether it will be on the test or not.

## Commenting and questioning moderately

Comments and questions are active learning — the stuff of which enduring learning is made — as opposed to the material that flies out of your head the day after the test. But you don't want to be one of those selfish students who takes up too much class time. Rule of thumb: Offer one or (maybe) two concise comments or questions per hour of class time. If you have additional questions or comments, email them to the professor or visit or call during office hours.

TIP

Be sure that the purpose of your question or comment is to enhance your learning, not to show off. Use a tone of respectful querying rather than trying to impress or even one-up the instructor. Here's how to tell the difference:

**Inappropriate:** Dr. Jones, you said that Erik Erikson speaks of a person's 60s as their age of transgenerativity: when people want to transmit their knowledge to the next generation. That's obsolete. We're living a lot longer now.

**Appropriate:** Dr. Jones, you said that Erikson speaks of the 60s as the age of transgenerativity, but he lived a long time ago. We live longer now. Do you think it's fair to say that the 70s are the new 60s?

## Remembering what you read

It's easy to read for 20 minutes and not remember anything you've read. To keep alert, try being an active reader: Read a paragraph or two, then turn away and, aloud, summarize what you just read."

## Reviewing feedback on your work and tests

There's a tendency to care only about the grade. But the comments and your errors on a short-answer test are individualized feedback, the stuff of which important learning is wrought.

## Adapting assignments to suit

Often, the standard assignment isn't well-matched to your career goal. Most professors welcome your proposing an alternative, as long as it's not so that you can do less work.

## Taking an independent study

Some professors will let you take a one-on-one course, studying something relevant to their expertise that intrigues you. Pick a professor whose course you've taken and with whom you click.

## Choosing career-relevant extracurriculars

Student government? Student newspaper? Interested in joining a club for students preparing for your career — for example, the Future Lawyers Club? Or do you want to become a student member of the faculty senate? That may help you figure out whether journalism, the law, or politics is really what you want to end up doing.

## Joining your future career's professional association

If you aspire to become, say, an organizational psychologist, you probably should join the Society for Industrial and Organizational Psychology and even propose to co-present with a professor at the next local or even national meeting. Hundreds of professional associations are out there, and more likely than not there's one associated with the field you're interested in. And students usually get a deeply discounted membership fee.

## Reaching out to potential employers early

Don't wait until the last minute to send those feelers out to folks who just might hire you. Start that process long before you expect to get hired. To find potential employers, use family and friend connections, LinkedIn, and the professional association's website. Describe what you're clear and fuzzy about regarding your career, and ask for advice. If, for example, the person suggests you read something, take a certain course, or attend a particular conference, let the person know when you've done that and what you learned. That often can pave the way to further mentorship and even a job.

## Using your college's career services

Using the campus career services can be valuable when it comes to career exploration, identifying target employers, reviewing your résumé and LinkedIn profile, examining cover letters, and conducting mock interviews, especially if you start early in your college or graduate school career. Part of what your tuition covers is career services. Not using them is like paying for a full tank of gas and not filling it to the top.

## Nailing down good fieldwork, internship, or co-op opportunities

It's difficult for programs to find a high-quality placement for all students. So consider asking whether you might unearth your own. Then look for a placement that's both on-target for your career and with a competent supervisor there who'd be glad to mentor you.

## Choosing your final project

Write your final project, thesis, or dissertation on a topic that helps prepare you for your career, would impress your target employer, and excites you. You'll be spending months if not longer on that project, so it needs to be sufficiently motivating that you'll stay with it to the end.

# Paying for It

Anyone smart enough to read a *For Dummies* book knows to fill out the federal FAFSA and, if required, the Profile, and to do it by the deadline — there are no extensions. So I won't waste your time with such basics. Here, however, are a few more advanced ideas:

**TIP**

The financial aid formulas penalize student income and assets much more than parents'. And assets held outside the family (for example, by grandparents) don't count against you at all. So if the family wants to make a major purchase or pay off debt, it might use money that's in the student's name. If the family wants to save money for college, perhaps save in the grandparents' name. (That said, institutions that require the Profile require reporting grandparent financial information, which could reduce the value of that income shifting.)

If you're 24 or under and an undergraduate, your parents' income and assets will be considered unless one of these is true: You're married, you have dependents other than a spouse, you're an orphan, you're a veteran or an active-duty member of the US Armed Forces, your parents are institutionalized, or you're *emancipated*, which means that you're on your own and receive no support from your family. Usually, that status must be verified by a third party such as a counselor or religious leader.

As mentioned, apply to as many as ten institutions, including a few in which you'd be an above-average student. To entice you to come, those institutions are more likely to give you a big discount.

Carefully compare offers. Of course, compare how much cash you'll actually be required to pay. Also note the renewal requirements for any scholarship or discount. The award letter may say that the scholarship is renewable, but the fine print could say that a high GPA is required for renewal. Or it might give you a generous discount in Year 1 without mentioning that, starting in Year 2, some of that cash discount will be converted to loan, which of course, you must pay back with interest.

Consider playing one offer against the other. Colleges' financial aid officers understandably don't like hardball negotiators, even though that's certainly your right. The sweet spot may be to negotiate but gently, as in this example:

> I'm pleased to have received your offer of admission, but my family and I are nervous about taking on all this debt. You see, our family's financial situation isn't as rosy as implied in the FAFSA. We have unusual medical and housing expenses, and Dad's job is tenuous. Also, another good institution has offered generous financial aid, which is tempting. I'm hoping you might be able to convert the loan portion of my financial aid package to grant. I'm confident I'll do well at school, so I don't mind its renewal being contingent on my getting a B+ average or higher. Thank you for considering my request.

**REMEMBER**

That may or may not work, but you have nothing to lose by asking. Indeed, that's related to the broader advice that's been given at Harvard's new-student orientation: "Key to success at Harvard is to ask for what you want. And if they say no, ask someone else."

# Chapter 12

# Getting Trained Without a Degree

A mid the criticism (and cost) of college and graduate degrees, many people wonder if they might get at least some of their career preparation away from the ivy-covered walls.

Add to this the fact that, especially in technology fields, more employers are caring less about the diploma and more about finding candidates with the needed expertise and personal characteristics.

Sure, if you're aiming for certain careers, you must get the required degree. For example, you can't be a social worker without a degree. But even in fields in which a degree is normally required, there may be alternative routes. For example, in California, Virginia, Vermont, and Washington, aspiring lawyers can train by apprenticeship rather than law school.

This chapter will discuss non-academic ways to gain career expertise, what I call *You U* — some combination of mentorship, tutoring, self-study, workshops, and in-person and online short and long courses.

**REMEMBER**

Academic and non-academic training are not mutually exclusive. Even a lover of school might want to supplement with a bit of You U.

# Good Reasons to Get a Degree

You might well have good reasons to pursue a degree:

>> **For your enlightenment:** A degree program can help you become an informed citizen and experience life more richly. A humanities course taught well can broaden and deepen your worldview.

>> **Some fields require a degree:** For example, if you want to be a physician, the government won't let you treat patients just because you had a mentor, read some articles, and attended a couple of conferences. In fields like management consulting and investment banking and at top law firms, employers generally ignore applicants who aren't waving a prestigious diploma.

>> **If you aspire to an academic career or as a researcher in industry:** Universities are good places to train to be a researcher. Nearly all professors have a doctorate.

>> **If you tried and failed to change careers without that degree:** You tried You U, but it didn't work. You may need a degree.

>> **You need the structure of school:** To design and follow through on a You U education requires self-motivation, even if you have a mentor. (See "Getting Mentored, Being Mentored" in Chapter 19 on how to find and make the most of one.) Many people need the structure of school, as in "Be there from 7 to 9 p.m. on Tuesdays and Thursdays."

>> **You want the social contact that comes with being in class regularly.**

# Poor Reasons to Get a Degree

These reasons for getting a degree aren't so good:

>> **To help you decide what career to pursue:** Most degree programs expose you only to a small fraction of the career options. Better to choose your career using the methods in Part 2 of this book.

>> **To postpone looking for a job:** No need to spend years and serious money to postpone that task. Part 4 of this book shows how to find a rewarding job without experiencing undue pain.

>> **Because you think it will lead to a good job:** Internet research and perhaps interviewing a few people in that career can reveal whether it's wise to consider a nondegree approach to achieving your goal.

>> **Impress friends and family:** Might you find less costly and time-consuming ways to do that? Wouldn't landing a good job years sooner than if you had gone back for that degree be even more impressive?

>> **To feel legitimate:** As I explain later in this chapter, in some fields you can be at least as legitimately trained at You U as at standard U.

>> **To dazzle employers:** In some fields, employers may end up being truly impressed with your You U career preparation, as long as you adequately explain You U's benefits, as I describe later in this chapter.

# More Reasons to Consider You U

Some people recognize the drawbacks of getting a degree, yet insist that it's worth the time and money because of what the piece of paper can do for them. Will that be true for you?

Yes, people with degrees do earn more over their lifetimes than do other people, but the degree may not be the main reason for that discrepancy. They may earn more mainly because degree seekers are, on average, more capable and more motivated to begin with. If you locked degree seekers in a closet for four years, they might earn more than people who don't pursue degrees.

**REMEMBER**

It's true that many employers' job ads specify that you need a degree. But if your application letter is like the one I recommend later in this chapter, at least some wise employers will consider you, just as they may consider a candidate who lacks another requirement. Might it be worth trying to land that job with You U preparation instead of a degree? If that doesn't work, you can pursue that degree with greater confidence that you really do need it.

In her book *Success Without College*, the *New York Times* editor Linda Lee cites a *Newsweek* article by Robert Samuelson that says even "[G]oing to Harvard or Duke won't automatically produce a better job and higher pay. Graduates of these schools generally do well. But they do well because they are talented." The article was titled "The Worthless Ivy League."

What do you think the following people have in common: Richard Branson, TV chef Rachael Ray, Malcolm X, Jessica Alba, Facebook cofounders Mark Zuckerberg and Dustin Moskovitz, *Vogue* editor-in-chief Anna Wintour, Mary Kay Ash, Oracle CEO Larry Ellison, Maya Angelou, Tumblr founder David Karp, Oprah Winfrey, Simon Cowell, Ellen DeGeneres, JetBlue founder David Neeleman, advertising legend David Ogilvy, designer Steve Madden, Yahoo! cofounder Jerry Yang, David Oreck (Oreck vacuum cleaners,) Barbra Streisand, Hollywood mogul Barry Diller, PBS *NewsHour*'s Nina Totenberg, Ted Turner, Whole Foods founder John Mackey, Vidal Sassoon, Bank of America founder A.P. Giannini, former governor Jesse Ventura, IBM founder Thomas Watson, architect Frank Lloyd Wright, former Israeli president David Ben-Gurion, Dell Computer founder Michael Dell, Woody Allen, Warren Beatty, Domino's pizza chain founder Tom Monaghan, folk singer Joan Baez, Digg founder Kevin Rose, MGM owner Kirk Kerkorian, Conair founder Leandro Rizzuto, Microsoft cofounders Bill Gates and Paul Allen, *Pulp Fiction* director Quentin Tarantino, ABC-TV's Peter Jennings, Wendy's founder Dave Thomas, Holiday Inn founder Kemmons Wilson, Thomas Edison, Blockbuster Video founder and Miami Dolphins owner Wayne Huizenga, Etsy founder Rob Kalin, William Faulkner, Jane Austen, McDonald's founder Ray Kroc, Coca-Cola CEO Charles Culpeper, Henry Ford, cosmetics magnate Helena Rubenstein, Ben Franklin, Alexander Graham Bell, Coco Chanel, Walter Cronkite, Walt Disney, Bob Dylan, seven U.S. presidents from Washington to Truman, Rolls-Royce founder Sir Henry Royce, Leonardo DiCaprio, cookie maker Debbi Fields, Sally Field, Jane Fonda, chocolatier Milton Hershey, Buckminster Fuller, DreamWorks cofounder David Geffen, *Roots* author Alex Haley, Ernest Hemingway, Dustin Hoffman, famed anthropologist Richard Leakey, airplane inventors Wilbur and Orville Wright, Madonna, satirist H.L. Mencken, Auntie Anne's Pretzels founder Anne Beiler, Colonel Sanders (KFC), Martina Navratilova, Rush Limbaugh, Rosie O'Donnell, chef Wolfgang Puck, Robert Redford, oil billionaire John D. Rockefeller, Eleanor Roosevelt, NBC mogul David Sarnoff, Apple Computer founder Steve Jobs, and thousands of computer whizzes?

Not one has a college degree.

Of course, these people are exceptions, and it can be argued that only brilliant or very weak students can afford to forgo a degree. But you need to know one of higher education's secrets. Many college websites trumpet the careers that are *possible*. That misleads prospective students into thinking that if they spend the years and the money, they're *likely* to land one of those careers. Alas, in many fields, as you will see, nowhere near enough professional jobs exist for the number of degree holders.

For example, I was sitting in an executive suite in the Time-Life Building meeting with four editors of one of Time-Warner's major magazines. In the course of the conversation, someone said, "It's obscene what these schools of journalism are doing. They're accepting thousands of students into journalism programs, knowing full well that 90 percent of them will never make more than McWages from journalism." Everyone nodded.

Table 12-1 makes the case for You U.

**TABLE 12-1**      **Degree Program versus You University**

| Degree Program | You U. |
|---|---|
| It usually involves acquiring a massive amount of information at one time, when you don't have the opportunity to apply it. | You learn what you need when you need it, especially if you learn on the job. |
| It can require many courses. Sometimes a course is required mainly because a professor likes to teach it. | Study only what you need and want. Often, you get what you need in a fraction of the time it takes to earn a degree. |
| Often you get a degree, only to find that you don't remember — let alone *use* — much of what you were taught. You own an often valuable piece of paper. | Because you learn what you want, how you want, at the pace you want, often when you have the chance to apply it, you remember more. |
| You're forced to learn when it's convenient for the professor, like Mondays and Wednesdays from 9 a.m. to 11 a.m. | Learn when it's convenient for you. |
| Learning is passive. You focus on what the professor wants to teach, and fear a low grade if you don't. Many students leave school with poor self-esteem. This is often because some professors teach material of limited value outside the classroom, yet it's difficult, so students feel dumb. | You are empowered. You study what you want, to the level you deem necessary. You U builds self-reliance and self-confidence. A key part of what makes a career feel good is the sense that you're an expert in your field. In some careers, you're as likely or more likely to feel like — and be — an expert with a "degree" from You U. |
| The material, especially in science or technology, is often obsolete. As long as professors continue publishing articles in their microniches, many universities will tolerate their not updating their course material. | You can get up-to-the-minute information: on the Internet, from periodicals, by talking with people in your field, and from short and longer classes offered by your profession's leading practitioners. |
| Costs range from $20,000 to well over $100,000, not to mention the loss of what you could have earned had you not been in a degree program. | Costs are 50 percent to 90 percent less than in a degree program. |

# SOME BAD NEWS

**WARNING**

*Phi Delta Kappan*, a prestigious education periodical, provides this discouraging information:

A Rand Corporation report concluded that the number of new doctoral degrees in science and engineering average 25 percent *above* appropriate employment opportunities. A National Science Foundation study found a 41 percent oversupply of PhDs in the supposedly in-demand electrical engineering field and a 33 percent oversupply in civil engineering. Rand charged that universities are oblivious to the job market.

Thousands of other graduates trying to gain entrance to other professions face the same situation. Even graduates from America's most prestigious business schools are finding no guarantee of a job. An amazing 16 percent of newly minted MBA graduates of Stanford University were unable to find jobs. Less prestigious business schools fared even worse: 40 percent of the graduates of Ohio State's business school could not find jobs; the figure for the University of Georgia was 30 percent; for the University of Texas at Austin, 24 percent; and for Tulane University, 24 percent. Experts project that, of the millions of university graduates, a mere 20 percent will find the well-paying, challenging jobs for which they were trained.

That data was collected in 1996. Now, graduate schools admit even more students at the same time as companies are shrinking middle management, automating, and offshoring ever more high-level jobs.

# Making You U Work

In more fields than you may think, motivated people can use You U for career preparation that offers at least equal net benefit compared with a degree program.

At You U, you decide (often with your chosen mentor's help) what you want to learn and then design a plan to learn it.

One of my clients, Phillip, wanted to learn how to create partnerships between corporations and schools. Rather than go back for a (largely ill–fitting) master's degree in education or business, he did a You U "master's." How?

>> Phillip searched the Net for articles on business-education partnerships.

>> He interviewed, by phone (yes it took persistence), people at companies involved in those partnerships. One person suggested materials he should read and mentioned an upcoming conference on business-education partnerships.

>> At the conference, our hero attended sessions, spoke with experts, visited vendor booths, and found out about an on-target newsletter and an Internet discussion group. He also visited companies that had model corporation/ school programs.

Now imagine that you're a corporate employer looking for someone to develop a partnership with local schools. Would you rather hire someone with a master's in education or someone like Phillip, who attended You U? Phillip was hired as a school liaison by a major telecommunications company.

Here's another example: When prominent nature sound recordist Jonathon Storm decided to switch from pursuing an architecture degree to becoming a sound recordist, rather than change majors, he left school to learn directly from a master. He asked the nation's leading nature sound recordist if he might study with him. Today, Jonathon is a master.

# Planning your You U career preparation

Planning your You U career preparation may be simpler than you think. If you follow the steps in this section, you'll soon graduate from You U cum laude.

## Finding a mentor

Start by finding a mentor who is an expert practitioner in your field — someone who can suggest resources, ensure that you're covering enough of the bases, and answer your questions. Expect to compensate your mentor with money or by volunteering as an assistant. The latter can be instructive in itself. Sometimes, though, people will mentor you for free. For example, many older people want to pass on their wisdom to the next generation.

Where to find a mentor:

>> Look for someone in your field whom you already know, like, and respect.

>> Attend a meeting of your field's professional association. Some of these associations have formal mentoring programs.

>> Post a request for a coach in your field's Internet discussion group. (LinkedIn, Yahoo!, or your professional association's website may well have one.)

>> Check out SCORE, the Service Corps of Retired Executives: www.score.org.

>> Track down someone who supervises interns. Don't know of anyone? Try www.myperfectresume.com/how-to/career-resources/intern. It's a portal to a variety of databases of internships.

>> Approach a professor who has enough practical knowledge to coach you.

>> Post a flyer at the local senior center or an ad on its website or newsletter.

There's no need to limit yourself to one mentor — different people provide different expertise and opinions. Besides, you don't want to overtax your mentor.

**REMEMBER**

The book, and especially the article, are underrated learning tools. You can often find on-target ones simply by visiting your professional association's website or searching Google for articles and Amazon.com for books. Using these tools, you'll be able to quickly and efficiently search millions of books and articles to find on-target ones for you. Now tell me that's not cool.

**TIP**

Working with a tutor is another time-effective learning method. For example, rather than take a course in Java, get a study manual and then have a tutor start you off. You may find one at www.tutor.com or www.wyzant.com. Then keep a list of questions and problems, and use that as the basis of the next tutoring session.

## Figuring out what to learn

When talking with a potential mentor, ask this question: "I'm trying to prepare to enter a career in X using articles, books, in-person or online classes, webinars, and conferences. Are there any resources you'd particularly recommend?" In addition to asking your mentor(s), you can pose this question to other professionals in the field. Additional ideas can come from

>> A respected member of your professional association

>> Your association's website

>> Public, college, or corporate libraries and their librarians

When looking for courses to take, consider local colleges' extension programs and community colleges and local undergraduate-oriented colleges that focus more on students than on research.

At You U, you're not bound to one campus. You can find the best professor in your locale for each course — in major cities, you have a number of colleges to choose from. Check out individual instructors on www.ratemyprofessors.com, which aggregates student reviews. And because students may lack the larger perspective, many colleges publish a list of teaching award winners who usually are selected not just by students but also by faculty and administrators.

## Considering online classes

Some people are more satisfied with online, audio, or video classes. They're fast and less expensive, there's no hassle getting there, and there's no searching for a parking spot. Instead, you're at home in your comfies.

Online courses offer other advantages: With tens of thousands of choices from 1-hour quickies to semester-long comprehensives, you can pick one on the right topic and at the right length for you. You get to choose what you want instead of what your local college happens to be offering that semester.

When a question is asked, you get to answer it and without embarrassment, unlike in a live class, where only the called-on student does.

You can replay (and fast-forward!) audio and video lectures as often as you like. Some online courses allow you to play a lecture at half-speed, regular speed, 1.5 times as fast, or double speed. Try asking that of a live instructor.

**WARNING**

Online classes have low completion rates. One reason is that the physical presence of a professor and students is motivating. Perhaps more central, many online courses allow you to set your own pace. (That's an advantage and a disadvantage. Procrastinators beware!)

Still interested? Check out www.udemy.com, www.lynda.com, and www.udacity.com for practical courses, and www.coursera.org, www.edx.org, and perhaps www.thegreatcourses.com for instruction with a more academic focus.

Hey, don't forget about plain ol' YouTube videos. No, you don't get badges or course credit, but YouTube offers literally millions of videos on every imaginable topic.

# Adding a top college to your résumé — fast

**TIP**

How'd you like to put a prestigious college's name on your résumé without undergoing a rigorous admissions process and after less than a semester of class sessions? Many designer-label colleges allow the public to take in-person or online seminars, workshops, and courses — through Coursera and edX, for example. That's the easiest, fastest way to add a designer-label institution to your résumé.

Will such a shortcut improve your employability? Imagine that you're looking to hire an analyst and you happen to see the Education section of this applicant's résumé:

**Professional Development**

**2018 Massachusetts Institute of Technology (MOOC): The Analytics Edge (12 weeks)**

Analytics methods, including linear regression, logistic regression, CART, clustering, and data visualization. Implementing all those methods in R. Solving optimization models in spreadsheet software.

Final project: Reducing a fashion website's shopping-cart abandonment rate using a logistic regression-based predictive model. (*Link to that project would be included.*).

**2018 Harvard University, Harvard Business School, HBX (8 weeks): Business Analytics**

Describing & summarizing data, sampling & estimation, hypothesis testing, regression.

Grade "Pass with Honors." *Link to certificate of completion.*

Even if this person's degree is from No Name State or even if the person has no degree, don't those short MIT and Harvard online courses make you more likely to interview the candidate?

# Considering certificate programs

Certificate programs are hard to define. They can be as short as a half-day workshop or as long as a 12-course endeavor. They're offered by community colleges, universities, industry groups, professional associations, and training firms.

**TIP**

Looking to track down a certificate program? Thousands of such programs are aggregated on edX.org, Coursera.org, Udemy.com, Udacity.com, and Lynda.com.

When are certificate programs worth it? Some fields value certificates more than others. And that can change quickly. It wasn't long ago that a coding boot camp lasting a few months would land you a job. More recently, employers have concluded that too many boot camp completers have insufficient skills. To ensure that a certificate program still provides an edge for you when it comes to landing a job, do the following:

1. Scan job ads for your target job. Is a particular certificate often listed as desirable or even required?

2. If so, that certificate program may be offered by more than one entity. Google the name of the certificate and look for highly rated providers.

3. Visit that provider's website to examine the curriculum. Is that content what you want to learn and at the level you need?

4. If so, Google-search that provider's program, adding the word *reviews* — for example, *"App Academy" reviews*.

5. As with all education and training, quality varies with the instructor. Use the provider's Contact Us feature to ask for the name(s) of instructor(s) teaching it. Google-search on that person's name and the word *reviews*. Maybe even go as far as to email or phone instructors to get a sense of their style and how they implement the program.

## Assessing apprenticeships

An apprenticeship is a time-honored way to prepare for a career and is often a wise choice for people who learn best in hands-on situations under a mentor's supervision. It also enables you to get paid while you learn. Apprenticeships typically last from one to four years, usually including some coursework to accompany the on-the-job training.

Traditionally, apprenticeships have been for the building trades and manufacturing, but some white collar fields such as healthcare, hospitality, insurance, and IT are turning to apprenticeships. Long seen as the career preparation of choice in Germany, England, Denmark, and Switzerland, the number of U.S. apprenticeships is up by 50 percent over the course of the past five years, and the federal government is proposing doubling its budget for apprenticeships.

TIP

Focus on apprenticeships registered by the U.S. Department of Labor or by your state. Those require each program to meet curricular standards, students to be supervised by a mentor, and apprentices to be paid from Day One. Graduates of registered programs receive an industry-recognized credential.

Interested? Check out the Fed's clearinghouse of apprenticeship information, including an apprenticeship finder, at www.dol.gov/apprenticeship.

# Getting Employers to Hire You Without That Degree

Imagine that you are an employer. Would you consider the candidate who wrote this letter:

*Dear Ms. Hirer,*

*I know that when you're inundated with applications, it's tempting to weed out those without a prestigious MBA, but I believe I'm worth a look because I believe I've acquired learning more useful than what I would have in an MBA program.*

*I seriously considered getting an MBA, but after talking with a number of MBA holders and examining the courses I would have to take and their relevance (or, too often, lack thereof) to becoming a good software marketing manager, I concluded that the two full-time years (and $100,000) could be spent on career preparation that would make me a better employee.*

*I contacted directors of marketing at leading Silicon Valley software companies and offered to work for them for no pay in exchange for their mentoring. I figured that was inexpensive tuition for the on-target learning I'd receive. A marketing manager at HP took me on. After three months, I felt I had learned about as much from him as I could, whereupon I made a similar arrangement with a director of marketing at Cisco Systems.*

*In these experiences, I was fully involved in a number of projects similar to those mentioned in your ad — specifically, social media marketing and managing a national consumer branding campaign. In addition, I attend American Marketing Association conferences, read the best articles and books recommended by the AMA, and spend much of my commute time listening to career-beneficial audio classes and talks. To get the bigger picture, I've read a couple of books by leading academics — including on the ethics of marketing, an underexamined issue.*

*But now comes the moment of truth. In choosing a self-directed education over a traditional one, I believe I have prioritized substance over form. Now the question is, will you consider interviewing me?*

*I hope that you'll appreciate my having developed a beyond-the-box learning plan that I was assertive enough to make happen and persistent enough to see through to completion, even though I had no professor or deadlines forcing me to do so. Perhaps more important, in working at the elbow of top marketing executives, I learned a tremendous amount about how to do the job well. I recently discussed my approach with an MBA holder from Stanford, and he said that I probably learned more of real-world value than he did.*

*I'm hoping you will invite me for an interview but, as any good employee, I won't just passively wait. If I haven't heard from you in a week, I will take the liberty of following up.*

*I enclose samples of the deliverables I produced during my work at HP and Cisco.*

*Thank you for your consideration.*

*Sincerely,*

*John Jobseeker*

Again, imagine that you're the person in charge of hiring. Would you interview John? Even if other applicants had a designer-label degree? During a recent talk, I asked the 300-person audience whether they would interview someone like John. Almost everyone raised their hand. On my radio program, I asked the same question of the associate dean of the U.C. Berkeley Business School, and even he agreed that he would interview John.

So, before heading back for a degree at State U. — let alone Private U. — ask yourself whether a wise choice might be You U.

Again, as good as You U. can be for some people, it's certainly not right for everyone. Ready for a back-for-a-degree stint? Chapter 11 can help.

# Lifelong Learning

Lifelong learning has become a cliché, and it can sound daunting to forever continue upgrading yourself. But there's an upside. In past generations, after years on the job, many people felt bored — like they had been there, done that. There always have been new things you *could* learn, but in order to thrive today, you often *must* learn new things. Consider staying enrolled ongoing at You U. That can mean, for example, that you

>> Join or form a group of peers that connects live or electronically to discuss problems and solutions.

>> Read (rather than let stack up) the monthly issues of your professional association's magazine.

>> Attend at least one professional conference a year.

» Take an occasional academic course. Stepping back from the relentlessly practical to look at larger issues can enrich you as a professional and a person.

» Find one or more mentors. Times have changed. A mentor/protégé relationship used to be a one-at-a-time, time-intensive deal. Today, such a relationship is likely to be more fluid. You call with a question, exchange emails on a new development, and occasionally commiserate over a cup of coffee. Ideally, you'll have a few mentor relationships, some in which you're the mentor and others in which you're the protégé. Those can be among life's more rewarding relationships.

# Chapter **13**

# Getting Emotionally Solid

areer success requires not just knowing what to do but also being personally solid enough to do it: reasonably confident, able to avoid procrastinating (too much), and resilient to work's inevitable slings and arrows. This chapter can help.

## Avoiding the Imposter Syndrome

*Imposter syndrome* may be more common than the common cold, especially if you're just starting out in a career. You may think, "I have a professional degree, but am not sure I'm worthy of a professional paycheck."

It may help to remember that every human being, from cave dweller forward, began her career as a beginner. And beginners make beginner's mistakes — even life-and-death ones. At orientation, the chief of staff at a prestigious New York hospital told the new residents (newly minted doctors) something like this:

*Each of you is entitled to one clean kill. You'll take a patient who came in reasonably expecting to go home and you'll kill them: wrong diagnosis, wrong medication, botched procedure. You must forgive yourself because your worth as a doctor isn't defined by any single incident but by your net impact over your lifetime. Yes, be careful, yes, ask questions, but if you screw up, learn from your mistake and then please forgive yourself and move on.*

**REMEMBER**

You probably won't kill anyone because of your beginner's mistakes, but do follow that chief-of-staff's advice. Be careful, ask questions, learn from your mistakes, and move on. The more you wallow in guilt and self-doubt, the more likely you are to spiral down into insecurity. Not everyone can be a star, but you will probably grow to become at least good enough — although, now and always, you'll be human. Forgive yourself your humanness.

# Gaining Realistic Confidence

*Am I ever going to land a job? I know I need to network, but I don't want to look like a loser who needs to beg people for a lead. And I don't like imposing. I'm afraid I'll sound stupid. I'm not even sure what kind of job I want. Okay, I'll call one networking contact — Jen; she'll be nice. But does she really know anyone who could hire me? Probably not, and even if she does, I'd be terrified at the interview. The employer will realize I don't know enough. They'll reject me. And even if they hire me, I could absolutely fail. I'd get fired and then have even a harder time finding a decent job. I'll end up sweeping floors. I'll end up a bag lady. And even if I succeed, I don't want to be like those people who work a zillion hours a week. They have no life! Argh! I'm going to get something to eat. Maybe I'll think about looking for a job tomorrow. Maybe.*

Ah *the catastrophization spiral.* Like imposter syndrome, mentioned in the preceding section, this spiral is more common than you might think. After all, on Facebook and LinkedIn, everyone seems so successful, so happy, so downright perky. You ask someone how they are, and the answer is always, "Fine." Well, beneath the veneer, not everyone is fine. But the tips in this chapter can help improve your state of mind.

Sometimes, catastrophization is just a manifestation of imposter syndrome. The flashes of worry breed more and more worry, and, before you know it, the concern has metastasized into "analysis paralysis" and a straitjacket of inertial fear. The solution lies in remembering your beginner status. This, too, shall pass.

But sometimes that concern should be heeded. For example, is your anxiety a sign that you've chosen the wrong profession? For example, if your parents pushed you to major in business and you stuck it out but now hate the thought of a lifetime in business, you may be "nonprofit" at your core. Maybe it's time to cut your losses. Or your career choice seems reasonable, but you're worried that your skills and abilities aren't yet good enough, even for an entry-level professional position. In that case, maybe you need a volunteer gig or additional training, at Standard U or You U.

Whether or not you feel the need to address your catastrophization fears, after fixing what you can reasonably fix, remind yourself that — after making reasonable baby-step efforts — you'll get better. And if you don't, you still have plenty of time to find a better-suited career, even later in life. Hey, even half of married couples divorce — so much for "'til death do us part." That's certainly true for your job or career, too.

# Developing Drive

Procrastination is merely the symptom, not the disease. Just as a headache can be caused by anything from a migraine to a bonk on the head with a rolling pin, procrastination can come from fears, as described in the previous sections — though procrastination is, more often than not, just a bad habit you acquired in school. Think back to that 500-word paper on the thymus gland you had to write in 11th grade: You didn't care a whit about the thymus gland. So, because it wasn't due for a week, you procrastinated. You did everything but start on that paper. You even cleaned your room! Then, the night before the paper was due, an hour before bedtime and fueled by 11th-hour adrenaline, you thought, "I *gotta* get it done." So you searched Google for *thymus gland*, cut-and-pasted sentences from the first few search results, changed them into language appropriate for your grade, moved a few paragraphs around, and ended with a summary. And with your mother screaming, "It's bedtime, Binky!" you thought, "Well, it's better than nothing. At least I won't get an F." And lo and behold, thanks to grade inflation, you got a B+. And thus started your addiction to adrenaline.

Alas, grade inflation hasn't spread as much to the work world, especially among good employers, so it may be time to follow the advice your mother gave you back in the day:

>> **Get started as soon as you receive the assignment.** This tactic avoids the guilt that comes from procrastination and gives you time to get it done well — maybe even early enough to put it aside for a while and look at it with fresh eyes before having to turn it in.

TIP

>> **Start with the first 1-minute task**. Even if it's just to write, "The Thymus Gland, by Binky Binklestadt," do *something*. Objects in motion tend to stay in motion, so after the first 1-minute task or two, you may have progressed sufficiently into it that you breeze right on through it — or at least work on it for 20 minutes until you decide that you need a burrito break.

>> **Pace yourself.** Speaking of 20 minutes, one procrastination-beater that has helped many people is the *Pomodoro technique*, named after the tomato-shaped kitchen timer. Any timer will do, though, including the one on your phone — all the timer need do is ding. You set the timer for 20 minutes, work for the entire period, and then give yourself 5 minutes to do whatever you want: call a friend, watch a YouTube video, pour yourself a drink. (No, not an alcoholic one.) Then you do another 20-and-5, and then a 20-and-10. The three 20-minute units constitute a Pomodoro.

>> **Recognize that both winners and losers fail, though winners rarely wallow.** As I've said *ad nauseam*, winners learn from their failures and take the next step forward. Even if procrastination is caused by fear of failure, it usually hurts your career, and perhaps your personal life.

>> **Commit to a goal.** It might help to tell someone, even all your Facebook friends, that you've committed to crushing that monster task by Friday at 5.

>> **Ritualize the process.** I'm not talking about praying — I'm talking about calendaring a specific time each day to complete The Dreaded Task. Or you could tie the task to something you like doing — for example, before watching your favorite TV show, making yourself do a Pomodoro.

>> **Put your house in order.** Is substance abuse de-motivating you? Maybe it's time to rethink certain aspects of your personal life.

>> **Commit to a goal, Part 2.** When you feel stuck and about to procrastinate, set the timer for 60 seconds, and if you don't make progress by then, phone or email a friend. Or even remember (pushy parent alert!) that successful people accept the short-term deferral of pleasure for the greater long-term pleasures that come from accomplishment.

>> **Watch the clock.** Some people lose track of time. They space out, and by the time they realize it, they've wasted quite a chunk of the day. If that's you, try setting the timer to ding every 20 minutes and log what you did during the last 20 minutes on a memo pad, Word file, or an app like RescueTime, RememberTheMilk, or FocusBooster. That can serve as a wake-up call and help you gain a better sense of time so that the day doesn't get away from you.

>> **Get organized.** To keep track of tasks, it helps to have a system you use all the time. Most people will regularly maintain only a simple system. For example, you might use Google Calendar or a week-at-a-glance paper engagement calendar for formally scheduled events and also keep a memo cube on your desk for items you have to complete today but not at a particular time.

## HOW I CONTROL MY PROCRASTINATION

When I want to stop working, I usually do, guilt-free, but only briefly. I might stretch out on the floor with my doggie, Einstein, grab a cup of coffee, or take a walk around the block. The key to not letting procrastination control me is to keep the breaks short.

**TIP**

>> **Ritualize at bedtime.** Write to-do items every night before going to bed, or at least first thing in the morning. Then check your calendar and to-do list throughout the day. Most of my clients say that it feels comforting to check those items regularly so that they don't forget something important. It also feels good to cross an item off the list.

>> **Consider group support.** Some but not all people do better with group support. If that might be you, do you want to invite a few responsible friends to meet regularly, either live or on Freeteleconference.com or Google Hangouts, and report to each other on their progress, hear encouragement, and perhaps consider suggestions? Or join a ready-made job-search group, such as one you might find on Meetup.org, on your alma mater's website, or via your local government's unemployment office.

## Staying Upbeat

If your job search is taking longer than expected or that job you finally snagged isn't as cool as you'd hoped, your motivation can wane. Maybe one of the mental strategies in this section can help you:

>> **The playing-card metaphor:** Say I spread out a deck of playing cards face down and say, "If you pick the ace of spades, you get a good job, even if you have to flip through all 52 cards. Wouldn't you do it without feeling rejected when you pick, for example, the eight of diamonds? That's the mindset to adopt when your inquiries get rejected or, more commonly these days, when you receive no response.

>> **Fake it 'til you make it.** Behavior change can *cause* attitude change. If you *act* upbeat, you may actually start to feel upbeat. You certainly have nothing to lose by trying it.

>> **Stay in the moment.** If you look back at your unsuccessful efforts, you'll feel bad. And if you look ahead to all the reaching out and dues-paying that you may need to do, you may be tempted to watch the "Seinfeld" rerun marathon

instead. So stay in the moment: Ask yourself repeatedly, "What's my next 1-minute task?" As when climbing a mountain, if you simply put one foot in front of another, before long you'll look back and be surprised at how far you've climbed.

# Developing Emotional Intelligence

Many people can't understand why they struggle while other people succeed despite being less capable and hard-working. Here are a few tips for enhancing your emotional intelligence:

>> **Make others feel good about themselves.** If you're a job seeker, you should aim to appear to be a desirable employee without making the other person feel inferior. Bosses claim to want to hire people who perform better than they themselves do, and they claim to welcome disagreement. In practice, however, it's usually wiser to reserve disagreement for those rare situations in which it's critical, or when you're sure that the person truly wants you to "show your chops."

**REMEMBER**

At the granular level, having emotional intelligence means that you look for opportunities to say things like "That's a good point" and "Thank you" and avoid responding to other people's ideas with "But" and "No." It means touting your ability with softening terms, such as "People say they like working with me" rather than "I'm good to work with. You also make others feel good about themselves by using the standard politician's self-effacement strategy — "It was a team effort. I couldn't have done it without them."

Some advisors suggest that people, especially women, avoid such modesty, but I've found that as long as you don't make yourself sound like an overall loser, humility pays. My wife is a nationally prominent expert on technology in schools, yet in keynote speeches she proudly acknowledges, "No one would call me a digital native." People don't think less of her, and they aren't threatened. My wife is using emotional intelligence.

>> **Stay attuned to people's reactions.** Often, long before someone decides to reject you, they show signs of liking or disliking you. Examples of positive reactions are a natural smile, open body language, face-to-face positioning, and good eye contact. Examples of negative reactions are (especially if it's a change from initial positivity) furrowing the brow, sighing, folding arms, or

even pivoting part of the body away from you. The latter examples are signals that you've said something wrong or talked too much, for example.

Just a word about talking too much: Everyone believes that what they're saying is interesting, or else they wouldn't say it, but sometimes it's flat-out *boring*. Or they continue talking because they don't care whether it's interesting — talking out a topic often helps clarify your thinking. But talking too much usually turns people off.

Here's a rule of thumb: In a 2-person conversation, aim to talk 30 to 50 percent of the time and in short bursts (anywhere from a few seconds to one minute).

Always follow the traffic-light rule too. During the first 30 seconds of an utterance, the traffic light is green: Speak freely. During the second 30 seconds, the light is turning yellow: The chances are increasing that the other person wishes you would let them speak. At the 1-minute mark, the light has turned red: Unless you're positive that the other person is interested, stop talking or ask a question.

>> **Focus at least as much on the other person's needs as on yours.** To get what you want, it helps to give people what they want. Look for opportunities to be helpful, whether it's before or after you've received help or even if you never receive any. It really does feel better to give than to receive.

For example, whenever you're networking, interviewing for a job, or even working on the job, be a "help detective" — someone's statements may embed an opportunity to help. Think of every complaint you hear as a chance for you to give. For example, if your networking contact says, "I don't have time to talk," you might respond this way: "I'm sorry I've imposed. Would you rather I leave now? Forever? Or is there something I can do to help?"

Here's another example: During the small talk that often takes place at the beginning of a job interview, your interviewer mentions her upcoming leave of absence for childcare. You might ask, "How are you feeling about it?" She might hint at a possible problem — for example, "I'm looking forward to it, although the lack of sleep might not be so much fun." If you then send her an article with advice for newborn parenting, you've shown emotional intelligence — and that you're a caring person. Living life as a help detective is rewarding: It makes you feel good about yourself, distracts you from your own woes, and can possibly advance your career.

# Gaining Focus

If you can't force yourself to focus, you might consider adopting one of these strategies:

» **Create a reduced-distraction environment.** If necessary, hang a Do Not Disturb sign on your door. Or perhaps turn off the music. Maybe you should even set up a cardboard privacy partition on your desk. (If the partition sounds like a good idea, you can pick one up at www.officesupply.com/furniture/panel-systems-accessories/panel-systems/panels-partitions/pacon-privacy-boards/p105881.html.)

» **Accept yourself.** Some people can be sufficiently productive even if distractible. They may have to put in more total hours but think of those distractions merely as distributed recreation: mini-breaks in their workday.

» **Medicate.** Medication such as Adderall and Ritalin are effective for many people. (For more info, check out "The Right ADHD Treatment for You" at www.webmd.com/add-adhd/guide/adult-adhd-getting-right-treatment-you#1.) First, though, you might try coffee. As the popular commercial said, "Coffee, the think drink." For many people (including me), drinking coffee improves focus. (Besides, I like the comforting feeling of working while sipping that sweet, warm drink.)

# Gathering Equanimity

Just as a group of people's height might range from diminutive to towering, so does their predisposition to anger. Some go from 0 to 60 on the anger scale in 1 second, whereas others have a slow fuse. Part of the reason is physiological: If you put ten people in a room and suddenly bang a loud gong, some people will jump out of their seats while others will calmly peer sideways.

If you're predisposed to anger, it's critical that you control it. Hotheads, even if they show anger only covertly, struggle in most workplaces. Even the big boss today is respected more for equanimity under stress and treating workers firmly but without anger. Whether or not you liked President Barack Obama personally, nearly everyone respected him for his calm demeanor, even when discussing difficult topics such as healthcare and terrorism.

Here are several tactics for reducing anger:

>> **Most foundationally, live your life with a sense of perspective.** Even if this advice seems a tad airy-fairy, in the larger scheme of things, how important is that issue, anyway? Few situations are worth your being viewed as a hothead, not to mention the possibility of harming your health. (It's well-established that anger is unhealthy; check out "7 Ways Anger Is Ruining Your Health" at www.everydayhealth.com/news/ways-anger-ruining-your-health.)

**REMEMBER**

>> **Some people have a permanent chip on their shoulder.** They believe that the world has treated them unfairly or some horrible event has happened, and they can't look past it. Your best prospects for an improved life are to stop looking back, start looking for the positive aspects in your present and future, and take the next step forward. When I asked my father, a Holocaust survivor, why he rarely talks about his experience, he said, "The Nazis took five years from my life. I won't give them one minute more. Martin, never look back. Always take the next step forward."

>> **Put yourself in situations less likely to trigger anger.** Anger is usually caused by unexpected circumstances, and when you're dealing with people, the unexpected happens often. Computers behave predictably: Type the letter Q, and you see a Q (except, of course, when you see the blue screen of death). Plants behave predictably: Plant a zucchini, and you get a zucchini, never a rutabaga. With people, you get surprises, including unpleasant ones, and especially in stressful careers — customer service, for example, or teaching or sales. If you're an anger-prone person, you might want to consider a more predictable career — as an accountant, a pathologist, researcher, or an archivist, for example.

>> **Have a ritual for when you're *starting* to get angry.** The first second you feel yourself starting to get mad at someone, exit. Say, "Excuse me a moment — I need to use the bathroom," or make a similar statement. Then take a couple of deep breaths and ask yourself whether the upsides of getting angry will outweigh the downsides. Very occasionally, you'll decide that it *is* worth it: Perhaps a coworker, despite calm reminders, has been lazy, saddling you with his work, and you decide that he needs a bit of strong medicine to get shaken from complacency. But much more often, you'll decide that although your anger may let you blow off steam or get the person to do your bidding, you'll have won the battle and lost the war: You'll be dismissed, figuratively or literally.

# Managing Peter Pan Syndrome (or, It's Time to Grow Up)

It's understandable that a person might be tempted to defer growing up. Though you may have had to do schoolwork in college, most tasks were neatly laid out for you: "Read page 225 to 275 by Tuesday, study for the midterm on November 3, and take the final exam on December 22." And the aforementioned grade inflation mentioned in the earlier section "Developing Drive" helped ensure that you'd pass courses as long as you put in even moderate effort. Plus, the school year was pleasantly short. Most colleges have classes for only 30 weeks a year, and within that period are holidays and weekends.

But now you're reading this book, which implies that you're at least thinking about growing up — picking a career and working 9-to-5 (or longer), for example. What usually goes along with that is "the R word" — responsibility — and also thoughts about committing to a long-term relationship, and maybe even a house and kids. That's potentially exciting but also scary. It's tempting to capitulate to the Peter Pan syndrome, or refusing to grow up, at least for a little while longer.

And maybe you should refuse to grow up for a while. With the life expectancy of today's 20-somethings about 90 for women and 85 for men, you'll have plenty of decades as a grown-up. Would it really hurt to spend a few years mainly having fun? You can usually find a way to explain to friends and family that you aren't goofing off: "Um, I'm exploring options and getting some real-world experience before deciding on a career path."

But alas, Peter Pan syndrome isn't conducive to launching a good career. If and when you're considering shoving Peter to the back seat, the following information might nudge you into action.

>> **Many people who deferred starting their work lives end up enjoying life more *after* they enter the work world.** Not only are they making money and adding structure to their lives, but it also feels good to be contributing members of society. Of course, a person's career contentment depends on how well-suited the career and the specific workplace are, but this book can help with that.

>> **You don't want to fall too far behind your peers.** Two years from now, you'll not only be further behind in work experience and on-the-job learning, but your résumé will also have a Captain Hook-size gap. (And Tinker Bell may not be able to save you.)

>> **Taking too much time for exploration may backfire on you.** At least in my clients' experience, taking off more than a month or two, whatever non-academic experiences you had after you finished school, rarely results in additional career clarity — only more guilt about still living off parents' or taxpayer money.

>> **When other people are making money and contributing, you're unlikely to want to continue to tell your friends and family that you're "still exploring."** Picture yourself at the family holiday party a year from now and someone asking you, "So, how *is* your career coming along?"

>> **You don't want to be perceived as lazy.** It's socially unacceptable to call a person lazy to their face, but privately they may well describe you with the dreaded "L word."

# Managing Depression

Depression isn't just sadness. Though a person's depression may have better and worse periods, it's characterized by weeks or months — or longer periods — of not caring about much of anything. It's an indifference, a numbness, a lack of motivation — not exactly facilitators of career success.

Depression often has a physiological basis that is exacerbated by a personal problem. For example, someone could be predisposed to depression but function well and then lose his job, which triggers a crash. Or his romantic partner, the love of his life, dumps him. A person with depression may find that the episode doesn't relent, despite his trying to push forward. And sometimes an episode can originate without an obvious external trigger.

Many cases of depression are significantly improved when one or more of these strategies takes place:

>> Regular exercise

>> Cognitive-behavioral therapy

>> Prescription medication

   You have many options here — check out "Antidepressants: Selecting One That's Right for You" at www.mayoclinic.org/diseases-conditions/depression/in-depth/antidepressants/art-20046273

>> Electroconvulsive or brain stimulation therapy (for severe depression)

>> Baby steps to improve one's life (good advice, of course, for everyone)

# 4

# Landing a *Good* Job Faster

# Chapter **14**

# Writing Your Way to a Good Job

**A**pplying for jobs has changed.

Sure, you still need a resume, LinkedIn profile, and job-search letter, but with tons of career advice out there, rising to the top of the stack requires ahead-of-the-pack tactics. This chapter offers them to you.

First, a bit of good news: People spend too much time primping resumes, LinkedIn profiles, and job-search letters. They do that because it feels productive and is more comfy than, for example, networking. But after a relatively small amount of time spent on resumes and the rest, your job-search time can be better spent.

**TIP** This chapter's philosophy is that the perfect is the enemy of the good. It gives you not-so-obvious tips that quickly get you to "plenty good enough." If you want to go the extra mile, check out any of the books from Wiley Publishing on each topic — *Resumes For Dummies*, by Laura DeCarlo, *Job Search Letters For Dummies*, by Joyce Lain Kennedy, and *Answering Tough Interview Questions For Dummies*, by Rob Yeung, for example.

Here's more good news: More than 30 hours a week of job-searching is usually counterproductive. If you're working full-time, 10 hours is probably a reasonable goal. After you've put in that much time — make time for fun: sports, creative outlets, friends (platonic or otherwise).

# Creating a Winning Resume

Creating a resume should be Step 1 in your job search, and not just because most employers and referrers want to see one. The act of creating your resume reminds you of all the positive qualities you bring to the table. Many of my clients have said that creating their resumes helped them realize that they have more to offer than they originally thought. Creating a resume also helps you identify anecdotes to add to your job letters and interviews. Plus, it makes it easier to respond to common questions, such as "What can you tell me about yourself?" and "Why do you want this job?"

## Stay away from resume writers

A resume not only describes the candidate's work history but provides a sample of writing, organizational, and thinking skills. Though many job seekers hire someone to write their resumes, that's no more ethical than a college applicant hiring someone to write his college application essay.

Beyond ethics, resumes written by hired guns usually sound artificial. A resume writer tends to use stock "power" phrases like, "dynamic," team player," "unique," and "spearheaded" that scream "hired gun." Worse, the resume writer tends to write at her own intellectual and linguistic level and style, not the candidate's. So, in the interview, the candidate's language will likely differ greatly from the resume's. Thus, the employer will distrust the candidate, even if it's only subconsciously. And interview success is so much about building trust.

Nor do I recommend using resume software. Because such software is developed by resume writers, the software also usually suggests power phrases, and because such software has long been ubiquitous, these terms also announce to the employer that the resume was created a hired gun, in this case, a digital one.

Here is the summary at the top of an actual person's resume. I've changed just a few words because it's posted on the Internet and don't want to endanger her confidentiality. Would this summary make you want to hire this person?

> *Results-driven sales professional with proven track record of success in sales. Team-oriented, innovative, and self-directed at driving revenue-enhancement in corporate environments.*

P.S. In our first session, the creator of the resume admitted to me that she is a bad salesperson, detests the job, and is seriously thinking of changing careers and becoming a children's counselor. That's why she came to me.

Instead of a resume writer or resume software, just Google search on the term "resume templates," pick one you like, and recreate it on a blank document.

If you're applying for different types of positions, adapt your resume to fit the position — or even create two or three slightly reworded versions of your resume.

**TIP**

The most important aspect of your job search is to *put yourself in your target employer's shoes*. Ask yourself, "Would adding this info make me more or less likely to want to interview this candidate — or, if the info is in the interview, to hire this candidate?"

## Name and contact information

If you prefer to be called by your nickname, include it only if you don't mind if the employer searches for it on the Internet — you don't want that nickname leading to that JPG image of you partying hearty, for example. If you include your nickname, use this format: John "Jake" Jones.

**TIP**

Don't include your mailing address on your resume, and not just to avoid unwanted visitors: An out-of-town employer might wonder if you'd actually move for a far-flung job. Simply include the email address and phone number(s) that you want the employer to use.

## Summary, objective, or highlights?

After you list your name and contact information, conventional wisdom suggests that you add a summary rather than an objective. That advice, however, is too black-and-white for my taste. If you have rich work experience and are looking for a job similar to one you've done in the past, adding a summary is fine. Especially for people who are early in their careers or for career-changers, though, it's wiser to use an objective, and one that highlights your accomplishments. This strategy not only beefs up the intro paragraph, it also better helps employers assess whether you're a good fit.

**TIP**

Here's a principle (implicit in the previous paragraph) that is useful not just in resumes but also in job-search letters and interviews: If your past would more impress your target employer, tout it. If your future would be more impressive — what you can do and what you hope to accomplish — tout it instead.

An employer's first look at your resume may not even involve human eyeballs — the first look may be done by computer. So try to embed key words or phrases from the job ad into your resume. Don't put them at the end — that's transparently a ploy. Instead, embed them where they'd naturally fit.

If you've advanced past the computerized review or the employer doesn't use one, a live human will review your resume. Usually, this person makes her first toss-or-keep decision within a few seconds — she may never continue past the first few sentences. So, immediately after you list the objective or summary, add a section, labeled *Highlights*, of 1-line bullet points that describe a few of your most impressive accomplishments. If your objective is to score your first job as a software engineer, your highlights might look like this:

>> Earned a 3.5 GPA in computer science courses

>> Built (for senior project) a robotic hand using Python; see portfolio at PythonPerson.com

>> Created apps ranging from health trackers to casual games

You might also add these items to your list of highlights:

>> A quote or two of praise from your boss or customers or from your performance review.

>> A 50- to 100-word PAR story — a *problem* you faced, the clever or dogged *approach* you took to resolve it, and the positive *result*.

Even if this candidate had not yet worked at a job in programming — not even a volunteer internship — might you consider hiring him?

# Education

If information about your education would impress your target employer more than your work-related experience would, it's the next part of your resume.

In the Education section, include this information:

>> The institution you attended and your year of graduation or (if you didn't graduate) your years of attendance

>> Your major and (if it would impress your target employer) any minor

>> Your GPA, if it's above 3.2 overall and/or in your major

>> Any courses, projects, or extracurricular activities that would impress your target employer

# Choosing the Format

After you list your objective, summary, and/or highlights (and perhaps education) on your resume, choose from these two general resume formats:

» **Chronological**: List your work history — paid and volunteer, in reverse chronological order. For each job, list a few bullets documenting accomplishments that would impress the employer.

» **Skills:** Provide a few bullets of evidence for each skill that would impress the employer. Then list your employment history, using just one line per employer.

WARNING

If you use the skills format, you start with a strike against you. Though conventional wisdom suggests that you choose the format that puts you in the better light, that choice is no longer clear. Now many employers are aware that a skills–based resume is often used to hide an unimpressive chronology — the lack of recent relevant experience or a long gap in employment, for example. It's usually wiser to use a chronological resume, of course, highlighting info that would impress the employer.

# Work

If you're using a chronological resume, you have the opportunity to do far more than simply list where you worked and when. Here are a few tips for impressing a target employer:

» **Put the best face on your job title.** If your official job title understates the work you did, write your more descriptive title first and then, in parentheses, your official title. For example, if your job was to write catalog copy, but your official title was *office assistant,* write it this way:

Catalog copy writer (official title: Office assistant)

» **Describe the organization.** If your target employer is unlikely to have heard of the organization and, if knowing about it would be impressive, include a sentence to describe it. For example, if you're seeking an urban planning position and you completed an internship at a prestigious real estate development firm, write *Wilens Land Development, Inc., an award-winning, 400-person firm that is in its 43rd year of creating theme parks and mixed-use developments.*

» **Describe impressive accomplishments.** For each place of employment, add two to four 1- or 2-line bullet points describing your accomplishments. For example, if you're looking for a position as an accountant or a manager, you might say, "Revised the expense reimbursement system, resulting in faster reimbursements and fewer under- and overpayments."

**TIP**

Though quantification may impress, your accomplishments may not be quantifiable. In fact, excessive use of quantification may suggest dissembling.

>> **Mitigate employment gaps.** If you have a long gap in employment, list employment dates by *year* and on the right side of the page. If you have continuous employment, list them by *month* and on the left.

## Other sections

The resume sections described in the following list are optional, but often add heft to your self-description. Decide whether any of these areas will enhance your prospects:

>> **Special Skills:** Spell out skills that might impress the employer — for example, software you know how to use, computer languages you know, or foreign languages you can speak. For each one, state your level of proficiency: basic, moderate, expert, or native (if a non-English language is your native one).

>> **Honors and Awards:** If you've received at least two honors and awards, adding a separate section makes sense. If you've received only one award, embed it in the Highlights section and add it as a bullet point in either the Work or Education section.

**TIP**

>> **Personal Interests:** Conventional wisdom suggests omitting this section from your resume — because the employer doesn't care about your personal interests. I disagree. Sometimes, the tipper between the hired candidate and others is a personal bond with your boss or another key co-worker — people *enjoy* working with kindred spirits. Listing a few personal interests boosts the chances of having such a connection. In addition, it makes clear that you're a human being, not just a fungible work unit. Most good bosses like people who are more than simply work machines.

# Determining the Length

Don't worry about whether your resume fills one page or two. The rule of thumb is to include *any* information, concisely, if you think it would make an employer more likely to hire you over other candidates. And it's better to spread the resume over two pages, with plenty of white space, than to cram it onto one page.

# Getting Feedback

Show a draft of your completed resume to trusted colleagues, friends, and family members. Ask them to

>> Specify whether it would be attractive to your target employer.

>> Point out the most impressive and least impressive areas.

>> Make suggestions for improvement.

Don't necessarily accept all suggestions: Your reviewers are advisors to you, but you are the CEO of your life.

Save your resume in two versions: one formatted to be read easily in Microsoft Word and the other a more basic one that's in plain-text format so that it's readable by automated tracking system (ATS) software commonly used to process applications. To convert the formatted version to one that's easily read by computer, follow these tips:

>> Use a common font, such as Times Roman.

>> Convert boldface text to ALL CAPS.

>> Enclose italicized words in quotes (and remove the italics).

>> Replace bullets (•) with plus signs (+).

>> Use spaces instead of tabs for indents.

Then paste the document into an email and send it to yourself to see whether it looks as you intend.

# Posting Your Polished Resume

After you've done all the work, how can you use your resume to maximum advantage?

Of course, you should show it to people in your network and potential employers not advertising a job, and, of course, you should use it to answer job ads — if it helps your case.

## WHEN SENDING A HIGHLIGHTS LETTER MAY BE JUST THE TICKET

What happens if your resume lays bare a liability virtually ensuring that your application won't be the winner or that it would disincline a potential referrer from touting you? For example, you might lack the normally required training, have a long gap in employment, or show little or no recent experience in the job to which you aspire. Chances are good that showing your resume, no matter how you polish it, will hurt more than if you didn't send it.

Suppose that two years ago, you won a student award for something that might impress an employer, but since then your best employment has been as a burger flipper. Your resume would reflect that and hurt your chances — except for another fast-food job. But a *highlights letter* can include only what would impress your target employer and referrers, and even if those are slim, the letter can also talk about the future: what you can do, what you hope to do on this job, and why it matters to you.

Sure, at some point an employer may want to see your resume, but at that point your resume may matter less. If your resume won't be impressive compared with your likely competition, try to defer sending it. I call that the hide-the-resume game.

Of course, some employers and potential referrers will reject you for daring not to send your resume. But when day is done, the candidate whose resume would reveal a likely deal-killing liability will likely land a good job faster, by standing and falling with a highlights letter.

Post your resume on websites specific to your career goal or on megasites such as Indeed, LinkedIn, and Career Builder, and on USAJOBS.gov for federal jobs and Career One Stop (`www.careeronestop.org/JobSearch/FindJobs/state-job-banks.aspx`) for links to state government jobs.

Unless your resume makes clear that it's superior to most resumes out there for your target job, that may well not be how you land your job. You have nothing to lose by posting it, however. Even if you don't want your current employer to know that you're looking, most job sites have privacy settings to reduce your risk.

**TIP**

While you're on a job-search megasite, set up alerts to be notified whenever new jobs meeting your keywords and geographical settings are posted.

**WARNING**

Perhaps you believe that you have nothing to lose by sending your resume to external recruiters, or *headhunters*. Not necessarily. These external recruiters are paid by employers, and employers generally choose to pay them because the job they're trying to fill sounds undesirable, requires a rare skill set, or is simply unwanted because the *employer* is bad and no internal employee wants the job. So, even assuming that you fit the bill, you're more likely to interview for not-so-great jobs, and if one is offered to you, the recruiter may try to get you to take it, even if it's not really in your best interest. Just as bad is that some unscrupulous headhunters blast your resume to every employer under the sun, so if you get a job there, they claim a commission — that makes it more expensive to hire you than other candidates. In sum, unless you know that for your specific position, many jobs are filled by way of external recruiters and a recruiter promises to send your resume only to individual employers and only with your permission, I'd avoid them.

# Creating a Solid LinkedIn Profile

A LinkedIn profile is now pretty much a must-have item. Many employers troll LinkedIn's 500 million (can you believe it?) members to find people to invite to apply for jobs. And if you've applied for a job, employers may request the link to your LinkedIn profile instead of your resume.

A LinkedIn profile's disadvantage, compared with your resume, is that you can have only one. So if you have two or more job targets, you have to put all your LinkedIn eggs in your Plan A basket or have your profile straddle all your career goals.

## Your mugshot

We are a "lookist" species, so a photo of you is an important ingredient on LinkedIn. Follow these tips:

>> Use a head-and-shoulders shot with your eyes looking one inch above the lens. That raises your chin slightly, making you look more confident.

>> Wear your favorite outfit that would be appropriate on the target job.

>> The image must be well-lighted — no shadows.

>> Wear the smile that looks best on you. Try a few in the mirror, and then keep trying to reproduce the best one until you have it in muscle memory.

>> A selfie on your phone or pictures taken by a trusted friend might come out better than a professionally taken one because you'll be more relaxed. The resolution even on older smartphones is high enough for LinkedIn photos.

>> Take lots of shots, maybe 25 to 50, and pick your fave.

## Your title

LinkedIn allows you to give yourself a title. Give this some thought — it's the employer's first yea/nay filter. As always, put yourself in the shoes of your target employer: What title would make someone there want to read on? Also, try to embed keywords that a recruiter might search on, such as the reasonable ones in this list:

>> Food chemistry BS, cum laude, one year toward SFC, seeks product development bench position.

>> Political campaign operative serving as fundraiser, social media lead, and volunteer coordinator seeks management role.

## Career summary

The career summary can be as long as you want. Keep in mind, though, that in order to see beyond its first three lines, an employer has to click the See More link. Make those first lines compelling to your target employer. Here's my summary:

I love being a career and personal coach and writing about it. Specialties: intelligent, kind people facing professional or personal challenges. Many of my clients are referred to me by other career counselors.

## Experience

The Experience area on LinkedIn is like your resume: It shows your paid and unpaid work experiences, with bullet points describing accomplishments that would impress your target employer. You can add images and your portfolio, including links to online video.

## Skills

Though you can list as many skills as you want, only the first three display without having to click the See All link. Pick carefully!

## Career interests

The Career Interests area isn't easy to find. At the top of your home page, click on Me and you'll see, in tiny blue letters, View Profile. Click on it and then, in equally tiny letters in the gray box, click the career interests Voilà! You can specify the kind of job titles you're looking for, the industry, and the size of the employer.

## Recommendations

Find at least three people willing to sing your praises — the more credible their job titles, the better. For example, a person starting out is more likely to have a credible reference from an internship supervisor than from a CEO. On seeing some eminent's reference, the employer may think something like, "Aw, that's probably the person's parent's friend or relative."

## Personal interests

In the Personal Interests area, you can list LinkedIn forums and professional associations you belong to (a sign of being an involved professional), causes you care about, and avocations.

# Answering a Job Ad

The good news is that it's easy now to filter through millions of job ads. That's also the bad news: If it's easy for you, it's easy for anyone with an Internet connection. That's billions of people, from Aden to Zululand. So, even if you're a strong candidate, being the winning one requires savvy. I'll try to offer that to you in the following sections.

## Homing in on the right ads

How do you find the right ads? You probably need to check the heavy-hitting sites, which contain millions of openings: You can cover the largest number using just four: Indeed, Craigslist, LinkUp, and LinkedIn. Also check your professional association's website. It won't attract as many visitors.

**TIP**

Most of LinkedIn's job listings are *not* in the Jobs section. They're listed in Groups. That's because advertisers don't have to pay to put them there and by posting them in Groups, the audience is more targeted. So, joining groups not only enables you to learn what's new in your field, make connections, and be noticed by recruiters, but you may well also see on-target job openings. You also can search LinkedIn for on-target jobs by using the search bar and hashtags. For example, you type #jobs #Chicago #social media marketing in the search bar and then click on Posts.

## Before applying

Before you apply for a job, follow the employing organization on LinkedIn to see an ongoing feed of company-related posts from the organization's staff. Look especially at how people are filling your target role and see how their backgrounds compare with yours. This can help you as you position yourself in an application.

# The job-search letter

In Chapter 15, I discuss how to write letters to your networking contacts and to potential employers that aren't advertising a job. In this section, however, I offer a template for answering an *advertised* job opening — a template that has worked well for my clients. Here it is:

> Dear Employer,
>
> I was pleased to see your ad for an organizational development manager on Indeed.com because <specify something you like about that employer> and because the job description is a good fit for me.
>
> Major job requirement 1: <State it verbatim from the ad.>
>
> How I meet it: <If possible, state how you meet the requirement, and also supply evidence that you did it well: a quantitative or qualitative accomplishment or kudos from your boss, for example.>
>
> Major job requirement 2: <State it verbatim.>
>
> How I meet it:
>
> Major job requirement 3: <State it verbatim.>
>
> How I meet it:
>
> Of course, there's more to me than can be summarized in a chart. People say <insert a personal quality of yours that would seem important in this job — for example, you're calm under pressure or organized or pleasant to work with.> So I'm hoping you'll choose to interview me.
>
> In addition to my resume, I enclose <work sample, proposal, references, or white paper that would demonstrate current knowledge relevant to the job — for example, a 2-page report titled Five Keys to Excellence in Nonprofit Organizational Development.)
>
> Sincerely,
>
> Jane Jobseeker

A way to compensate for lack of experience is to write a *white paper*. This document, consisting of only a few pages, is similar to a school report — except that the topic must show your target employer that you have knowledge that's at least partially equivalent to experience. For example, if you're looking for a job in fashion marketing, open a Word file, which you'll use to store the nuggets you find. Search for the term *fashion marketing* on Google, and read a few of the resulting articles. Copy and paste not-obvious nuggets into the Word file. Perhaps watch a couple of YouTube videos and add any nuggets there to the Word file. You might also search for nuggets amid the posts on a LinkedIn or Yahoo! forum for fashion marketers. Then arrange the nuggets in a logical order, adapt them as needed, putting them in your own words or quoting with attribution where necessary, write a brief intro and conclusion, and — voilà! — you have a white paper that may impress an employer enough to give you a shot at fashion marketing. Even if it's only a job as an assistant, *that's* your needed launch pad.

# Chapter **15**

# Getting an "In"

I n any random room filled with 100 well-employed people, more than half of them got their jobs with the help of an "in." For example, they answered an ad and were touted by an insider. Or they contacted an employer who had no openings but created a temporary or permanent gig for them anyway or remembered them when a job eventually became available.

How do you find an "in" that's powerful enough in a way that is thorough, "head and heart" (as mentioned in the following section), and well suited to who you are? Enter this chapter. Although it's one of this book's shorter chapters, it's packed with some difficult-to-implement ideas. Be patient with yourself. Hey, in school, they probably spent two years teaching you algebra. Getting good at this chapter's content will take far less time and, hopefully, yield you far more benefit.

First, a bit of good news: Even if you're not a schmoozer, networking can work for you. You see, networking comes in flavors. There's usually at least one that works well for a given person. And if, after learning about them all, none appeals, it's not a deal killer. Many people succeed without networking.

# Prepping for Networking Success

Here's how to maximize the chances of networking helping you land a good job:

1. **Create a good resume and LinkedIn profile.**

   Even if your resume wouldn't be top-of-the-heap compared with other applicants, creating one teases out your best accomplishments, which you can mention to networking contacts so that they believe you're worth touting.

2. **Especially if your resume doesn't suggest that you'll be a solid candidate, write a *highlights letter,* which spells out what you want target employers to know about you.**

   Your resume lays bare everything, whereas a letter can put the focus on only what would impress that employer — for example, relevant work, courses, projects, or experiences, plus the reasons you've chosen this career path and what you hope to accomplish.

   In addition to facts, include feelings in the highlights letter, to help motivate a referrer to make the effort to champion you. I'm not saying that you should reveal desperation, but expressing a positive emotion can often help. For example, you might say, "I'm excited about pursuing a career in X because what I've learned about it says I'd be a good fit." Even a negative emotion can be helpful as long as you don't say that you're a stoned-out basket case. For example, you might say, "As someone just starting out, I'm a little nervous. After all, this would be my first professional job, and I'm guessing that other people have more experience. All I can say is that I'm eager and ready to learn and to do a good job." That vulnerability may turn off some people, but will motivate the right ones.

   **REMEMBER**

   To prevail in getting career help, you must connect with both head and heart. Every luxury carmaker knows that: Rationally, it makes sense to buy the more reliable, and less expensive, Toyota. Designer-label carmakers must fight that battle with both hands — head and heart — to entice customers to spring for a Mercedes or a Beemer.

   If your qualifications for your target employment are thin, it may be wiser to stand or fall on that highlights letter.

3. **Prepare evidence that you'd be good on the job.**

   Such evidence could include one or more of these items:

   - *A few brief PAR stories:* These describe a career-relevant *P*roblem you faced at work or school, your clever or dogged *A*pproach to solving it, and the positive *R*esult.

   - *A portfolio of work:* For people starting out, student work counts.

- *Your thoughts about the future:* If your past is light on impressive accomplishments, offer your thoughts moving forward — a 2-page paper on the future of your field or a proposal for what you'd do if hired, for example.

## Maxing your online presence

Before going to bat for you, people will likely check you out online. To ensure that online searches show you in the best (legitimate) light possible, be sure to follow these tips:

>> **Search for your name and nicknames on Google.** If you find information online that you believe is unfair, prepare an explanation. Or create articles or websites to help push any yucky stuff off Page 1, which is where most employers stop looking.

>> **Publicly post.** For example, post thoughtful questions, comments, and articles (and maybe even word of one that you plan to write) on their LinkedIn or Yahoo! groups or forums.

**TIP**

An additional reason to be active on LinkedIn Groups is that recruiters can post job listings there for free — and those ads are read by a targeted audience. So, no surprise, a majority of job listings are in LinkedIn Groups rather than in its Jobs section.

>> **Post thoughtful Twitter tweets.** Twitter now allows 280 characters per tweet, which allows a bit of room for nuance.

Having a good online presence helps not only in networking but increasingly, employers don't want to have to review oodles of applications. Instead, employers troll the Net, including various forums and groups (plus their personal and professional networks), and invite a small number of people to apply.

## Practicing your pitch

Create two pitches — one 10-second, one 30-second — that summarize the sorts of job you're open to, why you'd be a good hire, and why you're looking for a job. Here are the baby steps:

1. **Script it.**

2. **Reduce it to a few bullet points.**

3. **Practice in front of a mirror and then into a recorder (such as Voice Memos on the iPhone or Smart Voice Recorder on Android.)**

   Don't memorize it — even teleprompter-reading news anchors have a hard time sounding like they're not reading a script.

4. **Try out your pitch on a trusted friend.**

    Have someone role-play by asking follow-up questions — especially those you're afraid they'll ask — such as "What have you been doing since graduating?" or "Do you have much background in this field?"

# Lining Up and Growing Your Network

Networking is a crucial part of a job search, but one that many clients resist, understandably. For people who aren't natural networkers, it's hard work, and you have to overcome the fear of imposition, embarrassment, and rejection. Remember, though, that you're imposing no more than when you stop a stranger on the street, and you can survive *any* embarrassment or rejection.

Are you ready to use your network and, if needed, enlarge it? Here are the steps:

1. **List the people in your network.**

    Use a spreadsheet, a site such as JibberJobber.com, or even an index card file to keep track of your contacts. In the first field, list 10 to 30 people — the more, the merrier — who like you and who might also have a job lead for you: relatives, friends, family members, family members' friends, people you've worked with, fellow volunteers, fellow alumni, former classmates, and even distant ties such as your spiritual leader or haircutter. These folks talk to lots of people every day and, if they like you, can tout you to them. You certainly have nothing to lose by trying even tenuous connections. Remember that these people needn't be in a position to hire you — you just need for them to *want* to refer you — people know people. For example, I'm no dentist, but I know a few dentists.

    **TIP**

    Alumni from your college or even your high school, especially if you attended a small or private institution, may be a useful source of job leads. People tend to feel a bond with others who have done what they've done, especially if it's unusual. LinkedIn offers an alumni directory that specifies the kind of work people do and where they're employed. You can request to connect with someone on LinkedIn, and that person may end up giving you a job lead. If you're not a premium member of LinkedIn, you can message the person if you're both part of the same LinkedIn group. Or, you can usually find someone simply by typing *site:LinkedIn.com* and the person's name at Google or another search engine and then adding, in quotation marks, the first few words of their LinkedIn profile's title — for example, *site:LinkedIn.com, Jane McAllister "director, SME credit control."* To see how powerful this can be, check out the directory at www.linkedin.com/alumni/.

    In making your list, think especially of any "connectors" you know: people who know lots of people and enjoy connecting them.

**2.** **Place the names of those 10 to 30 people in order, from most likely to help to least, and then start reaching out.**

TIP

First contact the people least likely to help you — your first few reach-outs won't be as polished. When you feel you've got your act together, jump to your top leads so that you still sound fresh. That's analogous to the printer who uses cheap paper for the first few copies and then, when the pages are printing well, substitutes the high-quality deckled vellum.

**3.** **Expand your network.**

If you don't have enough well-placed people in your network, grow it with "planned serendipity" — put yourself in places with well-placed people in abundance. This list gives some examples of where to expand:

- *Start an alumni group.* If you've worked for a large organization, even as an intern, but no longer do, join or start an alumni group. One may exist as a LinkedIn or Yahoo! group. Its members share an affinity with you and so are more likely to introduce you to prospective employers or otherwise be helpful.

- *Look on LinkedIn.* In the search box, type in a job title, employer name, or person. When the results appear, to the right, you'll see ways to filter. That enables you to find people with your target job title (or a title two levels above it, the likely level of the person who will hire you) or with the specified industry, current employer, past employer, or location. Review their profiles, follow them, and look for an opportunity to engage — for example, by commenting on one of their posts. Then offer to connect. Or start by typing the name of the organization and working from there to identify people to connect with.

- *Volunteer at a nonprofit.* Pick one that you believe in. Political organizations are particularly good choices because political kinship tends to be a strong bond.

- *Get involved in your career's professional association.* The American Copy Editors Society is one example. A particularly potent form of involvement is to get on an organization's program committee, which meets multiple times. Then you can get to know its members better and, possibly, get to invite speakers to the next conference, which is an opportunity to interact with heavy hitters.

- *Attend your profession's regional or national conference.* It's perhaps *the* best networking opportunity, from the breakfast line to the exhibit area to the wine-and-cheese mixer.

REMEMBER

Network-building is usually more fruitful than attending events explicitly labeled as networking events. Attendees at such events tend to be looking for help rather than being in a position to provide it.

Regardless, many job seekers find connections, emotional support, and job search skills in a support group. Many such groups are provided by local and regional governments, religious institutions, nonprofits, Chambers of Commerce, and other outlets.

### 4. Record your attempts to reach out.

In the second field of your spreadsheet (refer to Step 1), list the best way to contact each person: by phone, email, text, or even "bumping into" them. In the third field, specify any activities you can invite them to — for example, lunch, coffee, hiking, shopping, ballgames, drinking, whatever. In later fields, list the date of contact, a date to follow up, and notes on the voicemail or email conversation you had.

### 5. List target employers.

List 10 to 30 organizations you'd like to work for. (Of course, you might be open to work somewhere else, but it helps to focus.) How do you find the 10 to 30? Unless you feel that you're competitive for jobs at top-of-mind employers such as Amazon, Citigroup, or United Way, search for under-the-radar employers that most job searchers don't jump to. To that end, try these options:

- *Google-search for the term* fastest growing companies. Your results will include lists of the national and regional up-and-comers as well as companies growing quickly in a specific field — for example, high-tech or healthcare.

- *CrunchBase.com* lists newly funded high-tech companies, those with the most money, and those trending upward on Chartbeat, which ranks pages by the number of visitors.

- *Check out LinkedIn's Top Startups.* It's at www.linkedin.com/pulse/ linkedin-top-companies-startups-50-industry-disruptors- daniel-roth?trk=eml-mktg-top-startups-2017.

- *LinkedIn has discussion groups in a wide range of fields.* Interesting, growing companies are often mentioned.

- *There are dozens of local editions of Business Times* (www.bizjournals.com). Each one contains information on companies in growth mode, often including the names of contacts associated with that growth.

- *Your local newspaper.* Yes, read the Business section, but note that the rest of the publication — even the advertisements — can lead you to growing businesses. *The online version may be more robust.*

- *The big job-ad sites, such as Indeed, LinkedIn, and Craigslist.* Employers that you've never heard of that have multiple job listings are likely to be in hiring mode. Use keywords and zip codes to narrow your list. Also, search job sites specializing in your field. Here's a link to 20 such sites: https:// www.thestreet.com/slideshow/13621473/5/15-best-niche-job- boards-for-job-seekers-and-recruiters.html.

Here's a list of specific sites to visit:

- **VentureLoop.com,** which claims to be "the worldwide leader in job postings focused on venture-backed companies," says that many of its job postings cannot be found on any other job board.

- **ThomasNet** profiles 650,000 distributors, manufacturers, and service companies within more than 67,000 industrial categories.

- **ReferenceUSA.com,** available on many public library websites, contains millions of U.S. businesses, including a section with 4 million new ones, where job openings are more likely and less competitive than in established companies.

- **Ward's Business Directory,** also usually on library sites, profiles 100,000 U.S. companies, 90 percent of which are private, mainly smaller.

- On shopping sites like **Amazon, Etsy, and eBay** search for a category of product you care about — for example, garden seeds. Does any company stand out for you?

- Drive around in local business areas and look at the **lobby directory** in office buildings.

- **The alumni directory at your college and even high school:** The alumni directory could unearth useful contacts.

**TIP**

Need help? A librarian often can provide it.

And don't forget about human sources of leads, such as these examples:

» **Officers at local organizations:** Rotary, Kiwanis, Lions, Chamber of Commerce, and so on. There you might ask which local businesses are growing.

» **Job-seeker support groups:** These folks often feed each other leads for which they personally are inappropriate. Again, the government, religious institutions, nonprofits, and Chambers of Commerce may sponsor such groups.

» **Your friends (last but definitely not least):** This group includes not just your wafer-thin friendships on Facebook but also your real-life friendships. Also look at where your LinkedIn connections and Facebook friends are working or have worked.

Sometimes your first job isn't for an organization — it's for one person. So don't forget about individuals who could hire you, such as a 1-person-shop business owner or your lawyer or writer friend who's a solo practitioner.

If you have guts, a surprising number of people have gotten an instant job offer by walking into a business that intrigues them and telling their story to the first friendly face. No, that won't work for a job as an investment banker, but especially for people starting out, it's worth a shot. Yes, you can survive the befuddled looks and rejections.

# Tracking Down the Names of People with the Power to Hire You

It's one thing to have a nice list of target organizations, but you also need the name and contact information of someone there with the power to hire you. The good news is that you don't need anywhere near a 100 percent hit rate. Here are ways to maximize your chances:

» **Check the employing organization's website.** It may list key employees and their contact info.

» **Search LinkedIn.** You may find someone in your network who works at that company.

» **Search Google for a target employer, using words that might elicit the name of the person with the power to hire you.** For example, you might search for *"Western Widget Waxing Co" "vice president marketing."* If that doesn't generate contact info, search for as much of the following information on a potential lead as you have: name, title, organization, area code, and the word *email*.

» **Phone the company's main number and use its automated directory to find a likely candidate.** You might hear, "For accounting, press 202; for marketing, 203," and so on. If you end up with an inappropriate person, ask whether she has a company directory handy and say that you're looking for the operations manager (for example) who handles your geographic area.

» **If you have a name but not the contact information, phone the organization's main number.** You'll get a live operator or a dial-by-name directory. Either way, you may get the person's contact information. For example, the automated system might say, "Connecting you with extension 203."

» **Connect to the mail room at a large organization.** Call the main number and get connected to that mail room. The person answering the phone probably doesn't have gatekeeper responsibility and so may give you the names and contact information of people with the power to hire you.

# Making the Ask

Whether by phone or email or in person (whichever way you're most comfortable with), this section describes the sort of pitch you might use. Note its informality and that it comes right to the point.

If you start out with, "How's the family?" or some such greeting, it will be clear that you're just buttering up the person for The Ask. The time for chitchat is *after* you've finished the business part of the call or email. Here's an example:

> "Hi Jamie. I'm probably the last person you're expecting to hear from. After all, it's been two years since we were in that study group in that economics course with that professor who spoke such poor English. You might wonder why I'm contacting you now. I'm looking for my first job after graduating, and they say that your best shot is to reach out to people you like. By any chance, might you know someone who could offer me advice or even a job in consumer advocacy? I'm especially interested in medical consumer advocacy because my degree is in biology and I really enjoyed my senior project on that, but I'm open. I've identified ten organizations I'm particularly interested in. Here they are. Might you know someone there or at another appropriate organization?"

Saying "I enjoyed this" rather than "I was excellent at this" suggests that you're good without bragging.

If the person suggests someone, ask if he might set up an introductory 3-way meeting over coffee or by video- or teleconference. That's the most potent introduction. If that method feels like you're asking for too much, ask if he'd forward your highlights letter (refer to the earlier section "Prepping for Networking Success"), and perhaps your resume, to that person. If even that feels like asking for too much, ask if you could let that employer know that he referred you.

Usually, the person says that he has no leads. If he has none, say, "I understand. Would you mind keeping your ears open and, if I'm still looking in a month, allow me to circle back?" The person almost always agrees and — voilà — you've recruited a scout and gotten permission to call or write back. And thus you've assembled a team of scouts. The odds are far greater that, over the month, rather than at the moment of making The Ask the first time, people will come across a lead for you.

The Ask can be one or more of these actions:

>> A lead

>> Advice on your job target or resume

>> A discussion of a collaboration, partnership, or joint venture

>> An offer to chat by phone or to get together socially

Usually, you get at least a few leads that way. And such leads can make you a less anonymous candidate whenever a job at that employer comes up. The employer may even create a job, or at least a temporary project, for you. And once you're hired, you're an insider, and subsequent jobs become easier to get.

After discussing your job needs, *then* it's appropriate to ask about them. For example, you might say, "Enough about me. What's doing in your life?" Look for an opportunity to help the other person. For example, if he says that he's moving this weekend and dreading it, offer to lend a hand or at least to dig up a good article on how to making moving easier.

TIP

If the person is someone you might want to work for, ask the magic question: "Are you or your team grappling with something difficult right now?" If the person tells you about such a problem, if possible at that moment or after your call, try to come up with a suggestion that might help. That shows your abilities and your kindness, and it creates indebtedness, all of which make the person more likely to help you get a good job.

If, in knowing about their problem, you feel you can help, you might even make The Ask: "You know, in listening to you, it seems like it might make sense for you to hire me. (Explain how.) What do you think?" A next step might be for you to offer to submit a 1-page proposal to describe what you'd do.

## Boosting your chances of a callback

With people you're unsure will return your query, try this phone-email-phone technique:

>> **Phone:** Call after hours, saying in a brief message on voicemail that you'll email a summary of what you've said so that the person has it in writing.

>> **Email:** Immediately email that note and, if you think it would help, your resume.

>> **Phone again:** If you haven't heard from the person in three to seven days, phone again — this time perhaps during business hours. You still may get voicemail. It's okay. Your message should sound something like this:

"I'm John Smith, that recent geology graduate who's interested in starting a career in natural gas exploration. Not having heard from you, I assume that you're too busy, though I know how things can fall between the cracks. So, like any good employee, I'm following up. If you're willing to offer any advice on what I might do, and even discuss how I might be helpful to you and your organization, I'd welcome that. I won't be a pest, so if I don't hear from you, you won't hear from me again. My phone number is . . ."

## Going direct

Whether or not you have an "in" from your network, reach out to someone at each of your 10 to 30 target organizations, *whether or not it's advertising an appropriate job*. First check the organization's website, and apply for any appropriate positions.

Your approach to contacting such an employer is the same as with your network. The only exception is that if you've gotten a lead from your network, start your ask with this: "Mary Jones suggested I reach out to you."

If you've just applied for a job there, keep in mind that some managers may see your following up with a call or email as pushy. Many, however, welcome a statement such as this one: "I've applied for a position at your organization as a data analyst but I'm particularly enthusiastic about it, so although I am concerned it might be pushy, I thought I'd reach out to you."

**TIP**

Search your LinkedIn connections to see whether any of them work or worked at your target organization. If they can attest to your abilities, ask whether they might email or phone someone there with a message like this: "I've heard that Joe Blow has applied for a position as finance analyst. I've worked with him at B of A, and he's terrific, smart, thorough, and low-maintenance. I just thought I'd throw my two cents in."

# Keys to a Great First Impression

It's a cliché: You never get a second chance to make a first impression, but it's true, and of course, a first impression is important.

Shallow as it may be, posture and a smile really help. If you're hunched, with arms folded and eyes averted, you look closed down, which is the opposite of what you want. You want connection. So, the second before you're about to enter the room for an in-person meeting, networking or otherwise, remind yourself: Open body language plus eye contact. No, don't stare all the time — you'll look psychotic. Three-quarters of the time is about right.

How do you make a smile more genuine? First, realize that you don't need a grin permanently plastered on your mug. The key is to look for the positive aspects of the person you're talking with and the topic you're talking about. That will help make a natural smile emerge at the right times.

# Making the Most of a Networking Event

Let's say you're at an event where it would be inappropriate to jump right in to your pitch — an alumni mixer, for example, or the coffee break during a professional association meeting, or the pre-lecture milling at a conference, volunteer organization, or singles event.

First, use your intuition to pick out someone who seems nice and with a better-than-average chance of being able to hire you. Perhaps it's a person who's well-dressed or older than you and who looks approachable.

Many people find it scary to approach a stranger, but once you get used to the idea, it's easier — kind of like riding a bike. To reduce the risk of rejection, test the waters. For example, try to establish eye contact from a distance — maybe 10 feet or maybe just a half-second's worth every 10 seconds or so with a pleasant look on your face. If the eye contact is met without a grimace — or even better, with a smile — it's a clue that you can approach the person without their biting your head off.

If the person is part of a group conversation, it's easier. Stand a couple feet outside the group, facing the person. Again, try to establish that eye contact. If you're lucky, she'll invite you to join the conversation or, more likely, just return the eye contact, in which case you might take a step closer to the group and listen.

So now you're face-to-face. Of course, you can't launch right into your job-search pitch. Assuming that the other person doesn't take the lead, it's standard procedure to start with an environmental comment (no, not about climate change) about the room, the event, the speaker. Here are some examples: "Hi. It's my first time at this event. How about you?" or "It's hot outside but certainly comfortable in here," or "That's quite a spread they've put out for us."

From there, listen — and comment or ask a question that builds on what was said. If that peters out, you might say a little something about yourself, even something a bit revealing, like this: "It seems like everyone knows each other here (implying that you feel like an outsider) or "This is my first time at a professional association meeting" or, simply, "My name is Jane Jones. You?"

Continue listening and responding until you sense that it's time to turn the conversation to your job search. For example, you might say, "I've enjoyed my internship in human resources, and now I'm hoping to launch a career in that field. I've applied to a few jobs, but, as is the experience of many job seekers, the usual response is no response. I'm wondering whether you might have any tips?"

If you'd like to end the conversation, just stick out your hand and say, "It's been good talking with you. I'm going to get something to drink" <or run to the bathroom or whatever else you can think of>. If you'd like to recruit the person as a scout, say something like this: "Of course, if you have any further advice for me, I'd welcome hearing from you. May I give you my contact information?"

# Special Opportunities for Networking

You can find plenty more sources to help open the door to a job than just the ones described earlier in this chapter. This section looks at a few.

## At an online professional forum

After joining a professional forum, read old threads and lurk for a while, to get a sense of the forum's culture: How much consists of giving advice versus providing information? How overt can the desire for career help be? Then, before asking for help, you might, each week for a few weeks, post a comment that shows your intelligence, knowledge, or caring, but without being hubristic. So you might post a link to an article by an industry luminary, plus a key tip from that article. Or ask a thoughtful question or comment in response to a previous post. Then you might make The Ask — for example, "I'm looking for a job that requires psychologically attuned copy writing — perhaps for a politician, nonprofit cause, or good product. By any chance, might you know of someone I should reach out to?"

## At a party

You: So, anything interesting happening in your work life?

The target says something.

You then make a follow-up comment or ask a question that transitions into your giving your pitch, as in this example:

> "You must be proud of your progress. I'm also eager for that. I just graduated and am looking for my first accounting job. It's been a little frustrating because every ad asks for three to five years of experience." (Without your having to ask, you've hinted that you're open to career help.)

# In class

You make a point in class of sitting, perhaps regularly, next to someone who intrigues you professionally and/or personally. Or, during the pre-class milling, you approach him:

You: What did you think of the reading?

He: It was a little long.

You: Yeah. Are you taking this course because it's required? I've elected to take it. The course title is relevant to my career goal: organizational psychology.

He: Frankly, I took it because it fits into my schedule and doesn't meet early in the morning.

You: This is the last course I need to finish my major. Now I need to start looking for a job, or at least an internship.

Again, without asking for help, which would be premature, you've opened the door for it. When you sense that it's time to ask, there's little risk in doing so, and there's a good chance that the person has some advice or knows someone you should talk with.

# In the supermarket

At the supermarket, pick your checkout line purposefully: Observe the last person in each line. Which one do you sense you might best connect with professionally or personally? Get in that line.

Or (and this may be more planful than you want to be, but here it is for your consideration). As you're walking up and down the aisles, keep your antennae out for people with whom you feel some sort of affinity. Try to establish flickers of eye contact — each one arouses a bit of curiosity and connection. When it comes time to choose a checkout line, see whether you can — without seeming like a stalker — get in line behind one of those people. Look in their shopping cart for an item you can make a positive comment about. For example, maybe you use that item and love it, or the flower bouquet is beautiful.

You (pointing to the Port Salut cheese in the person's cart): I love that cheese. It's worth the calories.

She: Thanks. It's my first time.

You: I shop at Trader Joe's all the time. Love it. You?

She: Yes.

You sense that she doesn't know what to say, and neither do you, but you know that you've signaled being open to conversation, so you wait. If you were lucky, she'd say something, but let's make it difficult: She remains silent, and you have only a minute before she's literally and figuratively checking out.

You: What do you do when you're not on a Trader Joe's line?

She: I'm a sales rep for Moet champagne.

You: Wow, that's sexier than my career, or I should say, my aspiring career. I'm trying to get my first job after graduating from college as some sort of qualitative researcher — you know, like doing research for a book writer, nonprofit, or government agency.

The sales clerk (to your counterpart:) "Will that be cash, credit, or debit?"

You: You're busy. Sorry.

If you're lucky:

She. No it's fine. Let me just pay.

You: Sure, I'll wait.

And if you're really lucky:

She: My cousin is an assistant director at Planned Parenthood. I could give you his email.

You: I'd love that.

**REMEMBER**

Of course, most times, reaching out in this way doesn't have a fairytale ending — but you have nothing to lose by making informal networking part of your existence. These opportunities can be fun, and can often enough yield a lead that could turn into a job offer or a relationship.

# Does Everyone Need to Network?

Most people do. Here are the possible exceptions:

» Simply, you abhor networking.

» You believe that your resume will, often enough, be top-of-the-stack for your desired position, or you're already well employed and positioned to move up.

» You've made major efforts to improve your networking skills, you've tried them out extensively, and they've yielded too little fruit to justify further effort. You'd be wiser to focus on creating excellent applications for advertised jobs.

» You find networking ethically unacceptable. A case can be made for networking being a ploy for getting a job you wouldn't deserve on the merits. Such people might want to try hard to land the job the traditional way, by simply answering ads responsibly and, only if feeling desperate, using this chapter's methods.

# Chapter 16

# The Relaxed-Yet-Successful Job Interview

The terms *relaxed* and *job interview* seem to go together as well as a fish and a bicycle. Though I can't promise that a job interview will be as relaxing as a massage on a Bora Bora beach, it can be less stressful than the medieval torture chamber that many people fear.

## Preparing for the Interview

Your main task in preparing for the interview is to assemble evidence that would impress your target employer.

### Preparing, not overpreparing

If you overprepare, you'll be tight. Especially don't memorize any answers. Many candidates script answers to such questions as "Tell me about yourself." But usually, even if the interviewer asks such a question, it's often a variant, and the memorized answer can seem nonresponsive. Plus, under the pressure of an interview, you could easily get thrown off your script and become tongue-tied. And even if you stay on-script, you'll sound scripted. That doesn't build credibility.

**TIP**

Sure, if you need to, script your answer to help flesh it out, but then reduce it to a few signpost words. Practice using those few words as your "cheat sheet," and then without it. Don't overpractice, or your recitation could resemble high school students reciting the Pledge of Allegiance.

## What to prepare

Preparing for an interview can seem overwhelming: "They could ask me anything!" Focus only on the following tactics and you'll likely be ahead of the pack:

>> **Wear appropriate attire.** Dress one notch above what you'd wear if you were hired for that position. Not sure? Call the employer's office and ask.

>> **Prepare answers to the two or three questions you're most afraid to be asked.** Perhaps it's the wide open statement "Tell me about yourself." *Hint:* Don't start from when you were born. Start with the first moment you thought you might like a career or job like this one, and then walk the interviewer, in about a minute, through the key moment that made you eager to apply for the job. Here's an example:

> "I thought I wanted to be a doctor, but after reading a medical textbook, I too often found myself thinking, 'Do I have this disease?' That bit of hypochondria made me pivot to hospital administration. I took a course in that and liked it, did some job shadowing and liked that, and now that I've graduated, I'm excited about launching my career in hospital administration. That's why I applied for this job."

>> **Get technical-minded.** Ever more jobs require one or more technical skills, for example, coding, and so interviews may include a technical test. Take the time to bone up. For example, regarding coding, one good resource is Gayle McDowell's book *Cracking the Coding Interview: 189 Programming Questions and Solutions* (www.amazon.com/Cracking-Coding-Interview-Programming-Questions/dp/0984782850).

>> **Prepare a few talking points.** These illustrate attributes you bring to the table that might give you an edge over other candidates. For example, if you wrote a paper in school on a topic related to the job, look for an opportunity to briefly describe it. Or let's say that your relative suffered from a disease that the company's device helps; explain how that situation moves you to want the job. Or maybe you just attended a boot camp on using Spark with Python and are excited to get to use it on a real-life project on artificial intelligence.

>> **Have three PAR stories ready.** These are 30- to 60-second stories of a *Problem* you faced, the clever or dogged *Approach* you used to resolve it, and the positive *Result*. No surprise: Pick three stories that would impress your target employer. If you can't think of three from work, volunteering, or school, even consider something from your extracurricular life, as in this example:

"When I was co-captain of my school's lacrosse team, we had one guy who played dirty. Everyone was scared of him. Even the coach seemed to look the other way. But it bothered me that he would do things like poke opponents in the eye intentionally! So I figured I'd give it a try. I asked if he'd go out for ice cream with me — I knew he liked ice cream. After some small talk, to avoid sounding like his father, I told a little lie. I said, 'My father told me that he'd rather see me lose honestly than win by cutting corners.' I saw his face get angry and then his eyes dropped. I felt I didn't need to say any more and changed the topic to the upcoming game. I can't tell you that turned him into a saint, but he seemed to play a little cleaner after that. That sort of experience is motivating me to have a career in people management, which is why I applied for this job."

TIP

Tell your stories at the right level of technicality. People like to feel good about themselves, so if you're talking tech, tell your story in a way that's technical enough to impress but not so technical that the person doesn't understand. Generally, unless the interviewer is a specialist in your area, it's wise to use the grandparent rule: Tell it so simply that your grandparent would understand it.

>> **Show, don't tell.** Be prepared to demonstrate what you can do. Of course, that works especially well in sales positions: Offer to show how you'd sell the product. But demonstrating can be useful for many other jobs. You might bring in work samples that would be relevant to the job. You might offer to go to the whiteboard to lay out how you'd structure your planning for a problem they say you'd be tackling. Or you might offer to role-play. Let's say you're applying for a job in child protective services. You might role-play how you'd try to convince a reluctant parent to allow you to come to their home. If your job would include teaching, training, or explaining and by the end of the interview they don't ask you to do a demo, offer to do one.

>> **Be prepared to discuss salary.** Better for you to preempt the question "What's your salary requirement?" than to answer it. Answering it risks stating too high or low a number. Right after you've given your first good answer in the interview, say, "By the way, what salary range has been budgeted for the position?" If the interviewer refuses to answer and instead asks for the amount you're looking for, it's best to say, "I'm confident that if we both want each other, we'll come to a fair agreement." If he pushes for a number, give a wide range — for example, "$65,000 to $80,000 depending on the nature of the position, the benefits, and so on."

>> **Prepare emotionally.** Even if you're dying for the job, remind yourself that you can always find other jobs, and that this one may not be as good as it sounds. Also remember that if you're rejected, it may well mean that the job wasn't a sufficiently good fit or that some factor beyond your control made them choose another candidate. Yes, *prefer* to get the job, and do well in the interview, but be yourself and let the chips fall as they may. If it's not meant to be, it's not.

I had a client who was "dying" to get a job working for a company that helps make buildings greener. He didn't get the job, but later got one working on converting wave power to usable electric power, and he is grateful he didn't get the green-building job.

For many people, such advice helps, but is insufficient to keep you calm enough in the interview. It may additionally help to physiologically tire yourself out: Exercise before your interview, leaving enough time to shower and get there, including a little cushion for the unexpected: traffic, parking problems, and even getting a bit lost.

Immediately before entering the building, review an index card with key words reminding you of your PAR stories and answers to tough questions.

**REMEMBER**

The dating mindset: Just before opening the door to the interview, remind yourself one more time that although you might prefer to get the job, perhaps in learning about it in the interview, you won't. And even if you do want it but don't get it, there are always other jobs, probably ones that are a better fit. This is a date — you're both checking each other out.

# Excelling in the Interview Situation

Ever more interviews are conducted remotely using Skype, Zoom, or Google Hangouts. Here are a few tips:

>> Position the webcam so that it's a head-and-shoulders shot and none of the frame is in shadows.

>> Pretend that your interviewer is an inch above the lens. Looking at that spot raises your chin slightly so that you look more confident and have better eye contact.

>> Increasingly, interviews are conducted asynchronously: The interviewer has prerecorded the questions, and you answer them, clicking a key when you're done. Why do employers do that? It enables you and the interviewer to complete the interview when convenient. It also ensures that all applicants see the same questions and interviewer body language. If the employer wants to ask follow-up questions later, she can.

>> When the interview begins, ask your interviewer if the video and audio are okay.

If the interview takes place in person, stride in, stand straight with good posture, hold your chin just slightly above 90 degrees, and wear a slight, pleasant smile that doesn't appear forced. Shake the interviewer's hand (or interviewers' hands), and wait to be invited to sit down.

Again, don't focus so much on yourself that you forget it's a date — you're both checking each other out. Listen intently to the questions while maintaining eye contact most of the time. Get in touch with how you're feeling about that boss. How are you feeling about the job as the questioning reveals it? Such thoughts can help you avoid a bad job *and* keep you relaxed because you're not obsessing about the nanodetails of how you're coming across.

Follow the traffic light rule: During the first 30 seconds of an utterance, the light is green: They're listening. All's good. During the second 30 seconds, the light is yellow: The chance is increasing that they've heard enough. After 1 minute, the light is red: You probably should stop or ask a question. If they want more information, they can ask.

Following the traffic light rule ensures that you're leaving your interviewers enough time to talk. If you end up talking more than about three-quarters of the interview, it tends to deenergize the interviewers and can make you seem too eager or even desperate. In contrast, when they talk, they gain investment in you.

The free video "Interview Simulation" (at https://www.youtube.com/watch?v=2zKsBfsrxrs) may be helpful. It shows an interviewer asking typical interview questions, allowing you 60 seconds to answer each one. That can help you get a sense of pacing — 30 to 60 seconds is about the right length for answering most interview questions.

When answering, if you're facing more than one interviewer, try to do this: Begin answering the question while looking the questioner in the eye for a second or two. Then talk to the person to the questioner's right. Continue moving right until you reach the last person, and then reverse directions. Eye contact makes people feel valued.

Applicants who are asked a question that's difficult to answer, such as "Why have you been unemployed so long?" or "Why should we hire you when you have no experience in this field?," tend to give long answers to dig themselves out of trouble. Usually, it's wiser to do the opposite: Give short answers to difficult questions, and longer answers to easy questions, so that more of the interview is spent in areas you'd like to talk about.

Many interviews contain simulation or case questions: "How would you handle this issue?" Often, there is no single correct answer. The interviewers are looking to see how you structure your thinking. So take a moment to think, and then describe how you'd tackle the problem, step by step. Don't be afraid to say, "I'd like to take a moment to reflect."

For legal reasons, some interviews must be identical for all candidates. In such cases, you're not allowed to ask questions until the end. If you're permitted to, it's wise to ask two or three during the interview. That shows enthusiasm and helps you decide how much you want the job. The best questions tend to build on something the interviewer discussed or asked about, though a canned question or two may be okay. Here are some examples:

>> If I turned out to be an excellent employee, what would you hope I'd accomplish in the first week or month?

>> Every office culture is different. What would you say differentiates yours?

>> Every boss has a different style. How would you describe yours?

>> What should I know about the organization (or workgroup) that might not appear in the employee handbook?

Especially if it's an internship or volunteer gig, you have a particular right to ask vetting questions. You're donating your time for little or no pay, so the gig needs to be more than envelope-licking. You might, for example, ask:

>> What might a typical day look like?

>> Can you tell me about any training and mentoring I'd be receiving?

>> What percentage of interns and volunteers get a paid position within six months?

After hearing the answers, ask yourself whether this volunteer or internship gig is likely to be a dead end or a career launcher.

**TIP**

Early in your career, you're likely to have less relevant experience than do other candidates. In such cases, it's wise to shift the conversation from the past to the future. The interviewer may focus on what you've done, for example, by walking you through your resume, but that won't help you. So talk about what you would do if hired. Make it impressive enough, and it may trump your lack of background.

If you're good at thinking on your feet, try to convert the interview into a conversation about the challenges your prospective boss or the organization are facing. Ask questions, listen carefully, and perhaps tactfully offer suggestions, all in a relaxed, conversational, and even slightly playful manner. Even if the job you're interviewing for is tactical — for example as a graphic artist or administrative assistant — asking bigger-picture questions and, if it feels right, offering an idea or two can make the employer think *the* most important thought: "This is a person I'd like on my team."

At the end of most interviews, you're asked, "Do you have any questions?" Here are a couple of canned ones to consider if you think you want the job:

>> "I am more interested in the position than ever, and I'm wondering whether you think I'm a good fit?"

That gives you a chance to counter any objections.

>> "Do you have a sense of when you'll be getting back to me?"

If no one contacts you when promised, you have a basis for following up with a phone call. That gives you a chance to not only connect again but also, if they're hesitant to hire you, to ask whether there's a concern that you may be able to address.

# Foiling Employer Ploys

Job seekers need to watch out for employer ploys. This section looks at common examples.

## Hyping the job

First out of the gate is the infamous "hyping the job" ploy. Here's how it works:

>> **The ploy:** In the job ad and interviews, employers may inflate the job's wonders. It needn't mean that they were intentionally misleading — we all have a hard time reconciling our disliking our job with staying there, let alone touting it to others. So, to avoid cognitive dissonance, we tell ourselves that the job is good. If we're interviewing candidates, our job is to encourage applicants to want to work for us, so we're particularly likely to highlight the job's positives. Besides, we could get in trouble with our boss for bad-mouthing the place.

>> **Foiling the ploy:** The job-seeker needs to be a sleuth. During the interview, ask questions like those mentioned in the earlier section "Excelling in the Interview Situation." The words in the answer may not reveal as much as does the speaker's tone of voice and the other interviewers' facial expressions. For example, you may end up in a group interview in which you ask your prospective boss, "Every boss has a different style — what's yours?" If the boss responds, "I try to be collaborative and have an open door policy," but you notice one of the other interviewers' lips purse and another one flash a hint of a grin, that's a warning sign.

You may get an even better indication of whether the job is being hyped after you've been offered the job but haven't yet accepted it. Offer to come to the workplace to discuss terms. This action signals that you won't just roll over and accept the employer's first offer, and you get a chance to assess in context whether you want the job.

**TIP**

When you arrive for the interview, take in the workplace's vibe: Are most people engaged, but not harried or sad? Hang out in the break room and glance at employees' faces — their eyes can be windows to the soul. Also, you might ask a question such as this one: "I've just been offered a job here as a such-and-such. Is there anything I should know about working here that might not appear in the employee handbook?" Again, the answer itself may or may not be revealing, but you often can get a sense from tone: An enthusiastic, "It's fine" means something different from a monotonic "It's fine."

## Extracting free labor from the applicants

Here's an employer tactic that's especially nasty:

>> **The ploy:** The employer asks all candidates to provide a work sample: a difficult task that the employer needs done, such as creating a marketing plan for a new product. That gives the employer free work from many motivated people. In that ploy's worst incarnation, the employer doesn't even have a job opening — she just wants free high-level work, knowing that all those job seekers will do their best.

>> **Foiling the ploy:** Provide a work sample large enough only for the employer to judge your competence. At the end of your sample, write, "Hire me and I'll show you the rest." Perhaps you can even add a smiley emoji, like this: ☺ If your boss objects, you have to decide whether to capitulate or to explain that it feels unreasonable to ask for more work than necessary to ascertain your competence. Yes, that takes guts, but it also shows moxie. Besides, the employer who takes advantage of candidates will probably take advantage of you after you're hired. You may be better off working elsewhere.

## Making vague promises

Making vague promises is also known as the blowing-smoke ploy:

>> **The ploy:** As when an employer oversells the job, sometimes the deception is unconscious. Like many people, your boss may simply be unrealistically optimistic about the candidate and the chances of a promotion, of the

company getting a big new client, and so on. Alas, at other times, the employer consciously figures, "It can't hurt to err on the side of optimism."

>> **Foiling the ploy:** The antidote to vagueness is to ask for specificity. For example, when offered the job and you're not happy with the salary, ask the employer to commit in writing to an automatic 10 percent raise, for example, after the first three months unless you're terminated for cause. If you're taking the job on the assumption that you'll soon get a plum sales territory, ask that the contract give you a 15 percent compensatory fee if you don't get that territory within six months.

# Employing Post-Interview Tactics

Jobs are often won or lost after the interview. This section looks at ways you can make a win more likely.

## Writing an influencing letter

Writing a thank-you letter won't distinguish you from many other applicants. Also, it can make you seem toady: Do you really want to thank them for putting you through the wringer with no guarantee that it will pay off?

Instead, write an *influencing letter.* Yes, you can begin with "Thanks for the opportunity to meet with you to discuss the position. I'm more interested than ever because (*Insert something said in the interview that makes the job more appealing.*) But instead of going right to the phrase "Hoping to hear from you," you have opportunities to do the following:

>> **Present new information:** For example, in light of the interview, you might realize that a key factor in the hiring decision is to pick a candidate who's good at streamlining office processes. If so, you might say something like this: "I've reflected on your comment that you'd like the candidate to streamline some of the office's processes. I hadn't stressed that in my interview, so I thought I'd mention my relevant experience." Or, "I had a thought about how you might make more efficient the linkages between the salespeople, warehouse, and office. I could well be off-base about this because there's so much I don't know about the way you do things, but it at least offers a window into the way I think."

>> **Take a second swing at a question:** If you flubbed a question, your influencing letter gives you a second chance at answering it. You might write, "I've reflected on your question about such-and-such, and here's my new-and-improved answer."

>> **Include new collateral material:** Consider attaching a piece of collateral material that might be impressive, even if it's only someone else's article that you know would interest the employer. Or send a list of actions you'd take to get off to a good start on the job. Or include a reference letter, custom tailored to the position, that highlights how you'd be a good fit, particularly with regard to a factor that the interviewers said would be important.

## Following up

As mentioned earlier in this chapter, at the end of the interview, ask when you'll get the employer's decision. If the employer doesn't keep the promise, send an email or, better, phone. Whether you get the person or the voicemail, say something like this: "You had mentioned that you'd be getting back to me before now, so, like any good employee, I figured I'd follow up. I'm enthusiastic about the position, and although I have other irons in the fire, I wanted to check back with you."

TIP

I know that you're eager, but it's usually wise to wait a few days beyond when you feel like following up. When you reach out first, it can feel too eager, even desperate. People like to feel that they have to chase you. If you follow this chapter's advice, they may well do that.

# Chapter 17

# One (Hard) Week to a Good Job

I n trying to put myself in your shoes, dear reader, if I had read Chapters 14-17 of this book, I might be feeling overwhelmed into inertia. Perhaps a summary is in order.

So, here, day by day, is what one might do. Though many employers take their sweet time deciding whom to hire, you can put all the balls in motion in just a week — a difficult week, but still just a week.

To provide a little insurance against a how-to writer's tendency to ask other people to do what he himself wouldn't do, I am writing this chapter in the first-person voice — that is, in words that reflect what I believe I personally would do.

## Monday

Monday is the killer day.

Get coffee, and then force myself to shuffle to my desk by 8 a.m., or 9 a.m. at the latest.

I'd think hard about my job target. I wouldn't want something too broad, like this: "Anything that uses counseling skills and oral and written communication." That over-broadness would make it too difficult to sound expert enough in interviews. And it could sound a bit desperate, or at least like I'm a "dabbler" — a jack-of-all-trades and master of none. That would motivate too few people in my network to tout me to potential employers.

On the other hand, I wouldn't make my target too narrow — for example, "Career coaching for a nonprofit in Oakland, California." Too few open job listings would be available, and my network would be unlikely to know someone who could hire me for that job.

A middle ground might be, "Career counselor working for a quality company, nonprofit, or university in the San Francisco Bay Area."

At that point, I might give myself a 3-minute break to reheat my coffee or freshen my thoughts. But I'd keep it to three minutes. I want to get my job search *done!*

I'd write my resume and post it on my professional association's website. I'd adapt my resume for LinkedIn and post it. While on LinkedIn.com, I'd set up an alert to receive an email every time an appropriate job is posted.

**TIP**

I'd allocate only two hours or so to writing the resume and adapting it for LinkedIn. Most people spend too much time on creating resumes, LinkedIn profiles, highlights letters, and other job-search items. Generally, additional tweaking beyond the first couple of hours makes little difference — the time is better spent net-working, cold-contacting target employers, and answering ads. Also, quickly completing letters, resumes, and other documents enables you to complete the compressed job search that I've been advocating in this Part of the book. Writing time-effectively not only completes the job search more quickly — it also maximizes the chance that you'll receive more than one job offer at the same time. That's your strongest lever for negotiating a higher salary and perks.

If I were tempted to procrastinate, I'd try the Pomodoro technique: First, set a timer for 20 minutes. Then work for 20 minutes, and then relax for 5 minutes; work another 20, and then relax for another 5; work another 20, and relax for 10.

At this point, it's probably lunchtime. Because I want to avoid the sluggish feeling of overeating, I'll eat something light and quick. (Full disclosure: I have been known to cheat.)

After lunch, I'd assemble any collateral material I'd want to send to my network or prospective employers, such as good evaluations from my previous bosses, letters of recommendation, thank-you notes from clients, and papers I'd written that would impress my target employer.

I'd write a short letter to my network, something like the following (because someone reading this book is likely to be just starting out, I've worded it here as though I were a new graduate):

Hi, <insert the name — no mass mailing allowed>:

I'm looking to start my career, and I often hear that answering ads usually doesn't work — that it's better to reach out to people you like. That, of course, brings me to you.

I'd love to have a job as a career counselor working for a quality company, non-profit, or university in the San Francisco Bay Area — for example, Google, Apple, Facebook, Amazon, Berkeley, Stanford, or United Way, or even a lesser-known organization. Might there be someone you think I should talk with? And if not, would you mind keeping your ear to the ground? Because I'm just starting out, my resume is a little thin, so I'm instead attaching a letter to prospective employers that lists the things I've done that might make them want to give me the time of day.

And now that the business part of this note is done, the last time we spoke (it has been a year!), you mentioned that you were starting your first job at that high-tech start-up. How's it going? Are all the stories true about ping-pong tables and Red Bull in the break room and a massage therapist who comes in once a week?

All the best,

Marty Nemko

**TIP**

I'd write the following *highlights letter* to prospective employers. That will enable me to tout the things that might impress the employer. In contrast, a resume buries those amid materials that highlight my inexperience. (I'm making up details, rather than using my own, so that it's more typical of this book's readership.)

Dear Employer,

I am hoping to launch my career as a career counselor. Here are

highlights of what I've done so far:

- A bachelor's degree in psychology (3.3 GPA) and an M.A. in career counseling (3.6 GPA) from California State University at Northridge.

- In a career counseling internship, worked with 17 clients and received 14 five-star evaluations, 2 four-star evaluations, and 1 one-star evaluation. I've learned some things from that experience.

  (Acknowledging some weaknesses or imperfections adds credibility to your letter and displays your openness to input.)

- Shadowed two in-house career counselors in their jobs — one at 3M and the other at Citi.

(That supports my argument that I prefer to do career counseling from within a corporation.)

- Special interest in helping employees strategize their next steps — up is not the only way.

- Though it may not be relevant, I'm an avid hiker and sports fan.

(I've found that it helps in building a bond with certain clients.)

Of course, there's more to me than can be stated in a few bullets. My clients and coworkers at my internship say that I'm easy to work with, and although I take my work seriously, I bring an upbeat attitude. I'm attaching a couple of evaluations from my boss and thank-you letters from clients.

I'm hoping to have the chance for you to get to know me a bit better, and to offer some career-launching advice — or even consider me for a job.

In any event, thank you for reading this.

Sincerely,


Marty Nemko


At this point, I've put in a full day's effort, and it's time to call it quits and start enjoying a pleasurable evening. To ensure that I can hit the ground running tomorrow, I make a to-do list:

1. Get back in the saddle by 8 a.m. or, at the latest, 9 a.m.

2. Create a list of people to network with and a list of target employers.

3. Create a one-pager of collateral material.

4. Send the letter to my network and to target employers.

5. Increase my participation on forums.

# Tuesday

I'd make a list of the 20 people most likely to help me obtain my target job. Of course, the list would include friends, family members, and colleagues in that field, but would also include anyone who likes me and isn't a hermit. That's because people know people. Even if my old college buddy is now a haircutter, he has customers and friends, and one of them might be a useful lead.

Then I'd make a list of ten or so organizations that I'd love to work for. As when I applied to college, I'd choose some "reaches," like Google, Apple, Facebook, and Amazon — plus, some less well-known choices, for which competition for jobs wouldn't be so tough. (Google gets 1,500 unsolicited resumes per *day!*) Of course, this is a reminder that, in order to have a chance at a job, especially at a prestigious place, I need to focus my efforts on getting my network to refer me.

I'd Google-search a career-counseling topic to find articles I could invoke when talking with an employer. I'd convert them into a 1-page list of bullets that would impress my target employers.

Lunchtime. I'd do something fun so that I don't feel deprived having to get back to work.

I'd reread my letters and send them, my resume, and collateral to my network and target employers.

I'd lurk, ask questions, or make comments on career counseling forums on LinkedIn or Yahoo! Groups.

I'd look for any upcoming job fairs or on-campus recruiting events hosted by the career center or alumni services. I'd put them on the schedule.

Done for the day!

The plan for Wednesday:

1. Back to work at 8 or 9 a.m.
2. Comb ads for on-target jobs to apply to. Apply.
3. Identify job fairs and on-campus events.

# Wednesday

These days, if people are going to respond, they'll do it within a day. If they don't, the chances decline with every day that passes. So today I follow up with a phone call, text, or email to each person who hasn't responded.

For example, here's the follow-up letter I'd send to my network:

> Hey Jude,
>
> I'm just following up on the email I sent you. If by any chance you know someone that you think I should talk with, I'd love to hear from you. And, even if you only feel like chatting or getting together, let me know that, too. I'd like that. My number is 311-555-2368.

Then I'd search for on-target job ads, using the websites of the American Counseling Association and the National Career Development Association. I'd also look on Indeed, LinkedIn, Craigslist, USAjobs.gov, and governmentjobs.com for government-related jobs. I'd answer one or more ads using a point-by-point cover letter, which shows how I met each of the major requirements listed in the job ad. I might also include a piece of the collateral material I assembled on Monday. While I'm at a job site, I'd post my resume.

# Thursday

I'd follow up with the ten employers I identified on Tuesday. If they have an appropriate advertised job, I'd be sure to apply. Then, for especially desirable jobs I've applied for, I'd email someone other than an HR rep to explain that I'm reaching out because of a particular interest in the position.

Also, I'd respond to more of the job ads I identified yesterday, search for more, and apply.

# Friday

At this point, I should have received at least a few positive responses from my network of employers. I'd respond promptly, of course, if only to say, "Thanks for offering to keep me in mind. I hope you don't mind if I circle back in a month if I'm still looking."

And so, in time to prepare for the weekend, a job seeker has done more than the vast majority of job seekers do in three months to land a job. And now you have that task lifted from your shoulders, and you can wait for employers to do their part.

If your job target has been reasonable, that strategy should yield one or more job offers — of course, not in a week, but you will have put all the necessary balls in motion.

# The Job-Search Troubleshooter

Here are some common reasons that people don't land a good job, and some tactics for dealing with each one. This section also serves as a summary of some of this chapter's best points.

## Overcoming fear

Fear is a major reason that people don't vigorously search for a job.

### Fear of failing on the job

Let's not prematurely dismiss the fear. Do you need additional training — on a hard or soft skill — before applying for jobs? One approach is to enroll in a course from Lynda.com, Udemy.com, or Udacity.com. You could even try for a certificate. Some aspiring managers would be wise to attend a management or leadership boot camp. But many people will find it faster, more customized, and cheaper to hire a tutor — perhaps the instructor of one of those courses. For example, people who are light on technical skills might hire technically oriented tutors to gain at least basic computer literacy.

Or is the job likely to be beyond your intellectual, knowledge, or emotional capabilities, at least at this point in your life? There's no shame in scaling back for now — and maybe forever. There are many paths to the life well-led. "Upward" is only one. Or maybe you need to accept that you're not expected to be an expert yet. Nearly every inexperienced person suffers from imposter syndrome. You don't yet know a lot about how to be a master practitioner. You will make mistakes, but if you learn from them — and, indeed, continue learning, you'll gradually grow in competence. Be patient with yourself.

### Fear of seeming like a loser because you're looking for a job

True, top candidates may have jobs come to them, but most people need to look for work. That doesn't make them losers. *Not* looking for a job is less impressive. In pitching yourself, as long as you use a tone of motivation rather than desperation and say that you're looking for a fulfilling job (and not just any job), most people will think more, not less, of you. Imagine that a person contacted you and said, "I've been out of college for a year, trying to figure out what I want to do. Now I've become clear that a good match of my skills and interests would be to work as a people manager in a nonprofit. I might or might not yet be hirable in that position, but I'd love to find a launchpad job that would send me in that direction. Might you know someone I should talk with?" Wouldn't you gain respect for that person?

## Fear of imposing

Haven't you ever stopped someone on the street and asked for directions? Asking someone for a bit of career advice or a job lead imposes no more than that. If people want to give you more than a minute, that's their choice, and many people like to help others. If you still feel guilty about asking, maybe it would help to promise yourself that whenever you're in a position to help someone with their career or otherwise, you won't blow them off.

## Fear of sounding stupid

A reasonable amount of preparation, as described in this chapter and in Chapter 16, will reduce the risk of appearing like a lightweight. Honestly, though, you almost certainly will write or say one or more dumb thing — though you'll also say some smart things. Truly, to be well-employed and well-liked, you need-n't be perfect. I understand that people's Facebook pages and party conversations make them seem godlike, but remember that half of people are, by definition, below average, and most of them find jobs. Forgive yourself your idiocies — we all commit them, of course (me included).

## Fear of rejection

Almost all job searchers get rejected in their requests for informational interviews or in applying for jobs — you name it. Even after getting hired, most people also eventually get laid off or are out-and-out fired (me included). Get used to it. One difference between successful and unsuccessful people is that the successful ones may fear failure but push through it anyway. Then when they fail, they process it, only to see whether lessons can be learned, and then move on and try again.

When I was let go as a career columnist at the *San Francisco Chronicle*, after an hour (yes, only an hour) of anger and mourning, I said to myself, "I am going to get a better job." And so, the very next hour, I sent my clips to 20 national publications. I received 19 rejections (or no responses), but *U.S. News & World Report* hired me. I've since gone on to write for the *Washington Post*, *The Atlantic*, *TIME* magazine (20 articles), and *Psychology Today* (1,300 articles).

## Fear of success

Some people fear that if they land a job, it will swallow their life: They'll no longer have time for a personal life. The antidote is to realize that, in most jobs, you can set limits. You can work part-time or make 5 o'clock a relatively inviolate quittin' time. In your interviews, you can ask, "Approximately how many hours per week are people in my position expected to work?" Have the strength of your convictions to nix an employer with expectations beyond the ones you want to meet. If the employer continues to insist that you work too many hours, you probably should leave and find a more compatible employer. They do exist. On the other hand, I've had many clients who feared excessive work hours, only to find that if they're good at their work, they prefer working extra hours even over recreational activities.

## Fixing your job target

A job target can be inappropriate for a number of reasons, each with its own fix:

>> **Your target work has too few openings.** So expand it. For example, if your job target is to be a lawyer for a nonprofit and you're getting nowhere, expand to government. If your job target is to be a physical therapist with children, expand to physical therapist at a senior rehab facility.

>> **The competition in your job target is too intense.** Some fields are hyper-competitive: investment banking, management consulting, the environment, sports, fashion, entertainment, broadcasting, and high-status companies like Google, Johnson & Johnson, and Apple. Less sexy options can be as rewarding (or more), although less cool to talk about at parties.

>> **Your job target is at too high a level, or your salary expectations are too high.** In moderating your salary expectation, it may be comforting to remember that half of the top part of your earnings would go toward taxes. So, aiming for a salary that's $20,000 lower probably won't affect your lifestyle much.

>> **Your job target is at too low a level or doesn't pay enough.** Okay, what's the highest-level job you could aspire to obtain and have a reasonable chance of landing — and succeeding at? Should you increase your goal to meet that mark?

>> **You have too little experience for the target job.**

TIP

If you don't have time for the standard education or experience, take a crash course. For example, in an extreme case, you're an administrator and you want to be the proverbial rocket scientist. After work, instead of spending the usual amount of time on TV, video games, and chatting, you search Google for some specialty in rocket science — say, propulsion fuels. Take notes and write a 2-page white paper on the topic, and then submit it to employers that are *not* advertising a job. If they would hire someone with no experience, they wouldn't have placed an ad. They would have hired cousin Gomer. In inter-views, move the conversation from your past, which won't help your case, to the future: what you could contribute to that rocket science employer. That strategy works . . . occasionally.

# Improving your interviewing skills

Your networking meetings haven't led to good leads, and your job interviews haven't yielded a decent job offer. Might any of the following factors be causal?

>> **Lack of preparedness:** Prepare a few PAR stories that demonstrate your potential to do the target job well: a *Problem* you faced, the clever or dogged *Approach* you used to address the problem, and the positive *Result*. Prepare answers to the two or three questions you're most afraid they'll ask, such as "How come you've been unemployed for five years?" Prepare, but don't memorize the answers. You don't want to sound scripted.

>> **Excessive nervousness:** It may help to remember that the interview is like a date: You're both checking each other out. If you're not right for each other, fine. There are lots of fish in the sea and probably one with whom you're more likely to proceed swimmingly. It may also help you relax if you realize that it's fine to be yourself in the interview — yes, your best self, but still yourself. If the interviewer doesn't like the real you, the heck with him. You certainly don't want anyone to like you based on a phony persona. You'd then have to keep up that persona on the job. Yuck. Again, there's probably a more compatible employer for you.

>> **Annoying personality in the interview:** Usually, this means being too aggressive or indulging in too much "yes-butting." In a small percentage of workplaces, aggressiveness and arguing — even in an interview — is seen as a positive. But in most U.S. organizations, especially larger ones, disagreement must be the exception rather than the rule, and it needs to be tactfully dispensed. Look for opportunities to find agreement, and perhaps once, maybe twice, in the interview, you can tactfully raise a counter — for example, "Looking at your firm's major competitor's price sheet, I'm a little worried about your pricing versus theirs. Is that a valid concern?"

>> **Lack of enthusiasm for the job being interviewed for:** Sure, if you're naturally taciturn, you might want to ratchet up your enthusiasm to your highest-level *natural* self, though more enthusiasm than that can come across as phony, and then you'll have to appear phony on the job to avoid being perceived as having put on an act in the interview. If you're not perky enough for that employer, know that plenty of employers out there are wise enough to not overvalue that quality.

# Boosting your motivation

Lack of motivation is only the symptom of job-searching half-heartedly. It has many causes:

>> **Your job target is too mundane:** Should you make it more high-status? More intellectually challenging? In a more competitive field?

>> **Your substance abuse problem is demotivating.** Is it time to moderate, or even quit? If so, would supportive people help you? For example, some people are sufficiently helped simply by letting their friends and family know (maybe even on Facebook) that they're committed to getting back on the wagon. Other people are helped by 12-step programs or by one-on-one cognitive-behavioral therapy.

>> **Depression:** Depression is different from sadness. Most people would be sad if they didn't have a good job or a good romantic partner, for example. But clinical depression is more like numbness or indifference or being in a haze — it feels almost impossible to motivate yourself. The standard prescription for garden-variety depression is a combination of making yourself exercise regularly, staying busy, and focusing your attention on others rather than on even more "navel-gazing." If those activities don't sufficiently address the problem, the standard next step is short-term cognitive-behavioral therapy, perhaps supplemented by an antidepressant such as Prozac.

>> **Laziness or lack of desire to work:** It's not politically correct to call someone lazy. Inertia is typically deemed a symptom: fear of failure, fear of success, and so on. But some people simply *are* lazy. They probably came out of the womb laid-back, practically quaffing a brewski. Others are lazy because they just don't value work, and someone — a spouse, parent, or taxpayer — is supporting them. I've found that flogging, or even gently encouraging such people to work harder to get a job, usually fails. So, might it be the case that you should stop your job search for now and focus on what you're more motivated to do?

>> **Not realizing it would take a great deal of effort:** Sure, some of my clients get a job right off the bat — they were unusually good candidates, had a powerful network, or simply lucked out. Yes, luck matters. Luck favors the well-prepared, though some lazy people do have good jobs drop into their laps.

**REMEMBER**

For most people, a job search takes some time. That's normal. The odds are tiny of any single attempt to reach out leading to a job, but a few months of reasonable networking and answering ads usually works. A typical job search looks like this:

No response, no response, no, maybe later, no response, no response, no response, no response, maybe later, no, no response, no response, no, no, no response, no, maybe later, no, no response, no response, no response, no response, no response, no, no, no — *yes!*

# Chapter **18**

# Negotiating Wisely

Negotiating with a prospective employer is understandably scary. After all, employers do it all the time and you're a novice.

Yet negotiation is learnable. Enter this chapter.

## Practically Preparing

In this chapter, I focus on negotiating after you've received, but haven't yet accepted, a job offer. Most of the principles I describe here also apply in later negotiations, though you rarely have as much leverage as when an employer says "I want you!" but doesn't yet have you and may be concerned that you'll turn down its job offer.

Of course, some of the principles described in this chapter also apply outside of work — for example, when negotiating with friends, parents, or romantic partner.

### Gaining leverage

I'll lead with the most important aspect of negotiation: gaining leverage.

Of course, part of your leverage comes from factors that are hard to change. If your skills are rare and in demand — if you're a data scientist with expertise in machine learning, for example — you have more leverage than does a dropout with an undeclared major from Marginalia Community College whose biggest selling point is that he's "good with people."

But most people can gain leverage in a few ways.

**TIP**

You gain powerful leverage if you have another job offer in hand (or a few in the skillet). That's why it's wise, as described in Chapter 17, to make a thorough job search, all compressed into a busy week or two. Reaching out to every prospect in just a week or two maximizes the chances of having another job offer at the same time as you're negotiating for the first one.

That's also why, even when you're feeling relieved that your job search is finally over, you shouldn't stop looking. And when you have an offer, or even sense that one might be coming (when you're a finalist, for example), trumpet that news to all your leads. Having one employer want to hire you often motivates others to want to — and perhaps at an accelerated rate to avoid losing you. Everyone wants what's hot. That would be you.

The second most potent tool for gaining leverage is *a list of comparable compensation:* research the amounts that others are earning for similar work in a location with a similar cost of living. If you're lucky, you know someone who works at your prospective workplace or at a competitor who will give you the scoop. With or without that, you can get comparables from the Internet. Standard sources are `Glassdoor.com`, `Salary.com`, `Payscale.com`, `Indeed.com`, and `SalaryList.com`. Plus, if your professional association publishes a salary survey, that may yield even more targeted information. The more data points on your list, the more credible you are to your employer. Someone in HR, for example, may have done less work to establish the position's salary than you would — for them, you're just another employee. For you, you're *the* employee.

Make a list of all your comparables. At the bottom, make an adjustment based on the nature of your specific position: its difficulty, the rarity of skill set required, the potential for making money for the organization, and the local cost of living.

Later in this chapter, in the section "Negotiating with Wisdom," I show you the right time to show it to the employer.

Another lever: Can you think of a way that you can add value beyond what's in the job description? If so, that can justify better compensation.

## Determining your priorities

Don't focus too much on cash in the negotiation. Additional amounts over the initial offer are taxed at your highest rate. When you're considering federal and state income tax, Social Security, workers' compensation, and contributions to employer-paid healthcare, for example, you may lose half — assuming that the employer agrees to your request and doesn't pull the job offer. A client came to me after he was offered $65,000 and he had asked the employer, "What's your best offer?" They said $67,000. When he said he'd take $70,000, they pulled the offer: "We don't want a disgruntled employee. Our second-choice candidate is pleased to take $65K. Our offer is hereby retracted. Thanks for your time." Rule of thumb: If you feel that the first offer is too low, show your comparables and ask for the best offer. Whatever it is, you might then ask, "Maybe we should turn to a couple noncash items?"

TIP

Again, in negotiating benefits, moderation is probably wise: Pick just the two or three items that are most important to you and that have a good chance of yielding a yes.

Here are some sample benefits:

>> **Permission to telecommute a day or two a week**: Telecommuting saves you the time, cost, and stress of a commute and gives you private time to get your work done — yet you're in the office as needed and to make connections. Meanwhile, the employer gets an employee who doesn't start the day emotionally drained from the long commute. The employer may even welcome having the extra desk space.

>> **A training budget**: Again, both you and the employer benefit. And this benefit isn't taxable. (Ideally, this training should take place in Hawaii.)

>> **A better-sounding title**: A better-sounding title attracts more respect and is a better launchpad for positions of greater authority and money within and outside the organization. For example, having the title of Management Trainee may serve you better than simply Coordinator.

>> **A better-tailored job description**: For example, if the job description has you doing just a bit of research work and a lot of customer service and you'd prefer the reverse order, you might explain that research better plays to your strengths. Or perhaps there's work that would allow you to acquire a desired skill. The boss may be able to make that adjustment, to the organization's benefit — and yours.

>> **An expedited salary or title review**: If you've stalled in negotiating your salary or title, you might propose this: "In three months, if I turn out to be as good as you hope, will you bump my salary 10 percent and my title to Project Lead?"

>> **An employer-paid computer and/or smartphone**: The cost and monthly fees of these items are significant. If the employer gives them to you, that's another nontaxable benefit.

>> **Stock options**: Stock options give the owner the right to buy a stock at a given price. If the company does very well, that can mean serious dollars.

**WARNING**

But beware of focusing on this. Most stock options end up being worthless. Unless you know that the company is going public and that its core product is outstanding, think of stock options as, at most, the cherry atop a sundae.

>> **A flexible start date:** After all that time in school, and perhaps in your job search, you might want a month or so to just play, and not have to worry about whether it will hurt your job prospects.

>> **A more compatible person to report to:** Sometimes during interviews you meet someone you click with who has perhaps lots of expertise and power. Try to negotiate getting to report to that person.

**TIP**

Before you're in the heat of the negotiation, set three benchmarks:

>> **The best realistic deal:** With regard to both salary and noncash items, this is the most you can realistically ask for without likely alienating the employer.

>> **Your statesmanlike deal:** What King Solomon would deem fair to both sides.

>> **The least you'd accept:** Anything less than this amount and you'd walk.

# Preparing Psychologically

Even if you use a restrained approach to negotiation, many employees and would-be employees feel insecure in negotiations. Perhaps one or more of these reminders will help you keep your anxiety under control:

**REMEMBER**

>> **Most employers don't want to lose you.** After you reach the negotiation stage, the employer has probably undergone quite a process of deciding that you're the one. She doesn't want to have to tell her boss that she lost you simply because she refused your reasonable requests. And, if you walk and she has no other candidate who's essentially as good as you are, she's forced to hire someone less qualified or to reopen the job search — which means that the position will go unfilled for a while. That situation can cause problems and requires more effort to screen additional applications and interview other candidates. Plus, if the employer negotiated equally rigidly with the next person in line, that person could also walk. Once you're offered a position but haven't yet accepted it, you have real leverage.

>> **It may be all for the best.** If the employer treats your fair-minded negotiation as a sign of weakness to be taken advantage of, you probably don't want to work for that person.

**TIP**

>> **Role-playing can help.** Nervous or not, you might ask a trusted friend to play the hiring manager. Brief your friend on the job's basics, and ask her to be tough but realistic, throwing fairly tough statements at you now and then. After playing out the first five minutes of the negotiation, pause to get your friend's feedback, and give it another five minutes. The goal is for you to become comfortable being uncomfortable, practice how to draw on your preparation and throughout, stay positive, polite, and optimistic.

# Negotiating with Wisdom

You've already done the hard part: You've prepared, practically and psychologically. Now you have just a few things to remember.

**REMEMBER**

Conventional wisdom suggests that you try to negotiate in person. That's because even a tough employer is more likely to say Yes to a human being than to a disembodied email or text. One way of making it happen lies in your response to a job offer. You might say something like this: "I'm pleased to get your offer. I'm wondering if I could come in to discuss the terms." This response shows that you won't simply accept the first offer and gains the chemistry of an in-person negotiation. Also, negotiating in person gives you the chance to check out the vibe in the workplace, and even to talk to employees to help assess how much you'd like to work there.

Many people, on the other hand, do better at negotiating by email. Why? Because, if you're afraid of getting thrown by things a more experienced negotiator says, you have time to reflect and get advice before responding.

You may be wondering how soft or tough to be. A conventional rule of thumb in a negotiation is to be soft on the people and hard on the terms. But more nuance may be helpful. Your stance should depend on the situation: for example, how much you want the job, how good the first offer is, and your sense of whether your negotiation counterpart is focused more on fairness or on winning. So, the more you want the job, the better the first offer, and the more fair-minded your counterpart, the kinder your demeanor should be. As the negotiation proceeds, the person's stance can evolve. It's sometimes wise to mirror that evolution to avoid coming across as too wimpy or too stubborn.

It's usually best to start the negotiation by listening carefully. You may learn a lot about tone, which factors are important to the employer, which terms aren't negotiable, and to what extent. It rarely hurts to gather information.

But because negotiation really is about nuance, occasionally you get the sense that you'd fare better by being fair but tough — for example, stating your demands and perhaps even your highest quasi-reasonable demands. Some employers react well to strength: They view it as your being a good-enough candidate that you're willing to risk the employer pulling the offer. Or, your apparent confidence could intimidate an employer into being more flexible than if you were nice. But it's risky. It's poker. Does he call your bluff?

**WARNING**

Inexperienced people who try to be tough with experienced professionals can come across as cocky and off-putting. Generally, it's wiser to aim for moderation.

If you want to discuss your salary, bring it up before the employer does. You might say something like this: "I am interested in the position and, as you said, I would do a good job. I'm not wedded to a specific number — I'm flexible as long as we work out a fair deal, and I know you want to be fair. That's why I've tried to make sure my requests are reasonable. One possibility is X number of dollars, based on the salary data I've found on the Internet. (Show the negotiator your comparables sheet.) Another option is Y number of dollars, plus creative option Z. Any of those would be fine with me."

Here are some possible additions:

>> If true, add that you have a better offer in hand or that you're a finalist for one or more other positions.

>> If you've prepared an example of how you might add extra value to the employer, explain how it would work.

>> If you're already well-employed, add this factor: "Because moving to a different position (and locale?) requires significant effort, an extra 10 to 15 percent would seem appropriate. (If the negotiator balks, you might propose it as just a one-time bonus.)

**TIP**

My rule of thumb is this: Reject the first offer, accept the second. Generally, any additional cash that you negotiate after the first counteroffer is too small (after taxes) to risk alienating the boss, which could harden her in negotiating the deal's often more valuable noncash components. Worse, if the second offer is granted, it could heighten expectations for your near-term job performance — which, if not met, could result in early termination. Or it could alienate the employer for having her arm twisted into paying you more than peer employees. Occasionally, as mentioned earlier, it can even result in a withdrawn offer of employment.

Whether or not you're satisfied with the cash part of the negotiation, say something like this: "We're making progress on the salary. Should we put it aside and look at the few noncash items I wanted to discuss with you? Then we can pull back and consider the whole package."

You'll likely get the person's assent. Now you have two choices: You can ask about the item that the employer is most likely to agree to, which moves the discussion in a positive direction, or you can first ask about your most important issue. That's a matter of "feel" — do what feels right in that situation.

Retain perspective. Don't let your ego interfere with reaching agreement. Many people become too rigid in the negotiation, which can make it blow up. It also can mitigate against either of you proposing creative win–win solutions that you couldn't have anticipated in advance. For example, the employer may make clear that she is under pressure to build the bottom line. Perhaps you could propose a performance bonus instead of cash: Only if you meet (or your workgroup meets) the profitability goal do you get more cash or a training budget, for example the workgroup exceeds its fundraising goal.

If you reach impasse, muster the courage to suggest taking a break. It not only can provide a useful cooling-off period but also serve as a nonconfrontive sign of strength. I routinely tell my clients to sit tight for a day or two. Often, the employer comes back with a better offer without my client having to do a thing.

# Foiling Employer Ploys

For pragmatic reasons or for sport, some employers use ploys to try to wheedle a better deal for their side. Here are a few common tactics:

>> **The higher-authority ploy:** The employer says that he agrees with your proposal, but claims to need approval from a higher authority in the organization. He then puts you on ice for as long as possible, to maximize your insecurity. Finally, he returns and apologetically (using the good-cop/bad-cop routine) says that he fought for your terms, but the boss said No.

*A possible prevention:* Upfront, ask whether the person has the power to negotiate. If you get an equivocal response, you might ask, "Can you tell me which terms you and I can negotiate?"

*A possible cure:* If, in the negotiation, the employer invokes the need to get a higher authority's approval, you might try this: "Alas, in the past, whenever I've heard that an employer needs to check with someone else, the answer is usually No. Am I worrying unnecessarily? And, by any chance, can you make the decision yourself?" Or, if the answer is unsatisfactory, ask whether you can speak directly with the ultimate decision-maker.

**The lowball:** Sometimes, the employer starts with a poor offer. That way, if he ends up giving you a bit more, you'll *feel* that you received something in the negotiation, when in fact the employer could have given you much more.

*A possible prevention:* Ignore the conventional advice to let the employer make the first offer. Instead, you make one that's on the high-side of fair.

*Three possible cures:*

The tough-minded approach: "Well, it seems we're very far apart on the terms. Perhaps we're not meant for each other."

The kinder approach: Act as if he hasn't made a poor offer and, instead, show your list of comparable salaries and say, "In light of the comparables, X dollars seems fair. What do you think?

The flinch: If the employer makes a poor offer, flinch and wait a few seconds. Sometimes that response can result in the best-paid few seconds of your life. Without being overtly confrontive, the flinch can invoke enough guilt or fear that you'll walk to inspire a better offer.

**The feigned-anger ploy:** Sometimes the employer flashes true anger in response to your unfair or rude request. Thus, it isn't a ploy. So, first, be sure that you're being reasonable in substance and tone. Sometimes, though, you can be a statesperson and the employer *feigns* anger. It could be as subtle as an exaggerated sigh or a steely look in person or a curt tone in email. Or it can be as overt as the wording "Absolutely not" or "I don't think this is going to work." In that case, the employer may be trying to shake your confidence, by softening you up for a lowball offer.

*A possible cure:* I know it's not easy, but try to stay on the facts and avoid emotion. Take a deep breath and say, for example, "You may be right and we can't work it out. In the interview, however, you've shown a can-do attitude, so I'm wondering if we might try. For example, there's the issue of telecommuting a day or two a week. Can you see a way we might make that work?" (You've then picked an issue on which you think he might be flexible and, instead of wording it as "I'd like to telecommute a day or two a week," you *ask,* "Can you see a way that we might make it work?"

# Sealing the Deal

Fortunately, few negotiations are too tough to be worked out successfully. Chances are, if you use a kind, statesperson–like attitude toward discussing your pay and two or three noncash items, you'll end up with an agreement that both sides can accept, and you start your work together on a positive note.

He who wields the pen wields the power. Often, even when you've agreed on all the negotiated issues, gray areas often remain. If *you* write the summary of the terms that have been agreed to, you can nudge the gray areas in your favor. So, at the end of the negotiation, offer to summarize the terms. For example, you might say, "Okay. This all seems fair. How about I send you an email summarizing what we've agreed to? If there's anything I get wrong, just let me know."

TIP

Get the negotiated terms in writing. Doing so is important for another reason: Bosses come and go and, after the current one has left the organization, others there may not remember — let alone feel obliged to keep — earlier promises.

# 5

# Succeeding in Your Career

# Chapter **19**

# Becoming a Beloved Employee

B eyond being successful, many people wish they could become beloved by bosses, coworkers, and customers. That's a tall order but, as Norman Vincent Peale said, "Shoot for the moon. Even if you miss, you'll land among the stars."

## Smart Onboarding

As they say, you never get a second chance to make a first impression. Here's how to make a good one on day one of your job:

>> **Dress thoughtfully.** Some people dress to stand out (even by having green hair) but — except in unusual workplaces — that can cost you. Employees tend to like coworkers who dress within the workplace norm. If your interviews occurred in the workplace, you may know that norm. If you don't, before your first day on the job begins, email and ask one of your interviewers.

Within those norms, it's probably safer to dress at the top of the range for your position. For example, if your peers in the workplace wear nice shirts, perhaps with a jacket, you might try the latter. If you're aspiring upward, you might even want to dress like employees who hold the job to which you aspire.

After the first day or two, you can adjust your attire based on what you see and how others react to you. An enthusiastic "Nice tatts!" tells you something very different from a sarcastic "Nice tatts."

**Get clear on expectations.** Your boss will probably soon meet with you to discuss management's short- and longer-term expectations of you. If not, request this meeting. If your boss doesn't make your marching orders sufficiently clear, ask something like this: "What would you hope I'd accomplish in this first week? In the first month?" "Is there anything beyond what we've discussed that I can do to make your work life easier?"

TIP

When you're starting out, your perceived value is high, and you and the employer are in the honeymoon period, so that first meeting may be a good time to get your job description molded to fit your strengths. Consider tactfully proposing an idea — for example, trading some spreadsheet time for a people-facing activity. Even if a trade isn't possible, you may feel it's worth taking on a little extra work to get to do something that you'd enjoy or that would enhance your career.

» **Talk with your stakeholders.** Meet one-on-one (in person, if possible) with key coworkers and customers. Explain that you want to get off to a good start. Ask a few questions. For example:

"What should I know about working here that might not appear in the employee handbook?"

"Is there anything I should know about how to work effectively with you?"

"Is there anything I can do to make your work life easier?"

» **Scope out the organization's culture.** Because you're observant, you may quickly learn a lot about the organization's culture. For example:

- Some organizations are all about the bottom line. Others care a lot about processes, rules, or avoiding hurt feelings.

- Some employers welcome lots of questions. Others feel that you should be able to hit the ground running.

- In some workplaces, you're expected to give and receive lots of direct feedback. In other workplaces, there's a lot of beating around the bush.

- Though most workplaces officially claim to expect a 40-to-50-hour workweek, the truth is that in some workplaces, people who work more than the standard 40 hours are disliked by their coworkers. In other places, people who work less than 50 hours are viewed as insufficiently committed.

- At some workplaces, you're expected to take a full hour for lunch; at others, you get brownie points for eating at your desk.

>> **Work well, but not too well.** Most organizations reward good to very good performers. Though excellence may be rewarded, organizations are ecosystems: If you stick out too much, a predator is more likely to eat you. If you fit in, the team hums along, and organizations are all about the collective yielding more than the sum of its parts. For example, you might make your goal to work just slightly more than your workplace's average: If most of the employees work 45 hours a week and take a full hour for lunch, aim for 47 or 48 and take that full hour.

>> **Don't overwork early.** If you start out putting in 60 hours a week and later cut back, you may appear to have lost interest in the job. If you want to work extra hours to get up to speed, try to do that away from the workplace.

>> **Map the power players.** Every organization has official and under-the-radar power players. By observing and getting the scuttlebutt, map who's who and subtly ingratiate yourself. Understand and keep in mind the hot buttons of higher-ups. For example, if your boss dislikes other people taking credit for his work, be careful to assign due credit. If he believes deeply in work-life balance, don't try to make your claim to fame with 14-hour workdays.

>> **Get small wins first.** For example, you've just received the agenda for a meeting and, while thinking about it, you have an idea that you'd like to share. It may be wise to run it by a trusted colleague first. Your idea might have been tried already, or it might contain a landmine, such as violating the boss's core belief. If your idea passes muster with your confidant, reduce risk at the meeting by couching it as a suggestion: "I'm wondering whether X is a good idea. What do you think?" Then go bigger. After you've gotten your sea legs, think of a major (perhaps highly visible) project that would excite you to participate in or lead. A good time to propose that idea to your boss is right after she has praised you for something.

# Unspoken Keys to Workplace Success

Sure, you'll find lots of dos and don'ts in the employee's handbook, but some of the most important are rarely written down.

>> **Be *quietly* assertive.** In most workplaces, being too overtly aggressive is off-putting, or seen as too willful. For example, when presenting ideas at a

meeting, consider couching them as suggestions, not mandates. If you want a promotion, rather than sell your ideas to higher-ups, see if you can get a trusted colleague to say things to them to imply that you'd be great in that position.

>> **Make your accomplishments visible.** If you'd like one of your work products to gain more visibility, consider emailing a draft of it to staff "for feedback." Also, try to get placed on projects with powerful group members or projects in which the product will be highly visible or core to the organization's priorities.

>> **Embrace office politics.** It's sad that even competence isn't enough. Good treatment, plum assignments and, alas, promotions often require being championed by a power player and not having someone trying to tear you down.

Certainly, start with *positive politics.* Socialize moderately. Be cordial to everyone but friendly to only some — more could make you seem like a glad-hander. Once or twice a week, take a break or lunch with coworkers and, if possible, your boss. Doing more than this may seem like you're trying too hard to network and deprive you of the private time many people need.

**TIP**

Another manifestation of moderation is your role in the gossip vine. If you totally avoid the gossip vine, you may be seen as haughty — yet, if you're at its center, the vine can strangle you. Listen to gossip and make occasional gentle, safe contributions, but no more.

Alas, despite practicing positive politics, at some point you may sense that someone is trying to hurt you: Perhaps it's a peer vying with you for a promotion or someone jealous of your looks. Of course, don't jump to conclusions, but let's say that you and perhaps a trusted colleague verify that sabotage is afoot. Here's a real-life example: A coworker withheld information that my client needed to do her job. I suggested she tell the coworker, "I've heard that when material comes in for me on your printer, you toss it rather than send it to me. Is that true? (The other person denied it, but she now had put the person on notice.) She finished with this statement: "I don't like running to the boss, but I want you to know that if I get wind of further sabotage, I will." That was enough to make her rival turn her nefarious attentions elsewhere.

>> **Be low-maintenance.** Of course, occasionally it's wise to raise a concern to your boss — when you see something that could be done more efficiently, for example, or when a coworker is gumming up the works. But generally, keep your complaints rare — speak up only when the matter is important. Save most of your grumblings for your journal.

>> **Stay in reasonable shape.** Rightly or wrongly, being very overweight is often perceived negatively by those who evaluate employees. And cigarettes, alcohol, marijuana, and other mind-altering substances — especially if used

heavily — can take a toll on an employee's productivity, even if used only after work hours. For example, the recent National Academy of Science metaevaluation of hundreds of studies on the effects of marijuana conclude serious risk: yes, of memory and motivation impairment but also of more profound mental and physical diseases.

» **Prioritize just-in-time learning over degrees and certificates.** Of course, having a degree, or even a certificate, enhances your employability, but the opportunity cost of the time and money can be too high. It's sometimes wiser to engage in your professional development on a just-in-time basis: Read articles and forum posts, hire a tutor, or attend a webinar, boot camp, or pre-conference workshop. Hey, you might see whether you can get your boss to spring for that training in Hawaii.

» **Form a board of advisors.** Four years ago, I invited the seven colleagues or friends I most respect to form a board of advisors. Since then, we've met monthly on Google Hangouts for one hour, from 7 to 8 p.m. The structure is simple: After three minutes of small talk, I ask, "Who'd like to take the floor?" Someone volunteers and shares a problem on which she wants the group's input. The group asks questions and tactfully offers suggestions until the person cedes the floor with, for example, "Thank you. Who'd like to take the floor?"

» **Where appropriate, delegate.** Sure, you may perform a task better than the person to whom you'd delegate it, but delegation will not only free you up for more important tasks but also empower others. The result is that your workgroup's overall productivity may well increase. No one to delegate to? How about finding an intern or a co-op education student?

» **Be in the moment.** Stay focused on doing your task well, not on an outcome that's beyond your control nor on the other tasks you need to do inside or outside the workplace. I am reminded that during Bill Clinton's second term as president, the nation's number-one topic was his affair with Monica Lewinsky — yet, whether you agree with his politics or not, most people admire that he was able to compartmentalize that issue and fully fulfill his responsibilities as president. I'm guessing that your issues are less dramatic.

» **Retain your personhood.** Your decision to work in an organization makes an implicit contract to suppress *some* of yourself in favor of the organization's norms. Yet there are opportunities to retain your personhood at work, at least partially:

● Do you have an avocational interest you could bring to work? For example, a photographer might adorn his cube walls with his creations; a gardener might bring her flowers to the break room; or a baker might share his brownies with everyone on his floor.

- As discussed in the "Smart Onboarding" section at the beginning of this chapter, you might try to tweak your job description to capitalize on your strengths and skirt your weaknesses. Occasionally, you can do that on your own, although usually you'll need your boss's okay.

- If you see a serious ethical problem, consider raising the issue with a higher-up — though you're safer if you invite one or more coworkers to join you in that action.

If you feel that your personhood is too squelched in your current job, might a transfer within your organization help? For example, should you angle for a transfer to a more respected boss or workgroup? If so, try to "run into" the boss you prefer — for example, in the break room. Say something like this: "I've heard good things about you. If you ever need an extra person on a project or need to hire someone, I'd be pleased if you'd consider me." Or maybe you should be putting out "feelers" to your network for a better-fitting workplace. Or have you, like me, come to the conclusion that your wisest option is self-employment?

# Mastering Meetings

Your performance in meetings can enhance your influence, reputation, and advancement.

First, review the agenda and if you can, prepare a comment or question in advance. You may or may not end up stating it, but it can't hurt to have it at the ready. That way, you won't need to come up with brilliance out of thin air.

**TIP**

Be the last to chime in on an important topic. Your silence may generate curiosity about what you're thinking or may make some wonder whether you're thinking at all. So, when you finally speak up, your comment may attract particular attention. Also, by waiting until others have had their say, you make them less eager for you to finish just so that they can add their two cents. Perhaps most important, waiting enables you to incorporate the best of the already stated input and avoid making an obvious mistake. Of course, by then someone else may have made your good point, but it's generally worth taking that risk. Besides, it's not all about you. If a good idea is brought up, that's to everyone's advantage, even if you weren't the person who offered it.

Brevity indeed is the soul of wit. Especially in meetings, in which many attendees' primary goal is to get the meeting over with as quickly as possible; remember *the traffic light rule:* In your first 30 seconds of speaking, the light is green — you're good to go. In your second 30 seconds, the light is yellow — your risk increases of being seen as a Joe Blowhard or Chatty Cathy. After 60 seconds, the light is red: Only rarely should you run a red light and continue speaking.

# Managing People

Though many people are happy as individual contributors, others strive to become managers. They may, however, feel ill-equipped to manage people. That's understandable: People are not as predictable as text, numbers, or computer code. And managers are often limited in what they can do because of employer policies, laws, regulations, and their supervisees' human frailties. Entire books and courses are devoted to the art and science of managing people. Here are just some of the (perhaps not-so-obvious) keys:

>> **The vision thing:** You must come up with a worthy vision for your workgroup, if only for the next project, and be able to compellingly explain that vision. That can be true even for mundane yet ethical work. For example, the head of an accounts payable department might remind employees this way: "Getting the right amount of money without delay into people's hands ensures that they can feed their families and businesses can pay their bills. That's important."

>> **Walk the talk.** A lazy, unethical, or otherwise low-standards boss can't expect the employees to do any better. If you slack, your employees are likely to slack, too. As a supervisor, you might even want to go the extra mile. For example, ask whether a person needs help and then offer it, even if it's outside your job description.

>> **Give only earned praise.** Too many leaders and managers give praise so easily that it's devalued. Others give too little, for fear of engendering complacency — or a request for an excessive pay increase. Be liberal with earned praise. Offer a hand-written note, for example; employees love taking those home to show to family members.

Gary Chapman offers other lovely ways to praise:

- *Offer a small gift.* It can be as simple as an extra ticket to a local concert or sports event.

- *Provide quality time.* Give your undivided personal attention, either one-on-one or in small groups. Yes, that can include a TGIF event at the local watering hole.

- *Provide the physical touch.* It's riskier in these sexually sensitive times, but if it feels safe, accompany your thank-you for a job well done with a 1-second resting of the palm of your hand on the person's arm.

These kinds of behaviors are key to going from good to beloved.

>> **Criticism isn't a dirty word.** Tactful criticism accompanied by a suggestion for improvement should be part of the manager/supervisee relationship. With in-office employees, manage by walking around, giving in-context feedback. Strike a balance: Criticize too rarely and you're not providing enough feedback. Criticize too often and you'll likely demotivate.

>> **Don't rely on excessive pay to motivate.** Generally, as long as compensation is at least adequate, employees are motivated primarily by their jobs being ethical, not too demanding or too easy, and by receiving earned praise and tactful, helpful feedback. If employees are demanding more pay and you think they're already reasonably paid, that can signal problems within your workgroup. Investigate.

**REMEMBER**

>> **Treat everyone not equally, but in ways that bring out each person's best.** For example, even if two of your supervisees have the same job title, the wise manager adapts their job description to reflect the person's strengths and skirt their weaknesses. Also, employees vary in their need for autonomy, supervision, personal talk, praise, criticism, training, flexibility, and other factors. Wise managers and leaders realize that one size does not fit all. Though some of your supervisees may complain about unequal treatment, explain that your goal is to treat everyone equally in the important sense: that which will help each person be her best.

To that end, in the first day or two as manager, meet with each supervisee one-on-one. In that meeting, make clear that you do care about your people, their goals, and what brings out the best in them. For example, more structure or less? More accountability or more freedom? Training in a certain area? And really listen. Sometimes, managers so focus on asking the right questions that they don't fully listen to the answers.

>> **Help each employee develop an exciting yet realistic career plan.** To avoid losing their good supervisees, poor managers don't help them move up or out. Good managers realize that among their job's most important functions is helping supervisees flourish, and if that means that they leave, so be it. Even if your priorities are more pragmatic, encourage your supervisees to grow, even if it means their leaving will make it more likely that the person will tout you and your place of employment as a good place to work.

>> **Foster a humane but not group-therapy workplace.** Encourage a humane workplace, but not the expectation that it will act as a surrogate family. Yes, give earned praise. Yes, ask your people about their lives. Yes, if there's a personal problem, perhaps offer a bit of counsel. But ineffective managers go

too far: They encourage so much openness that the workplace turns into a cross between a pity party and a therapy group. It can also encourage an office culture in which even a small slight (real or perceived) is cause for a meeting or backstabbing.

## Getting crisp

Crispness is an underdiscussed key to great management and to creating a vibrant workplace culture. Here are several examples of how you can manage crisply:

>> **Weigh the pros and cons of making a decision on your own or getting input.** We live in an era in which decisions made unilaterally are often viewed as too hierarchical. But I've seen many workplaces ground into torpor and tepid decision-making through too-frequent use of group input, let alone decision-making by consensus. On a case-by-case basis, decide whether the speed and boldness of a unilateral decision outweigh the benefits of group input.

>> **Use teams judiciously.** Some managers too quickly assign a project to a team rather than to an individual. Teams use lots of staff time and delay decision-making, and decisions made by teams are rarely bold — usually, it's only a middle-of-the-road plan that everyone can agree to. Just as serious, many capable, hardworking team members often resent being on a team because their efforts go unrewarded or are mitigated by lower-performing team members. Managers often get the most from strong performers by giving them challenging assignments to tackle by themselves. The good manager uses teams only when the benefits of group input and buy-in outweigh those risks.

>> **Use meetings judiciously.** Meetings use up a lot of time: Everyone must stop work to sit there and listen. Often, a meeting agenda item could more time-effectively be addressed by sending an email and asking for reactions. A regular monthly meeting is often a good idea for *esprit de corps* and a predictable opportunity to raise questions and issues. But additional meetings should be reserved for when group input is needed fast.

**REMEMBER**

Solicit requests to add or change the agenda, but as the manager, the buck stops with you. When you do schedule a meeting, send the agenda in advance with, if needed, instructions on how to prepare.

Often, the best time for a meeting is right before lunch. People will be motivated to get through the agenda on time, reducing unnecessarily long spiels. At the meeting, for each agenda item, when you sense that the discussion is starting to yield diminishing returns, summarize key input and, if appropriate, make a decision. For example, you might say, "In light of Mary's idea A and David's idea B, we're going to do X."

>> **Consider having stand-up meetings that last no longer than 30 minutes.** Meetings tend to move crisply and participants tend to be more engaged if they're standing and know that it will be over expeditiously.

If a person makes a sidetracking comment that you think isn't worthy of the group's time, at least at this meeting, ask the person to talk with you about it after the meeting, email you about it, or, if he still feels it's relevant, request that it go on the next meeting's agenda.

>> **Pivot promptly.** When a project is flagging, the effective leader quickly assesses how to adjust, often gathering input from the employees. Then, if she feels that the project should continue, she inspires the troops to persevere by expressing fair-minded optimism that the revised plan will likely improve results and that the benefits to the workers, customers, and even society as a whole are worth the persistence.

## Hiring wisely

A core Western assumption is that people are extremely malleable: that with persistence, most people can accomplish most things. Alas, as every teacher and psychotherapist knows, even years of effort rarely can turn a phlegmatic into a charismatic, a technophobe into a computer geek, a dullard into a brainiac. So it's critical to hire people who have — without requiring a personality transplant — the ability and drive to do the job.

And in today's litigious society, you may well find it painful to attempt to replace an unsatisfactory employee. That's why most top management books urge managers to hire slow and fire fast. Here's how.

For most positions, intelligence, drive, and being low-maintenance trump specific experience or skills.

You may be forced to keep some employers that you'd rather not. But wherever possible, replace employees who aren't A, or at least B, players with stronger performers. You, your employees, and your customers will appreciate it. And you have a high probability of finding at least B players — if you search wisely:

>> **Recruit by asking for referrals from trusted colleagues.** Relying on respondents to a job ad is risky. As someone who has coached countless job seekers, on average, weaker applicants do more to hide their weaknesses — papering over employment gaps and poor performance on previous jobs, for example. Some weak job seekers do remarkably unethical things that, to avoid promulgating, I won't list here. But beware.

» **Screen initial applicants with a short online or emailed quiz** that taps candidates' ability to do a few of the job's common, difficult tasks. To avoid applicants' hiring a ringer to answer the questions, let them know that interviewed candidates will take a parallel quiz at the interview.

» **The interview should consist mainly of simulations.** For example, if the person will be running meetings, have him lead a brief mock meeting with the interviewer(s) playing the role of the meeting attendees. Also, probe claimed accomplishments, stating, for example, "Tell me the details about how you saved the company $200,000." Avoid questions that can be coached in advance, such as "Tell me about yourself," "What's your greatest strength and weakness," or "Why the long employment gap?"

» **Before hiring, ask the top candidate or two for a half-dozen references**, including phone numbers. Call each after-hours, saying something like this:

> I'm hiring for an important position, requiring good intelligence, drive, and a low-maintenance personality atop the ability to extract useful information from Oracle databases. I'm considering Sally Jones for the position. If you think she'd be very good on that job, I'd greatly appreciate a call. If not, no need to call back.

Most people are reluctant to give a bad reference but are willing to not call back to get that point across. Of course, there are reasons other than disliking a candidate for not calling back, but unless at least half of the people call back, beware.

» **Cut your losses.** Usually, within weeks if not days of hiring, it becomes clear whether an employee is likely to — without spending too much time coaching them — be at least a B player. If not, it's wise to counsel the person to find a better-suited position. Doing that, instead of starting documentation for a termination procedure, can be less painful for all concerned.

Here's how you might try to counsel someone out: Take the person out for coffee or lunch, perhaps at a nice place near your workplace. There, after a little small talk, say something like this:

> I appreciate <insert one quality you like about the person, perhaps even about their work performance>. But your job doesn't seem the best fit for your strengths, <insert one of their strengths>. This job places a premium on <insert the thing(s) he does poorly>. I'd like to try to help you find a better-suited position within our organization or give you a helpful <it can still be honest!> reference for outside."

That can sometimes avoid a painful, costly, time-consuming termination process.

>> **Ethics really must be Priority One.** Yes, cheaters sometimes win, but so that you can sleep at night and proudly tell your family what you do, don't let profit or expediency trump ethics. Management guru Warren Bennis describes managers as people who do things right, and leaders as people who do the right thing.

# Converting an Internship or Volunteer Gig into a Good Job

Many of this chapter's points will boost your chances of converting a no- or low-pay gig into a job, but the following tips are particularly likely to make that happen:

>> **Brand yourself starting on Day One.** Come in on time, dressed for the job to which you aspire, and in the first meeting with your boss, ask such questions as these:

- "Are there hard or soft skills I should work on to succeed here?"

- "What can I do to make your work life easier?"

- "What should I know about this workgroup's culture that will help me fit in?"

- "What else can I do to boost my chances of getting hired?"

If your tasks are too low-level, to avoid being inappropriately branded, ask your boss, "I realize I may need to pay some dues, but I'd welcome your keeping me in mind for some higher-level work — for example, <insert a task that you'd do well and enjoy>. Is that possible?"

>> **Be visible.** When you're proud of one of your work products or ideas, bring it up if only "for feedback" at a meeting or in an email. Also, you might ask permission to sit in on important meetings. If you have a good comment or question, offer it tactfully — for example, "I wonder if X is a good idea. What do you think?"

>> **Develop a power schematic.** Every workgroup and organization has power distributed not necessarily by title. Sometimes an administrative assistant has outsized influence, whereas a pooh-bah could be on the way out. Chart the power distribution and have a tentative strategy for currying favor with the great and powerful. One power player might be most impressed by a no-nonsense, get-it-done person. Another might be mainly about the relationship. Still others

respond to praise or to your offering to help beyond the call of duty. Something that sounds like this could even work wonders: "I have a little extra bandwidth. If you could use a helping hand on a project, I'd welcome the opportunity to do some work for you."

>> **Avoid the gossip vine.** Many people who swing on the gossip vine get chopped down, especially interns and volunteers. After you're well-employed in the organization, you might nibble at the vine's periphery, but until then, it's wise to steer clear.

>> **Put out feelers.** Keep looking for paid work. If you get a nibble, share it with a coworker or two at your current gig. They may leak that information to higher-ups, which makes the employer more likely to offer you paid work: Sometimes, the only way to extract money from employers is to make them afraid of losing you.

There are no guarantors of getting a good job beyond being smart, knowledgeable, likeable, hard working, low-maintenance, and lucky. But those tactics should boost your odds not only of getting hired but also of becoming successful and even beloved.

# Chapter 20

# Building a Name for Yourself

G oethe wrote, "Dream no small dreams for they have no power to move the heart." I wouldn't go that far, but many people — secretly or not secretly — would like to develop a name for themselves, to be publicly recognized.

This chapter helps you do that: build charisma, get good at giving talks, and use the media to build your brand — and make a difference.

## Cultivating Charisma

Sometimes a person's persona makes others admire them, want to do their bidding, and promote them. Fortunately, charisma isn't as ineffable as it may seem. Here are several ways to build yours:

>> **Grow in competence.** People admire a competent person more than they admire someone who's more sizzle than steak. For example, many fine leaders are introverted: Proctor & Gamble's A.J. Lafley or Charles Schwab or Avon CEO Andrea Jung or Berkshire Hathaway's Warren Buffett. Their secret sauce? Expertise. What step should you take toward building yours? A course? A mentor? Self-study?

>> **Improve your physical presence.** Stand straight, with shoulders back but relaxed. Stride rather than trudge, but don't rush — careening isn't charismatic. Barack Obama, especially when asserting a controversial statement, raised his chin slightly — that suggests confidence. Of course, lifting your chin too much can make you appear pompous. Dress to bring out your best and to be attractive to your target audience.

>> **Speak moderately.** *Moderate* refers to pitch, volume, and pace:

- *Pitch:* Fast talkers are viewed as dishonest or out of control, and are more difficult to understand. Though your pace should be moderate, occasionally slow down or even pause for emphasis.

- *Volume:* Use moderate volume as your baseline and lower, and raise the volume to emphasize key words and create drama. But don't sound like an actor. Spencer Tracy's advice to actors was, "Never let 'em catch you acting."

- *Pace:* Don't talk too much or too little. In a 2-person conversation, aim to talk 30 to 50 percent of the time and in relatively short bursts.

>> **Remember not to try too hard.** Jokesters and glad-handers are usually dismissed. So are people who gesticulate broadly in an attempt to appear passionate. Within your natural personality, just try to connect with people. At a party, Hillary Clinton chatted briefly with my wife and gave her full attention, even though many more important people were in the room. It made my wife feel valued. That's an example of low-key charisma.

>> **Have your best smile at the ready.** Practice different smiles in front of a mirror, and when you find one that's maximally engaging (no, not the salesperson's too-broad smile), practice it until it's in muscle memory and can be summoned when appropriate.

>> **Become a good storyteller.** Practice a few stories, perhaps 30 to 60 seconds long, that are inspiring, funny, or educational. Having developed those, you'll have boosted your ability to tell other anecdotes that pop to mind in conversation or in giving a talk.

TIP

>> **Err on the side of positivity.** Of course, there are times to criticize, but most charismatic people emphasize the positive. Just don't take it too far: It's not charismatic to be chirpy and Pollyannaish. Moderate optimism is what most Americans deem charismatic.

>> **Speak of *we* rather than *I*.** No one likes an egotist. Even if you've done something for which you deserve credit, it's usually wise to focus on what *we* did and the opportunity that *we* have.

REMEMBER

Amid these techniques, retain your authentic essence. If you're introverted, don't try to be Jimmy Fallon. If you're intellectual, you ain't gonna come across as Paris Hilton.

In sum, aim to sound calm, moderately upbeat, and confident, yet moderately self-effacing *and* authentic. Want examples? Watch C-SPAN, which presents a parade of America's most influential people: Congress members, generals, Fortune 500 CEOs, and political activists. Even if they're talking about terrorist attacks, their demeanor is usually measured and cautiously optimistic.

# Becoming a Compelling Public Speaker

Public speaking is a top fear of many people, but many formerly reticent souls now crave opportunities to hold forth. Here's a step-by-step plan:

1. Ask yourself, "What does my audience really want and need from my talk?"

    If you're not sure, ask the person who asked you to speak. Jot down the important points that aren't obvious. If you don't have enough solid, not-so-obvious content, find some by reading or contacting people. And, might there be a behavior change that you'd ask of your audience?

    **WARNING**

    Beware the tyranny of content. Think of all the talks you've attended. From most, you probably remember only a few points. Include only what's important.

    For each point, ask yourself whether you should add an example, a compelling statistic, or an anecdote. Don't have an anecdote, but would like one? Concoct a fictional one, and acknowledge it as such — for example, by prefacing it with something like this: "I can imagine a scenario like this." Or use Google Search to find good anecdotes. Or get in the habit of maintaining a Word file with stories from your life that might work in a talk.

2. Write a minimalist outline of your talk's major elements, as in this example:

    Intro: A shared experience — for example, a wonderful speaker who preceded me. If an "introducer" didn't share my mini-bio, do it.

    Major point 1: Statistic from Department of Energy.

    Major point 2: The Betty anecdote.

    Major point 3: Have them turn to the person next to them to discuss it.

    Summary

    Conclusion that inspires, gets them to try my three points, and puts the talk in a larger context: Anecdote about my father.

3. Write a script based on the outline.

   Do not read your talk, let alone try to memorize it. Unless you're a terrific actor, you'll sound scripted, which is a turn-off. If your audience wanted a scripted talk, you could have emailed them the text. Also, memorizing it leaches the chemistry that's the key to an effective talk. Plus, under stress, you'll likely be thrown off your script. Finally, you'll be wedded to your script and so be unlikely to add good ideas that pop into your head — something you heard from your audience during your pre-talk mingling, for example.

4. Insert your major points.

   Within the outline you created in Step 2, insert your script's major points — just a word or phrase to remind you of what it is. Even for a long talk, that should all fit on one, or maybe two, index cards.

   Though I've occasionally used PowerPoint when I have compelling images or video to show, I generally don't. People come to a talk to connect with the speaker. If they're looking at a screen, they're not connecting with you. If you have important text for them, put it on a handout and distribute it as late as possible in the talk — when you're summarizing, for example. Or leave it on a chair at the exit for people to take when leaving.

5. Practice wisely.

   I recommend using a recorder — your iPhone's VoiceMemos feature or Android's Voice Recorder, for example. Practice your talk using your index card(s) as a guide. Use a conversational tone — unless you're a pro, if you try to sound like a motivational speaker, you'll sound forced. The only differences from the tone you'd use in conversation is that if you tend to talk quickly, slow down; and if you tend to be monotonic, vary your volume and pace. Listen again to your recording, and revise it based on what you hear.

**REMEMBER**

   Even if you go blank and take 15 seconds of silence to recover, people will gain more from your talk and like you more if you proceed by ad libbing — using only your index card(s) and without having practiced your way into boring perfection, let alone attempting to memorize your talk.

6. Arrive early at the venue.

   Do this for a sound check and to mingle with your attendees. That will make you more comfortable and make them more receptive. You may even garner an anecdote to insert into your talk. People love such currency. While mingling, if appropriate, ask people what they're hoping to get from your talk. That might give you a clue for a tweak — you needn't slavishly adhere to your outline.

   To help ensure that you connect with your audience, don't deliver a talk from behind a podium. It's a barrier between you and your audience. If possible, use a lapel mike. That will free you to use your arms and to move. Just don't be constantly moving. It's distracting. Take a few steps and talk. And then take another few steps and talk.

7. **Psych yourself up.**

   Just before you begin, take a few deep breaths and remember that you do not need to be perfect. Indeed, in the attempt, you'll likely drain that crucial chemistry from your talk. Connection requires being conversational, making off-the-cuff asides, hesitating when stuck, and being someone they can relate to — in short, being human.

TIP

   On my radio program, the minute before going on the air, I usually tell my guest, "Key to the interview working well is to pretend that we're at a bar and on our second beer. Not our fifth, but our second, and we're having a conversation. That's the right tone."

8. **Talk to one person at a time.**

   This may be tough for a beginner to pull off and, to be honest, I don't always remember to do it, but it's helpful. For a second or two, talk to a friendly-looking person at your far left, and then a friendly-looking adjacent person, and so on. After you've reached a person on your far right, reverse the order: Talk to someone friendly immediately to the left, and so on. People like to feel special, and if you spend even a second or two talking directly to someone, he will feel cared about. By focusing on friendly-looking people who are smiling or nodding (no, not nodding off), you're more likely to feel relaxed and connected to your audience. In Step 2, I suggest asking audience members to turn to the person next to them to discuss a point you've made. No matter how large the group, you can get everyone in the audience fully involved by having them turn to the person next to them to discuss an important point you've just made. That doesn't replace a question-and-answer period. It's just an effective tool for breaking up a passive lecture.

9. **Finish with connection.**

   At the end, smile and establish eye contact with everyone. That leaves them with a more positive feeling about your talk and you, it may trigger applause, and, when you get really good, it may even inspire a standing ovation, which is one of life's lovelier moments.

# Mastering the Media

Today, branding requires you to be *mediagenic*, able to use traditional and social media to convey your expertise. This section deals with how to become mediagenic.

## Branding in bits and bites

It used to be that the most likely path to fame was to write a book and have it sell lots of copies, at least to people in your field. But people are increasingly learning in bites: tweets, blog and forum posts, YouTube and Instagram videos, and articles. So, if you're a writing sort, every time you get a fresh idea that might interest people in your field, post it. If you're telegenic, talk it into your webcam, maybe prune it to the best bits, post it on YouTube, and send it to your colleagues and to thought leaders.

TIP

You needn't be the fount of all expertise. Why not ask a few of your field's biggies for their opinion about a hot topic? For example, if you're in PR, you might ask PR experts their favorite ways to use Instagram. Then write up the suggestions as an article. Send it to your field's most respected trade publication. In PR, that might be *The Public Relations Strategist.* Or create a podcast or video in which you interview them. Google Hangouts allows you to record video with multiple interviewees for free.

## Landing media interviews

As with so many interactions, the key is to put yourself in the other person's shoes. What might you talk about that a leading blogger, podcaster, broadcaster, or article writer would be excited to discuss? Here are a few examples to trigger your own ideas:

>> An economist might want to talk about the implications of a Democrat or Republican winning the White House in 2020.

>> A fashion designer might want to list her votes for the three best and worst new fashions.

>> A software engineer specializing in artificial intelligence might want to talk about the three most exciting new apps for staying healthy.

## Being an engaging interviewee

Much of what it takes to be an engaging interviewee is the same as to be an engaging public speaker. Follow my suggestions in this section and you'll impress your audience *and* boost your chances of being asked back:

>> **Have two or three talking points ready.** These are the fresh, not-obvious yet important ideas that you most want to convey. To bolster each one, prepare a compelling statistic or humorous anecdote. To avoid your humor falling flat, first try it out on a friend.

See whether you can reduce at least one talking point to a sound bite. For example, a school superintendent was lobbying to build a new headquarters. A journalist asked her, "Why spend the money?" Her response, which carried the day: "As we all know, in the long run it's cheaper to buy than to rent." Rhyming is particularly memorable: Even though it was decades ago, don't you remember, "I like Ike," "Mend it, don't end it," and "If it doesn't fit, you must acquit?"

>> **Answer the question.** Sure, look for opportunities to make your talking points, even if it requires redirecting the interviewer with these words: "If there's one thing I think your audience really would benefit from, it's <insert your talking point>." But in general, answer questions directly. Interviewers and listeners are turned off by nonresponsiveness. You don't want to be like those politicians on the Sunday news shows who answer difficult questions by giving their stump speeches.

>> **Be concise.** Today's audiences are turned off by missives and diatribes. Keep your answers to less than a minute. If the interviewer wants more, she can ask.

# Podcasting and broadcasting

If you believe that you can keep the interesting content coming and can think on your feet, consider podcasting. Choose topics at the intersection of your expertise and the information your colleagues are hankering to know about it. You needn't know it all yourself. Interview experts. You'd be amazed at how many eminent people will agree to be interviewed by you.

Here are the keys to interviewing people well:

1. **Put yourself in your colleagues' shoes.**

   What are the half-dozen questions they'd most like your expert to answer?

2. **Pre-interview the interviewee.**

   Tell the guest about the traffic light rule (mentioned in the "Mastering Meetings" section of Chapter 19) and the second-beer metaphor (mentioned earlier in this chapter). Ask ten questions. That will help you identify the worthwhile ones to ask and will give the interviewee a rehearsal.

3. **Front-load your best content.**

   Put the good questions in a logical order, but start with one that the listeners would especially be curious about and to which the guest has an important, not-obvious answer.

**4. Listen carefully to the interviewee's answer.**

If possible, amplify, politely disagree, or ask a follow-up question. Only after that thread feels sufficiently covered should you go on to your next question.

**5. Don't try to sound like a radio talk-show host.**

It will probably come off as insincere. Be conversational, as though you were having that beer with the person. The only deviation from normal conversation is that if you tend to speak too quickly, slow down a bit. Most people are listening with one ear. Or if you're monotonic, add a bit of dynamism.

Many people would like to be a recognized expert. This chapter's advice on gaining charisma, public speaking skills, and media savvy can help you get there.

# Chapter **21**

# Managing the Bugaboos: Time and Stress

Oh, to have more time and less stress. Okay. Let's make it happen.

## Managing Your Time

When I give a talk to successful people and ask them to raise their hands if they manage their time well, about 90 percent do. But when I ask that of an audience of unemployed people, only 10 or 20 percent do. The good news is that you *can* learn to manage your time better. And I won't make you use some complicated system. (Those rarely work, anyway.)

### Caring enough to manage your time well

Not everyone cares to manage their time well. They figure it won't improve their life enough to make it worth the effort. For example, if your life is in the toilet, it's hard to believe that time management tactics will catapult you from the crapper to the crown.

For example, many people fear they'll never meet a romantic partner or even have a friend who really understands them. Or they think that they're ugly. Or they have no money and fear that they'll always have to decide whether they can afford tomatoes *and* toilet paper. So they figure, "Why bother with time management?"

Might any of these be holding you back?

>> **You have no romantic relationship.** Would a baby step be to sit down with a friend and create a good online dating profile? Or to tell all your friends that you're finally ready to meet a good person for a long-term relationship? Or to break up with that partner whom you know you should have dumped long ago?

>> **You don't have a bff/gff.** Have you ever had a best friend? Is it time to reach out again? Or do you have a casual friend you might try getting more deeply involved with? Should you have a good talk or even take a road trip with your parents or stepparents?

Okay, let's say that none of these sounds promising. What does your intuition say would be the most likely way you'd meet someone who'd turn out to be a good friend? Volunteering? Attending a sports event? Taking a class? Something or somewhere else?

>> **Your parents or stepparents just don't "get it."** Unless your parents really are nuts, they may be your best support system. One or more of them knows you well — maybe even better than you know yourself. Is it time to forgive them?

Honest disclosure: My mother used to beat me with a strap almost daily, thinking that was the best way to control her hyperactive son. I resented it throughout my mid-20s and then one day, just like *that,* I told her, "It really was stupid of you to hit me all the time, but I believe you were doing what you thought was best. So I'll forgive you as long as you promise not to hit me again." (Yes, that was a joke. At the time, I was 25 and much stronger than she was.) She cried, I cried, and we became buddies after that. So, is it time to forgive?

>> **You think you're physically ugly, and you're aware of how lookist people are.** Don't you know at least one unattractive person who's doing okay? And even if you look like the Elephant Man, clothes and hair can help a lot. Need to lose weight? Try this strategy as a baby step: The next time you're hungry, stay present — savor each bite, note *not* when you're full but when you're no longer hungry, and stop then. Think how virtuous you'd feel and how much better you'd look if you stopped rather than "porked out" until you're bursting. I know it's not easy, but maybe it's a start.

» **You think you're too stupid or lazy to find and keep a decent job.** Maybe you're no Einstein, but you're smart enough to have picked up this book *and* enough of a go-getter to have read most of its chapters. That probably makes you smart enough and motivated enough to succeed in many of the hundreds of good careers profiled in this book. Especially likely are the careers you picked out. Not sure which career to pick? Take a baby step and watch YouTube videos that highlight a few of them. Afraid no one will hire you? Take a baby step and call a few friends or family members to ask whether they know someone you should talk with. What happens if you've gotten hired but feel like an imposter? Most beginners do. In that case, ask questions, learn from your screw-ups, and give it some time. You'll get better.

## Time tactics

Assume that you care enough to manage your time decently. Might any of these suggestions help?

» **Keep a voice whispering in your ear.** The tool that helps me get a lot done is to have a little voice always whispering in my ear: "Is this the best use of my time?" Might that help you avoid "time-sucks" — for example, watching TV for three hours in a row, listening to your whiney friend yet again, or going to your second cousin's third wedding in Altoona?

When doing a task, might it help to ask yourself questions like this: "Will this approach be the most time effective?" For example, when writing, I recognize that more research will yield a better result, but I try to stop after I've reached the point of diminishing returns.

» **Log your activities.** If you don't seem to know where the hour, day, or even year went, how about keeping a log for a few days? Okay, one day. Set a timer — maybe the one in your phone or watch — to chime every 20 minutes and, on a memo pad, write what you did during the past 20. After each day, review your entries. Anything you want to change?

» **Take choice out of the equation.** Given a choice, many people too often choose not to work. So if you foundationally accept that you need to prioritize work, contribution, and getting stuff done, do you want to try to get into the habit of not even thinking about whether you should do your work? To make it not a choice?

» **Tend to the To Do list + calendar.** Sometimes, the simple-and-obvious method works best. Indeed, many of my clients have profited by simply placing a memo cube on their desk with today's to-do list on it, on which items get crossed off and added throughout the day. For formal appointments, they use Google Calendar, an app on their phone, or a paper week-at-a-glance engagement calendar. (Yes, that's the method I use.)

>> **Learn to use the Pomodoro technique.** I mention this technique in other chapters, but it deserves a reprise. The Pomodoro technique uses a timer — any one will do, including a web-based one like www.marinaratimer. com — though this technique is named after those tomato-shaped kitchen timers. When you have to work on an unappealing project, set a timer for 20 or 25 minutes. Work that stint, and then rest for 5. Work another 20 to 25, take 5 more off. Work another 20 to 25 — and take 10 or 15 off.

>> **Picture the benefits and liabilities.** At the moment of truth, when you're deciding whether to start the dreaded task or to procrastinate, it may help to picture the benefits of getting it done versus the liabilities of procrastinating until the last minute or not getting it done at all.

For example, if you get that report done early and well, you'll have gotten it off your plate, made a contribution, pleased your boss, helped secure your employment, boosted your chance of promotion, helped yourself (if this is a dead-end job) score a recommendation for a better one, and even provided a work sample to show to future employers. On the other hand, if you procrastinate and then, at the last minute, race to turn something in, you not only won't get those benefits, but it could also be a step toward losing your job and having to face another job search. (Not that!)

>> **Do it for something bigger than yourself.** Some people aren't sufficiently motivated by picturing benefits to themselves. Maybe what will light a fire under you is to find something outside yourself to work toward — a mission — whether it's your children, to help a business or nonprofit succeed, or to change the world. That *pulls* you to achieve, which is more sustainable than to *push* yourself to. You can only push yourself for so long.

>> **Banish fear of failure.** Many people procrastinate for fear of failure and its analogues: fear of embarrassing yourself and of being rejected. If you believe that the risk/reward ratio of tackling a task is poor, perhaps don't do it.

If you think it's worth trying but you still are resisting, might it help to remind yourself that not trying is the one way to ensure failure — and that, if you fail, even if you've embarrassed yourself in the process, you can survive? Picture what would happen if you failed. Might you still have learned something from it? Might that failure be a necessary prerequisite for success? Except for end-stage disease, you always have another chance.

**REMEMBER**

Even multiple failures don't make you a loser. Many successful people have failed a lot. *Preachy parent alert:* You won't be a loser as long as you try to learn from failures, perhaps redirect your efforts elsewhere, and keep taking that next step forward. You're more likely to be permanently unhappy and unsuccessful if you consistently give up before trying.

>> **Become comfortable being uncomfortable.** This is an analogue to the previous suggestions. Often, when afraid of failure, you decide, "I need a break, or "I should call my friend," or whatever. Successful people realize that if a task should be done, (here's *another* preachy parent alert) it's worth enduring the short-term discomfort for the long-term gain. Of course, if the work is too hard, see whether you can forgo or delegate it. Or try the *1-minute struggle*, described in the following paragraph.

>> **Take advantage of the 1-minute task.** Often, a big project is daunting, so it's tempting to procrastinate doing it. But one minute is a friendly, not-intimidating amount of time. So it may help you get the ball rolling to ask yourself, "What's my next 1-minute task?" Do that and then force yourself (yes, force yourself) to do the next 1-minute task, and the next. Often, a simple 1-minute task or two is enough to keep you going. As you may have learned in high school physics: Objects in motion tend to stay in motion; objects at rest, to stay at rest.

>> **Limit the struggle to one minute.** When you reach a task's hard part, it's tempting to try for only a moment or, at the other extreme, to keep staring at it, which is frustrating and can make you want to forgo the entire task. A middle-ground rule of thumb is to struggle with the roadblock for just one minute. If you haven't made progress then, decide whether to phone a friend, figure out a way to complete the task without doing that hard part, or come back to it later with fresh eyes.

>> **Build in rewards.** Many people are motivated to plow through a boring or difficult task by promising themselves a reward after completing a small chunk of work. The reward might be to take a 3-minute walk around the parking lot if you finish the next piece of the project. Or play on the Internet for a few minutes after making that scary phone call. Or phone your honey when you solve that spreadsheet problem.

>> **Use The Thermometer.** Especially for a big project, you might try what my wife says helped her complete her PhD dissertation. Using my crude artistic skills on a piece of plain paper, I drew one of those thermometers, like the ones nonprofits use to show progress in meeting a fundraising goal. (See Figure 21-1.) On the side, instead of writing numbers, I wrote the steps she needed to complete toward getting her dissertation done. Every time she finished one, we celebrated in some way.

Yay!

Revise draft

Write draft

Analyze data

Collect data

Find subjects

Get Human Subjects' approval

Revise proposal

Write proposal

Outline proposal

**FIGURE 21-1:** Keeping track of goals.

Review literature

>> **Ritualize.** Build unappealing-but-necessary tasks into your routine. I had a client who is a photographer of wine bottles — yes, that is a real niche. She hated sending and paying bills, so she would let months go by. She solved her problem by setting a fixed time: every Friday between 11 a.m. and noon. She chose that time slot because right after that, she'd get a reward: her weekly Pilates class.

>> **Engage in "sponge" activities.** Life imposes stretches of dead time. Sure, sometimes you just want to veg out, but you may want to sponge up that time and use it. For example, in the car, you might listen to an audio course. When you have a few minutes between required activities, answer an email or three. When you might have to wait — at the DMV, for example, or haircutter or doctor's office — bring a magazine or a book or a Kindle.

>> **Multitask.** Multitasking is widely disparaged, but in certain circumstances it's helpful. For example, most days I hike with my doggie, Einstein, to Trader Joe's and bring my thorniest problem to think about. That enables me to do some undistracted thinking, get some exercise, get Einstein some exercise, and do my shopping, all at the same time. It's maxi-multitasking with no downside.

# Managing Your Stress

Stress is unavoidable, and moderate stress may even be good for you. But especially in today's faster-paced life, stress can hurt you — psychologically and physically.

Stress can originate directly from what's going on at work: The work is too hard, too easy, or too much. Your boss can micromanage and play "gotcha." Your coworkers can refuse to hold up their end and even blame you. A coworker might spread rumors about you, or even threaten you.

And, of course, stress from outside the workplace can affect you at work: a fight with your sweetie, your child experiencing the terrible twos, your favorite stock tanking, your doggie dying, your feelings about suffering from imposter syndrome, your stress-prone and worry-prone nature — even the evening news makes you anxious. Even positive events can take a toll: You're getting married, buying a new car, or moving to a new home. Argh! Try some of these stress reducers:

>> **Take stock of whether you're generally an anxious person.** By this point, it may be ingrained, so the best option may be to simply accept your basic self and put yourself in situation with as little anxiety as possible, inside and outside the workplace. Then do regular moderate exercise. It's amazing how calming a few deep breaths and a 3-minute walk can be.

>> **Quell the imposter syndrome.** Remember that most people feel that way. So, at the risk of being repetitive, ask questions, learn from mistakes, and forgive yourself. You'll get better.

>> **Manage that micromanaging boss or coworker.** Should you give your boss so much accountability that he soon gains confidence in you and turns scrutiny to some other poor soul? Or should you just be avoidant, for example, communicating crisply by email?

>> **Change your tasks or your job.** Sometimes, all the stress reducers won't sufficiently help if the job is too demanding or too boring. Do you need to tell your boss that you can't do a particular task? Do you need a different job?

>> **Maintain perspective.** How important is this in the long run? A week from now, will it matter to you? To your boss? To your sphere of influence? To the world? Yes, try, maybe even try hard, but at a certain point do you need to remind yourself to give yourself a break? That this too shall pass and you will survive?

**TIP**

>> **Take lots of few-minute breaks.** Many of my clients have found that taking a few-minute break every half-hour or hour reduces stress more than engaging in longer relaxing activities before and after work. For example, one of my clients used to do yoga for a half-hour before and after work, meditate for a half-hour at lunch, and then meditate again when she got home. She also went on weeklong meditation retreats. Yet she still felt stressed much of the time.

Then she decided to try taking a few-minute break every half-hour, and now she feels sufficiently destressed to cut back on the yoga and meditation.

>> **Get out of your chair for those breaks.** They say that sitting is the new smoking. So take a walk around the building, call a friend, stretch at your desk. At lunch, if the weather is decent, take a longer walk. Appreciate nature, even if it's just the few street trees in an urban block.

>> **Take even more 10-second breaks.** Whenever you're feeling even a bit stressed, take ten seconds to slowly inhale and even more slowly exhale. Even doing it once will help. It's like instant Xanax with no side effects.

>> **Write on.** Write out your problem, describe how you might solve it, and specify what your best self might tell you to do about it. Or keep an ongoing stress journal: Throughout the day, on a memo pad or in your phone or computer, write when and why you're feeling stressed. That may evoke a solution.

>> **"Hobbify" your life.** A hobby can relax you when doing it and give you something to look forward to when you're stressed. Here are some examples:

- *Join a community theatre on-, back-, or off-stage.*

- *Plant a garden.*

- *Volunteer.*

- *Get a doggie.* Even better, ask whether you can bring him to work. My doggie, Einstein, is my receptionist. (I couldn't pay a receptionist to kiss every client. Einstein does it for kibble.)

- *Get creative.* Paint, juggle, do magic tricks, join a rock band, make videos, or write the great American novel or a local short story.

>> **Compartmentalize.** Of course, sometimes your personal problem takes over you and you can't distract yourself. But more often than you may think, you can distract yourself. I recall a client who has two young kids and both grandparents who are seriously ill and she said, "Work is the only thing that keeps me sane."

>> **Let go of what you can't control.** After you've done your part, there's often a waiting period to get the results. Maybe you've made that sales presentation and they say they'll get back to you. Or you've applied for another job and, despite weekly follow-ups, they're not responding. Or your grandparent is ill. Or you're waiting for the results of the definitive pregnancy test. I know it's not easy, but try to let it go. The Serenity Prayer is wise: "Grant me the serenity to accept the things I cannot change, courage to change the things I can, and wisdom to know the difference."

>> **Face the worst case.** As I mention earlier in this chapter, you can survive anything but end-stage disease. You may even ultimately be better for getting fired or losing your romantic partner. That probably wasn't the right fit. There may well be better things awaiting you in the future.

» Fifteen careers that are somewhat
easy to transition into

» Four approaches to a successful
change

» If you decide to stay in your current
career

# Chapter **22**

# The Career Changer

Whether you were careful in choosing your career or fell into it by chance, you may be wondering whether you should change careers. That could be scary: Will you have to take a pay cut? How long will it take to retrain and then to get hired over people with experience? And will all the effort be worth it? This chapter should help with all these questions.

First, I'll ask you questions to help you figure out whether it's wise to stay put, perhaps with a minor pivot. If you decide that's not enough, I'll show how best to benefit from the four ways that most people use to successfully change careers.

## Will a Career Tweak Do the Trick?

A career tweak rarely yields ecstasy, but you may decide that its ease outweighs a radical move's challenges. This section looks at some options for you.

### Tweaking your job description

Maybe within your current job you could, on your own or with your boss's permission, adjust your job description to replace tasks you dislike with those you'd like better. For example, a middle-management client of mine enjoyed, and was far better at, resolving conflicts and giving talks than supervising employees and making budget forecasts. She found a coworker who was the opposite, so both of them went to their boss and got approval to trade some of their tasks.

## Changing bosses

Your boss is a fire-breathing, micromanaging taskmaster. Or he's not a troglodyte, but simply has a personality that drives you nuts — he loves lots of small talk and processing, whereas you like to just get the job done. Perhaps a change of boss is enough, at least for now.

## Changing employers

Sometimes, your malaise can be adequately addressed by changing employers but still doing what you do. For example, an HR specialist hated the chaos in her small nonprofit. She wanted more processes in place but didn't have the ability, let alone the power, to implement them. So she moved to a larger company, where all that was in place, and though she still doesn't feel that her career was made in heaven, it works on earth.

## Moving to management

Perhaps you're a computer programmer who's had enough of sitting in front of a computer all day and having to learn the latest version of the software. Might it help to find some management training, let your boss know that you're interested in moving to management, and (if you sense that it won't happen at this workplace) look elsewhere?

# Time to Change Careers?

Sometimes a tweak just won't do, not only because a career is a misfit but also because, sometimes, a career misery's cause lies within the person. In those cases, a person brings the cause of her unhappiness to her new career, having expended a lot of time and, usually, money for nothing. These questions can help you decide whether you need a career change:

>> **True or false:** You're confident that your unhappiness in this career is unfixable — it won't help to simply change your employer, adjust your job responsibilities, or gain a new skill or attitude. For example, a psychologist gets consistently poor results despite being well-mentored. Or a salesperson

gets more and more call-reluctant, even though the product is a good one. Or a journalist finds it impossible to make a living because of all the "citizen journalists" willing to write for free.

>> **True or false:** After sufficient reflection, Internet research, and perhaps informational interviewing, you're confident that you'd be happier and more successful in a particular new career.

>> **True or false:** You have the time and money to afford retraining and, often, a pay cut.

>> **True or false:** You're confident that with (or even without much) training, you'd be employable in your new career. For example, you know that the job market is good for people newly trained in this field, or you know someone who'd likely hire you whether the job market is good or not.

>> **True or false:** You're confident that if you made the aforementioned career change, you'd be happier and more successful.

# Fifteen Ideas

Sure, more than one social worker has, in midlife, relaunched her career to become a rocket scientist. But those people are rare enough that they're the ones who appear on "The Oprah Winfrey Show." Here are 15 careers that a higher percentage of people have switched to and found satisfying:

>> **Government employee as manager, analyst, or coordinator:** Many people change careers to find security, and its last bastion is government.

>> **Politician:** Many people want to make a difference. And though the wheels of government turn slowly, its massive size allows the potential for broad impact. No, you won't start out as chairman of the House Ways and Means Committee, but many people make at least a part-time living in entry-level political careers — for example, as members of the local school board or parks commission.

>> **Political campaign manager:** Are you intrigued by being in politics, but are better at handling details and managing people than being the front person?

>> **Grant writer:** Money is a nonprofit's lifeblood, and a key vehicle for getting money is to answer requests for proposals from government or foundations. Grant writers write those proposals. You get to live in the world of new ideas, projects, and hope, and it requires a nice blend of writing and human interaction.

>> **Fundraiser:** This is another revenue-enhancing job in the nonprofit sector, and because of that, the pay tends to be better than for most nonprofit jobs. You may or may not need to be the person who makes The Ask. Nonprofits use organized types to develop dossiers on prospective donors, plan fundraising events, and manage the donor database.

>> **Personal assistant:** Many people like being the right arm to a kind, respect-worthy person.

>> **Nurse:** Being a registered nurse (RN) requires at least two years of training but affords myriad options. Some people find satisfaction, however, just in being a licensed vocational nurse or even a nurse's aide or medical assistant. (The latter two require only brief training.)

>> **Teacher or teacher's aide:** If you can deliver lessons enjoyably, get kids to want to behave for you, and inspire parents' confidence, this can be a rewarding career.

>> **Employee trainer:** This is a good option for people who like teaching but are daunted by the challenge of classroom management with kids. For that matter, are adults always well behaved?

>> **Personnel recruiter:** This sales job requires the ability to persuade employers to consider the candidate you've unearthed. Of course, you also need a nose for finding a good person for the particular job.

>> **Technician:** Here's a chance to work on cool stuff like wind turbines, ATMs, smartphones, or industrial machinery — for example, robotic welders.

>> **Flight attendant:** Many career changers would rather trade money for the adventure of meeting lots of new people and seeing new places. Oh, and there's the free travel.

>> **Bookkeeper:** This job can be especially rewarding if you specialize in doing small-business bookkeeping for professionals in a specialty you like: for example, for professional photographers, psychologists, or boutique owners.

>> **Communication specialist for a company, government agency, or nonprofit:** This job could be in internal communication, media relations, or public or community relations.

>> **A low-pay but easy, pleasurable job allowing plenty of time and energy for an avocation:** For example, it might be a sport or performing or art or writing. A variation: a portfolio of such jobs, each part-time. Here are some examples: Teach a college or adult education course, work Saturdays at a bookstore, sell handmade jewelry at street fairs, walk dogs, plant and maintain gardens, or officiate sporting events.

Up is not the only way. Indeed, status can be the enemy of contentment.

# Effecting the Change

It's all well and good to have a goal, but as they say, a goal is a dream with a plan. In this section, I lay out four ways to make a career change. One size does not fit all. Which do you think might work best for you?

## Changing by retraining

If you have the time and money, retraining gives you the most options. For example, have you been in corporate America and want to become a teacher? Many colleges offer teacher training programs, and school districts may offer alternative certifications, learning mainly on the job.

Or vice versa: You have been a teacher and you want to leverage that experience by becoming a manager in an educational technology company, preparing with an MBA or an MS in educational technology development.

Or you've worked for an environmental nonprofit and you love the cause but not the pay and you want to leverage your fundraising skills. So you take one or more sales training courses and do "ride-alongs" with excellent and ethical salespeople. That training gives you a shot at a well-paying career selling big-ticket environmental products to businesses.

A side benefit of taking career-preparatory courses is that it provides the opportunity to make career-door-opening connections. Your instructor, fellow students, and fieldwork and internship supervisor can pave the way.

The following few sections look at retraining options details.

### University-based training

Even many people willing to take the risk of changing careers are risk-averse when choosing how to get retrained. They know that most employers are more comfortable with a traditionally trained person, if only because a third-party has awarded grades and because a boss is less likely to get in trouble if a well-credentialed employee doesn't work out than if someone informally trained proves to be a disaster.

Here are the keys to making the most of university–based courses:

**»** **Choose a program.** Yes, consider the university's brand and rankings. We live in a brand-name society, but don't let that overshadow the quality of career preparation. A university may have developed its reputation and ranking based on research productivity, which, ironically, may be antithetical to its career preparation's quality. When professors are hired and promoted and gain a reputation primarily on their research, they often have less ability and motivation to focus on helping you become a practitioner.

Here are criteria for selecting a career-preparatory program that deserve weight:

- *Specialize in a career area that excites you.* Here are some signs that a career specializes in that: Does the website's program-summary focus on it? Do the required, or at least elective, courses address it? Do at least a few of the faculty's bios indicate that they specialize in your target career?

- *Before applying, reach out to the professor who seems most aligned with your career interest.* Does she respond promptly to messages? When you chat with her, do you sense that she'd be a good advisor for you: a person who could teach you the inside baseball that will help you become a better practitioner and who might even, on graduation, open career doors for you?

- *Solicit student opinion.* Visit professor-review websites such as RateMyProfessors.com and ULoop.com. Even better, if you can, check the class schedule for the program's thesis or project seminar, email the instructor, and ask to sit in. At a break or at the end of class, explain to students that you're considering becoming a student in their program and wondering what they think of it: the learning, graduates' employability, the enjoyability — yes, that counts too.

**»** **Get in.** Of course, grades and scores on the GRE, GMAT, LSAT, MCAT, and other tests count. I recommend only moderate test prep: Spend a half-hour a day for a month using software you've picked as feeling right for you. Amazon offers many, each with user reviews.

If you "click" with the aforementioned potential advisor, ask, "I'd be pleased to be one of your students — do you have any advice on how I might enhance my admissibility?" If she truly likes you, that may even motivate her to write the admissions office a letter of support. That's golden.

Write an admissions essay or cover letter explaining how this particular program is a well-suited next step in your career. Start with how you first became interested in the field and what you've learned along the way — transferrable skills from your previous career, for example, or articles you've read and experiences you've had — but make it clear that you're eager now for a more thorough education in the career so that, afterward, you'll be in a better position to do a good job at it, not just to make money but to make a difference.

>> **Pay for it.** If cost is an issue, and it certainly is for most people, have a candid conversation with both a financial aid officer and the head of the program. Why both? Because the program head may have discretion over separate funds. Also, as a longshot, peruse the third-party scholarships in the FastWeb.com database. If you're a particularly well-suited candidate, it's worth the effort to apply. For example, David Letterman funds a $10,000 scholarship for telecommunications students at Ball State for average students.

>> **Make the most of it.** You boost your chances of your retraining paying when you

- *Choose an advisor who can open career doors for you.* For example, choose someone who does a lot of outside consulting. Of course, your advisor must not only respect but also like you, so be sure to pick an advisor you click with. If you've picked wrong, you may not be stuck. Check out another advisor and, as on a first date, if it feels good, ask whether you can switch.

- *Choose professors and courses with your career goal in mind.* Sure, there may be required courses with only one professor teaching it, but where you have discretion, resist the temptation to dabble excessively. Choose courses that you could see listing on your resume and, in job interviews, describing what you learned. That said, when in doubt, it's usually better to choose the better instructor than the more appropriate course title. A good instructor can help you grow as a professional and as a person, even if the course title is Medieval Indo-European Linguistics.

- During lectures and student comments, listen for statements that might be relevant to your career. For example, you're in an MBA program and a student asks, "How do you strike the balance between making evidence-based decisions and using intuitive judgment?" If you're aiming for a career in the healthy-foods industry, you might ask yourself how you'd deal with a new food concept that the focus groups loves and you don't.

## Informal training

It's often possible to get more practical career training that's faster and cheaper by forgoing State U, let alone Private U, in favor of what I call *You U.* You see, in a typical graduate program, you take 60 or more units, many chosen for you, and you have to listen to lectures, read material, and be graded on information that you'll never use, that you've forgotten by the time you need it, or that has become obsolete. For the privilege, you have to show up at a prescribed time (maybe even in online courses) and pay. In contrast, at You U, you pick the articles, webinars, conferences, short courses, mentorships, and volunteer work that work best and most practically prepare you for your specific career goal.

Here's a real-life example. My client (I've changed only irrelevant details to protect his anonymity) had been a store manager at a Peet's Coffee and wanted to move out of retail and into a corporate job as a manager of store managers as a stepping stone to even more advancement. He looked into MBA programs, but the only one he could find that focused on retail management was at Michigan State, and he wanted to stay in California. So he asked his boss, the district manager, what she thought about his enrolling in You U. She was supportive, suggesting that he attend some Peet's University workshops, spend part of some Saturdays helping that district manager with this and that, taking a leadership and management course on Udemy, and waiting to hear "We'll see." Six months and less than $100 later, that manager recommended him for three assistant district manager positions, and he landed one. Of course, not every You U "graduate" gets the gold ring, but neither does every State U grad. Especially if you're a self-starter, it's worth considering You U.

## Documenting your You U learning experience

*You U* students don't receive transcripts, so you have to document your learning. Fortunately, a portfolio of your work is more compelling to many employers than is a university transcript: Marketing Theory and Practice: B+; History and Systems of Data Analysis, A−," and so on.

From Day One, get in the habit of saving material for your portfolio. Maybe it's a word processing file with the not-so-obvious nuggets you'll use in your career, or the culminating project you completed at that boot camp, or the master list of all you did: articles and book chapters you read, conferences you attended, one-on-one meetings with mentors. It might even be worth the effort to write a few sentences on the most valuable things you learned from each one. Of course, you'll remember more if you do it right after you've completed the activity. A portfolio can be compelling to employers.

## Helping employers understand why a You U "graduate" is worth hiring

Before you can expect an employer to look at your You U portfolio, you need to make your case in a cover letter.

Many applications, especially online forms, don't have room for cover letters, so, simply append it atop your resume.

Imagine that you're an employer who is reviewing job applications and you see this letter:

*Dear (If possible, insert the employer's name rather than say, "Dear Sir or Madam" or "To Whom it May Concern."),*

*I'd imagine you're tempted to toss my application in the trash, seeing that I don't have the master's degree in sports management, as your job ad specifies. But I'm hoping that you view my decision to have attended "You U" rather than State U as making me more qualified and more of a self-starter.*

*I started my You U education by seeking out the most outstanding sports manager I could find. I was fortunate that Suzanne Michaels, an award-winning sports management executive, agreed to help me craft a self-learning plan, which I have implemented. It included six articles, three book chapters, two Udemy short courses, and four videos — and attending chapter meetings of the American Sports Management Association. I have completed all, and I append the list as well as a list of career-valuable nuggets I learned. As the culminating project of my You U "master's degree," I co-presented with her at the American Sports Management Association conference. I also append the white paper she suggested I write in preparation: "Five Thorny Issues Sports Managers Must Face in the 2020s."*

*I hope you'll choose to interview me so I can demonstrate that I'm worthy of consideration.*

*I'm particularly interested in working for your company. I've googled it, and the reviews are impressive.*

*Hoping to get to meet you.*

*Sincerely,*

*Jane Jobseeker*

If you were that employer, might you interview that candidate? Sure some, or maybe most, employers would reject this candidate, but enough would consider Jane — and probably the kind of employer one would want to work for. And, Jane will have started on her new job, perhaps better trained than had she gone the traditional route. Plus, she'd have a lot more money in her pocket — not just the saved tuition but because she would be earning income during the time she would have still been in the master's program.

## Using your network

Especially for people who lack the time and money for a long retraining effort, the best chance of making a successful career change is to invoke and, if necessary, build your network.

You see, if you rely only on answering ads, you'll probably fail. Few employers would go through the hassle of screening oodles of applicants if they wanted to hire someone with no experience. Someone who wanted to do that would simply hired his wayward cousin.

So with, and especially without, solid training in your next career, you really boost your odds of landing a good launchpad job if you fully invoke your network and, if it has too few people likely to refer you to an employer, to build your network. Don't worry. That can be fun, sort of — well, if you're an extrovert. Otherwise, it can still be tolerable and worth the effort.

## Invoking your network

Most people, even introverts, have a larger network than they think. Sure, if you've just moved to a new city and if in your previous one you were a hermit or universally despised, maybe your network isn't gargantuan. But do any of the following suggest people you might reach out to?

REMEMBER

A person doesn't need to be in a position to hire you. She just needs to know one person he might introduce you to. Here are some examples of lead sources:

>> Your family. (Even that wayward cousin might know someone.)

>> Your current and past coworkers.

>> Your college alumni.

>> Your high school alumni.

>> Your elementary school alumni. (Okay, that's reaching.)

>> Your former romantic partner. (Be careful here.)

>> Acquaintances in your group hobby: basketball team, theatre group, book club, dive-bar-hopping.

>> People who perform services for you: your haircutter, your bookkeeper, your house cleaner.

>> People from your religious or spiritual affiliation, whether it's a leader or a flock member.

>> Your social media friends and sort-of friends. You could send out an all-points bulletin to your contacts on Facebook, Twitter, Instagram, and, of course, LinkedIn, like this:

*Hi, All:*

*Being a teacher has been okay, but I'm looking to pivot from that job into working for an ed-tech company. I've done a fair amount of retraining and am loving it. Do you know anyone you think I should talk with? Here's the link to my LinkedIn profile, which contains a portfolio of some relevant work I've done.*

Note the reach-out's informal tone. When people don the job-seeker persona, it's off-putting: It sounds desperate or fake, and usually both. How would you feel if someone wrote to you: "I'm a self-starter but team player who delights in exceeding customer expectations and seeking to join a dynamic company"? About now, I'd be vomiting.

## Building your network

Despite the long list of sources of leads in the preceding section, if you feel that the odds of generating enough useful leads are dim, you'll need to build your network. Do any of these ways appeal, or at least not repulse you?

- >> **Join or start a club.** There are all sorts of clubs, from book clubs to motorcycle clubs, although I'm not sure the Hell's Angels would be the most promising source of professional job leads.

- >> **Join or start a political organization.** Political affinity is among the strongest bonds. Your organization needn't be big. It could simply be folks who support a candidate for school board. Or join the local Democratic or Republican club.

- >> **Join a nonprofit board.** Sure, big nonprofits expect big donations from board members, but small nonprofits may be grateful just to have people to steer the operation. That's a potent networking opportunity because boards do tend to have successful people on them, and you're getting to work with them, on an ongoing basis, on a cause you all believe in. That's fertile ground for job leads.

- >> **Join a sports team.** This, too, affords repeat opportunities to engage with the same people. Just as in dating, it normally takes multiple get-togethers before you get comfortable with someone.

- >> **Join or start a group creative activity.** Examples here would include an artist's collective, a community theatre group, a rock band, a chamber group, and a chorus.

- >> **Take a class.** Most likely to yield fruit for the career changer is a class that people in your prospective career might take. For example, if you're an aspiring accountant, perhaps you'd take a continuing education course on the new tax law changes. But even recreational courses can work. Again, this affords an opportunity to see the same people again and again — plus, you share a joint interest in something fun: A course in magic? Dressing for success? Tattooing? Tip: Don't practice that on your forehead.

No matter the vehicle, the pitch is still the same. At a time when it feels right and not prematurely, say something like this:

*I used to be a lab chemist but couldn't see spending my life at the bench, mixing chemicals and peering into a microscope. So, because I've always loved the outdoors, I took a certificate program in forest management and really took to it. Now I'm looking for my first job in that field, perhaps for the government or perhaps for a private company. By any chance, might you know someone I should talk with, if only to get some advice — if not a possible job lead?*

## Working up from the bottom

Sometimes people try to change careers by working their way up from the bottom. Perhaps they tried for a higher-level job to no avail. Or their self-esteem is in the toilet. Or as a beginner, they prefer to do their learning concretely, on the job.

Here's an example: A former corporate drone and aspiring tradesperson took a job handing nails to a kitchen countertop installer. He watched, asked questions, learned, and soon got to be in charge of simple jobs in which someone handed *him* the nails. Then his boss gave him more complicated jobs, and, finally, he opened up his own shop. It's Sullivan Countertops in Oakland, California. Look it up. It's there.

## Becoming self-employed

Some successfully self-employed people didn't choose to be their own boss; they were forced into it: They couldn't land a good job, and so they figured they'd try their hand at self-employment. That enabled them to go from novice to CEO in one fell swoop, and many people appreciate the control of being their own boss. That's especially likely if they've spent time in a large organization where they may have needed three signatures to blow their nose.

Chapter 9 offers many self-employment ideas. In this section, I discuss a common self-employment option for career changers: becoming a consultant on the kind of work they did as employees.

You needn't have been a higher-up to be a consultant. You just have to have been good. A good administrative assistant who was tired of being an underling started giving workshops for admins at the local chapter of the administrative support association, at libraries, and at churches. She also pitched the training departments of local large companies, government agencies, and nonprofits, and occasionally got to do workshops for them. At the end of each workshop, having strutted her stuff, she explained that she was available for one-on-one consultations in which she'd visit an admin on the job and make suggestions in context.

Of course, the woman enjoyed public speaking, so she marketed her consultancy by doing public speaking. If she were more of a writer, I'd have suggested that she write articles or a tip-of-the-month article for a publication read by admins, even if it were just the newsletter or website for the local chapter of a trade or professional organization. If she were more of a networker, I'd have had her join clubs like Rotary or the Chamber of Commerce and, when the time was right, explain what she was looking for. Of course, if you're an effective networker, you may not need to join anything new. Your existing covey may provide all the leads you need to kick-start your consultancy. After that, word-of-mouth from satisfied clients may be enough.

# If You Decide to Stay in Your Current Career

Some people conclude, either before really trying to change careers or after an attempt, that for now at least, they'll stay in their career and even in their same job. If that's you, please know that you're not doomed to eternal misery. For example, might one or more of the suggestions in the following sections make your current career tolerable, if not forever, at least until you're more ready to change jobs or careers?

## Learning a new skill

If you're unhappy in your career, it probably won't help to learn something you dread, even if it's important. But maybe, for example, you've always been daunted by public speaking but would like to see whether you might learn to give a presentation without vomiting or at least to speak up more authoritatively at staff meetings. If so, you might try Toastmasters, which is inexpensive and has a long-proven method for improving people's public speaking. Or if you need more private and personalized training, even if you're not rich, you probably can afford a few sessions with a tutor.

## Pitching an exciting project

Sometimes part of the problem is that your job is stale — it's the same-old. Even if you have to work a little overtime, might it be worth asking your boss if you can work on a project that would excite you and use your best skills? Who knows? If it's something that the boss thinks is valuable, she might even temporarily release you from one of your odious tasks so you can do it without taking the time out of your hide. Here are a few examples to stimulate your ideas:

>> Take photographs of everyone from the janitor to the CEO to post on the company's intranet site.

>> Interview the staff for up-close-and-personal articles to be posted on that site.

>> Make site visits to your competitors and write a report as a way to get out from behind your desk, get out of the office, and learn cool things that others are doing.

## Taking a sabbatical

Only a few workplaces offer actual *sabbaticals* — that is, months off with pay to learn something new or otherwise refresh. But occasionally, if you make a strong case that it will benefit the employer, your boss might say yes — you have nothing to lose by trying. For example, here's a pitch that a logistics manager might make to a boss:

*We've been doing logistics pretty much the same way for a long time. Now, there are many good new tools, high-touch as well as high-tech, that I know little about, let alone how to use or train others to use. I think it would be a good use of company dollars for me to take a 2-month training leave to become knowledgeable about those. I'd come back with a proposal for how we might take our operation to the next level. I think it would generate more in profit than the cost of my sabbatical. What do you think?*

## Finding an avocation

Occasionally, a mediocre work life can sufficiently be compensated for by having something to look forward to after work — for example, one of the topics I mention in earlier sections: a creative outlet, a cause to advocate for, or, perhaps most common, a romantic and/or family life.

## Changing your attitude

Changing your attitude is both the hardest to do and perhaps the least likely to result in career contentment. But for completeness, I should mention it. Might a conscious, sustained effort to change your foundational attitude from half-empty to half-full sufficiently address your career malaise? For example, when you see something annoying, should you ask yourself, "Am I better off letting it go, or stewing or complaining about it?" "Should I force myself to look for the positive? To feel a sense of gratitude?" As my mother would say, "People really are starving in Africa." I'm guessing you're not feeling it.

Chapter **23**

# Finding Your Foundation

f I were starting my career, I'd be tempted to skip this chapter. I'd be thinking, "It's probably just a bunch of high-minded urging of work-life balance and ethics."

Not quite. For example, yes, some people look back on their work lives and think, "I wish I had spent less time at the office." But other people wish they had devoted more. Some people wish they had been more ethical, and others feel they were foolish to be purist. Some wish they had worked for a nonprofit, and others wonder whether having sacrificed income for "the cause" yielded less benefit than if they had worked for a for-profit, which enables people to get good products.

## Unearthing Your Work Life's Core Principles

There's no one-size-fits-all set of work-life principles. You can adjust yours as life proceeds, but it can't hurt to think about them so you can try to live those principles rather than be buffeted by external events.

# The pay continuum

Many people overestimate money's importance:

>> Beyond a middle-class income, money doesn't buy happiness.

>> In many locales, you end up paying half of your income above $75,000 in taxes, so you generally have to earn $125,000 or more a year to significantly improve your material lifestyle.

>> For an employer to pay you big money, you need to make the employer bigger money, and that can bring ethical temptations.

>> Few careers pay big money, so your options are limited. Unless you have a shot at being the next Madonna, you may need to forgo artistic careers as well as nonprofit work, unless you're a major fundraiser or director.

For some people, however, major money is important:

>> It's tangible evidence of how much the world values your work.

>> Big money buys things like a nice house in a nice neighborhood.

>> All things equal, it's better to go for more money than less. For example, if you like selling and can land a job selling a great product, and if you're committed to not cutting ethical corners, why not?

How much money would *you* like to make near-term? In five years? And how important is that amount to you?

`<_____<`

$30,000                                                    $200,000+

# The people-contact continuum

Some of my clients complain about being isolated at work — they crave more people contact. On the other hand, some of my clients would rather work mainly solo. Relatedly, some people like workplaces with lots of social interaction, even if work productivity suffers. Others prefer a minimum of chitchat, let alone inter-personal drama.

There is no right or wrong. The question is, "Where on the people-contact continuum would you like to be, and how important is that to you?"

>_____<

No people contact                                    Lots of people contact

## The status continuum

Even though status is ineffable, many people are driven by it. After all, why would someone buy Gucci, Pucci, Coach, or Chu when they could buy less tony brands that look and perform essentially as well, still looking good by the time most people decide to change styles? Status. Why do people buy a "Beemer," Mercedes, or Jaguar that costs oodles more than a Toyota, even though they break down more? Even though there's no status in standing on the side of the road and waiting for a tow truck, many people buy designer-label cars, even going into debt to do it. Why? Status: It makes some people feel good to be associated with a status name. Of course, that concept extends to career. It feels good to know, and for others to know, that you're a physician rather than a physician assistant, or a lawyer rather than a haircutter, even though surveys find that haircutters have higher average job satisfaction. Oh, and physician assistants and many haircutters do make a solid living. The question for you is (be totally honest with yourself), how important is status?

>_____>

No importance                                          Great importance

## The workload continuum

Work-life balance is high priority for many people. They want to be able to succeed while leaving plenty of time for family, fun, and personal maintenance. For them, a 40-hour workweek is pretty much tops, and it's even better if those hours are flexible, that they can take lots of breaks, and that when they leave work, they're done with work. Rarely will they engage in professional reading or attend professional workshops or answer their email after work hours.

Other people find work more rewarding, contributory, and even pleasurable than what they otherwise might be doing.

Where are you on the workload continuum, and how important is that to you?

>_____<

Fewer than 20 hours; not unduly
productivity oriented

More than 60 highly productive hours a week

## The ambition continuum

No one blames a person for wanting to climb the status-and-income ladder. If you say you're an individual contributor and your goal is to be a vice president, the response is usually "You go, girl" or, I guess, "You go, guy," although I've never heard that sentence uttered by anyone.

But some people strive upward more because of praise than because they simply want to. Privately, they'd rather trade the money, power, and prestige of a big-time job for less stress and more free time. Or they may realize that if they push upward, they'll rise to their level of incompetence. You spend too much time at work to let societal pressure dictate your level of ambition. Consciously decide how ambitious you want to be:

>_____<

A basic job is fine.

I want to rise as far as I can.

## The ethical continuum

Most people claim to be ethical, but in real life, as in most human characteristics, there's plenty of variability.

For example, some people believe that any sales or fundraising job is unethical because, in order to be more than an order taker, you have to manipulate the prospect into buying when he otherwise could buy from another vendor or donate to another charity. On the other hand, some people, as long as they don't commit egregious ethical violations (like overtly lying about a product or the benefits a charitable donation will yield), prioritize putting bread on the table.

Another example: For one person, anything this side of selling tobacco or mind-altering substances is ethical. For others, ethics requires clear societal improvement. Of course, that can occur in all sectors: for-profit, nonprofit, and government. For example, someone who works for a company that makes best-in-class products such as Toyota, Apple, or Google, as long as their day-to-day behavior is ethical, can lay their heads on the pillow with pride. So can someone who works for a nonprofit that has demonstrated it makes a bigger difference than do peer non-profits. A person who works for a government agency that belies the stereotype "Government does everything poorly but expensively" can, of course, also be proud.

So now I again turn to you. Where on the ethical continuum do you want to be, and how important is that to you?

>_____<

Anything more ethical than selling addictive drugs                    Mother Teresa

## The redistribution-versus-merit continuum

The New Testament urges us to prioritize "the least among us." Indeed that's the core principle of liberal/progressive politics and economics: "How can we sit by when some people live in mansions while others live in squalor?" Other people operate from the battlefield medic's triage principle: When you have limited resources, you help more people by allocating medical supplies not to the sickest but to those with the greatest potential to profit.

Translating that concept to the career world, some people want to be social workers, inner-city teachers, community activists, or nonprofit employees, who usually focus on "the least among us." Others are dissuaded from that view, arguing that, despite significant funds set aside by the United States to close the achievement gap, in their opinion that gap remains as wide as ever. Such people choose to work in organizations that employ and serve high ability/high achievers: high-quality companies or private schools serving intellectually gifted kids, for example.

So, what about you? Where on the continuum do you want to focus your career efforts, and how important is that to you?

>_____<

On "the least among us"                    On high-achievers, the "best and brightest"

## The hedonism-versus-contribution continuum

This continuum is embedded in some of the previous ones, but is central, so it deserves separate attention. This continuum spans three philosophies of life. One end on the continuum is the belief that the life well-led is about the pursuit of happiness: Strive to do as little work as possible so you can have as much fun as possible. On the other end of the continuum is the belief that the life well-led is defined by spending as many heartbeats as possible making the biggest contribution possible: Work long hours using your best skills, even if some of the work is unpleasant, because greater good accrues from that than from spending discretionary time, for example, watching TV, playing video games, or even having family time. Between those two lies the most commonly held value: balance, the Aristotelian golden mean. It's often referred to as *work-life balance*.

So, where on the continuum do you want to aspire, and how important is that to you?

<_____>

Hedonism                                        Maximum contribution

## Your choices are cast in Jell-O

Of course, your choices aren't cast in stone. They're cast in Jell-O: You can change them, although it may get sticky. But thinking consciously about your core principles may give you a head start on living the life you want to live now and a life you'll look back on feeling good about how you lived it.

# Chapter **24**

# What's Ahead?

**E**xperts differ on whether the work world's changes will end up a boon or a bust. In this brief chapter, I offer both a quite pessimistic and a quite optimistic perspective on the work world's future. That wide range should help you in developing your own vision. And it's important that you have one, both in planning now and as you proceed in your career.

## A Pessimistic View

Some pretty smart people — including Elon Musk, Stephen Hawking, and Bill Gates — worry that artificial-intelligence-driven robots will take over the world.

A more widely held pessimistic view is that, because of automation, offshoring, and part-timing, most jobs that will provide even a modestly adequate income will require a skill set too few people can attain, even with ratcheted-up spending on education. And the United States already spends in the number-one or number-two spot in the world in per capita spending on education and arguably has yielded too little result.

So the pessimistic view contends that a large percentage of the population will not sustainably earn a sufficient income. The most widely proposed solution is a guaranteed basic income (GBI.) But questions have been raised about it: How severely will the increased taxes that are intended to pay for a GBI impede job growth? To what extent would a GBI, as previous welfare programs did, increase the so-called welfare mentality: reluctance to look for work when one would get paid for not working? To what extent would a GBI cause the bite-the-hand-that-feeds-you phenomenon?

Another proposal is to resurrect the Work Projects Administration (WPA). In the Great Depression, taxpayer dollars were used to create the WPA to provide income to the unemployed while building U.S. infrastructure. WPA2 would mitigate the "welfare mentality" problem, but not the problems of paying for it nor the bite-the-hand-that-feeds-you phenomenon.

Perhaps the pessimists' biggest fear is that the lack of jobs will increase crime, drug abuse, and civil unrest.

# An Optimistic View

For time immemorial, technology has advanced — from the wheel through the next-generation iPhone, and despite the naysayers, more jobs have been created than lost.

And these jobs won't be only for brilliant creators. Even software, which can be manufactured in unlimited quantities with the push of a button, requires, for example, marketers, salespeople, and support staff. And even in the current technocentric era, many products and services will not be created so autonomously, and so will continue to require many employees.

It's true that many boring, repetitive jobs will be automated, but few people crave those. We will continue to need high-touch people — for example, managers who understand the nuances of data and people. We'll need nurses and teachers augmented by (but not replaced by) artificial intelligence, enabling them to focus on the human side of their work. We'll need government employees using ever better software to use tax dollars more efficiently.

Technology will benefit lives in other important ways. It will cure more diseases. It will bring greener, cheaper energy. It will reduce the cost of most items and services, reducing some of the pressure that people feel to earn a substantial income. For example, next-generation premanufactured homes will be desirable and affordable.

There's a silver lining, even if people's buying power decreases: People could be redirected from a too-materialistic lifestyle to one that ultimately is more rewarding: centered around quality of work, relationships, creative outlets, and service to society.

Plus, the world is becoming ever more educated: There will be more people to come up with innovative ideas for improving life and for creating jobs. For example, here are two of mine:

» **The assistance army:** Rich people have long known that they free up time by hiring personal assistants: helpers with their newborns, homework helpers, tech tutors, personal assistants to run errands and wait for the cable installer, and elder companions for their aging relatives. That practice needs to be brought into working- and middle-class people's consciousness.

People of moderate means won't be able to pay big wages but can afford to hire help part-time. Members of the *assistance army* could piece together a few such assistant jobs and make an acceptable living while being of real help to people.

» **The entrepreneurship army:** Perhaps the most important subject that schools ignore and may even disparage is entrepreneurship. After all, that is the only way in which jobs are, net, created. Government-created jobs are paid for with taxpayer dollars — money that otherwise would be spent creating jobs, or indirectly so, when people buy goods and services.

What is needed is more entrepreneurs, at least ethical ones. Kindergartens might have their children develop lemonade-stand-type businesses. In higher grades, the businesses and the planning and analysis required would, of course, grow more sophisticated. At the college level, more institutions would offer an entrepreneurship major. In job retraining, instead of preparing people for jobs that soon become obsolete or oversupplied, people could be trained to be ethical entrepreneurs, which puts them more in control of their income and their lives.

This section bases its optimism by looking forward. Harvard's Steven Pinker finds reason for optimism by looking at humankind's track record:

> Look at history and data, not headlines. The world continues to improve in just about every way. Extreme poverty, child mortality, illiteracy, and global inequality are at historic lows; vaccinations, basic education, including for girls, and democracy are at all-time highs . . . believe it or not . . . violence has declined over long stretches of time, and today we may be living in the most peaceable era of our species' existence. In the "pre-state" era, you had a 1-in-6 chance of dying in conflict. In the last century, for all its horrific violence, that number fell to just 3 percent. And the current period is the most violence-free in history.

# My Prediction

I would like to be optimistic, believing that progress has always been two steps forward, one step back — but inexorably forward. So, emotionally, I prefer to bet on humankind.

But if I am to walk my talk about radical honesty, which throughout the book I've implied as central, my bet — and I wouldn't bet the house — is moderately pessimistic. Automation will kill too many jobs, and the remaining ones will require a too-rare amalgam of tech chops, soft skills, and emotional solidity. So I'm concerned.

But importantly, just because society as a whole may have a tough time doesn't mean that you as an individual can't thrive. Indeed, this book's purpose is to help individuals thrive in a tough world. So, though I may not be able to bet on society, I'm willing to bet on you.

Let me close by coming full circle. At the beginning of this book, I say that I welcome your comments and questions. That's particularly true for people who've gone this far with me on this journey. I can be reached at mnemko@comcast.net.

# The Part of Tens

Chapter **25**

# Ten Ultrafast Ways to Land a Job

The approaches outlined in this chapter could help you avoid a long job-search slog.

## Just Walk Right In

Imagine that you're awakened in the middle of the night by a phone call from a stranger asking if you would take in a baby. If you're like most people, you'd decline. Yet if the doorbell rang and you opened the door to find an infant on the threshold, you'd take it in. Right?

REMEMBER

The power of showing up applies to job seekers. Today, when ads for good jobs attract gobs of applicants, walking into workplaces can be a faster way to land a job. It won't get you a CEO gig but it can work for jobs other than burger-flipper.

But what if there's a gatekeeper? This story may be inspiring. A client wanted to work for a large employer in Oakland, California. She showed up outside its doors a few minutes before 9 a.m. and approached a friendly person who was about to walk in. She said something like this: "I know this sounds weird, but I'd love to work here, and applying the traditional way is a brick wall. I'm wondering if you'd be willing to tell the security guard that I'm with you so that I can perhaps find a nice person willing to give me some insider advice." After three negative replies, including one who said "Are you nuts?" one person said yes. When the job-seeker advanced past the security guard, she asked her escort: "I'm interested in being an analyst. Is there a floor you think I should try?" She got off the elevator at that floor, looked for people who looked friendly and not busy, and told them her tale. No, she didn't get a job on the spot, but she formed a relationship with one person who gave her hints. A few months later — that's fast for large employers — she was hired.

Another example: A client wanted to work at UC Berkeley. She didn't care much what she did there. She was a soft-skilled person: friendly, detail-oriented, bright. She simply went to department offices that she found appealing — alumni relations, physical education, English, and student housing, for example. At the student affairs department, she was told of an upcoming opening, given tips on what to say in the application, and — voilà — two months later, given a coordinator job in a favorite department at her dream employer.

# Get Outrageous

Most people have seen a job seeker's outrageous tactics on TV or in a YouTube video. That's just what the job seeker wanted: Media coverage for a job-search shenanigan yields exposure that he couldn't buy with a lifetime premium membership in LinkedIn. Common outrageous approaches are to stick an enlargement of your resume on a sandwich board and then, in your would-be work getup, parade up and down a street crammed with rich people — for example, in the financial district or on a Pucci, Gucci, hoochy-koochy block.

An even more flamboyant variation would be to wear a costume — for example, prison stripes while holding a sign: "Unemployed — I'm a prisoner in my parent's house."

Pitch a half-dozen TV and radio stations, newspapers, and local websites such as NextDoor, and maybe one will pick up your story. Even if none do, your eagerness to work will be on full display for lots of well-heeled passersby. And to boost the potential benefit, have a friend record your pitch, edit it to the best or funniest clips (all lasting a few seconds apiece and no more than 1 minute total), post it on YouTube, and send the link to your immediate universe.

Or try the standard desperate-job-seeker's tactic: Include a gift with a mailed-in job application, perhaps sent overnight so the packaging stands out. Its potential innards might say, "I'm a hotter salesperson than this salsa." Or an envelope full of Hershey's Kisses might state, "I'm sweet to work with." A vertically challenged person could send a photo of himself, taken atop a box of nuts, saying, "I may be a peanut, but I'm not nuts. Interview me and you'll see."

Such audacity might (or certainly might not) also work at the interview stage. Imagine that you're interviewing engineers and an applicant comes in with a coffeemaker he has designed. He offers to make a pot for the interviewers and, as the final touch, pulls out yummy pastries. You probably wouldn't want your entire team to be gamesters, but mightn't you want one?

# Call-Email-Call

Walking in may be the fastest way to get hired for an entry-level job. The *call-email-call* tactic may be the fastest route to a not-so-entry-level job: After hours, you leave voicemail for, say, a dozen target employers, immediately email them, and three days later, phone to follow up. You select those employers without regard to whether they're advertising an appropriate opening.

**REMEMBER**

Starting to get cold feet? You're imposing no more than if you asked a stranger on the street for directions. If the person doesn't want to help you, she can (and often will) say no. Nor should you let your fear of sounding stupid stop you. In the worst case, you flub — there are *so* many other employers. Just start with your least desirable employers so that if you do blow it, you've lost only your worst prospect. It may also help to remember that many sales reps make 50 to 100 sales calls a day and are usually selling something they care less about than about themselves. You, the job seeker, are selling yourself, and if you close just one sale, you make thousands of dollars.

So, can you suck it up? I'm asking you in one shot (yes, one shot) so you can get your job search over with, to call-email-call the 10 or 20 target employers. Don't know who those people might be? Search LinkedIn on those places of employment.

**TIP**

Look for people with a job title that might hire someone at your level. For example, if you're looking to be an individual contributor, you might look for people in a large company with the title of *manager*. If it's a small company, *director* might also be an appropriate title. Do prefer someone from the desired division rather than HR. For example, if you're looking for an analyst position, you might look for a title like *director of research* rather than *HR director*.

Here's an example of how you might use call-email-call — of course, employers may well press Delete before you finish your first sentence, but you're calling umpteen possibilities, and you only need one:

> "Barbara, I suspect that you hate unsolicited calls but against the odds, view my assertiveness, as a plus. I'm a recent computer science graduate, and I seem to have a knack for explaining technical topics to nontechnical people. I'd imagine that your company trains its paraprofessional staff on, for example, the elements of software development, and I'm wondering if you might be willing to talk with me about the possibility of being a trainer of such topics for your employees. I've made a little YouTube video called "The Internet of Things For Dummies" to give you a sample of what I can do."

"Of course, I'd love it if you called me to discuss a possible job, but I'd also be happy if you simply had some advice for me or a referral."

I'll email you that video. Hoping to hear from you. My name is Nate Green, my phone number is 510-555-2368, and my email address is Nate2020@gmail.com."

Send that video and a nice note immediately, and if in three days you haven't heard back, phone again and — whether speaking to the person or to voicemail — say something like this:

> "Hi, this is Nate Green, that CS grad who's eager to become a trainer. Not having heard from you, I assume you're not interested in talking with me, but I know how things can fall between the cracks. So, like any good employee, I'm following up. If you're open to speaking with me about how I might be of help to you, or even if you just have advice for me or a referral, I'd love to hear from you. But I won't be a pest. If I don't hear from you, I won't bother you again. My phone number is 510-555-2368, and my email address is Nate2020@gmail.com."

# Phone a Friend (Okay — Ten Friends)

Reach out. Your friends may even welcome the chance to help.

**TIP**

Phoning is more powerful than email or text. It's harder for even your marginal friends to turn down the sound of your voice than to ignore the disembodied bits and bytes of an email or text message.

So list a dozen or two people who like you who could possibly hire you or refer you to a potential employer — everyone knows people. Sure, each person is unlikely to have something for you, but if you phone a bunch, you put the numbers game in your favor. Then call them all in one (okay, two) sittings, leaving voicemail as necessary. Here's an example:

> "Hi, this is Greg Michaels. I'm trying to find a first job in database management, but because job searches these days can take months, and because I could use the income and structure, I'm open even to interim jobs of whatever sort. As you know, I like work that requires good reasoning skills. By any chance, might you know someone who might want to hire someone like me or refer me to someone who could? If so, I'd love to hear from you. Actually, I'd like hearing from you, even if it's just to chat; it's been awhile. My phone number is 510-555-2368."

This method may yield only an interim job. That's okay. You wouldn't be reading a chapter on ultrafast ways to land a job if you wanted to hold out for the dream position. Many people would be wise to take such a job. Just don't work there so long that it vitiates your motivation and energy to look for something better.

I had a client, a UC Berkeley grad who worked as a Starbucks barista for seven years. When I asked why he stayed so long, he said, "Just inertia." If you have to take a low-level job but aspire to something loftier, start developing relationships with higher-ups at your workplace and perhaps at headquarters — after all, many employers give employees a directory of internal phone numbers. Plus, continue networking and answering ads for good positions elsewhere.

## Blast Your Social Media

An even faster and wider-reaching version of the phone-a-friend tactic from the preceding section is simply to send that email to all your LinkedIn connections and Facebook friends — you'll see how good these friends really are. If you're on Twitter, post a few-sentence version. If your friends are on Instagram or follow you on YouTube, you might even make your pitch on video.

Need to expand your social media network, and fast? On LinkedIn and Twitter, follow ten or more organizations that interest you and individuals there who could hire you. In inviting to connect with someone on LinkedIn, don't use the standard invitation. Rather, in a sentence or two, explain what you like about the person or organization: for example, "I am an avid user of Evernote and would certainly consider working there. Might you add me to your LinkedIn connections?" Over the next week, post a few smart, occasionally flattering comments and questions on the Evernote feed. Then ask for an interview as described in the previous paragraphs. That should add some fresh folks to that blasted email blast.

## Make 'Em an Offer They Can't Refuse

Imagine that you're an employer and someone comes to you, describes her skill set, and says,

> "I'll volunteer for a week for free. At that point, you can hire me or not. No risk. At minimum, you will have gotten a week's worth of volunteer work to make your life easier."

Of course, there are a million reasons an employer could say no: She doesn't need anyone; that place of employment doesn't allow volunteers except for college students; the organization's insurance wouldn't cover you if you slipped on a banana peel. But the fact is, the stars occasionally align: The employer is drowning in work and there's no prohibition against volunteers. So you're manna from heaven.

## Use the Government

All those tax dollars that you or at least your parents pay are used for something. One is the labyrinth of federal, state, and local entities whose mission is to get you a job. In fact, the long arm of the law often strong-arms businesses wanting to expand to give government job-search entities the first crack at finding new-hires — that would be you. Fortunately, there's a one-stop that knows about lots of those government agencies and programs, cleverly called CareerOneStop. They're all over the United States. To find your nearest one, check out this link:

```
www.careeronestop.org/LocalHelp/AmericanJobCenters/find-
    american-job-centers.aspx
```

## Pitch Parishioners

Religiosity is in decline, but many people still participate in religious institutions, if only for a sense of community and to support each other in times of trouble. Well, your needing an ultrafast way to land a job may qualify as trouble. Give your pitch, striking the balance between confidence and humility, to parishioners and pastor alike. Strongly consider lay leaders, especially those in charge of fundraising. Usually, they have money and know people who do — the kind of people most likely to hire you or to know someone who can.

## Start at the Bottom

I'm not saying that you need to take a McJob, although many successful people, looking back, were glad they did. But nearly always, there are can-you-start-now? openings in retail, especially around the holidays, as sales clerk, security guard, janitor, and warehouse person. Some may even be career launchpads: Plenty of pooh-bahs started as receptionists or in retail. Delivery services such as UPS and FedEx also hire for the holidays. Even if you omit that job from your resume, lest it restrict your career options, even a low-level job can be worth taking: It gets you out of the house and feeling better, if only because of the confidence you get from doing a good job. I had a client who was a chemist and needed out. She took an interim job as a Starbucks barista and loved it because, as she says, "I succeeded with every customer." And, of course, you get paid — and low-pay jobs are minimally taxed.

## Start an Instant Business

Let's say it's a few weeks before a holiday for which people buy stuff: Halloween, Christmas, Valentine's Day. Rent a well-located space for a month, or simply set up in an outdoor space near a busy intersection with a long traffic light, and sell. You can choose cool masks for Halloween or for Valentine's Day go traditional with flowers, candy, or teddy bears, or get personal. (Use your imagination.)

The following idea takes a special kind of person, but is even faster and simpler and costs little to start. Find a manufacturer of the hot local sports team's caps. Buy 100 at a good price, perhaps $2 apiece. You or a friend stands where fans will be walking to the day's game, for example, in or near the train station near the stadium or in the parking lot, if allowed. On the head, stack as many caps as can stay steady, maybe 20. The caps sticking up will be seen from all around and attract attention, and you probably can sell lots at $10 a pop. As your stack gets low, add more from your warehouse (your plastic bag). You could clear a few hundred bucks in a few hours. Once you've polished your system, build a team of people doing hat sales for all the major local teams. Or branch out: When that superstar performer comes to the stadium, sell the swag.

I've saved the perhaps most offbeat instant business idea for last. This one is for counseling types: Set up a table on a street with busy foot traffic and, like Lucy did in the "Charlie Brown" cartoons, post a sign: "The Coach Is In. 5¢." Try $5 or even $10. Nothing to lose.

Of course, most people find jobs in traditional ways, but especially if you're feeling desperate, one of these Hail Marys could give you a prayer.

# Chapter **26**

# Ten Career Myths

We're all subject to groupthink, but that can be dangerous at every stage of your career, whether in choosing it, landing a job in it, or trying to succeed at it. In this chapter, I alert you to conventional wisdom that often isn't so wise.

## Career-Choosing Myths

**The myth:** Working for a start-up is great.

**The reality:** Sure, the break room may have a ping-pong table, and the fridge may be stocked with Red Bull, but working at a start-up often has big minuses. For example, work processes are usually developed on the fly by people who've never before developed them. People have to wear multiple hats, none of which they've worn before. Plus, the seductive promise of stock options usually remains unfulfilled.

Not only does working for established organizations avoid such problems, these companies usually have the resources to try innovations and, yes, to give you good benefits. Plus, in our brand-name-driven society a resume that says *Procter & Gamble* usually attracts more attention than one that says *CrushIt.info*. Of course, large organizations can have labyrinthine bureaucracies, but after the initial rush of being in a cool start-up environment, many people end up being happier in an organization that's had time to become smooth-running.

**The myth:** Self-employment is wise.

**The reality:** Most self-employed people have the freedom only to work any 60 hours a week they want. That's because they usually can't afford to hire others to do all that must get done. You probably will have to do at least some of the sales, sourcing, HR, and even accounting and IT, lest you run out of money before sufficient profits roll in.

More broadly, unless you can do all that, and unless you're good and quick at practical problem-solving and are entrepreneurial, welcome long hours, and can work diligently without someone cracking the whip, your instant CEOhood may well devolve to schlepperhood.

# Landing-the-Job Myths

**The myth:** Everyone should network.

**The reality:** Most people should, but there are exceptions. For example, if you're a hotshot, employers probably come to you with good work opportunities. So you have better things to do than schmooze. Or you've networked a lot and it has yielded insufficient benefit or pleasure over what you otherwise could be doing with the time.

TIP

Sure, you might decide it's worth trying to improve your networking skills by reading up on the topic (for example, check out Chapter 15). Or you might try role-playing some networking situations with a trusted friend. But some people just aren't sufficiently prepossessing and glib to make networking worth a lot of time, especially if they don't enjoy it. If such people follow the standard exhortation to network, network, network, the likely result will be dispiritedness. Better to spend your time elsewhere.

**The myth:** Allow yourself a few extra months to figure out who you are.

**The reality:** Most of my clients who trekked through Europe or Latin America or sought enlightenment in India ended up no clearer. More of my clients found it more helpful and, of course, cheaper to figure it all out by using the approach outlined in Part 2 of this book.

**The myth:** You'll do better in a new city.

**The reality:** Alas, many people bring their problems to the new locale. Worse, moving adds the hassle of finding a place to live, needed services, and contacts who will assist in finding good employment in that new city. If a person were good at doing all that in the first place, she might not have felt the need to move. Sure, a new city provides a fresh start, but it may be wiser to change what you're doing than change where you're doing it. For example, taking the stereotype of being a pot-addicted slacker, doing that in a new city will be less helpful than committing to self-improvement.

**The myth:** Negotiate hard.

**The reality:** Maybe not. Because extra salary is taxed at your top rate, you may well lose half to taxes (federal, state, Social Security, and local) or to other costs, such as employees' share of premium contributions for employer-sponsored health care packages. And, in having squeezed more money from the employer, you may pay a price: unduly high expectations for your performance and your being more likely to get laid off because you're expensive compared with your peers.

TIP

Here's a rule of thumb: If you think the first salary offer is too low, ask for the employer's best offer, and then set aside the salary issue and try to negotiate one or two noncash items, which may be more valuable to you than taxable cash — and more negotiable. This list describes some examples:

>> **The job description:** You may be able to nail down one that's better suited to you.

>> **Telecommuting:** This one benefits the employer too, because you won't be drained by the commute.

>> **Training budget:** This one also benefits the employer, because she's getting a more qualified employee.

>> **Title:** A higher-level title not only feels good but also enhances your future employability — you're viewed as someone deserving more responsibility and higher pay.

>> **Whom you report to:** Perhaps in the interview process, you were impressed with someone other than your intended boss.

>> **An expedited salary review:** If the salary offer is still bothering you, push for this item.

## Myths about succeeding on the job

**The myth:** You gotta pay your dues.

**The reality:** Leapfrogging is more possible than you might think. That's why, more than ever, people are job-hopping. Someone who hasn't paid their dues can often make a jump.

After my daughter graduated from college, she was offered an internship in the Clinton White House. Her job? Answering letters to the Clintons' cat, Socks. She asked her boss whether she might gain more responsibility, whereupon she quickly became a researcher for Hillary. Yes, ask for what you want, including a way to leapfrog paying dues.

The more of these qualities you have going for you, the better your chances — you're

>> Bright

>> Self-starting and a reasonably hard worker

>> Low-maintenance and not a whiner

>> Physically attractive

   (I wish that this one weren't true, but I wouldn't be fully honest with you if I didn't include it. By the way, both my male and female clients have found this to be true.)

>> Good at office politics and willing to kiss up to power

>> Working for a growing organization in which the boss doesn't hold you back because he needs you in your current role

**The myth:** Good bosses like employees who disagree.

**The reality:** Alas, most of us are suckers for yes-people. You might want to occasionally disagree, but generally speaking, if you can ethically support your boss, it's wise to do so.

**The myth:** It's worth getting a degree to boost your career.

**The reality:** Of course, many employers demand a degree. And if your current employer reassures you that a degree will open career doors, then getting the degree can make sense (especially if the employer is willing to pay for it). But given a degree's cost in money and time, consider the likely payoff and the opportunity cost: what you otherwise could be doing with the time and money. For many careers though, most people take the traditional route — earning degrees — some needn't do so. For example, a bright, assertive person might be able to jump from zero to a fairly high-level position using only smarts, self-study, and moxie. The question is, for *you*, is it worth trying such a shortcut before pursuing a degree?

**The myth:** Good managers are collaborative and supportive.

**The reality:** Too often, such managers are viewed as wimps to be taken advantage of. Of course, the era of the autocratic manager is long over, but today's good manager decides how collaborative and kind — versus individualistic and tough — to be, depending on the employee(s) and the situation. One size does not fit all.

# Chapter 27

# Ten (+ 5) Preachy Pleas

M any people say, "I wish I knew then what I know now." You might prevent that situation by considering the parent-like pleas in this chapter — career-related and beyond.

## Stop Looking Back . . .

. . . and take the next step forward. More than a little reflecting on past problems will likely leave you mired in "analysis paralysis," not help you move forward.

## Ask for What You Want (As Long As It's Ethical)

Don't be unduly afraid of imposing. The person can say no. Remember that you can survive rejection. If you don't ask, you almost assuredly don't receive.

# Be with People at Least As Good as You Are

Being with people at least as good as you are can mean accepting a lower-level job at a workplace with quality employees. It can mean playing sports with players a bit better than you. It certainly means having personal relationships with people you look up to. It also means that if you're treated poorly in a relationship, after giving the person a chance, or maybe two chances, you probably should get out. Your time will likely be better spent with others.

That's also true for a job that doesn't live up to your expectations. It's even true of stocks: The stock picker's axiom "Never catch a falling knife" sums up that idea rather well. Or, as Warren Buffett said, "Most turnarounds don't turn."

# Prioritize Work

Your time is wisely spent doing work that you're good at, that you enjoy, and that improves your sphere of influence.

# Expect to Not Always Be Passionate About Your Work

This is the necessary addition to my plea to prioritize your work. If you strive for ongoing passion in your work, you'll probably not get it and, as a result, you'll always be discontented. If you can find good, ethical work that pays reasonably well, you're ahead of the game.

# Remember That It's Better to Be Honestly Mediocre than Dishonestly Successful

A corollary was taught to me by my dad: Respect but suspect.

## Control Your Procrastinating

Do tasks *now*, even if they're unpleasant. The short-term discomfort will likely earn you much more long-term comfort. Stay busy. Feel good about crossing tasks off your to-do list.

## Males are Neither Inferior nor Superior to Females

Both sexes bring plenty to the table.

The sexes are different, and each brings strengths. And more important than group differences are individual ones. Compared with your race or gender, your abilities, work ethic, and integrity better define who you are.

## Consider a Government Job

Unless you're a born entrepreneur, consider a government job. With companies and nonprofits converting ever more full-time jobs into freelance gigs, government is the major source of stable, full-time, benefited careers (with paid holidays and vacations) requiring only a 40-hour work week.

## Contribute to a Retirement Plan Such As a 401K, 403b, or IRA

Put that money and other savings into a single low-cost, diversified investment, such as a Vanguard Life Strategy Fund (investor.vanguard.com/mutual-funds/lifestrategy). This approach is easy to keep track of, is very low cost, and has performed well. (But as they say, past performance doesn't guarantee future results.) And while I'm disclaiming, I am not a licensed financial advisor. This is merely avuncular advice from someone who has been around the block and has long been a student of investing.

# Enjoy the Simple Pleasures

Movies, TV, your creative outlet(s), food, professional sports, amateur sports, nature, reading, and, yes, romance — the corollary is that you can't spend your way to contentment. That more likely comes from doing quality work, having good relationships, engaging in a creative outlet(s), and taking care of your body.

# Get a Sweet Dog

The hassles of getting a dog are usually outweighed by the benefits: unconditional love, enforced exercise, reduced stress, a nice vibe in your home and, if your boss will let you, in your workplace. Get a dog from a pound or rescue: www. petfinder.com offers a nationwide searchable database.

# Marry Only If You're Quite Confident You'll Stay Married

The 50 percent who divorce too often find dissolution painful, expensive, and protracted.

# Stay Off Drugs

Don't do drugs — for example, don't decide whether to use marijuana based on propaganda funded by Big Tobacco. It's wiser to make your decision based on the recent National Academy of Sciences metaevaluation of 200 solid studies:

www.nationalacademies.org/hmd/~/media/Files/Report%20Files/2017/ Cannabis-Health-Effects/Cannabis-chapter-highlights.pdf

That metaevaluation points to increased risk of everything from IQ loss to memory loss, social anxiety to severe mental disorder, cardiovascular disease to cancer.

# Be Nice — but More Importantly, Be Good

TIP

Many people smile, engage in chitchat, and hold the restaurant door open for little old ladies, but when it comes to money or power, they choose expediency over ethics. Judge people not by easy niceness or what they claim but rather by what they do when something significant is at stake.

# Index

# C

# Notes

# Notes

# About the Author

Marty Nemko's first job was as the 12-year-old security guard at his dad's tiny store in Brooklyn. At 13, he was a barroom piano player in the Bronx, and, in college, a cab driver in Manhattan. After receiving his PhD from the University of California, Berkeley with specializations in educational psychology and the evaluation of innovation, he has gone on to be career coach to 5,300 clients. He enjoys a 95% client-satisfaction rate and 4.5-star average Yelp reviews. *The San Francisco Bay Guardian* rated him "The Bay Area's Best Career Coach" and *U.S. News & World Report* called him "career coach extraordinaire."

He hosts *Work with Marty Nemko* on KALW-FM (NPR-San Francisco) and has been interviewed multiple times in outlets from *The New York Times* to *The Wall Street Journal* to *The Los Angeles Times*, from NPR's *Talk of the Nation* to *CosmoGirl* to *The Daily Show*. And he was the host of a one-man PBS Pledge-Drive Special: *Eight Keys to a Better Worklife*.

He has taught in the U.C. Berkeley graduate department of educational psychology and currently teaches medical students at the University of California, San Francisco School of Medicine.

This is Marty's tenth book and he's written more than 3,000 nationally published articles, including many in *TIME, The Atlantic, The Washington Post, U.S. News & World Report, Psychology Today,* and *The San Francisco Chronicle*.

He is married to Dr. Barbara Nemko, the Napa County Superintendent of Schools. They have one daughter and one dog, Einstein, whose name is false advertising: He is dumb as dirt but sweet as they come.

# Dedication

To my clients, listeners, and readers who have taught me a lot.

# Author's Acknowledgments

Thanks to the people who read drafts of chapters: my wife, Dr. Barbara Nemko, Bryce Walat, Mia Bruch, Jonathan Wai, Bayard Nielsen, and Katharine Brooks, Director of the Vanderbilt University Career Center and author of *You Majored in What?* who also, without fee, graciously agreed to write this book's foreword.

I appreciate that the *For Dummies* people at Wiley expend great effort to ensure that their books are of high quality and do so with an efficient process that minimizes the time between when the manuscript is submitted until you read it. That way, you get the most up-to-date information possible. I have written books for other major publishers and Wiley stands out. The people behind that effort in this book include Acquisitions Editor Amy Fandrei, Project Editor Paul Levesque, Copy Editor Becky Whitney, and Proofreader TK. Additionally, Wiley hires an outside technical editor to validate the book's content. This book's was Santina Pitcher, assistant director at the University of California-Berkeley Career Center.

Finally, I want acknowledge my dad, Boris Nemko, who is my life's most powerful influence and the inspiration for my becoming a career advisor. You see, he was a Holocaust survivor and what healed him was work. It distracted him from memories of the Holocaust tortures while providing for my mom, sister, and me, all while making a difference to others, even though his career was mundane. Plus, without my dad ever saying a word about work ethic, he demonstrated a can-do attitude that I continue to aspire to. My life is particularly guided by one piece of advice he offered. It's remarkable that even a Holocaust survivor could urge that we "Never look back. Always take the next step forward." I only wish he were still here for me to hand him the first copy of this book.

## Publisher's Acknowledgments

**Acquisitions Editor:** Amy Fandrei

**Senior Project Editor:** Paul Levesque

**Copy Editor:** Becky Whitney

**Technical Editor:** Santina Pitcher

**Editorial Assistant:** Matthew Lowe

**Sr. Editorial Assistant:** Cherie Case

**Production Editor:** G. Vasanth Koilraj

**Cover Images:** Door © denisik11/Getty Images; Office © imaginima/Getty Images

# Leverage the power

*Dummies* is the global leader in the reference category and one of the most trusted and highly regarded brands in the world. No longer just focused on books, customers now have access to the dummies content they need in the format they want. Together we'll craft a solution that engages your customers, stands out from the competition, and helps you meet your goals.

## Advertising & Sponsorships

Connect with an engaged audience on a powerful multimedia site, and position your message alongside expert how-to content. Dummies.com is a one-stop shop for free, online information and know-how curated by a team of experts.

- Targeted ads
- Video
- Email Marketing
- Microsites
- Sweepstakes sponsorship

**20 MILLION** PAGE VIEWS EVERY SINGLE MONTH

**15 MILLION** UNIQUE VISITORS PER MONTH

**43%** OF ALL VISITORS ACCESS THE SITE VIA THEIR MOBILE DEVICES

**700,000** NEWSLETTER SUBSCRIPTIONS TO THE INBOXES OF

*300,000* UNIQUE INDIVIDUALS EVERY WEEK

# of dummies

## Custom Publishing

Reach a global audience in any language by creating a solution that will differentiate you from competitors, amplify your message, and encourage customers to make a buying decision.

- Apps
- Books
- eBooks
- Video
- Audio
- Webinars

## Brand Licensing & Content

Leverage the strength of the world's most popular reference brand to reach new audiences and channels of distribution.

## For more information, visit **dummies.com/biz**

# PERSONAL ENRICHMENT

 **Staying Sharp**
9781119187790
USA $26.00
CAN $31.99
UK £19.99

 **Facebook**
9781119179030
USA $21.99
CAN $25.99
UK £16.99

 **Guitar**
9781119293354
USA $24.99
CAN $29.99
UK £17.99

 **Investing**
9781119293347
USA $22.99
CAN $27.99
UK £16.99

 **Beekeeping**
9781119310068
USA $22.99
CAN $27.99
UK £16.99

 **Digital Photography**
9781119235606
USA $24.99
CAN $29.99
UK £17.99

 **Meditation**
9781119251163
USA $24.99
CAN $29.99
UK £17.99

 **Pregnancy**
9781119235491
USA $26.99
CAN $31.99
UK £19.99

 **Samsung Galaxy S7**
9781119279952
USA $24.99
CAN $29.99
UK £17.99

 **iPhone**
9781119283133
USA $24.99
CAN $29.99
UK £17.99

 **Crocheting**
9781119287117
USA $24.99
CAN $29.99
UK £16.99

 **Nutrition**
9781119130246
USA $22.99
CAN $27.99
UK £16.99

# PROFESSIONAL DEVELOPMENT

 **Windows 10**
9781119311041
USA $24.99
CAN $29.99
UK £17.99

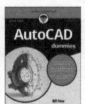 **AutoCAD**
9781119255796
USA $39.99
CAN $47.99
UK £27.99

 **Excel 2016**
9781119293439
USA $26.99
CAN $31.99
UK £19.99

 **QuickBooks 2017**
9781119281467
USA $26.99
CAN $31.99
UK £19.99

 **macOS Sierra**
9781119280651
USA $29.99
CAN $35.99
UK £21.99

 **LinkedIn**
9781119251132
USA $24.99
CAN $29.99
UK £17.99

 **Windows 10**
9781119310563
USA $34.00
CAN $41.99
UK £24.99

 **SharePoint 2016**
9781119181705
USA $29.99
CAN $35.99
UK £21.99

 **Fundamental Analysis**
9781119263593
USA $26.99
CAN $31.99
UK £19.99

 **Networking**
9781119257769
USA $29.99
CAN $35.99
UK £21.99

 **Office 2016**
9781119293477
USA $26.99
CAN $31.99
UK £19.99

 **Office 365**
9781119265313
USA $24.99
CAN $29.99
UK £17.99

 **Salesforce.com**
9781119239314
USA $29.99
CAN $35.99
UK £21.99

 **Coding**
9781119293323
USA $29.99
CAN $35.99
UK £21.99

**dummies.com**

**dummies**
A Wiley Brand

# Learning Made Easy

## ACADEMIC

**Algebra I** dummies

Mary Jane Sterling

9781119293576
USA $19.99
CAN $23.99
UK £15.99

**Basic Math & Pre-Algebra** dummies

Mark Zegarelli

9781119293637
USA $19.99
CAN $23.99
UK £15.99

**Calculus** dummies

Mark Ryan

9781119293491
USA $19.99
CAN $23.99
UK £15.99

**Chemistry** dummies

John T. Moore, EdD

9781119293460
USA $19.99
CAN $23.99
UK £15.99

**Physics I** dummies

Steven Holzner, PhD

9781119293590
USA $19.99
CAN $23.99
UK £15.99

1,001 Practice Questions
**SAT** dummies

Ron Woldoff

9781119215844
USA $26.99
CAN $31.99
UK £19.99

**Organic Chemistry I** dummies

Arthur Winter

9781119293378
USA $22.99
CAN $27.99
UK £16.99

**Statistics** dummies

Deborah J. Rumsey, PhD

9781119293521
USA $19.99
CAN $23.99
UK £15.99

2016/2017
**ASVAB** dummies

Rod Powers

9781119239178
USA $18.99
CAN $22.99
UK £14.99

Includes Online Practice Tests
1,001 Practice Questions
**Praxis Core** dummies

Carla Kirkland
Chan Cleveland

9781119263883
USA $26.99
CAN $31.99
UK £19.99

## Available Everywhere Books Are Sold

**dummies.com**

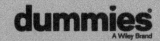
dummies
A Wiley Brand